RAISING PEACEFUL CHILDREN IN A VIOLENT WORLD

"A timely and compelling work.
Provides an indepth analysis of the roots of violence
in the lives of children . . .
and an action plan to counteract its influences.
Reminds us that peacemaking
is pro-active as well as a way of being."

—Mary Vixie Sandy, Parent Involvement Consultant,
California Commission on Teacher Credentialing

RAISING PEACEFUL CHILDREN IN A VIOLENT WORLD

by Nancy Lee Cecil
with Patricia L. Roberts

LuraMedia, Inc.
7060 Miramar Road, Suite 104
San Diego, California 92121

Cover Design by Dan Tollas, DeStijl Corporation, Doylestown, PA
Illustrations by Cynthia Lair

Library of Congress Cataloging-in-Publication Data
   Cecil, Nancy Lee.
      Raising peaceful children in a violent world / by Nancy Lee Cecil
   with Patricia L. Roberts.
            p.   cm.
      Includes bibliographical references (p.) and index.
      ISBN 1-880913-16-X (pbk. : alk. paper)
      1. Child rearing. 2. Nonviolence. 3. Communication in the family.
   4. Reconciliation.   I. Roberts, Patricia, date.
   II. Title.
   HQ772.C37   1995
   649' .1—dc20
                                            95-32351
                                              CIP

Grateful acknowledgement is made to the following for permission to reprint copyrighted
material:
'Ab du'l-Baha, The Promulgation of Universal Peace. Copyright © 1982 by the National
   Spiritual Assembly of the Bahá'ís of the United States.
Bernice E. Cullinan, ed, Children's Literature in the Reading Program. Copyright © 1987 by
   The International Reading Association. Reprinted by permission of Bernice Cullinan.
Marilyn Ferguson, The Aquarian Conspiracy. Copyright © 1980 by Marilyn Ferguson.
   Reprinted by permission of The Putnam Publishing Group/Jeremy P. Tarcher, Inc.
Etty Hillesum, An Interrupted Life: The Diaries of Etty Hillesum, 1914-1943. Copyright ©
   1981 by De Haan/ Uniebock b.v., Bussum. English translation copyright © 1983 by
   Jonathan Cape, Ltd. Reprinted by permission of Pantheon Books.
C.G. Jung, Psychological Reflections: A New Anthology of His Writing, 1905-1961. Copyright
   © 1953 by Bollingen Foundation, Inc. Reprinted by permission of Princeton University
   Press.
Carson McCullers, The Ballad of the Sad Café and Collected Short Stories. Copyright 1936,
   1941, 1942, 1950, © 1955 by Carson McCullers, © renewed 1979 by Floria V. Lasky.
   Reprinted by permission of Houghton Mifflin Co. All rights reserved.
B.F. Skinner, Notebooks. Englewood Cliffs, NJ: Prentice Hall, 1980, Reprinted by permission.
"Ruth Hill Viguers: A Reader's Tribute" by Joan Peterson. The Horn Book Magazine, May/June
   1991. Reprinted by the permission of the Horn Book., Inc.

To my peaceful and loving daughter, Chrissy,
who has been an excellent and enthusiastic coach
in my personal struggle to be a peaceful parent.

CONTENTS

SECTION II: PEACEFUL ENTERTAINMENT

SECTION III: PEACEFUL RELATIONSHIPS

FAMILY ACTIVITIES

FAMILY POSTERS

ACKNOWLEDGMENTS

The writing of *Raising Peaceful Children in a Violent World*, and the privilege of publishing and sharing it, has meant so much to me—more than any other writing project in my life. For the book has not only encompassed what I think and what I have learned, but what I deeply feel and believe.

There are many friends and colleagues, too numerous to mention by name, whose voices and spirits permeate these pages. In particular, I want to acknowledge the value of the child-centered conversations I have shared over the years with Sharon Alexander, Susan Mead, Phyllis Lauritzen, Patti Dusel, and Sheila Shapiro—all loving and wise parents who support and encourage me as friends and fellow mothers.

I would also like to thank my editor, Marcia Broucek, for her considerable skill and patience in bringing this book to print and for actually caring about the book as much as I do. Thanks also go to Dr. Lura Jane Geiger for her understanding of my personal vision and her unfailing support and guidance in every phase of the production of this book.

Finally, I must express my gratitude to my husband and partner in life, Gary, with whom I developed many of my beliefs about peaceful parenting, and to our lovely daughter, Chrissy, who graciously allowed me to use vignettes from our family life to share with other peace-seeking families.

PREFACE

I first began this book out of extreme frustration and outrage in the aftermath of the Los Angeles riots. My sense of hopelessness, indeed, my feeling of powerlessness, would simply not be quelled. I decided to take a proactive step with the most potent tool available to me: my pen. Convinced that violence begins at home, when children are not taught the skills necessary to resolve conflicts in a peaceful way, I decided I would write a book for parents.

"But wait a minute," I asked myself anxiously, "am I really an 'expert' in the area of child-rearing? My degrees are in education, not parenting. But, then again, are any of us who are raising children 'experts'?"

What I did know was that I could not simply sit by and do nothing. Thus began the odyssey that culminated in this book. I spent a long time thinking about my lovely daughter, Chrissy, and our years together. She has been my ultimate teacher. Chrissy was adopted when she was five years old, making it critical that I learn a great deal about child-rearing in a very short amount of time—"on the job training," some might call it. Truthfully, this child has often shown me the road to take as a parent and taught me more about the subject than I ever thought possible. I am *still* learning and, though a long way from being the consistently peaceful parent of my ideals, I can share what I have learned along the way. If any of what I have to say helps you in your quest to become a more peaceful parent of peaceful children, then the writing will have been truly a worthwhile endeavor.

In these very personal pages, you will be asked to undertake the same odyssey I undertook while researching the subject of peaceful parenting. You will be asked to consider very carefully who and what you are—why you think, believe, feel, and act as you do. You will be asked to listen in a new way and to see things from perhaps another point of view. You will be asked to explore some alternative ways to solve problems peacefully in your own life—because peace begins with you and me, in our own backyards. When we as adults are peaceful with who we are, we are able to radiate that peace to our children. They then have the best possibility of becoming the true peacemakers of the future—a future we pray will be in a harmonious global village.

—Nancy Lee Cecil

If there is a righteousness in the heart,
there will be beauty in the character.
If there is beauty in the character,
there will be harmony in the home.
If there is harmony in the home,
there will be order in the nation.
When there is order in the nation,
there will be peace in the world.

—Chinese proverb

INTRODUCTION

Is it possible to raise a peaceful child in a violent world? Our children are faced with violence and the use of force very early in their lives. For some children, this encounter may be relatively rare, but for others, it is a constant, grim fact of existence. Seemingly unprovoked attacks by other children on playgrounds, unpredictable adult behavior resulting from drug or alcohol abuse, a devastating rise in street crime promoted by the media, and even some unsavory police practices immortalized on video are a part of our society. Violence is also pervasive around the globe, as it escalates to war and is documented in the news, magazines, television, and on film.

There is simply no place to escape from violence. Even schools, which were once inner sanctums of innocence where children from violent homes could find peace and protection from the ravages of the outside world, are no longer such havens. Carrying handguns and wielding knives and other weapons is now *de rigueur* among children in schools around the nation. These days, instead of handling conflict through discussion, or even through the more prosaic "fisticuffs" that we as parents may recall from our youth, or through history's "honorable" act of dueling with "seconds" present to assure fairness, children are too often settling their arguments via the warlike alternatives that are being modeled for them on television, in films, and on the streets of their communities. Consider the following alarming examples that are by no means atypical:

- A fourteen-year-old boy, fed up with being teased by his classmates, brings his father's .357 magnum pistol to school and wounds two students.

- A disgruntled teen-ager opens fire in his former high school in a farming community near Sacramento, killing a teacher (who allegedly abused him) and three students.

- Two ten-year-old boys in Liverpool, England, lure a toddler away from his mother, who is busy shopping. The two boys beat the toddler to death and leave him near some train tracks. The boys are reportedly just "looking for something to do."

Though we might understandably wish we could bury our heads in the sand to avoid facing these grim realities, countless other examples keep cropping up in nearly every community, worldwide. There IS hope, but we must look at the facts, recognize that something must be done to stop violence NOW, and accept the idea that it needs to begin with us and our children.

But how *do* we help our children deal with the pervasive influences that are potentially so destructive to the kind of people we want them to become? How *can* we help them not only to remain untarnished by all the violence, but also to become peacemakers, and as such, part of the solution to these problems?

First, we need to understand what is meant by the word "peace." Contrary to popular belief, peace is NOT the absence of conflict. Conflict—disagreement, anger, hurt feelings—is an acceptable and inevitable fact of daily life. Internal, interpersonal, intergroup, and international conflicts are not in and of themselves violent. When individuals creatively deal with conflict so that it does not become violent, peace is the result.

Second, we need to understand what is meant by the term "peacemaker." Peacemaking is the mechanism by which the individuals work to resolve the conflict so that both sides feel good about the outcome. The resolution is "peace-full" if the participants want to cooperate with one another more fully and, as a result of the conflict and its resolution, find themselves more capable of doing so.

Third, we need to be clear about basic goals in raising peaceful children:

- to foster a sense of peacefulness and self-esteem within our children, as well as a sense of pride in their family and racial or cultural heritage

- to provide concrete examples of the common needs and values of ALL people, regardless of their income level, skin color, nationality, or language

- to teach our children to respect, be sensitive to, and aware of the beauty and richness of diverse groups of people in our communities and the global family of the world

- to offer a repertoire of peaceful alternatives to solving problems that arise interpersonally, within our families, and within the larger community

- to be a peaceful role model for our children—one who responds in peacemaking ways to frustrating situations, from disciplinary infractions at home to world events

- to help our children become involved in positive social action for peace by exposing them to advocates for peace and justice, as well as making them aware of the possibilities for their own involvement in creating peace in the global community

○ ○ ○

The intention of *Raising Peaceful Children in a Violent World* is to help parents, grandparents, teachers—anyone who is involved in raising children—to reach these goals. Toward that end, SECTION I, PEACEFUL COMMUNICATION, includes suggestions and activities to affirm family members, communicate peacefully, resolve conflicts within the family, and teach children to respond to potentially violent situations outside the family. Suggestions for peace-compatible discipline, strategies for creating positive racial and cultural attitudes, and ways to change prevailing sex-role stereotypes are also offered.

SECTION II, PEACEFUL ENTERTAINMENT, includes tips for counteracting the negative effects of television and offers a host of alternatives to warlike toys and games, with a strong emphasis on the value of children's literature for nurturing peaceful attitudes.

SECTION III, PEACEFUL RELATIONSHIPS, offers activities for celebrating family relationships, community activism, and global awareness and active concern. Avenues for effecting change in the world that are open to children, from letter writing to public expressions of concern, are suggested.

Finally, the APPENDICES include an extensive bibliography of additional readings for parents who are interested in further information about peacemaking, as well as an annotated bibliography of books concerning peace as it relates to children.

In a broad sense, *Raising Peaceful Children in a Violent World* is a philosophical perspective—an action-oriented one—that focuses on how we can create an atmosphere where peacemaking attitudes, values, and behaviors will be most effectively nurtured. When support and affirmation are openly expressed in our homes, our children will be free to try out new peacemaking patterns of behavior, to risk making mistakes, even failing. We can provide our children with the assurance that they can assume responsibility for peaceful resolution to conflicts, that they can create peaceful solutions to the inevitable conflicts that arise—in themselves, in their family, their community, and in the global village of the world. We can start them on the peacemaking path that is a lifelong process.

SECTION I

PEACEFUL COMMUNICATION

1

THE AFFIRMING FAMILY

First Steps toward Peace

"If there is something we wish to change in the child, we should first examine it and see whether it is not something that could be better changed in ourselves."
—C. G. Jung, *Psychological Reflections*

A Look in the Mirror

The place to begin to create a peaceful world is with ourselves: our attitudes, our word choices, our tone of voice, and our interpersonal behaviors, as well as the choices we make for our home environment. We need to look back into the mirror of our lives. In order to be active peacemakers, we need first to feel good about ourselves. We need a sense of peace about who we are. Only then can we raise affirming, loving, strong children who will be capable of becoming peacemakers in a most violent world.

There are times for all of us when we do not like what we see in ourselves as parents, times when we must admit we are not comfortable with our habits, behaviors, and resentments. We might find ourselves wanting to feel and think differently but seem unable to do so. Often we know with reasonable certainty that we are asking our children not only to behave better and more peacefully than we do but also to behave and think differently from the ways in which many people in our society think and behave.

To assist you in becoming more aware about your own attitudes and behaviors toward peace, a short questionnaire is provided at the outset of each chapter. This questionnaire will give you a moment to notice more reflectively how you think and feel about a particular subject, to "tune in" to yourself. Answer the questions as honestly as you can and discuss them with your spouse, other adults in your household, or a good friend. Careful self-inspections can sometimes be difficult, but remember that there are no "right" or "wrong" answers. With the questions below, take a few moments to think about your family, about the most important people in your life: your spouse, your children, your parents, your siblings, your close friends.

TUNING IN
How Affirming Is Your Family?

AFFIRMING BEHAVIORS

1. How often do you find yourself making peaceful and affirming comments to your loved ones?

2. How often are such things said to you?

3. In what ways do you consciously affirm your loved ones? Describe the "strokes"—such as praise, positive comments, or hugs—that you give and receive in your family.

4. How do you think the number of incidences of praise compare with the number of incidences of correction in your family?

5. How and how often do you let your children know that they are "the greatest kids in the world?"

6. In what ways do you support your children's activities to convey the message that they can participate in or achieve anything they want?

7. What are your children's particular talents, academic, and/or social strengths? In what ways do you show your support for these strengths?

8. What do you tell your children about their physical appearance?

JOKES, TEASING, AND PUT-DOWNS

1. What is the nature of jokes or teasing that occurs in your home?

2. How are put-downs and humor that degrades persons of a particular gender, race, ethnicity, or sexual orientation handled in your home?

3. What happens in your home when the person who is the object of a joke lets it be known that he or she is sensitive about the teasing and does not consider it funny?

4. How often are humorous activities and jokes occasions in which all family members laugh together?

POSITIVE EXPECTATIONS

1 What are your expectations for your children's academic achievements?

2. How do you determine when and if your children are doing their best school work?

3. In what ways do you give your children the message that they are loved unconditionally for who they are, regardless of achievement?

4. What are your particular talents, academic, social, and/or physical strengths? What are your particular academic, social, or physical limitations?

5. In what ways do you think your own strengths and limitations affect your aspirations for your children?

The Price of the Put-Down

Prime-time situation comedies, late-night talk shows, and even some highly regarded children's television programs are all rife with one-up-manship, sarcasm, and put-downs. The classic put-down has become the all-American pastime and is one of the few ways some people converse with one another. Jokes currently in circulation are also full of this negative attitude. Moreover, persistent teasing is a favorite form of recreation in many large families; this teasing habit can be passed through families from generation to generation. Once teasing is part of the family "tradition," its practice continues indefinitely unless family members make a concerted effort to change the behavior.

Looking back on my childhood experience, I can see how teasing can take a prominent place in the family circle. I am convinced my family's jibes were never intended to cause pain; they were just part of our family's good-natured "fun." As the youngest daughter of the family, I was repeatedly asked to pronounce words like "chrysanthemum" or "linoleum." Try as I might, I could not pronounce them exactly right. This brought such merry delight to my family that they would often ask me to "demonstrate" for the amusement of guests in our home!

Teasing can become an ingrained pattern that is easy to slip into. As an adult, I vowed never to laugh at anyone in my family, EVER. Yet, on occasion, I found myself teasing my English-born husband for his British accent and his diverse word choice. When this hurt his feelings, I would suddenly remember my own previous hurts and immediately regret my insensitivity.

The result of much of seemingly playful bantering is that, through our good-natured put-downs, we manage to keep an emotional distance from each other. We shun true intimacy; we actually avoid sharing with loved ones what we like or dislike or what we really feel is important about anything. By keeping our conversations peppered with put-downs of ourselves and others, or by constantly teasing, we put aside any possibility of honest discussion of who we really are. In a very real sense, such "infirming" behavior keeps us from genuinely relating to or being touched by others.

To counteract this supposedly benign verbal sparring, we can begin by shifting the patterns of communication from the negative, so prevalent in our homes and communities, to the positive. This can be a long and slow process; firmly established patterns of interaction do not change overnight. Being continually cautious is the necessary price to break the intergenerational teasing chain. The final evaluation of "fun quality" has to be made by the teased, not the teasers. The old adage, "If you had ten cents for every kind word you have spoken to your family members, but had to pay five cents for every thoughtless word you said to them, would it make you richer or poorer?" is still a good reminder.

Much has been written about the inability of children, adolescents, and even adults to say a kind word about another person, or their inability to make affirming statements about themselves. One way to change or enhance existing negative patterns of communication is to practice positive exchanges through family affirmation activities such as the "Naming Myself" activity that follows. Several affirmation activities are suggested throughout this chapter to give family members the opportunity to come together for the purpose of making very deliberate, positive comments to one another. Though such focused physical and emotional intimacy may be uncomfortable for some family members initially, such activities can gradually become a welcome way of sharing and helping one another to feel valued.

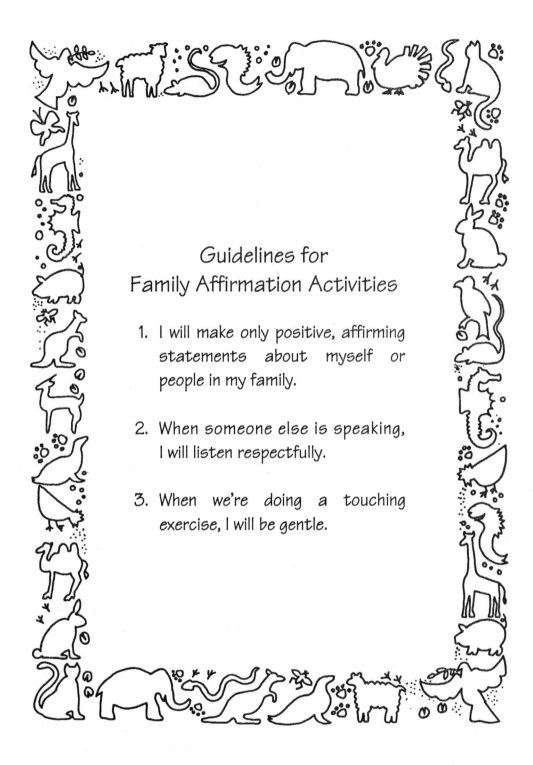

Guidelines for Family Affirmation Activities

1. I will make only positive, affirming statements about myself or people in my family.

2. When someone else is speaking, I will listen respectfully.

3. When we're doing a touching exercise, I will be gentle.

RAISING PEACEFUL CHILDREN IN A VIOLENT WORLD

Several simple guidelines apply to all of the affirmation activities in this chapter. A small poster listing these guidelines is provided on page 25 for you to cut out or photocopy to post for display. Your children may wish to color in the animal border with crayons or felt-tipped pens to make the poster more personal to them. Discuss the guidelines with your children. Refer to the poster often.

"Naming
Myself"

Supplies needed: *paper, writing utensils*

1. Gather around a table or sit on the floor.

2. Give each person a writing utensil and a sheet of paper.

3. Each person writes the letters of his or her first name vertically on the left hand side of the paper, like so:

C
H
R
I
S
S
Y

4. For every letter, each person writes positive, peaceful word(s) that describe her/himself. The letter can begin the description, end the description, or be contained in the middle, as in the following example:

<u>C</u>an draw really well
<u>H</u>as a pretty smile
w<u>R</u>ites wonderful stories
<u>I</u>s liked by others
<u>S</u>ees the best in people
likes rabbit<u>S</u>
<u>Y</u>oungest in the family

5. After everyone has finished writing, pass your papers around the family circle, adding more positive and peaceful comments to each other's papers.

6. Finally, read the papers aloud, sharing the affirming comments about each family member.

Unrealistic Expectations

Because we love our children, we want them to succeed in life, and we wish for only the best things to happen to them. Unfortunately, we may sometimes find ourselves getting "carried away" with our expectations to the point where the qualities and attributes we desire for our children's future do not gel with the reality of their existing qualities and attributes. When this is the case, our unrealistic expectations can make our children feel as if they are disappointing us, though this was never our intent. The two most common areas in which expectations can be conveyed are:

- how children look
- how children perform

How Children Look

Even if children are not teased or put-down, there are other, more subtle ways parents can make children feel less than peaceful about themselves. One of the more common ways of negatively affecting children's beliefs about themselves happens when we cause them to believe they are less than attractive. Unconsciously, we often give special attention to the attractive child. Intuiting this, the child with a face covered with acne, or the child with big feet, a hooked nose, crooked teeth, or prominent ears quickly gets the message that he or she is worth less than more attractive children. The child suffers additional pain when a well-meaning parent or relative observes, "You're so tall!" or worse, "Do you have to be so clumsy?" or "If you would simply cut out those greasy snacks after school, those pimples would go away." Tragically, children equate being physically unattractive with being unwanted and unloved by both adults and their peers. A significant cause of teen-age suicide is directly related to the youngster's conviction that "I am ugly" in the overly beauty-conscious world.

The following affirmation activity can help family members focus not only on their unique physical appearances but also on the many other ways in which each is unique. Through laughter, honest communication, and gentle physical affection, family members can observe and celebrate each other's unique qualities.

"Who

Has It?"

Supplies needed: none

NOTE: You might want to review the "Guidelines for Family Affirmation Activities" (page 25) about touching before you begin this activity.

1. Everyone stands in a circle.

2. Designate a caller. This person then calls out a quality, trait, or physical characteristic possessed by one or more members of the family.

   For example,
   "Touch someone who . . .
   . . . has dimples
   . . . smiles a lot
   . . . has a scraped knee
   . . . has black curly hair
   . . . has a mustache
   . . . likes to cook
   . . . listens to rap music
   . . . likes to work in the garden
   . . . doesn't like to get up in the morning
   . . . has a button collection
   . . . loves the color red
   . . . has read lots of Nancy Drew books

3. Everyone then touches, hugs, or embraces the person(s) having that trait or quality.

4. The caller continues to call out traits, making sure to include at least one or two unique qualities about every person in the family.

VARIATION:
You can include each member of the family by giving everyone a chance to call out one or two items. This process gives even the youngest children the opportunity to enter into the group decision-making. Remember to allow younger children more time to consider what to call. This extra time will also give the rest of the family an opportunity to practice patience in a small, caring way.

Children can also be made to believe they are supposed to learn *easily* in school. They are quick to conclude that if they want parental approval, they must succeed academically. Unfortunately, the minimum standard of most parents is that their children's performances must be at least "average." I have seen this in my own teaching experience. One day I was approached by a distraught mother about her son who was in my third-grade classroom. The mother's concern was that her son's grades were below the family's expectations. I carefully studied the child's academic history and test scores and conferred with the child's counselor. Together, we concluded that the child was making steady progress and was doing as well as anyone had a right to expect. After a lengthy discussion, the worried mother began to understand my careful interpretation of her son's learning potential. But the mother then reiterated her residual discomfort: "Well, I may be able to accept the fact that my son is 'average' in learning ability, but I will never be able to accept that any child of mine is *below* average!"

Difficult as it may be for most parents to accept, "below average" is every bit as normal as "above average." This is true whether we are considering a child's height, weight, running speed, musicality, artistic ability, or academic prowess. Therefore, parental pressures that encourage *every* child to be academically above average are not only unrealistic, but they can be rejecting. Simple statistics reveal that about half of all students in the nation will always be "below average" academically. If we do not accept this fact, some children, both at school and at home, are doomed to feel unloved and worthless, believing they have let their parents down. The truth is that everyone of us is below average in some of life's activities. I can, for example, personally attest to my "below average" abilities in several areas: sense of direction outside of a research library, auto repair ability, violin playing, certain sports, fly fishing, plumbing, nuclear physics, and oil painting—to mention only a few! It is important, therefore, to discover, celebrate, and prize the unique gifts that each of us possesses. It is especially important for us to realize that by decreasing pressures on our children to excel in areas where they are not particularly gifted, and by increasing attention and praise in areas in which they *do* have talent and aptitude, we affirm them. This not only builds personal self-esteem but also enables them to celebrate the successes of others.

The following activity will help you to focus on affirming who your children *are* rather than how much they have achieved according to some societal norm. The making of a sharebook can help each person record special things about her/himself to share with other members of the family. The sharebook has the added advantage of building self-esteem by focusing on ways each family member is special and unique. Over time, you will also find the sharebook an invaluable resource for heightening family communication.

 " 'I Am Special'

Sharebook"

Supplies needed: a notebook for each family member
                    writing utensils, crayons, or markers

1. Gather around a table or make a circle on the floor.

2. Each person writes or draws a picture in his or her notebook in response to a selected topic or question, such as:

   • one thing you really like about each family member

   • one thing you really like about yourself

   • one reason why you are proud to be a member of this family

   • one way another family member helped you recently.
     How did you feel?

   • one thing you did for another family member recently.
     How did you feel?

3. When everyone is finished writing or drawing, take turns sharing what each has drawn or written.

4. These 'I Am Special' notebooks can be kept in a special place to be used only for these family sharing times.

Characteristics of an Affirming Family

The word "invitation" comes from the Latin word "invitare," which means "to summon cordially, not to shun." Affirming families invite each other to be fully themselves. When family members feel "cordially summoned" or "invited," each is able to realize his or her unique potential; no one in the family is teased, put down, or shunned.

The affirming family is set apart by at least five recognizable characteristics:

- respect for individual differences
- sense of belonging
- cooperative spirit
- pleasant environment
- positive expectations

Respect for Individual Differences

In the affirming family there is an expressed appreciation for individual differences of members, a celebration of each person's unique qualities. Not everyone is expected to be alike, to do the same things well. There is tolerance for family members who are unable or unwilling to meet all family expectations or aspirations. "He's not heavy; he's my brother," reflects this attitude of unconditional support. There is also a great shared pride in those who exceed the fondest hopes of the family. Each family member is helped to move toward his or her own creative ways of being. In the eyes of the affirming family, the concept that "each is unique" determines all family policy. In such a family, love is never predicated on a preconceived notion of how each family member should behave.

Sense of Belonging

A most important quality of an affirming family is the deep sense of belonging of all members. This feeling is cultivated wherever and whenever possible. Family members spend time talking with each other and sharing their feelings and concerns. They each make a special effort to look beyond their own immediate gratification to the needs of other family members. Everyone is aware of the value of contributing to and receiving from "our" family, "our" home, "our" traditions, "our" responsibilities.

This loyalty to one another and the warmth shown toward family members results in mutual appreciation, positive self-esteem, a deep sense of family togetherness, and an ability to face the ups and downs of life.

Cooperative Spirit

"One for all and all for one" describes the major thread that binds together the affirming family. Parents and children learn from one another and seek ways of helping one another. The family is viewed by all its members as a cooperative enterprise in which unity is valued more than competition.

When one family member achieves something, ALL family members feel a part of that success; similarly, when one member is having trouble, it is a total family concern. Everyone pitches in and helps in any way possible until that family member is back on his or her feet. In the affirming family, a special watch is kept for those in the family who might need a special boost. This support is provided in a loving circle of unconditional caring and respect for the family member who requires the assistance.

Pleasant Environment

A relaxing, comfortable atmosphere is given a high priority in the affirming family. All family members are invited to take part in finding comfortable furniture, pleasing colors, attractive paintings, and meaningful "knickknacks" wherever possible. Changes in the family environment are made when all family members deem it necessary to ensure that the home is attractive and welcoming. In this soothing climate, the details of the home are designed to send the important message to family members, friends, and relatives, "We're very glad you're here! We want you to be as happy and comfortable as possible!"

Positive Expectations

Encouraging each family member to fully develop his or her own unique potential is also a significant feature of the affirming family. Parents notice when their children give up or say, "I can't do that" or "I'm stupid" and counter this with a positive attitude. Parents make every effort to offer opportunities for their children to enroll in sports, clubs, and other activities that will help the children to discover and develop their own natural talents and abilities. Every effort is also made to encourage family members to develop themselves in other more fundamental ways. Members are encouraged to practice self-control and individual responsibility and also to discover their physical, social, emotional, and spiritual potentials. Parents strive to model these attributes and introduce their children to other adults who also display these positive traits.

Ways of Affirming

When children feel good about themselves, they are more open to developing the skills of affirmation. When they have the ability to affirm themselves, they are also able to seek and find qualities in others that they readily affirm. They begin to evidence a belief in themselves and others; they have less need to judge, tease or put down others. Petty fights and sibling rivalries are lessened, too, when children learn the art of affirming themselves and others within the security of their own families. Finally, affirming people are more able to accept the challenges and risks involved in being peacemakers because compromising or "losing the battle" poses little threat to their healthy feeling about themselves.

In general, the positive self-esteem of children depends upon the extent to which they are affirmed rather than "infirmed," praised rather than belittled, recognized rather than ignored, and respected rather than ridiculed. A home environment that is characterized by an appreciation for the unique talents of each child enhances self-esteem and heightens the child's peacemaking capabilities. There are three important ways in which you can affirm your children:

- giving praise
- engaging in affirming deeds
- offering loving touches

Giving Praise

The most important element in showing appreciation is giving sincere praise for positive behavior, achievement, and effort. When I have asked parents to think back on the most empowering memories of childhood, their most uplifting and affirming remembrances invariably concerned a parent or a significant other who showed his or her appreciation in the form of praise for specific behavior or achievement. Here are some parents' memories:

> "My mother asked if she could send a copy of my cat poem to my aunt. I beamed."

> "My father said I was a 'compassionate listener,' and he felt that was an exceptional quality in one so young."

> "My mother always remarked that she wished she were as athletic as I was!"

> "My second-grade teacher once said that she liked to listen to me read because I had a 'twinkly voice.' "

> "My father said I had a real way with animals, and he said that was a 'gift.' He encouraged me to become a veterinarian."

Giving your children plenty of praise has a further benefit: What is taught at home carries over into the school. When children like themselves, their positive self-image strongly influences their creativity, integrity, and eagerness to learn.

The following affirmation activity can be helpful in fostering this positive self-image.

 ## "Positive

Messages"

Supplies needed: colorful self-adhesive notes
colorful felt-tip pens

1. Ask your children how they feel when another family member says, "I love you," notices something they did especially well, or offers a positive comment about their kind word or deed. Solicit examples of times when this has happened, and ask your children to describe how they felt.

2. Ask your children how they imagine they would feel if a family member not only mentioned a positive word or deed but also wrote or drew a message about it. How might the message, and the effort it had taken to write it, make it extra special?

3. Distribute colorful self-adhesive notes and felt-tip pens to each family member. Ask every person to be on the look-out for kind words or deeds that occur in the family and to be aware of appreciative or loving feelings that do not always get expressed.

4. Invite all family members to write or draw messages to give to other family members that could:

   • express love

   • offer encouragement

   • say "thank you!"

   • recognize an achievement or improvement

   • show caring and concern

5. Encourage family members to post their notes wherever the particular person to whom it is addressed would be most likely to find it—for example, in the briefcase of a parent or in the lunch box of a child.

Actions often speak louder than words in letting your children know they are valued. The gift of time that such actions take is especially precious when so many parents today have so little time to spend with their children.

Deeds are what the following parents remembered as being especially affirming in their early lives:

"I used to get 'happy notes' in my lunch box every single day. My mother always took the time to express different things that she loved about me, and I read them several times while I was eating my lunch. It made me feel incredibly loved."

"Every so often, my father would take me to work with him and 'show me off' to all his colleagues. That time with just him and me made me feel very special."

"We had a time set aside every night in our family called 'the day in review' where I would tell my parents about the best things that had happened during the day and share some of the decisions I had made. I used to really look forward to that time."

"Every summer, my dad and I would go camping for a weekend, just the two of us. On the four-hour drive up into the woods, I would share my thoughts about everything. He would just seem to listen and nod his head. I can't tell you what those times meant to me."

The following activity offers a way to help family members practice affirming each other.

"Body

Decorations"

Supplies needed: plain wrapping paper or butcher paper
marker
scissors
masking tape
felt-tip pens, crayons

1. Choose one family member to lie down on a large sheet of plain wrapping paper or butcher paper. Ask a second family member to use a marker to trace the outline of the person lying on the paper.

2. Cut out and tape the outline to a doorway or wall.

3. Every family member then states one positive word or phrase about that person and writes it on the silhouette. (Adults or older children may write younger children's ideas for them.)

4. The "owner" of the silhouette then colors and decorates it.

5. Keep the outline on the door or the wall for a week. During that time, family members—or visitors to the home—can add other words or phrases as they think of them.

6. Encourage the "owner" also to add more affirming statements about her/himself during the week.

7. Save the silhouette and display it again on subsequent birthdays, graduations, or other special occasions.

Offering Loving Touches

Children crave physical affection from their parents. A touch, a hug, a squeeze, or a gentle pat can go a long way toward showing children they are cared about and special.

I have seen many different ways in which touch is encouraged among family members. A friend recalls that her family had a "hug of the minute" in which any family member could walk up to any other and ask for a hug without any elaborate explanation or discussion. The "hug of the minute" always felt good and was a concrete way to demonstrate to one another that all were appreciated, loved. The tradition was considered an "11" on a "1-to-10" family scale. Other parents I spoke with recalled their own instances of special touches:

> "When my dog died, my father just squeezed my hand for the longest time without saying anything. I knew he understood."

> "I remember when I won a fourth-grade poster contest. When I left the stage after collecting my reward, my mother and father took my picture, and then they both hugged me really hard. I felt like a million dollars."

"When I got my tonsils taken out, I woke up in the recovery room, and there was my father standing over me. He told me he loved me and planted a concerned kiss on my forehead."

"I recall the first book I ever read. When I finished the last page, my mother put her arm around my shoulders, looked me in the eye, and told me what a great accomplishment I had made . . . I read everything in sight after that!"

The importance of physical affection in the life of a child—indeed, in the life of any adult—is well-documented. Often a hug or gentle caress can show a family member that he or she is loved and valued in a way that nothing else can.

The following activity can help children experience the positive, affirming value of touching a person they love.

 ## "A Gentle Touch"

Supplies needed: none

NOTE: Before beginning this activity, it may be helpful to review the "Guidelines for Family Affirmation Activities" about touch (page 25). Each family member should be touched according to his or her own level of comfort. Each person, therefore, needs to communicate clearly to his or her partner exactly what touch "feels good" and what does not. In this way the touching will be relaxing and pleasurable to all participants.

1. Every family member sits sideways in a circle facing the back of the person next to him or her.

2. Each family member gently massages the back of the person in front of him or her for three minutes.

3. Each family member then turns around and massages the back of the person who has just been massaging him or her.

VARIATION
Family members pair off. One person massages the other for three minutes, focusing on mutually agreed-upon body parts: feet, face, hands, arms, or head. Then the partners reverse and the "giver" becomes the "receiver" of the massage.

A Closing Word about Affirmation

There are many practical ways to make families more affirming by making gradual changes in attitudes about what affirmation is and by providing practice activities that families can do together to affirm one another through word, deed, and touch.

To the degree that our presence in the world is acknowledged by others with a warm smile, an affirming word, or a gentle touch, we grow in our own self-worth. And to this degree, we are then enabled to believe in and affirm others. Furthermore, we are empowered to become peacemakers in our society because we have become aware that by giving of ourselves we do not decrease: we *grow*. This is the true foundation of building trust among people and, eventually, creating peace.

2 THE COMMUNICATING FAMILY

Learning to Share Feelings Peacefully

> "An atmosphere of trust, love, and humor can nourish extraordinary human capacity. One key is authenticity: parents acting as people, not as roles."
> —Marilyn Ferguson, *The Aquarian Conspiracy*

Communication Breakdown

One day after school, a ravenous Jennifer is discovered eating her way through the last box of cookies in the house. Happening upon the scene, her mother fumes to herself, 'Typical! It would never occur to this child to leave any for anyone else in the house!'

When Jennifer bends down to tie her shoe, her mother spitefully grabs the nearly empty box.

"How considerate of you, Jennifer," her mother snaps sarcastically. "Your brother and I really appreciate your thoughtfulness in leaving us some cookies!"

Jennifer looks confused. Her mouth opens, but nothing comes out. Finally, she turns on her heels and walks out of the kitchen, mumbling under her breath, "Gosh, I was only getting a snack. Don't have a *cow!*" thus escalating the bad feelings between the two family members.

Not understanding her mother's sarcasm, yet hurt by it, Jennifer never discusses the incident, and the pattern of thoughtlessness that so incensed her mother continues.

How *do* we improve the channels of communication in our families? And how do we teach our children to be caring, yet open and honest with their feelings so they can grow up with the inner strength that will enable them to stand up for their beliefs?

Take a few moments to answer the following questions and discuss the answers with your loved ones. This exercise may help you take stock of how well your family members are currently communicating.

TUNING IN
How Does Your Family Communicate?

1. How do you express your anger or other strong emotions to your family members?

2. How do you deal with frustration?

3. How do your children express their anger or other strong emotions?

4. How do your family members express feelings of pride when one person has done something special or accomplished something?

5. In what ways do your family members laugh, have fun, and express happiness together?

6. How does your family share feelings in times of grief?

7. When you are angry with a person outside of your family, do you let your child see how you handle the confrontation? Explain.

8. How do you respond when your children tell you how they are feeling, particularly when the feeling is not positive?

9. How do you think your family communication patterns affect your children's peacemaking attitudes?

Family Communication Patterns

Though the effect of demeaning verbal punishment and frequent spanking is understood to be related to variety of negative emotional consequences, the profound effects of *lack* of positive family communication is less often considered. However, clear and honest communication among family members, when those members also actively listen to one another, is very likely THE pivotal factor in raising children who will later be peaceful within themselves and caring toward others. There are three fundamental communication skills and principles critical to communicating in a peaceful way:

- be clear
- be open and honest
- listen actively

Be Clear

It is important for children and parents to express their needs in clear action terms. Instead of discussing problems in vague generalities, it is most helpful to talk to one another about specific incidents, and the feelings that they create, as they occur. As parents, we can help our children learn this by modeling clear communication. When we have a problem with something one of our children is doing, we need first to recognize what *our* problem with the behavior is and then decide exactly what we want to do about it.

For example, I recently had the experience of trying to write a letter while my daughter, Chrissy, kept interrupting to read aloud what she considered to be funny passages from a book she was reading. I could have responded in either of the following ways:

> "Chrissy, go into the other room and stop bugging me! Can't you see I'm busy?"
>
> OR
>
> "Chrissy, I am trying to write a letter, and it is hard for me to concentrate when you are reading to me. Could you please wait a half hour until I finish? Then I would be happy to listen to your book."

While both of these statements would have reflected my desire, the second one conveys three specifics:

- It states clearly what the problem is:
  It is hard for me to concentrate with interruptions.

- It acknowledges what *both* of us need:
  I need to finish the letter, and
  Chrissy needs someone to listen to her book.

- It offers a compromise that can satisfy both our needs:
  a half-hour time delay.

The second message, expressed in a loving voice, kindly offered a solution that could be acted upon. Knowing I was willing to listen to her needs and feelings, Chrissy was not defensive when she replied. The second response avoided bad feelings and was much more honoring of the relationship than the first statement. It allowed for the problem to be clearly laid on the table, invited a cooperative response rather than an angry counter-attack, and paved the path for finding a mutually-agreeable solution.

Family members can gain practice in communicating their feelings by participating in the following activity.

 "Speaking

Clearly"

Supplies needed: none

1. As a family, consider the following scenarios:

   Scenario 1: Ten-year-old Laurie wants to get her ears pierced, but her mother and father feel she is too young.

   Scenario 2: Craig is late for school every morning. No matter how early his mother wakes him up, he ends up missing the bus, and his mother has to drive him to school.

   Scenario 3: Jennifer always eats all the food earmarked for snacks for the entire family.

2. Gather around a large open space. Invite different family members to try their hand at acting out various resolutions to these scenarios.

3. Afterward, discuss how each family member sees the following:
   - what the problem in each scene is
   - what each person in the scene is saying
   - what each person in the scene is feeling

   Practice stating each of these as clearly as possible.

4. Decide if each person in the scenes acted out had their needs met.

Parents and children need to express their feelings and desires in an open and honest way. Often our feelings are more important to us than our wants and needs, but sometimes it takes courage—and a modicum of tact and gentleness—to be able to express them freely in a relationship. Consider the following two messages where a parent is expressing himself to his child, and ask yourself what *real* message is being sent:

> "Taylor, get in here right now and clean up that pig sty you call your room! You know we agreed that you had to clean up your room on Saturday mornings before you did anything else if you were to get your allowance. I should have known you wouldn't keep your part of the agreement. I'm sorry I gave you your allowance; I really wasted my money!"

OR

> "Gosh, Taylor, I am feeling really disappointed. We made an agreement that you would clean your room on Saturday mornings before you did anything else. I want you to clean it right now and be thinking of a way we can help you to remember our agreement."

In the first message no feeling is named, although a frightening anger is communicated through the father's use of sarcasm. Of course, there are plenty of times when the primary feeling of parents or children *is* anger, and it is okay for both parents and children to admit they are angry. In the above scenario, however, the primary feeling of the parent was disappointment.

The second message clearly spells out the parent's feeling of disappointment and explains the reason for the feeling to the child. The honest identification of that feeling can be an invitation for the child to learn about different emotions. Communicating the secondary feeling of anger, especially when it is coupled with sarcasm, adds confusion to the exchange and, additionally, encourages resentment on the part of the child.

Furthermore, unless the real feelings going on in a situation are expressed openly and honestly, it is often impossible to deal with the underlying wants and needs. Hiding or sublimating or even ignoring our feelings ultimately leads to built-up resentments, and, in some cases, violence. We can help our children be open with their feelings by helping them learn to *identify* their feelings:

"I guess you're feeling angry [sad, jealous, disappointed, etc.] right now, aren't you? That's understandable."

When we verbally acknowledge our children's feelings, we help them recognize and sort out mixed emotions that might otherwise seem overwhelming. One way to gain experience in verbally acknowledging children's feelings is through Family Sharing Time (FST). This open communication activity provides family members with a safe forum in which they can practice sharing their hopes, dreams, fears, likes, and dislikes.

 "Family Sharing Time" (FST)

Supplies needed: none

1. Gather around a table or on the floor.

2. Each family member in turn responds to one of the following:

- What is your favorite work, idea, game, sport, color, animal, book, movie, song, place, time of day, subject in school, food to eat, season of the year, etc.

- What is one thing you would like to try someday?

- What is one thing you have done that you regret?

- Who is one person you admire and why?

- What is one thing you are looking forward to?

- What is one thing that makes you feel peaceful?

- Tell about a time you were afraid.

- Tell about a time you felt embarrassed.

- Tell about a time you cried with joy.

Listen Actively

Active listening is a style of listening that does not evaluate, belittle, warn, order, or even praise. Instead, the listener gives feedback, or paraphrases, the feelings and desires of the speaker as the listener heard them, checking out the accuracy of what she or he heard. This is an excellent way of helping children clarify their feelings and desires:

> "It sounds like you're feeling left out because Devon, whom you thought was your friend, did not invite you to her birthday party. Is that what you're saying?"

As parents, we need to understand that the more we listen to our children without judging their words (as difficult as that may be at times), the more we will enable our children to accept their own feelings, improve their problem-solving ability, increase their ability to listen to others, and expand their warmth and empathy. Such focused listening requires a certain attitude and considerable skill; as listeners, we must genuinely *want* to listen and be helpful, and be able to accept our children's feelings and separateness as unique persons. We also need to radiate trust in our children's ability to solve the problems(s) they are speaking about.

Many opportunities to practice active listening skills present themselves on a daily basis. At meal times, for example, family members can be encouraged to speak one at a time, while others practice listening. Special attention can be given to younger children so that they, too, are heard by the older children and adults.

In conflict situations, children can be shown how to listen to each other's feelings and needs. The following intervention in an argument between two children demonstrates a method of helping children practice active listening:

> "Chrissy, do you know why Laura is so upset with you?
> Laura, could you try to explain your feelings to Chrissy?"

Once Laura articulates her feelings, a follow up intervention might be:

> "Chrissy, do you understand how Laura is feeling? Can you tell her what you have heard, in your own words?"

Active listening can be promoted through active engagement in asking and answering questions about each other's daily routines and lives, as in the following activity.

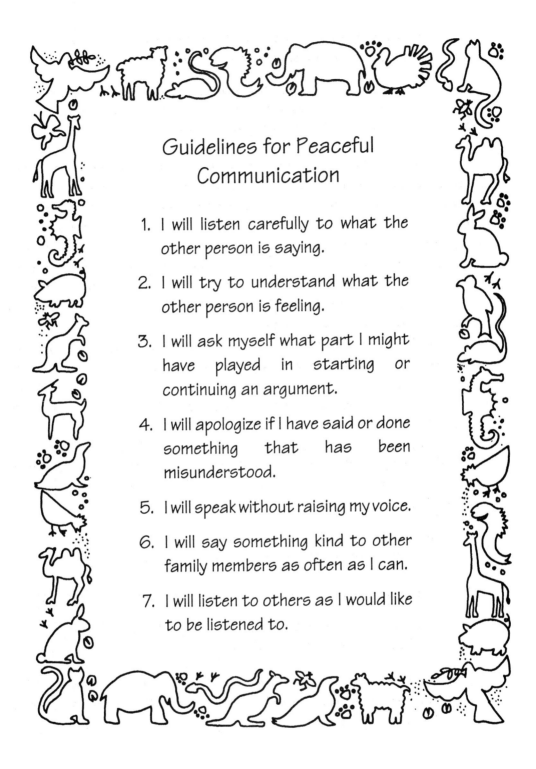

Guidelines for Peaceful Communication

1. I will listen carefully to what the other person is saying.

2. I will try to understand what the other person is feeling.

3. I will ask myself what part I might have played in starting or continuing an argument.

4. I will apologize if I have said or done something that has been misunderstood.

5. I will speak without raising my voice.

6. I will say something kind to other family members as often as I can.

7. I will listen to others as I would like to be listened to.

RAISING PEACEFUL CHILDREN IN A VIOLENT WORLD

"Listening to Each Other"

Supplies needed:　　none

1. Look for opportune times when the family could practice asking questions and listening: during meal times, while riding in the car, while doing dishes, while taking family walks, when settling in for bedtime, or during Family Sharing Time (page 45).

2. When the opportunity arises, suggest that each family member focus on another family member and ask very *specific* questions (rather than general questions, such as, "How was your day?"). Specific questions require particular information from the answerer, such as:

   - "What was the best thing that happened in school today, Chrissy?"
   - "Did your friend have her baby, Mom?"
   - "How did your meeting go with your client, Dad?"
   - "What was one new play you learned in football practice, Doug?"

3. Give each family member a chance to practice listening carefully, giving eye contact, and providing verbal feedback to let the speaker know that she or he is being heard. For example:

   - "Wow, that must have been some game!"
   - "Having a baby must be an amazing experience."
   - "It sounds like you felt good about the meeting, Dad."
   - "Gosh, that sounds like a complicated maneuver!"

○ ○ ○

Good communication is hard work and is time consuming, even in the most loving of families who care very much about one another. Family members may find the "Guidelines for Peaceful Communication" on page 47 helpful not only within the family but also as important reminders of how to treat others outside the family to promote more peaceful interactions. Cut out or photocopy the guidelines; post them where family members can refer to them often. Your children may wish to color the animals or decorate the poster.

Communication and Self-Esteem

The development of self-esteem is critical for several reasons in the overall task of nurturing young peacemakers. First of all, it is impossible for any of us to function effectively without a strong sense of self. Self-esteem has a dramatic impact on children's ability to function well in school and, later, in the broader society.

Second, self-esteem is necessary in order to be able to have compassion for others. No child can actually care about people who are homeless or starving in Somalia unless that child feels satisfied with who he or she is. To reach out to others, even with a sense of outrage about the causes of pain and victimization, requires a secure self-concept.

Third, peacemaking involves many instances where there is an element of risk, whether that risk is in the form of disagreeing with someone's opinion or breaking up a fight on the playground. A solid foundation of self-esteem that is begun with young children in a family setting can enable older children or adults to take a verbal or active stand on something they feel is important, even though risk is involved.

And, finally, self-esteem is critical in dealing with differences, whether those differences are cultural, racial, religious, or economic. Racism and intolerance fester in the minds and actions of people who feel less than positive about themselves and therefore need to find another person or group to be a scapegoat or to feel superior to.

Communication is the ideal way to foster positive self-esteem in our children. Our willingness to respect and accept our children's feelings will enable them to accept and trust their own inner beings. By discussing the guidelines for communication and practicing the communication activities contained in this chapter, you will be helping your children not only to learn to share their feelings more effectively but also to feel more content within themselves.

A Closing Word about Communication

The more we learn to listen without judging, the more we help our children accept their feelings, improve their self-image, increase their willingness to listen to us, and expand the peacefulness and compassion in all of us. Such active listening has certain defining features: a desire to focus on our children while trying to be helpful, an acceptance of their uniqueness, and a belief in their own abilities to solve problems.

Children, perhaps more than any other beings, must be provided with situations and opportunities where their ideas, feelings, and opinions can be affirmed and celebrated with caring others. As they try out their abilities at deciphering the many modes of communication possible in the human condition, they are learning the skills necessary to become active participants in the peace process.

3 CONFLICT RESOLUTION

Peace as a Process

"You can't shake hands with a clenched fist."
—Indira Gandhi

"Some Days Are Like That!"

A volley of screams erupt from an upstairs bedroom. "I'm telling Mom on you!" shouts an angry young voice, its owner descending the stairs two at a time.

"What's the problem now, you two?" asks the mother of the two siblings.

"Nicole took my best stickers and put them all over her notebook!" shouts Jessie.

"But you SAID I could have them!" retorts Nicole. "Mom, Jessie slapped me!"

"Did not!"

"Did so!"

"Will the two of you PLEASE stop arguing and try to settle your problem yourselves for a change?" pleads the harried mother.

If the above scene has a familiar ring to it, that is because the same drama, or one similar to it, is played out in thousands of homes across the country every single day. While this particular type of conflict may not be one that is evidenced in *your* household, your children certainly have their own conflicts with you, with their siblings, and in their everyday lives. Conflict in human relations is inevitable and not in and of itself a negative phenomenon; how we resolve interpersonal problems and how we learn from them is what really counts. With this in mind, take a few minutes to consider the following questions about family conflict. Discuss them with other adults in your household or with close friends to get a clearer picture of your own feelings about conflict resolution.

TUNING IN
How Does Your Family View Conflict?

1. Describe your feelings when there is conflict in your family. Give a recent example and your reaction.

2. How are conflicts generally resolved in your family?

3. In what ways do family members apologize to each other or try to rectify the situation if there have been misunderstandings or hurt feelings?

4. How do the adults in your household intervene when the children are quarreling?

5. In what ways do you problem-solve with your children when each have differing needs?

6. How do you handle your own anger with your spouse or partner? In what way(s), if any, are these conflicts and resolutions shared with the children?

7. In what ways do you model compromise and problem-solving behaviors when there is a difference of opinion between you and your spouse or partner? Give a recent example.

8. How do you remember conflict being handled in the home in which you grew up? How do you think this history has affected your current feelings about conflict?

| The Nature of Conflict | Most of us grow up thinking conflict is a phenomenon to be avoided at all cost. Until we truly understand the nature of conflict, we may have difficulty showing our children how to deal with it successfully. We need to start by asking ourselves how much we view conflict as a "negative": Do we see conflict as painful, as a situation that is threatening to |

our self-esteem? Do we believe conflict can be resolved only when there is a clear winner and a loser—and we are afraid to be the loser? Most of us, either consciously or unconsciously, share these feelings to some degree.

Conflict exists because we are all uniquely different individuals with diverse personalities, needs, talents, interests, strengths, and weaknesses. Conflicts often occur because of differing experiences, opposing needs or desires, limited resources, or because of real or perceived value differences between or among people. Conflicts, just like feelings, are neither right nor wrong; they just *are*. Rather, it is the way conflicts are handled, discussed, and resolved that can be positive or negative. There is simply no way to live our lives free of conflict, nor is it a "realistic" goal to set for our children. But how they choose to handle conflict can make all the difference in the world.

How we as adults experienced conflict as children generally determines how we perceive conflict and respond to it. In some homes, children never hear their parents disagree with one another about anything, and thus they learn nothing about how conflicts can be resolved constructively. In other homes, conflicts occur on a daily basis, but they are never resolved; often they may be accompanied by verbal abuse or even physical violence. Some adults "clam up" for hours, days, or even weeks when there is a problem. In extreme cases, children may witness the breakup of a marriage or a separation of some duration when the parents have not been able to work out their conflicts in a positive way. In all these situations, children have learned much about conflict but very little about its resolution; no positive skills have been modeled so the children have not learned to encounter everyday problems in a peaceful and constructive way. No wonder these children grow up thinking conflict is "wrong"!

Some conflicts are personal and internal. These can range from minor decisions, such as a father deciding if he will wear his grey or his paisley tie to work, to more far-reaching decisions, such as a seventh grader deciding whether she will or will not give in to peer pressure and accept a can of beer in the school parking lot at lunchtime. Other conflicts are interpersonal and affect relationships with others. Interpersonal conflicts can be also be broader in scope, such as conflicts between neighborhood gangs, cultural groups, or sports groups.

Regardless of the arena—personal or interpersonal, within a family or a larger community setting—if we think of conflict as a test of right and wrong, or as a situation where there is a winner and a loser, conflict becomes a negative, highly-threatening phenomenon that is both anxiety-producing and detrimental to self, the family, and the community.

If we have grown up in homes where conflicts were avoided or handled ineffectively, we might need some practice in order to model for our children positive and creative resolution of conflicts. We might even need to redefine what we mean by conflict. The rest of this chapter is devoted to offering some suggestions that will help you as a parent consider your attitudes toward conflict and encourage your children to confront everyday conflict situations with confidence.

Setting the Stage for Positive Resolution of Conflict

Parental guidance is probably the key factor in teaching children how to handle conflict as it arises. Children need to be taught early in life that conflict is not "bad," especially when an attempt is made to come to a peaceful solution. The following suggestions will help you as a parent provide a fertile environment for peaceful behavior and help you be a better model for your children in the peacemaking process:

- build positive images of conflict resolution
- acknowledge the problem
- foster an atmosphere of trust
- listen beyond the spoken word
- generate a feeling of empowerment
- encourage children to take responsibility
- distinguish viable alternatives
- include all family members

Build Positive Images of Conflict Resolution

Perhaps the best starting place is to consider and evaluate the role models we had as children for conflict resolution. When we take a look at where we have developed our strategies for dealing with conflict, we may find we are emulating the same behaviors that were used by our own parents or caretakers. Sometimes our conflict resolution strategies are the same ones we had hoped to avoid when we became parents, such as blaming, using sarcasm, yelling, or retreating. Or we may find we are repeating a family cycle of resolving conflict by "winning": the dominant, physically largest, or verbally most articulate family member always wins any argument. The problem with these models of conflict resolution is that they necessitate a scapegoat or a winner and loser. Someone ends up being "right" while others are "at fault."

For positive conflict resolution to take place, we need to consciously take a step toward erasing these negative images and seek more positive models that insist upon mutually-agreeable solutions that allow all parties involved in a conflict to "save face." A helpful peacekeeping motto to remember is that if everyone is working together toward finding a mutually-acceptable resolution, everyone "wins."

Acknowledge the Problem

Before any conflict can be resolved, it is necessary to acknowledge that a problem or conflict DOES exist. Denial that there is anything wrong, that friction or hurt feelings exist, often results in diminished communications. When family members stop sharing in an honest way, they begin keeping their real feelings to themselves because they are afraid to "rock the boat" or disturb the status quo. This creates a situation of avoiding conflict because it is perceived as threatening. When family members withhold themselves from each other, an emotional barrier is created that is often difficult to overcome. Family members can continue to grow in their relationships only when they are able to honestly admit to themselves and each other that there is a problem.

Foster an Atmosphere of Trust

Potential conflicts and problems will not seem as personally threatening when individuals feel truly affirmed for who they are, in an environment where they fully trust one another. Fostering an atmosphere of trust within the family means that each member feels valued and accepted for his or her own unique personality, strengths and weaknesses, likes and dislikes. In such an atmosphere, real communication—always a critical element in finding constructive solutions to problems—is possible.

Listen Beyond the Spoken Word

The inability to communicate is a primary contributor to many conflicts. The importance of good communication, including active listening, has already been emphasized in the previous chapter, but sometimes listening to the words is not enough. It is often necessary to delve beneath the surface of the words being spoken. In order to reach a peaceful coexistence, we need to be aware of messages conveyed by body language, facial gestures—in effect, what is NOT being said—in order to truly understand another human being's feelings and actions. Children, in particular, need to be made aware of these more subtle facets of communication because they often tend to believe every word that is spoken. They are therefore easily offended by shallow and vicious threats and meaningless bravado, as well as other language that is often not what it seems to be.

On the other hand, when children are communicated with kindly, with focused attention and eye contact, and with a caring heart, they are less likely to misinterpret spoken messages. They are then more amenable to listening in an unfiltered, open way.

Generate a Feeling of Empowerment

In an ideal situation, parents and children, brothers and sisters, and friends would relate to one another in ways that are mutually empowering. Children would entrust their parents or guardians with the power to influence, guide, direct, and inspire. Conversely, parents would enable their children to trust themselves, their siblings, and their friends, and would encourage their children to risk, inquire, share feelings, solve problems, and grow.

However, in this complex and violent society, parents often feel powerless themselves. When parents feel inadequate because they have not been taught how to empower their children in the ways just described, their children also often end up feeling like powerless victims. And because victims tend to become victimizers rather than peacemakers, an unfortunate cycle is perpetuated.

On the other hand, when children are taught to share, risk, trust, and relate to others in loving and supportive ways, they are able to tap their own creative abilities and talents and use them in peaceful ways in order to solve their own problems.

Encourage Children to Take Responsibility

The experience of being responsible may be as rare as it is powerful. The prevailing mind-set in the world in which our children are growing up is one of flagrant irresponsibility: "They are doing this to me!" "She hit me first!" "No one ever told me not to." "It's the government's fault!" "But I had an unhappy childhood." The context of irresponsibility has been around since Adam blamed Eve for his problems, who in turn blamed the snake in the grass. The buck just never seems to stop.

The shift from the context of irresponsibility to that of responsibility carries with it a profound sense of peacefulness and goes a long way toward eradicating a person's sense of powerlessness. When children learn to take responsibility for their actions and begin to seek alternative solutions to their problems, they make themselves stronger. They no longer need to manipulate circumstances, make excuses, or expend energy on scapegoating or wishful thinking. Instead, they are able to utilize a wide range of possibilities over which they have control and, ultimately, free will.

Distinguish Viable Alternatives

Children need to learn that, while most conflicts lend themselves to many creative resolutions, there are some methods of conflict resolution that are physically or morally unacceptable. A difference of opinion about where to go out for dinner, for example, would lend itself to a range of viable alternatives and, while many ideas may not be acted upon, any and all ideas should be solicited from children and considered. Certain other conflicts, however, such as how to deal with an antagonistic neighbor, may open up some suggestions from children that would not be appropriate actions. We need to teach our children that methods of resolution that are physically, emotionally, or morally harmful to another person or group of people—such as using violence as a means of resolving a conflict with an antagonistic neighbor—will never be considered acceptable.

Include All Family Members

Full acceptance of each family member includes inviting each family member to the decision-making process in the home whenever possible. Although children may not be capable of participating in certain critical family decisions (such as a parent's job transfer), there are many routine decisions in which children can participate and, by doing so, become empowered. They will learn to make responsible choices and also become aware of, and responsible for, the consequences of their choices, words, and actions. In group decision-making, children should be encouraged to express their feelings honestly and openly, and any suggestions they offer for the good of the family should be respected as valid contributions. While younger children's decision-making input may be limited to such basic issues as what dessert the family will have for supper, or what family recreational activities will be chosen, older children may begin to have a say in a broader range of issues, such as where the family will go on vacation or how the family budget could be cut.

Family Peace Meetings

A Family Peace Meeting is a practical, potent form of entire family consultation in which children can learn effective means of conflict resolution. It provides a forum in which children can experience being empowered, learn to take responsibility in the context of their actions, and begin to understand the nuances of effective communication. Used often and effectively, Family Peace Meetings can help children become familiar with the myriad of peaceful options available to them in nearly every conflict they encounter.

The Family Peace Meeting can be used for such varied purposes as the following:

- to decide where the family will take a vacation

- to consider an argument with your neighbors about their dog

- to renegotiate the amount of allowance each child receives

- to decide upon appropriate redistribution of household chores

The following activity outlines the format for Family Peace Meetings, with specific suggestions for implementing this important type of open forum with your family. Before trying the activity, however, consider the "Guidelines for Family Peace Meetings" on page 61 to assure that your meetings are conducted as fairly and openly as possible for the benefit of every member of the family. Review the guidelines with all family members. Cut out or photocopy them; create a poster to display in a public place when you have a Family Peace Meeting.

"Conducting a

Family Peace Meeting"

Supplies needed: table

chairs

1. A Family Peace Meeting may be called at any place, any time, by any member of the family. Those directly involved in the issue or conflict call the meeting.

2. All members of the family sit around a table facing one another.

3. With hands on the table, one person involved in the conflict begins by telling his or her point of view about what happened. The person removes his or her hands from the table to signal that the telling is complete.

4. Anyone else may then add to the presentation of the problem, adding details or other dimensions.

5. After the problem has been stated from all points of view, the adult(s) ask each family member to offer alternatives in a peaceful manner, without criticizing the participants or passing judgment on how the problem was originally handled.

6. The adult(s) then act as arbitrators to help the children develop concrete solutions or alternatives.

> For example, a child might suggest, "The girls should be nice to one another," and an adult might ask the child to elaborate on how exactly the girls could behave differently. The adult could then restate the options for the children, while avoiding saying which option should be taken or which one would be "the best." The adult never forces adult solutions upon children.

7. When a number of peaceful solutions have been articulated by the children and restated by the adult(s), a debriefing occurs. The adult(s) asks the children which option they can agree to, how they are feeling now, and how their actions in the future might change as a result of the ideas raised at the Family Peace Meeting.

8. The adult(s) may then end the meeting by asking the children to applaud themselves for being peacemakers. If the adult(s) so desires, special peacemaker stickers or badges could be given to children to concretize the experience in a positive way.

Guidelines for Family Peace Meetings

1. I will put my hands on the table when I am talking.

2. I understand that only one person may talk at a time.

3. I will not interrupt when someone else is talking.

4. I will not repeat what has already been said.

RAISING PEACEFUL CHILDREN IN A VIOLENT WORLD

To get an idea of how the Family Peace Meeting works, revisit the opening scene of this chapter in which Nicole, Jessie, and their mother were in conflict. Imagine them calling a Family Peace Meeting and consider how the meeting might help all of them feel more empowered, take responsibility for their actions, and communicate more effectively:

> Jessie, feeling she has a legitimate grievance, calls her mother and sister, Nicole, to the kitchen table for a Family Peace Meeting.
>
> Jessie begins the session by putting her hands on the table and explains what has happened from her perspective: "I was getting something from my bureau drawer, and I noticed that my package of troll stickers was gone. I asked Nicole if she had seen it, and she said yes. She showed me her notebook that was decorated with them. I got angry and told her I had said she could have SOME of the stickers but not all of them. She took every single one!" Jessie removes her hands from the table, signifying that she has finished speaking.
>
> Nicole puts her hands on the table and tells her side of the conflict: "Remember last week when it was your turn to set the table and you were rollerblading with Lisa? You asked me if I would set the table for you, and I said I would if you would let me have your new troll stickers. You never said how many I could take." Nicole removes her hands to show she is done speaking.
>
> Jessie puts her hands on the table to object: "I DID say how many you could take, sort of. I said you could have SOME of them. I never thought you would actually take them all! They were a birthday present from Lisa." Jessie signifies she is finished.
>
> Nicole responds: "I don't remember your saying I could have only 'some.' I just remember your saying if I would set the table, I could have the stickers, like a trade, a deal." Nicole removes her hands from the table.
>
> There is a momentary pause. Both sisters have carefully explained their sides of the story and both are considering what the other has said.

The mother puts her hands on the table. First, she restates the problem in an objective manner, pointing out the underlying breakdown in communication. She does not blame: "Nicole, you set the table for your sister in exchange for stickers that your sister said you could have. You thought you were entitled to all of them. Jessie, you noticed that Nicole had taken all of your stickers when you thought you had made it clear she was to take only some of them. No exact number was agreed upon. It seems that neither of you had a clear idea of exactly what the agreement was. What are some ways we could resolve this problem?"

Jessie immediately puts her hands on the table. "I think Nicole should buy me some more stickers. I'll give her some of them."

Nicole responds, "But we never agreed on how many stickers were a fair exchange for setting the table. I'll tell you what: If you will do one of my chores, I'll buy you some new stickers, and I'll just take one or two."

Jessie nods her agreement.

The mother restates what has been decided: "So the two of you agree that because no agreement was originally made about exactly how many stickers would be given in exchange for setting the table, Nicole will buy new stickers to replace the troll stickers she used and keep two. Jessie, you will do one of Nicole's chores."

The two children nod in agreement.

The mother then asks each girl how she feels about the resolution. Both girls smile and agree that they feel comfortable with how the problem has been resolved.

"How do you think the two of you could avoid a conflict like this in the future?" the mother then asks. "It seems as though there was a communication problem here."

Jessie answers, "Maybe when we make a deal with each other, we can repeat it to each other so each of us agrees with every word."

Nicole adds, "How about if we write down exactly what the agreement is? It's easy to forget what we said."

Jessie nods. "I think that's a good idea because in the deal we just made, I'd like to discuss exactly which chore I need to do for you so we don't argue about it later."

Nicole agrees and looks pleased. Both girls seem satisfied with the resolution.

The mother then restates the conclusion the girls have drawn and praises their peacekeeping accomplishments: "I am so proud of the way the two of you worked out your problem and the way you thought about how to avoid a similar future conflict. You did it so thoughtfully and peacefully. Pat yourselves on the back!"

Giggling, the two children pat their backs. Their mother is pleased and feels empowered herself, as she can see she has been able to guide them into taking an important step forward in their growth as peaceful beings who have considerable skills in conflict resolution.

Family Role Plays

In the case of Jessie and Nicole, a Family Peace Meeting could work well because the two children are mature enough to think abstractly and consider another person's point of view. However, for children who are not yet capable of seeing the argument from another perspective, a Family Role Play is often useful and can be a helpful transition activity in training for a Family Peace Meeting.

The objective for both activities is virtually the same: to help children to consider cause and effect relationships, allow them to evaluate several different behaviors, and demonstrate that there are often alternative methods of solving conflict. For younger children, role playing offers the advantage of illustrating these points more graphically, more concretely. The whole child—mind, body, and soul—is involved in the process of seeking a peaceful solution to the problem. As with Family Peace Meetings, Family Role Plays can occur whenever a child has had a conflict with a sibling, a parent or other adult, or a person from the school or community.

"Creating a Family Role Play"

Supplies needed: none

1. As in the Family Peace Meeting, any family member can call a Family Role Play session to order.

2. The person(s) who was involved in the conflict describes the situation as it happened, in detail, for the rest of the family members.

3. The person who called the meeting selects other members of the family to take the roles of the participants in the conflict. (In the case of a small family, members may need to play several roles.) The person may opt NOT to play a role, but to watch the performance.

4. The "actors" are then asked to prepare two skits. For the first skit, they portray the incident exactly as it happened, as authentically as possible. For the second skit, they create a scenario in which the same incident has a more peaceful ending.

5. Family members not assigned to the reenactment are asked to watch what the actors do and say, think how they might be feeling, and try to imagine yet another way the conflict might have been handled more peacefully.

6. After both skits have been performed, all the family members engage in a reflective discussion led by a parent or other adult. At this time, family members who watched the skits can give constructive feedback on how the actors solved the problem and can add their own ideas about ways the conflict might have been resolved. (If they wish to, they can role play their ideas.)

7. An adult restates the ideas that have been offered for solving the problem peacefully. As with Family Peace Meetings, no adult judgments are made on the relative merits of each idea, but each suggestion is carefully considered by each family member.

8. The adult then asks the person involved in the conflict to express his or her feelings about the optional solutions that were offered. If more than one family member was involved, they decide upon the solution that they feel most comfortable with.

9. At the end of the activity, the adult(s) praise the children for their peacekeeping efforts. The children leave the session empowered, knowing that there are several viable options open to them in any conflict. In addition, they have gained vicarious experience by seeing or role playing alternatives in the second skit.

A Family Role Play in Action

The following vignette demonstrates how role playing was used to reflect upon a problem that eleven-year-old Raúl encountered on the playground:

> Raúl was preparing to play baseball with his six friends. It was the boys' custom to take turns being captains, and those who were captains got to select which boys would be on their side. This day it was Raúl's and Denny's turn to be captains. When Raúl made his first selection, Jared got angry. He declared that it was his ball, and he had to be the captain or he would take his ball and go home. He had done the same thing several times in the past, and Raúl and the others were tired of his behavior.
>
> Denny suggested they simply take Jared's ball away from him, which two of the other boys proceeded to do. Angry words were tossed back and forth, culminating in a fist fight. Though Raúl had not participated in the physical fight directly, he had been badly bruised by a misguided punch meant for Denny. He was still feeling very angry with Jared.
>
> Raúl came home and called a Family Role Play session with his parents, a younger brother, and an older sister. He described for them in detail what had happened. He then asked his father to play his part and his brother to play the part of Denny; he decided to play the part of Jared himself. His mother and sister were asked to watch carefully to see if they could think of any other alternatives that would resolve the problem peacefully.

The three family members first played the scene as closely to the original as they could. For the second scene they modified the conflict, creating a scenario with a more peaceful ending that resulted from the brainstorming of the three family members. The second skit went like this:

Raúl [acted by father]: "C'mon, guys! Let's play ball! It's Denny's and my turn to be captains. Flip for first pick."

Jared [acted by Raúl]: "No way! It's my ball. I get to be a captain, or I take my ball and go home. No ball, no ball game."

Raúl [acted by father]: Jared, you've pulled that stunt a couple of times, and we're all sick of it. If you'd like to take your ball and go home, go ahead; the rest of us will play something else. Fred has a soccer ball he'll let us borrow. We'll play soccer for a change."

Denny [acted by brother]: "But we'd rather play baseball, Jared, and we'd like you to play with us. You have to wait your turn to be captain, just like everybody else."

Raúl [acted by father]: "Denny's right. Denny and I are captains today, and you and Fred are supposed to be captains tomorrow. Now, what do you say, Jared? Will you play with us?"

Jared [acted by Raúl]: "Yeah, I guess so."

The new skit showed the problem being solved with a high degree of diplomacy before the encounter escalated to verbal taunts. Justice was served, and Jared was able to save face. After all the actors had been duly congratulated for their fine problem-solving and peacekeeping skills, the role playing session then moved to the reflective discussion stage. The mother, who had carefully watched both skits, offered an additional alternative: Might Raúl or Denny have offered to switch turns with Jared in an effort to keep the peace? That is, Jared would be captain today but relinquish his turn tomorrow. The other family members discussed this alternative, but felt that, while it might have prevented an altercation this one time, the same problem might have occurred in the future, unless Jared happened to be in a more compromising mood. The sister then suggested the boys could borrow, or chip in and buy, another baseball so Jared would no longer feel he had special privileges because it was his ball.

The session came to a close with Raúl's mother restating the three options that had been created as a result of the role playing and subsequent discussions. Raúl chose his sister's idea of borrowing a ball from another friend as a way to solve the conflict. When his mother asked how he felt about this solution, Raúl said he felt "pretty good" about it. She praised the efforts of each family member. Raúl, who had been initially very upset, no longer felt powerless; indeed, he had the experience of considering several strategies that might be used to diffuse similar unpleasant situations when they occur.

<table>
<tr><td>

Frequently
Asked
Questions

</td><td>

Parents often have concerns about the "nitty-gritty" of instituting Family Peace Meetings and Family Role Plays. Therefore, here is a list of the most frequently asked questions and how each one has been addressed for the benefit of parents who may have similar concerns.

</td></tr>
</table>

Q. Won't some children be the subject of Family Peace Meetings or Role Plays disproportionately more often than others?

A. Yes, some children will use the forum of a meeting or performance to get attention. One child I know liked to cause minor problems just so he could talk about them at such times. Since children are pretty good at knowing what is fair, and since his siblings felt he was doing things just to get attention, they soon came up with a logical consequences: The family decided this boy could not call a meeting for one week.

Q. How much time does it take for a parent to become fairly good at leading a Family Peace Meeting?

A. Parents always seem to feel they could be better. But since all skills have to be practiced in order to improve them, it is important not to give up if your first couple of sessions don't go as smoothly as the examples in this chapter. Just as in learning to type or play tennis, practice is the key, and you will get better and better with experience. Parents improve with reflection upon their performance, and children improve as they become better at knowing what a variety of alternative solutions might be. Practice does make "perfect," in the respect that your ability to conduct the meeting gets better as your confidence in doing so increases.

Q. Are some of the conflicts children bring to a Family Peace Meeting or Family Role Play actually non-negotiable?

A. Some items ARE non-negotiable. This, however, does not mean they are not discussable. For example, if a child calls a meeting to complain about not being allowed to stay up until midnight on a school night, the child can immediately be told that the item is non-negotiable but that the adult will listen to the child's feelings in case there is something about the item that the parent is not understanding. The non-negotiable bedtime may have been put on the agenda because the child thinks that other children she or he knows can go to bed "anytime they feel like it." It is important for the child to be able to discuss her or his feelings about being "different" from friends, but parents can still reiterate their reasons for the non-negotiable rule while hearing and sympathizing with the child's feelings.

Q. What about parents putting things on the agenda for a family meeting or role play?

A. I have found that it can be extremely helpful for parents to put items on the agenda, especially problems involving specific discipline issues, such as children forgetting to do chores, keeping messy rooms, or not getting up in time for school. Such items are, in fact, often best handled with input from all family members.

Q. What if an alternative solution decided on by the family doesn't seem to work?

A. When this happens, bring the item back to a Family Peace Meeting or Family Role Play. Often the cause is that the family member did not carry out the plan as it was originally agreed upon. Further brainstorming or repeated restatement of the proposed solution usually will do the trick.

A Closing Word about Conflict Resolution

Children today are growing up in a complex world with a vast array of people each with differing ideas, customs, feelings, interests, and goals. In such a world, conflict is inevitable, but it does not have to end badly. Conflict can be healthy and lead to an important growth of character when it is approached creatively. When children *and* parents practice new ways of solving differences, this ensures that the environment in the home is a supportive one in which children can talk about problems freely. This not only helps children resolve conflict effectively but also helps them learn to become peacemakers in the world.

4

WHEN
PEACE
IS
THREATENED

Ten Responses to
Potentially Violent Situations

"[I]t isn't enough to talk about peace. One must believe in it. And it isn't enough to believe in it. One must work at it." —Eleanor Roosevelt, "Voice of America" broadcast

"Who Will Kill the Bad Guys?"

Several years ago my daughter, Chrissy, was watching television when an advertisement for an upcoming newscast revealed several young people being dragged off to jail by police. My six-year-old child asked why the people were being taken to jail. I carefully explained that they were protesting the opening of an atomic weapons plant in our area.

"What's 'atomic weapons'?" she asked earnestly.

In answering Chrissy's question, I expressed my personal view that the plant should be concentrating more on peacetime materials than on bombs and other war machinery. Little Chrissy had already formulated her own ideas.

"But, Mommy, we *need* bombs and guns and things like that to kill all the bad guys!" she exclaimed, her arms folded resolutely.

Obviously, I was somewhat dismayed at my daughter's seemingly cynical perspective on the world, as I had thought I was raising a "peaceful child." Yet her statement only underscored that the "might makes right" attitude prevalent throughout our society may not be easily eradicated simply by living in a peaceful home. Chrissy had already, in her six years on earth, established a viewpoint that life is pretty much an "us-against-them" preposition. And, more crucially, she seemed to think bombs and guns would merely kill the "bad people"—so "good people" should definitely use them! She had no understanding of the utter devastation produced by bombs and war.

I realized I needed to do something more to help my daughter grow as a peaceloving human being. My reflections at that time became the basis for the underlying question addressed in this chapter: How do we effectively teach peacekeeping skills to our children in a world that promotes—and even glorifies—violence?

Children's attitudes toward conflict, violence, and war are critically affected in the most subtle of ways by the views held by their parents or guardians. Children's ideas about a specific war—their attitudes toward the Rwandan conflict, for example—bear a close relationship to opinions gleaned from their parents, even when parental statements are not being directly addressed to children. We as parents, then, need to reflect carefully on our attitudes toward war and other violence. We need to be aware of the many different manifestations of "war mentality" we encounter AND perpetrate in our everyday lives. When we are confident that the attitudes we convey to our children are promoting peace and not war, we are in a much better position to offer our ideas about peacekeeping in regard to the problems children may encounter in their daily encounters with others. Finally, we need to determine what we are honestly willing to change in our own behavior in order to create the kind of peaceful environment we most desire for our children. With these thoughts in mind, take a moment to consider your attitudes toward violence in your community and in the world. Discuss your responses to the following questions with your loved ones.

TUNING IN
What Are Your Family's Views on Violence?

GUNS AND FIREARMS

1. What are your beliefs about keeping firearms in your home? Under what circumstances, if any, do you think this might be appropriate?

2. In what ways, if any, do you believe guns are contributing to the escalating violence in the United States?

3. How do you share your feelings and beliefs about firearms with your children?

4. How do you think your views on firearms affect your children's peacemaking attitudes?

WAR

1. Describe your beliefs about the necessity or the futility of war.

2. In your opinion, how is "patriotism" related to "fighting for one's country"?

3. What issues in the current conflicts around the globe are you familiar with?

4. How do you share your feelings about these issues with your children?

5. How do you talk to your children about the futility of assigning blame in any of the current global conflicts?

6. What are your feelings about nuclear weapons as a deterrent to war?

7. In what ways do you discuss your feelings about military defense, where age-appropriate, with your children?

8. What are your feelings about the amount of federal funds spent on military equipment versus the amount of funds spent on eradicating domestic ills, such as disaster relief and homelessness, and improving education?

9. How do you think your views on war affect your children's attitudes?

10. How do you think your children's view on war affect their peacekeeping strategies with others?

What Children Are Saying about Conflict and Violence

Several teen-agers from Eastern Senior High School near America's capital in Washington, D. C. were interviewed by Lynn Minton for *Parade* magazine.[1] They were asked the question, "Why is there so much violence?" Their responses were similar and centered around ten factors: anger, lack of self-esteem, lack of respect for others, excuses, lack of proper morals, temptation of material goods, imitation of violent peers, easy availability of guns, ascribing blame to others, and racial factors. These Washington teen-agers, speaking frankly, suggested in their interviews that parents needed to:

- Promote self-esteem and morals.
  They felt parents should bring up their children "right" and show their children they are loved.

- Encourage their children to strive for something.
  These teen-agers believed parents should teach their children to strive for something better than the parents had. However, these teens recognized that, sometimes, parents cannot strive for anything better—they are just trying to survive.

- Know their children's friends.
  The teen-agers thought parents should know who their children are hanging out with because the temptation for violence might come from the children's friends. One teen-ager said, "I try not to hang out with certain people that I know get into trouble."

- Watch who their children admire.
  The teens interviewed believed violence sometimes occurs because some young people admire the way violent people act.

---

1   *Parade*, Sunday, January 6, 1994, pp. 10-12. Parade Publications, New York, NY.

Ten Responses to Teach Children

The factors that these Washington teen-agers spoke about emphasize some things we as parents need to consider in creating a home environment that is conducive to peacemaking. However, for children to become independent peacemakers within and beyond the home, they need to have at their disposal a complete repertoire of responses that they are capable of using whenever they encounter a potentially violent conflict. Since it is not always possible for children to have the luxury of reflecting upon a host of alternative situations, as they might during a Family Peace Meeting for example, children need to have readily available some possible strategies for responding when problematic or potentially violent situations arise. The following ten responses, when they become so familiar that they are thoroughly ingrained, can help children respond spontaneously to a wide range of situations.

To help your children learn to make the best use of these strategies, consider introducing them in the following stages:

- Explain each of the responses.
- Study the "real life" examples given.
- Offer personal examples of when, how, and why each response might be used.
- Provide imaginary situations where your children can practice choosing a particular response to resolve a depicted conflict.
- Encourage your children to memorize the ten responses so the strategies are readily available (see page 83).

1. Talk It Over and Listen

Although these responses are not meant to be hierarchical, this first strategy is definitely "number one" because it is almost always a first step in resolving conflict before it escalates to violence. Many casualties could be avoided if young people would first talk out a problem *and* really listen to the other person's point of view before walking away in a huff, hitting, name calling, or even shooting or stabbing, to settle an argument. Young people are notoriously impetuous, often acting on the spur of the moment and later ruing their deeds. If they could internalize the concept of first discussing a problem in a calm fashion *before* reacting to it, many potentially explosive situations could be immediately diffused.

Example:

Chrissy, Gloria, and Laura are good friends. One day when these ten-year-olds are playing together, Laura whispers a secret to Gloria. Chrissy asks, "Laura, what did you just say to Gloria?" Laura replies, "I can't tell you; it's a secret." Chrissy is angry and hurt. Her first impulse is to slap Laura. Instead, Chrissy calls Laura aside and says, "I feel excluded when you whisper to Gloria right in front of me." Laura responds by saying, "We were talking about the summer camp that Gloria and I are going to in a few days. I was whispering so you wouldn't feel left out." Chrissy is able to hear that the whispering was not done out of malice, as she had thought, but out of concern for her feelings. Chrissy compliments Laura on trying not to hurt her feelings; however, she reiterates that whispering does hurt people's feelings and she asks Laura not do it again. Laura agrees. The three children resume playing, and the incident is quickly forgotten.

2. Walk Away

Each of us has experienced the need to "count to ten" in a situation where we have become extremely angry. As adults, we know it is usually best not to say anything or take any action until we have cooled down. Moreover, some individuals have shorter fuses than others: Their tempers flare, they react quickly, and then they feel sorry later for their actions or overreactions. Children need to be taught to understand and respect their own temperaments. If a short fuse is a problem, walking away is a strategy that may be a child's best response when confronting a conflict or potentially violent situation.

Example:

LeVon calls her best friend, Cynthia, to see if she can play. Cynthia says she is sorry but her mother has chores for her to do, so she'll be busy all day. LeVon wanders over to the park alone, seeking someone to play with. She spots Cynthia playing catch with two girls LeVon does not recognize. LeVon is furious, feeling she has been betrayed by her friend. LeVon is aware of her temper and can feel her face getting hot. She feels like going up to Cynthia and telling her what she thinks of her lies and her "friendship." Instead, she walks away and sits down behind a tree. She takes a few deep breaths and then silently talks to herself: 'Cynthia has been been my best friend for six months. She likes me and wouldn't deliberately hurt my feelings. I'm sure there is a good reason why she said she couldn't play and is playing with those girls. I probably have no reason to be upset.' LeVon then walks back to Cynthia and the other two girls and asks, "Hey, what's up?" Cynthia seems genuinely happy to see LeVon and introduces her two cousins, who unexpectedly came for a visit. The four children play together for a while until the two cousins have to leave. Cynthia goes back, reluctantly, to her chores. LeVon smiles to herself, glad she did not overreact and lose a very good friend.

3. Say, "I'm Sorry"

One of the premises of true peacemaking behavior is exemplified by a sincere "I'm sorry." Children need to learn that they, like every other human being under the sun, will make mistakes at times. Apologizing for the action shows remorse, a desire for forgiveness, and a real caring about accepting the responsibility for putting the relationship on track again.

Example:

José and Chad are on a lengthy bike ride, and the temperature is ninety degrees in the shade. As the boys stop to rest, Chad lifts their water bottle to his lips and takes a few large gulps, almost finishing the last of the two quarts of water they had brought with them. "Hey, dude, let me have some of that," José says. Chad doesn't answer as he thirstily drains the bottle. "There was only a little left," he finally says, wiping his mouth with the back of his arm. José is furious and tells Chad what he thinks about his greedy behavior. The two ride home in silence. Chad, reflecting on the incident during the ride, realizes how badly he has behaved and wishes he had shared the water with his friend. When the boys reach their neighborhood, Chad says, "José, I'm really sorry I didn't share the water with you. I was thirsty but so were you. I guess I was just being selfish. C'mon in my house, and I'll pour you the biggest glass of lemonade you've ever seen!" José shrugs and follows Chad into the house. There are no residual bad feelings.

4. Do Something Else

Children need to learn to be flexible enough to discontinue an activity or discussion if it is causing major problems among friends or within a group. Normally, the parents tell children to "break it up" or insist that the children stop the game or activity that is the source of the discord. But children can do this more effectively themselves by adding this important strategy to their repertoire.

Example:

Mary, Sarah, Courtney, and Jessie are playing Monopoly. Mary is complaining bitterly about being "in jail" for two turns and not collecting any rent on her properties. Sarah tells Mary she is being a poor sport; being in jail is part of the game. Mary loses her temper and deliberately knocks over the game board. Courtney and Jessie are furious and demand an apology. Mary apologizes, but she continues to sulk. Courtney realizes the game has ceased to be pleasurable for any of them. "Hey, let's go rollerblading!' she suggests, "I'm tired of playing Monopoly!" Without blaming anyone, Courtney has made everyone feel better. The girls all help to put the game away, and they head outside.

5. Take Turns

Children, particularly younger ones, tend to be somewhat egocentric and often believe the world revolves around them. Therefore, children need to be shown the positive outcomes of taking turns at an activity. By allowing friends to participate equally and watching friends as they take turns at an activity, children can learn to experience pleasure vicariously as they see the enjoyment of others. Such behavior, ingrained at an early age, can help ward off many minor conflicts before they can escalate to major battles, especially when the conflicts are over limited resources.

Example:

Ryan and Meg are playing on the slide. Since Meg is older and runs faster than Ryan, she appears to be getting more turns sliding than Ryan. Ryan, noticing this, sits down on the ground and begins to scream, as he is too young to put words to what is he feeling about the injustice he thinks is taking place. Meg figures out that Ryan is crying because he is not getting in enough slides. "Okay, Ryan, let's do it this way. When you slide, I'll wait for you at the bottom and cheer for you. Then you wait at the bottom for me and cheer. We'll take turns sliding and watching each other." The two children try this, and the activity is enhanced for both as each begins to share in the other's pleasure as well as his or her own.

6. Share

My mother used to instruct my sisters and brother and me that when we shared something such as candy, we should offer the larger piece to the other person. Such an "other-directed" attitude would go a long way toward easing some of life's conflicts.

Moreover, as children learn early in life to share, they will be building a foundation for becoming charitable adults, with a propensity for sharing what they have with those who are less fortunate. Therefore, such important behavior, internalized very early in life, is yet another technique for confronting conflict.

Example:

Ted and Jeremy have just returned from a camping trip, and they are famished. They go to a restaurant and order a pizza, but they have enough money for only a small pie. Just as they are sitting down to eat their pizza, their friend LeRoy happens by. He sits down with them, and they all begin joking and laughing together. They ask LeRoy if he is hungry, and he answers, "Starving!" Ted and Jeremy had been looking forward to three pieces each, but instead they divide the pizza so each of them gets two. They eat their slices slowly, savoring the company as much as the food.

7. Ignore Certain Behaviors

Even very young children can be taught a fundamental principle of psychology: If you continue to ignore undesirable behavior, it will soon extinguish itself. This is especially true if a child's behavior is an attempt to get attention or "a rise" out of someone. The offending child will continue to behave in the same manner as long as his or her "victim(s)" become upset or fight back, for that is exactly what the child wants. If we can help our children learn to develop the ability (and restraint) to simply ignore unwanted behavior, and learn to spot the sort of individuals who are most prone to perpetuate such antics, we can help them lead a more peaceful life.

Example:

Jennifer is watching television. Her younger brother, Todd, walks through the living room, slowly lingering in front of the television so that her vision is blocked. Jennifer first politely asks him to move. He appears to comply, leaving the living room, but he immediately comes back and repeats the behavior. Jennifer realizes that, for whatever reason, Todd is trying to annoy her. She picks up a magazine and starts to leaf through it. Todd turns to look at her, sees that she is paying no attention to him, and leaves the room—this time, for good.

8. Compromise

Because peacemaking is concerned with resolving a situation so that everyone can feel good about themselves, the art of making compromises is pivotal to the process. But children need to be taught, also, that reaching a peaceful, mutually-satisfying agreement often means all parties involved need to give up something so everyone can feel comfortable with the solution.

Example:

Twins Judy and Jane each want to enroll in a different Friday afternoon sports activity. Unfortunately, the activities take place at opposite directions of the city, and the twins' mother, a single parent, has only one car. Their mother tells them they cannot both go, but if one wants to go, they will have to work it out between them which of them it will be. The two sisters first consider drawing straws but decide against that option because they feel the girl with the best luck would "win," while the unlucky other girl will feel she has clearly "lost." They decide instead upon a deal or a compromise. They had earlier been told there would be no summer camp for them that year because the increase in price had made it impossible for their mother to afford to send both of them. Judy had been the most disappointed. Remembering this, Jane suggests, "How about if you go to summer camp, and I go to Friday afternoon soccer?" Judy readily agrees to this plan. They check with their mother, who is also delighted that her daughters were able to amicably reach a compromise that gave each twin something she wanted.

9. Give the Person a Hug

One lesson that can be difficult for children to comprehend is that human beings—children and adults—are prone to a variety of good and bad moods. These moods may depend upon a variety of environmental factors, but often a bad mood is brought about when there is more than the normal amount of stress in the person's life, such as an experience of loss, or a time when life just seems momentarily "out of control." Children need to be helped to understand that in conflict situations where someone is simply in a bad mood, reasoning with or negotiating a compromise with that individual may not be the best approach. Sometimes the person may just need a hug, a pat on the back, or some reassuring words, such as, "I'm really sorry you're feeling bad." Of course, if the bad mood occurs frequently, the child needs to be aware that there may be a deeper emotional or psychological problem. When this is the case, it may be impossible to resolve a conflict without outside help, and the child should be made to understand that he or she did not fail. But for the ordinary "bad mood" situation, an embrace or warm pat on the back can go a long way toward keeping a relationship on track.

Example:

Chrissy goes over to her friend Laura's house. Laura's cat has just died, and she is quite upset. The two decide to play dress up, but Laura insists upon wearing the best hat, the finest gown, and the shiniest shoes. They try several other activities, but Laura's behavior is the same. She will not compromise, take turns, or share, though these are the ways the girls normally resolve conflicts. Chrissy asks Laura what the problem is, but Laura insists nothing is wrong. Finally, sensing that Laura is still really sad about losing her cat, Chrissy gives her friend a big hug. Laura sits tearfully for a few moments, then starts giggling. "Thanks, Chrissy, I needed that," she says, drying her eyes.

All of these suggested strategies are geared toward teaching children how to solve a wide range of conflicts *independently*. Such an orientation is deliberate for, in far too many instances, parents or teachers tend to intervene in situations where children could learn much more about peacekeeping if they were encouraged to solve the problem themselves. Sometimes, however, a conflict is too large, too sophisticated, too dangerous, or too violent for children to take matters into their own hands. At that point, they need to solicit the help of a parent or other adult in authority. It is important that we teach them to recognize when this is the case.

Example:

José and Chad are selecting a video at the nearby video store. An older boy whom they do not know walks over to them, grabs the video away from them, and walks away. They try to ignore it and choose another video, but the same thing happens again. Frustrated, Chad asks the boy to leave them alone. The older boy sneers and exposes a knife that is partially hidden in his jacket pocket. "Meet me outside, and we'll decide if you deserve to be left alone!" the boy mutters menacingly. Chad and José realize the situation is beyond what they are capable of handling by themselves. Chad and José tell the store manager what has happened, and the manager quickly calls the police. An officer gives the older boy a stern warning, the knife is taken away from him, and Chad and José are safely escorted home.

○ ○ ○

Learning these ten responses to conflict or potentially violent situations will go a long way toward helping your children be prepared to handle conflict when it occurs. These responses are summarized in the "Guidelines for Peacekeeping" on page 83. Cut out or photocopy the page for your children. Post the list in your children's favorite place where they will read it often.

Guidelines for Peacekeeping

1. I can talk the problem over and listen to what the other person has to say.

2. I can walk away.

3. I can say, "I'm sorry."

4. I can do something else.

5. I can take turns.

6. I can share.

7. I can ignore the behavior.

8. I can compromise.

9. I can give the other person a hug.

10. I can ask for help.

RAISING PEACEFUL CHILDREN IN A VIOLENT WORLD

Practice in Peacekeeping

To assist your children in internalizing responses that will help them keep the peace, you may want to utilize the following specific family activities to give your children practice in dealing with violence, potential violence, or even perceived violence. The activities can be easily integrated into Family Sharing Time (FST) (see page 45) as the need arises.

"Make-Believe Peace Monster"

Supplies needed: paper plates
crayons
popsicle sticks

A "make-believe monster" can be a helpful prop that allows children to let go of their angry or hurt feelings by using the "monster" to intercede.

1. Talk with your children about any time that a parent or other adult hurt their feelings because the adult's anger was expressed in yelling.

2. Have your children create monster masks out of paper plates, crayons, and popsicle sticks.

3. Explain to your children that the "monster" can tell the adult how they wish the adult would behave.

4. Allow your children to keep their "monsters" in a special place to use whenever a situation becomes too intense or frightening and they would like to keep the peace.

"Puppets for Peace"

Supplies needed: two hand puppets

Puppets can be used to promote your children's peacekeeping behaviors by helping them act out possible solutions to a problem before it becomes a harmful conflict. Children are often able to recognize themselves in a puppet who won't share, won't wait for a turn, won't pick up after her/himself, tattles, bullies, shows off, whines, or does something that is unsafe.

1. Using two hand puppets, present a short skit depicting an undesirable interaction or behavior.

   Example:

   Jason: "Hi, Ralph. I'm going bowling."

   Ralph: "But, Jason, you don't even know how to bowl!"

   Jason: "I do *too* know how to bowl!"

   [Jason leaves angry.]

2. Invite your children to offer ways to avoid or resolve the problem.

3. Discuss the pros and cons of your children's problem-solving ideas.

4. Continue the skit incorporating your children's resolution to the problem.

   Example:

   Jason: "Yes, I *do* know how to bowl. It hurt my feelings when you said that."

   Ralph: "I'm sorry, Jason. I didn't mean to hurt your feelings. I wasn't thinking."

   Jason: "That's okay, Ralph. You are usually very kind."

   Ralph: "Are we still friends, Jason?"

   Jason: "Of course! Let's go bowling together. Maybe you can teach me how!"

5. Ask your children to describe how the puppet's actions might be similar to a real event in their lives and to share what they have learned.

6. Once your children have seen you using this puppet activity to act out potentially violent situations, they may want to take over and act out their own situations and solutions.

 "Apologizing

Promotes Peace"

Supplies needed: hand puppets (optional)

With or without the puppets from the above activity, invite your children to act out scenes such as the following as a way of practicing saying "I'm sorry" without being defensive or blaming:

Scene 1:

A child has messed up a parent's desk. The parent happens along and sees this. The parent gets very angry and yells at the child. The child apologizes for having messed up the parent's work place; the parent apologizes for having lost his or her temper.

Scene 2:

In a rush to get out the door for school, a child knocks down his younger sister, leaving a painful bruise on the little girl's leg. The brother helps his sister up and says, "I'm sorry. I shouldn't have been in so much of a hurry." The sister responds, "That's okay. I know you didn't mean to knock me down."

"Confronting Hurtful Situations"

Supplies needed: none

You can help your children learn to handle hurtful situations by teaching them to confront the situations in a variety of ways, as demonstrated by the procedures below:

1. Explain to your children, in simple terms, the psychology behind bullying or "name-calling" behavior. Explain that children may do this to get attention or because they feel bad about themselves and want others to feel bad, too.

2. Explain to your children how to avoid the conflict by not giving the teaser or bully what he or she is seeking.

3. Use the following example to discuss some specific strategies that could be used to diffuse bullying situations.

    Example:
    A child taunts you, calling you "four eyes" because you wear glasses.

Ask your children to consider the following responses:

Response 1:
Ignore the behavior.

Response 2:
"Sticks and stones may break my bones but names can never hurt me" (or a similar response that suggests the name calling is having no effect).

Response 3:
"It's too bad you are calling me a hurtful name because I would really like to be your friend."

4. Discuss the three responses with your children and ask them which one they think would be the most likely to bring about a peaceful resolution to the problem.

5. Ask your children to suggest some other "bullying" situations and possible responses.

"Effecting a Cease-Fire"

Supplies needed: notepad
                    writing utensils

A "war" among family members can be constantly raging in the homes of some children. Children can use the "talk it over and listen" response to help ease the situation. Children can also learn to bring about a "cease-fire" by diplomatically telling members of the family what has been observed and how destructive the resultant feelings are to all other members of the family.

1. Select one child to be a family "war correspondent." Assign the child the task of watching when a family conflict occurs. The child's job is to write down exactly what happens as it occurs.

2. Ask the child to bring his or her observations to a family meeting. In a calm, deliberate voice, read out loud what your child has written.

3. Invite other family members to describe how the feelings generated by the conflict affect them. In a helpful and caring fashion, brainstorm with the family alternative ways the offending family member might behave. Listen carefully to the responses of that family member and try to understand what he or she is saying and feeling.

A Closing Word about Violence

Children can be given a constellation of peacemaking strategies that will them learn to handle discordant situations within and outside of the family in a constructive manner. By discussing when each strategic response might be appropriate, and even role playing specific scenarios, children will recognize they are capable of bringing about harmony in their daily lives.

It is important to acknowledge that these strategies are by no means easy to carry out; doing so requires maturity, sensitivity, and restraint on the part of any child—or adult, for that matter. Moreover, peacemaking is tremendously hard work and takes a good deal of practice. But by practicing these strategies to the best of their abilities, children will be doing more than merely giving lip service to wanting a peaceful world in which to grow up. They will be actively working toward making it happen.

5 WHEN PARENTING GETS TOUGH

Peace-Compatible Discipline Strategies

"[T]he hearts of small children are delicate organs. A cruel beginning in the world can twist them into curious shapes."
—Carson McCullers, *The Ballad of the Sad Café*

The Valleys of Parenting

I have seen incidents similar to the following scene many times in my family over the years; I am certain you will recognize similar situations from your own family life:

Mother marches into Molly's room to deliver clean laundry and notices Herman, the golden hamster, gnawing on the metal bars of his cage. Upon closer inspection, Mother realizes the tiny animal has no food to eat nor fresh water to drink. Mother angrily thinks back to the many promises her daughter made, all the BEGGING, that had finally convinced her to relent and purchase the furry creature. As Mother watches Herman frantically searching the sawdust for a scrap of wilted lettuce or a stray hamster pellet, she feels her anger rising. Through clenched teeth Mother silently tells Molly (who is blissfully playing outside) how cruel and irresponsible she is; how she broke her promise and doesn't deserve to have a pet; how maybe she should go without supper tonight so *she* could see how it feels to go hungry! Then Mother sits down on Molly's bed and takes a few deep breaths. She tells herself that Molly is a child, and children are, by definition, childish. Molly needs, and will continue to need, reminding for many years to come—often about the same recurring issues. The least enjoyable part of one's commitment as a parent, Mother muses, is to guide, remind, and then take action—in other words, to discipline.

Perhaps the central problem in disciplining our children is how to do so in a peaceful and loving way so we do not encourage resentment and anger (theirs or ours!) or an "us-versus-them" mentality. Take a few moments to think about how you discipline your children. Discuss your answers to the following questionnaire with other adult family members or friends. Remember: There are no right or wrong answers; you are simply "tuning in" to your current beliefs and practices as a basis for later consideration.

TUNING IN
How Do You Discipline Your Children?

1. How are issues related to discipline decided in your family?

2. How are consequences for undesirable behavior decided upon?

3. How do you attempt to make the consequences match the undesirable behavior?

4. Do you believe that spanking is a reasonable punishment for undesirable behavior? What are your reasons?

5. Describe an incident where you have apologized for a punishment you meted out too rashly or later decided was too harsh or unreasonable.

6. How does your discipline differ when you are in a good mood as compared with when you have had a "bad day"?

7. How do you attempt to keep your discipline consistent, regardless of your mood?

8. What "delay" techniques do you use when you are really angry to avoid meting out a punishment that is too severe?

9. After you have punished your children, how do you show them you still love them?

10. How do your discipline techniques compare with those your own parents used on you?

11. How do you feel about how you were disciplined? How has it affected the way you discipline your children?

12. How do you think your methods of discipline affect your children's peacemaking attitudes and capabilities?

A Peace-Compatible Parenting Style

There are many styles of parenting, but we may never have stopped to analyze what our particular style is. Studies are finding, however, that parenting style not only impacts children's daily behavior but also strongly influences the kind of people they eventually become.

Parenting styles range from one end of the spectrum, where children are afforded almost total freedom, to the other end, where parents have total control over all decisions concerning their children. In general, this continuum of parenting styles can be summarized by the following three descriptions:

- permissive parenting
- authoritarian parenting
- authoritative parenting

Permissive Parenting

Permissive parents appear loving and warm; they cannot stand seeing their children unhappy or deprived of an event or object. Their parenting style is indulgent, and they usually allow the children to set their own limits, offering them almost complete freedom. While the idea of raising "free" children may sound wonderful, the result is often children who are self-centered or overly insecure. Feeling they are in charge of their lives, yet very aware of their immaturities and inadequacies, these children often see the world as a frightening place.

Authoritarian Parenting

The "authoritarian" style of parenting is almost the exact opposite of "permissive" parenting. Parents who display authoritarian guidance are stern and maintain almost total control over every aspect of their children's lives. Rules in such a family are handed down arbitrarily and are expected to be followed perfectly, without exception. Behaviors and consequences are rarely open to negotiation; a "because-I-said-so" attitude prevails. Children raised in such a family are usually "well-behaved" but are often incapable of thinking for themselves. Unused to initiating rules or ideas, such children are very susceptible to peer pressure and are the most likely to be induced into gang membership, religious cults, or other groups that dictate what they should do.

Authoritative Parenting

Authoritative parents are warm and affectionate while still being definitely "in charge." They set firm guidelines, but such guidelines are reasonable and are often developed with solicited input from all family members, including the children. They also change the rules and guidelines as the children grow and their needs change. Authoritative parents trust and respect their children and, while giving much input and advice, offer many opportunities for their children to make choices about their lives. Such children grow up knowing they are loved and respected, and they become empowered to make decisions and solve problems on their own.

Authoritative parenting offers children a secure emotional foundation to begin their lives as peacemakers. It is a style that validates children's feelings: "You must have felt hurt when you weren't invited to Mary's party." It is also a style that includes children in the reasoning process, offering them explanations of why they are being asked to do something, inviting cooperation with the rules: "Please don't dawdle on your way home from school because I get very worried when you are very late." And finally it is a parenting style that works with any age child in any culture or ethnic group, a true precursor to democracy and peaceful conflict resolution.

Strategies for Peace-Compatible Discipline

Discipline is probably the most challenging facet of nonviolent child-rearing. As parents, we have all felt the frustration of trying to balance affirmation and correction, freedom and structure, and the uncertainty of wondering if we have made the mixture effective for our children. We also have the incredible challenge of balancing what we believe to be right with performing those actions consistently, especially when we are tired, stressed, or frustrated.

Hundreds of books have been written about discipline, as coming to terms with fair and just ways of disciplining is a Herculean task. Yet fewer tasks are more important in raising peaceloving children. The following suggested strategies offer some possibilities for enhancing peace-compatible discipline:

- give more compliments than corrections
- give choices but have the final say
- be consistent and fair
- be united
- assume the best
- check your motives
- remove your child from the situation
- remove yourself from the situation
- apologize when you are wrong
- go easy on yourself

Give More Compliments than Corrections

Compliments (positive reinforcement) are infinitely more potent than corrections (negative reinforcement). Children who are praised for good behavior tend to repeat that behavior. Therefore, when you are supervising your children in any task or situation, note how often you use compliments. You do not want your praise to be so plentiful and vague that it sounds insincere, but on the other hand, you do not want to be so overly critical that your children feel they can do nothing right. Then they will stop listening. Consider setting yourself the goal of having compliments outweigh corrections approximately four to one. Another way to ensure that the ratio is positive is to "pass" on every other item that you are tempted to correct in regard to such items as table manners, tidiness of room, and so forth.

Give Choices But Have the Final Say

To the extent that your children's ages and the situations allow, encourage your children to give their input and make their own choices. However, make it clear that you, as the parent, have the final say, especially about important matters. For example, instead of asking, "Do you want to go the dentist now?," which is not a negotiable decision, frame the choice by asking, "Do you want to stop by your friend's house before or after going to the dentist?"

Be Consistent and Fair

Be consistent in adhering to the principle "let the consequence relate to the behavior." Look for a punishment that is immediate and as close to the "natural consequence" of the behavior as possible. Not answering or coming when called for dinner, for example, may mean that the child misses all or part of dinner. Getting in trouble at a friend's house may mean that the child is not allowed to accept a friend's future invitation or not allowed to have that friend over for a week or so. Losing a sibling's sweater may mean the child pays for it from his or her allowance or offers a suitable replacement from his or her own wardrobe.

Children, especially as they grow older, are hypersensitive to any parental unfairness, so it is especially important to keep the consequences at the same level of seriousness as the behavioral infractions. Discuss with your children how the punishment was determined and how, in your estimation, it matches the behavior. However, remember that what works well at one age may not work well at another age; what works with one personality may not work with another. What works for your even-tempered older daughter may frustrate and anger your hot-tempered younger son. You will need to individualize or customize your interactions. In addition to modeling fairness in your discipline style, you can help your children grasp the concept of fairness by asking them, "How would you feel if this happened to you?"

Finally, try to be consistent in the manner that you mete out punishment so that your children develop a feeling of security about the cause and effect nature of breaking rules in your house; inconsistency will tend to teach children that punishment is whimsical and dependent upon your moods.

Be United

We all know children can play one parent against the other, so it is important, if there are two decision-making adults in the household, to be united when it comes to discipline strategies. To do this, you will want to settle any differences of opinion in private, including compromising on issues about which you each feel strongly. It is also important to agree ahead of time on your expectations for children's responsibilities at home, bedtimes, homework priorities, entertainment, and such family values as prohibiting stealing, lying, and hurting others.

Assume the Best

The German philosopher Goethe once mused, "If we take people as they are, we make them worse. If we treat them as if they were what they ought to be, we help them to become what they are capable of becoming." While this is sage advice for ALL human interactions, it is especially critical for our children.

Make it a practice to assume the "best," not the worst, where your children are concerned. If your children are having problems, first listen to their point of view. Give your support so they will stay calm but help them see the situation from the perspective of all the persons involved. Let them know you are always their advocate even though you may be disappointed in their behavior at this moment.

Check Your Motives

Certainly we have all experienced uncomfortable episodes—in a store, at church, or in someone else's house—in the form of tantrums, disruptive, annoying, or rude behavior that young children are especially good at. When disciplining your children for an incident that takes place outside the home, make sure you are doing it for them, not for yourself. Ask yourself several questions before you take action:

- Am I worrying about what others will think about my children's behavior?

- Am I overly concerned that my children's behavior is reflecting badly on me?

- Am I overtired or stressed and therefore need to take extra caution in my disciplining?

Checking your motives will ensure that any disciplining, especially that which is done in public, is carried out with the best interests of the child in mind.

Remove Your Child from the Situation

When children are "acting out" or unwilling to cooperate, sometimes it is simply best to remove them from the situation until they can regain control of themselves. This "time out" practice allows both parties an opportunity to calm down. Removing a child from a situation can be done without shouting or reprimanding, although a measured explanation of why you are doing so will help convey a sense of "fair play" to the child.

Remove Yourself from the Situation

If you are afraid you will lose your temper with your children, take a break. If you are alone, it may be time to call a friend and ask the friend to come over. Additionally, you can ask your spouse or someone else to take charge while you go for walk, take a relaxing bath, and do some other activity that will help you deal with your anger in an appropriate manner.

Apologize When You Are Wrong

If you do "lose your cool" and yell at or spank your children, as most of us who have raised children have done at one time or another, approach your children as soon as possible and apologize. Hug them and explain how their behavior caused you to become very frustrated. When you tell your children you are sorry, you are sending the message that you respect them. You are also teaching them to apologize when they are wrong instead of fighting back aggressively.

Go Easy on Yourself

Finally, it is important to understand that parenting is probably the most rewarding but also the most demanding job in the world. There are no easy, pat answers; children do not come with instruction manuals! While there are some good basic DOs and DON'Ts, every child is different and every parent is different. You will make many mistakes—we all do—just as *your* parents did. But go easy on yourself when you feel you are not the world's most perfect parent. Do your best, but remember that perfection is neither possible nor required.

Approaches to Discipline

There are many approaches to discipline, and certain approaches go in and out of style like hemlines and teen-age crazes. Offered here are three approaches that are NOT "trendy" but that can be used together or separately according to the personalities of your family members, the severity of the behavioral infractions, or your personal preferences:

- a preventive approach
- a whole-family approach
- a problem-solving approach

Each approach is presented with an activity to allow you to "try out" the approach while you experiment with a variety of discipline styles.

A Preventive Approach

Perhaps the best way to handle discipline is to prevent the need for it, to prevent the problem behavior before it happens. One of our tasks as parents is to encourage our children to stop and think about their behavior before they act. For example, a sign near the sink helps Chrissy remember to put her dirty breakfast dishes in the dishwasher. A checklist for nighttime hygiene reminds Molly to make sure her face is washed and her teeth brushed. A sign on the towel rack helps Gavin remember to hang up the towels in the bathroom.

Use the following activity to provide a gentle reminder to children about what the rules in your family are and why they are important.

 "Rules Help

Keep Peace"

Supplies needed: none

1. Review with family members what the important rules and expectations in your family are.

2. Ask your children to consider carefully whether they feel MORE peaceful or LESS peaceful when there are rules and they know exactly what the rules are. Invite them to give their reasons.

3. Ask your children to consider the following hypothetical situations (or others that you create). Invite them to express whether they think your family would be MORE peaceful or LESS peaceful if these rules were in effect in your household.

   - We will have ice cream and candy—nothing else—for dinner every night.

   - Each person can have whatever they want for dinner.

   - Everyone can go to bed when they choose.

- If someone in the family doesn't don't feel like going to work or school, they don't have to.

- Each person can put things away or not, as they choose.

- Everyone can sleep as long as they like.

- Everyone can watch television as long as they want, whenever they want, whatever they want.

- It is no longer necessary to let anyone in the family know when you are going out or where.

A Whole-Family Approach

If positive approaches fail to prevent a problem behavior, then some kind of consequence needs to be decided upon, and some punishment imposed. As much as possible, bring family discipline issues to a Family Peace Meeting (see Chapter 3). Here, children can participate in deciding what the natural consequences of continuing an unacceptable behavior will be. For instance, in my household, it was a group decision to withhold one weekly television program for every chore that was forgotten.

Although the Family Peace Meeting may be an ideal vehicle through which to confront undesirable behavior, unfortunately, if left to their own devices, children may be inclined to mete out punishment that is far worse than the parents had ever imagined. If they are to participate in deciding punishment, children may need your guidance in learning what constitutes a "natural consequence" (refer to page 95). Discuss the "Guidelines for Consequences" on page 101 with your children. Cut out or photocopy the poster to create a helpful reminder. Post these guidelines in a public place whenever you call a Family Peace Meeting to decide disciplinary action.

Following is an activity that can help children practice deciding what consequences are natural or logical and help them internalize the concept of a "logical match."

"What Is a Logical Consequence?"

Supplies needed: none

1. Review the "Guidelines for Consequences."

2. Ask your children to offer their ideas for some "logical consequences" that would be appropriate for the following misbehaviors:

   - John is told he can go out to play only after he cleans up his room and does his homework. He tells his mother he has finished his work, and he goes out to play. His mother later discovers he hasn't finished either task.

   - Nicole, annoyed at her sister for constantly interrupting, tells her sister to "shut up." This phrase is never allowed in this family.

   - José leaves the door open continually, though he has been frequently admonished not to do so. One day when José leaves the door open, the dog runs into the street and is hit by a car.

   - Although she has an alarm clock, Martha is late for the school bus almost every morning, and her mother ends up having to drive her there.

   - Chrissy leaves her new watch in the park.

   - Mark ruins the jacket he borrowed from his dad.

A Problem-Solving Approach

As children grow older and their reasoning capacity increases, it is possible to arrive at the solutions to discipline problems together:

> "Chrissy, you keep misplacing your school assignments, and I am getting extremely frustrated. Nothing we have come up with so far seems to have worked. What do you think we can do about it?"

This problem-solving approach differs from the "whole-family approach" quite markedly: In this strategy no one is imposing consequences on the child. Rather, the child is being asked to figure out what to do about the problem on her own, with guidance but not directives, from the parent.

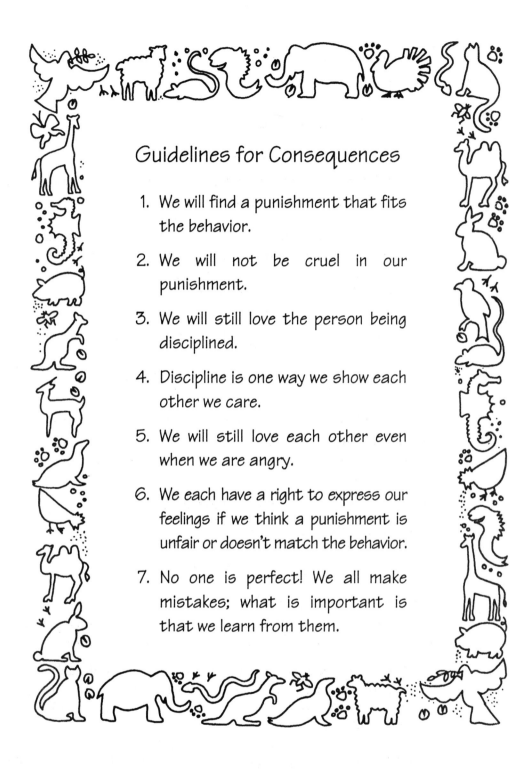

Guidelines for Consequences

1. We will find a punishment that fits the behavior.

2. We will not be cruel in our punishment.

3. We will still love the person being disciplined.

4. Discipline is one way we show each other we care.

5. We will still love each other even when we are angry.

6. We each have a right to express our feelings if we think a punishment is unfair or doesn't match the behavior.

7. No one is perfect! We all make mistakes; what is important is that we learn from them.

Not only can this approach help build a sense of self-esteem and instill an accountability for behavior, but also it can help children prepare to become independent and solve problems on their own.

The following activity, and others like it that you may devise, will help children practice thinking for themselves about their behavior and how it affects others.

 "Thinking about

Others in the Family"

Supplies needed: none

1. To help your children develop rational self-disciplining skills, discuss the following concepts:

   • what we do affects other people

   • only *we* have the power to change our behavior

2. Ask your children to consider, "What happens when a family member does something nice for you? What happens when a family member refuses to cooperate? How long do the good or bad feelings last?"

3. Suggest that your children role play one or more of the following situations portraying actions of children who care about only themselves:

   • You are playing outside, and it is time for supper. No one knows where you are. Your father has called every house in the neighborhood.

   • You make cookies for the family but you do not clean up. There is cookie dough everywhere, the oven has been left on, and you have gone out to play.

   • You are busy playing with your baseball cards, and your little brother comes along and looks at them. He accidentally rips your favorite card. You yell at him and he starts crying.

   • Other scenarios that match common occurrences in your home.

4. Ask your children what they might do to change the thoughtless behavior portrayed in each scene.

A Word about Corporal Punishment

No discussion of discipline would be complete without a word about corporal punishment. It is a rare parent who has never spanked or slapped the hand of a child, but this very issue is at the heart of this book: What are we teaching our children when we resort to physical or verbal violence to correct their behavior? The answer is sobering. Physical punishment can backfire. Here are some possible long-term effects of regular spanking:[1]

- Children who are frequently spanked or hit tend to become quiet, less articulate, and more sullen.

- Spanking tends to make children nervous and may slow down learning.

- Harsh physical and psychological punishment can lead to social distance among family members. As social distance increases, honest communication decreases.

- Frequent use of physical and psychological punishment is strongly associated with low self-esteem in children.

- Spanking is related to chronic passivity in children.

- Children whom parents attempt to control through physical punishment tend to develop an overdependence on outside rewards and punishment rather than an internal conscience. They often become followers, dependent upon the watchful eye of an overseer.

- Violence begets violence. Physical punishment meted out to a child for participating in a fight, for example, will teach the child that hitting back is the answer to conflict.

The negative effects of long-term physical punishment speak loudly: Physical discipline appears to lead to resentment and possibly violent behavior, perpetuating a vicious cycle that we, as peacepromoting parents, wish to avoid. Therefore, if spanking or other forms of physical punishment are a part of your current approach to discipline, consider initiating some of the other alternative approaches offered in this chapter.

---

1   From "Effects of Spanking," *Bows and Arrows*, Vol. 3, No. 4 (Winter 1980).

Discipline and Parental Moods

No one denies the need for consistency when interacting with children. Probably the most eagerly offered advice my husband and I received as young parents was, "Be consistent!" This, of course, is ever so much more difficult than it sounds. To suggest that we as parents should react to our children's every rule infraction with complete consistency would be tantamount to asking us to be parental robots, totally devoid of whims and moods! Moods are a reality of life. Therefore, while a certain stability and predetermined consequences for breaking the rules is critical when disciplining children, it is also true that our moods influence our reactions. On any given day, we may react to a child's misbehavior in myriad ways, based upon such diverse factors as how much sleep we had the night before, how our work life is going, how we are feeling about other relationships in our lives, or even how much caffeine we have consumed that particular day!

Remember the "hungry hamster" incident at the outset of the chapter? Here is the same scene revisited from three different perspectives, each time taking into account a different parental mood:

- mildly irritated
- harried
- in a rage

Imagine you are the disciplining parent and consider the following suggestions for various ways the situation might be handled.

If Your Mood Is "Mild Irritation" . . .

You are in a relatively good mood and/or this is the first time the hamster has not been fed. You can:

- Call your child to her room and point to the empty food and water dishes.

- Remind her graphically by taking the empty food dish from the cage and handing it to her.

- Give your child a note that reads, "Emergency!! Hamster dying of starvation!! Who will save him?"

- Offer a riddle: "Who is light brown, likes to play, and is very, very hungry and thirsty?"

- Describe, without evaluating, what the situation is: "Herman is gnawing hungrily at the bars in his cage." (This statement can be repeated if it receives no response.)

- Ask your child to help you to problem-solve: "Something is bothering me, and I need your help. When we first got Herman at the beginning of the summer, he always had food and fresh water. I have noticed now, perhaps due to your homework load and volleyball schedule, that Herman is no longer getting fed regularly. Do you think you could work out a schedule so Herman will get food and fresh water every day?"

If Your Mood Is "Harried" . . .

It has been a very trying, tiresome day and/or this is the second or third time Herman has been without food and water. You can:

- Let your child know you are annoyed by using firm words: "I am extremely disappointed. You made a promise that you would take care of a hamster if we got you one, and you have not followed through on your promise. That makes me angry."

- Share your values: "Animals are helpless. I believe that when an animal depends on us, it is wrong to let him down. Having an animal is a commitment, and not following through on a commitment to an animal is very unkind."

- Clearly state your expectations: "I expect that if a child in this family asks for an animal and receives it, (s)he will then take care of that animal's needs!"

- Make your child aware of what has occurred: "This poor animal is really suffering, and I am sure you don't want that to happen; *I* don't."

If Your Mood Is "Rage" . . .

You have had an absolutely horrible day in which everything seems to have gone wrong and/or this behavior has occurred countless times and is representative of all your child's other chores that are not getting accomplished. You can:

- Jolt your child out of her complacency: "The choice is yours. One, you can feed Herman right now and continue to do so on a regular basis. Two, we can give Herman away. Three, you can put up with a very angry and frustrated mother. Which one shall it be?"

- Let her know how angry you are: "When I ask you over and over again to feed your hamster and I am ignored, I get really angry. I am going to feed Herman myself right now . . . but understand that I am furious that I have to do *your* job!"

- Ask for some distance so you can vent: "When I see a helpless creature suffering from hunger and thirst, I become enraged! I feel like giving the hamster away to someone who will take better care of him. As soon as Herman is fed, we can talk about how to deal with this problem. Until that time, please let me be by myself because I am in no mood to talk with you pleasantly!"

Perhaps some of these suggested responses—particularly the "rage" reactions—may strike you as "unloving" or even too strong to appear in a book that purports to focus on raising peaceful children. Note carefully, however, the way the language has been chosen. The messages avoid evaluating the child's character or ability, and steer clear of damaging, deflating terms such as "stupid," "bad," or even "thoughtless." Such terms escalate bad feelings, get in the child's way, and allow the child to ignore the *real* message. Instead, the suggested responses use words that describe the child's behavior in a straightforward, honest fashion and the parent's feelings in an authentic, nonjudgmental way.

Since it is not humanly possible to avoid conflict in a family, the most realistic goal for a peaceful family is to confront issues as honestly as possible. As parents, we need to accept the fact that we have moods and become angry on occasion, but we also need to understand that expressing our feelings openly and honestly need not result in harm or abuse to our children.

A Closing Word about Peace-Compatible Discipline Strategies

The aspect of child-rearing that is often the most painful and problematic for parents longing to raise peaceful children is discipline. When we are praising our children for good behavior, or enjoying happy times of fun and togetherness, or savoring a stable period of family tranquillity, the task of instilling peacekeeping values seems reasonably simple. But as every parent knows, raising children consists of a great many "valleys" along with those blissful "peaks."

To make the valleys more bearable, there are many parenting styles from which to choose when disciplining children. "Authoritative parenting"—where parents and children make decisions about behavior and natural consequences together, but where the parents have the final say—can be very effective and has many positive outcomes. This moderate style is more compatible with raising peaceful children than a more "permissive" style, where children are allowed to do exactly as they want, or a more domineering "authoritarian" style, where children's opinions are not solicited. When children are invited to contribute to discussions about discipline, they are invited to take responsibility for their actions. This burgeoning sense of responsibility can lead to enhanced self-esteem, feelings of competence, and inner security. Authoritative parenting allows us to discipline our children without incurring anger or resentment, making it truly compatible with raising peaceful children.

6 CELEBRATING DIVERSITY

Creating Positive Racial and Cultural Attitudes

"Unity in variety . . . Each creature is only a modification of the other; the likeness in them is more than the difference."
—Ralph Waldo Emerson, "Nature"

Out of the Mouths of Babes

How do children grow up to be racists? I asked myself that unsettling question as I walked through a nearby park and saw a multiracial group of preschoolers playing together in a sand box. When an African-American boy picked up a plastic pail that a white child had just had his eye on, the white child suddenly began screaming at the top of his lungs, letting forth an angry stream of racial epithets as he did so. It was disturbing, if not downright painful, to hear such horrific words emanating from the mouth of such a seemingly innocent babe.

Recent studies have shown that by the age of two years, most children *do* recognize differences in skin color, but they will generally play peacefully with children of other races—unless they have been taught, directly or indirectly, to do otherwise. The youngster in the park may have learned from significant adults in his life—either from what they did or said, or from what they did *not* do or say—that differences and diversity are not good.

How is it possible to multiculturalize a family, to make a family more appreciative of other races or cultures? The place to begin is with ourselves: our attitudes, our behavior toward other races and cultures, the people we choose to befriend, and the choices we make about our lifestyle.

Use the following questions to get in touch with your feelings about other races and cultures. Talk them over with your friends and family.

TUNING IN
How Does Your Family View Racial Difference?

PERSONAL PREJUDICES

1. List three attitudes or beliefs you hold that might be examples of stereotypical thinking; for example, "All Asians are good in math."

2. What are some ways you tolerate the stereotypical thinking around you; some ways you challenge the stereotypical thinking around you. Give examples.

3. What are some stereotypical ways of thinking that you would like to change in yourself?

4. Describe any racial or cultural awareness workshops or training sessions you may have attended. What was your reaction to them?

5. What notable African Americans, Hispanics, Asians, Anglos, and Native Americans do you admire nationally? Locally?

EXPERIENCES WITH OTHER RACES AND CULTURES

1. What were the racial and cultural attitudes of your family as you were growing up?

2. What were the racial and cultural identities of your fellow students and teachers when you were in school?

3. What are the racial and cultural compositions of the people with whom you work? With whom your children go to school?

4. What are the racial and cultural compositions of the people in the neighborhood in which you live?

5. What are the racial and cultural identities of your current closest friends and acquaintances? Of your children's friends?

6. How does racial and/or cultural identity influence your decisions about making friendships?

7. Have there been any racial incidents in your neighborhood or your children's school that concern you? How have your responded? How have your children responded?

8. How do you respond when friends, relatives, or colleagues make comments with negative racial or cultural overtones? How do your children respond?

HOME AND FAMILY ACTIVITIES

1. How do the pictures and other decorations in your home reflect a world in which there are a variety of races and cultures?

2. What movies, books, magazines, and other entertainment do you and your children enjoy that reflect our multicultural world?

Creating Positive Multicultural Attitudes

In many ways, the task of creating positive racial and cultural attitudes seems an overwhelming one: There are so many examples of racial prejudice and unfortunate racial and ethnic stereotypes in the media and every other part of our society. But a heart-felt attempt to multiculturalize our families can also bring easily discernible results, such as when I heard my young daughter report, "I don't like the book we are reading in class. It makes fun of Native Americans and tries to make us believe they were all savages." Or when the same child, trying to select a birthday gift for an African-American friend, lamented the fact that there were no black Ken dolls. "Can I write a letter to the toy manufacturer?" she asked, with righteous indignation.

Times like these are reminders that the steps we as parents take to instill positive racial and cultural attitudes really can make a difference. Helping young children appreciate diversity is the foundation for building *positive* multicultural attitudes. Ultimately racism, prejudice, and bigotry cannot survive in homes where differences and diversity are welcomed, honored, and celebrated. Positive racial and cultural attitudes will flourish when family members work toward answering the following questions:

- How can we create an environment in our family that encourages respect for people from every race, culture, and ethnic background?

- How can we do this in a society that works to keep groups of people apart from each other and promotes the growth of false ideas and fears about anyone who is the slightest bit different?

There are five pivotal steps you can take that can help your family, and ultimately our world, achieve the goal of positive racial and cultural attitudes:

1. Build a strong sense of self in your children and a feeling of pride in *your* racial, cultural, and ethnic heritage.

2. Provide concrete examples of the basic needs and values that all people have in common, no matter what their race, culture, or ethnic backgrounds.

3. Promote a deep appreciation for the beauty of racial and cultural differences and an ability to rejoice in and learn from these rich differences.

4. Help your children become attuned to the world as one human family, preparing them to eventually live more fully as interdependent beings.

5. Help your children become aware of how racial and cultural differences are unjustly handled in our society, of what prejudice is, and of their ability to take steps to stop it.

It is never too early to begin to instill these awarenesses. These five steps are summarized on the next page. Cut out or photocopy this list of positive attitudes. Post it for your children to look at often and consider carefully. Discuss the beliefs frequently.

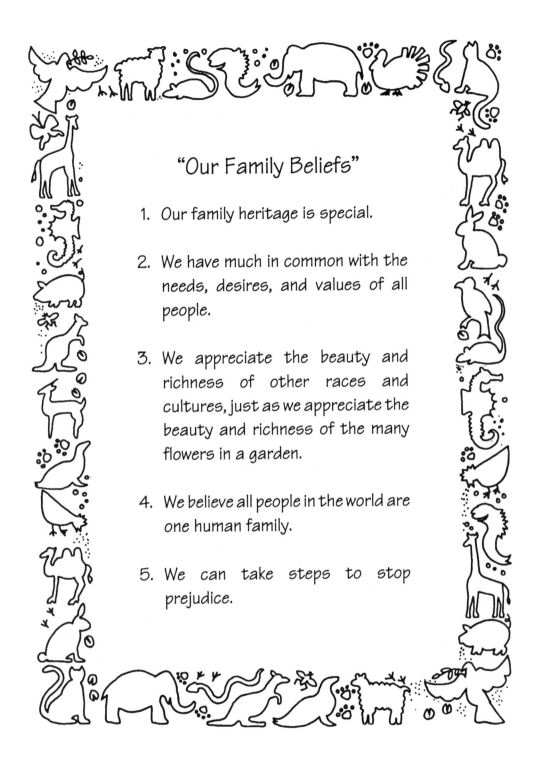

"Our Family Beliefs"

1. Our family heritage is special.

2. We have much in common with the needs, desires, and values of all people.

3. We appreciate the beauty and richness of other races and cultures, just as we appreciate the beauty and richness of the many flowers in a garden.

4. We believe all people in the world are one human family.

5. We can take steps to stop prejudice.

RAISING PEACEFUL CHILDREN IN A VIOLENT WORLD

Appreciating Family Roots

In America, almost all of us are the children, grandchildren, or great-grandchildren of immigrants from some other country. We have unique ethnic backgrounds and heritages. Unfortunately, many of us "baby boomers" grew up with the idea that to be lacking in prejudice meant to be "color blind" in a "melting-pot" society. While this popular post-World War II notion has its proponents exclaiming, "It doesn't matter to me if a person is black, white, or green!" in an effort to demonstrate their positive racial attitudes, the truth is, it *does* matter. Color-blindness is *not* a solution to racism. Ignoring differences denies the obvious uniqueness of others. Embracing diversity and celebrating differences is the real key to combating racism.

To begin, you can help your children celebrate diversity by teaching them about their *own* diversity. Many of us are multicultural by birth, though we do not always think of ourselves in that regard. Our ethnic heritage may be English, French, and German. Or it may be African, Native American, and German. Or it can be Jewish, Argentinean, and Mexican. We are living examples of "unity in diversity." When children are taught to respect the uniqueness of their own ethnic heritage, they not only build their self-respect but also become more open to respecting the uniqueness of the heritages of others.

The following activity can help your children appreciate their unique ethnic background and heritage.

"My Family Heritage"

Supplies needed: pens, crayons, markers, notebook
(for Family Book)
tape recorder, blank tape
OR video camera, blank tape
(for Family Tree)
family photos, materials for framing
(for Family Pictures)

1. Encourage your children to explore the facts of their history in one or more of these ways:

- *Family Stories*

Have your children ask adults in the family to share personal stories and anecdotes about their history. Create opportunities for your children to retell these stories to other family members and their friends. Ask your children how they feel about their family heritage. What makes them feel particularly peaceful and proud?

- *Family Book*

Write down stories that family members tell and encourage your children to illustrate them. Accumulate them over the years to create a family "series," e.g., the de Cordero Series, or the Chung Series, and so forth. Make these stories the focus of family reading sessions before bedtime and at other times. Pass them on to your children who, in turn, can pass them on to their children.

- *Family Tree*

Have all family members, particularly the children, participate in creating a "family tree." Using video or audio tape, have the children interview relatives by asking them to recall ancestors who are no longer alive. Encourage relatives not only to answer specific questions about their memories but also to include family stories handed down through the generations.

- *Family Pictures*

Collect photographs of your family's ancestors. Ask family members in other cities or countries for their photographs. (If the photographs are valuable or need to be returned, have them copied.) Then create a framed display or pictorial record of as much of the extended family as is possible. Such pictorial family histories can be cherished as heirlooms and/or given as special gifts to other relatives during the holidays and other special family celebrations.

2. To help your children continue exploring their ethnic backgrounds, here are some additional suggestions:

- Organize a family reunion that brings together as many different branches of the family as possible.

- Discover the major holidays celebrated by each of the ethnic groups within your family's heritage.

- Find books in the library about the history of the ethnic groups within your family's heritage. Read them aloud together as a family.

- Discuss stereotypes that society holds about ethnic groups within your family's heritage. Explore how such stereotypes got started and flourished, and brainstorm some ways false ideas could be squelched.

- Help your children draw pictures or make lists of what they like most about different aspects of their ethnic background.

- Ask your children to consider how their ethnic background affects who they are. In what way does it affect their personalities? Interests? Life styles? Appearances?

As you help your children come to appreciate the richness of their heritage, discuss ethnic differences openly. Children are fascinated with their own appearance and the appearance of others; they are naturally curious about people with different skin color, hair texture, and other various physical characteristics. This curiosity often embarrasses parents, particularly when children ask questions of strangers or stare at a person who is unlike them, but this curiosity is an extension of children's wide-eyed wonder about the world and should be actively encouraged. Generating personal discussions about human differences will help them feel more comfortable with diversity.

Honoring Differences

Multiculturalizing our families is a part of creating a peace-filled future for our children. It is a way of helping them develop the skills necessary to become agents for that peace. In family life we have many opportunities to learn about and practice the acceptance of others who have different physical characteristics, beliefs, and ideas.

As parents, we can show our children—through our lifestyles and our home environments—that we have a strong commitment to the ideals of celebrating diversity and honoring differences. From the books we read, to the people we invite into our homes, to the movies and plays we see, to the music we listen to, our homes can model an environment free of prejudice—an atmosphere of embracing diversity.

Take a good look around your home to discover how many symbols there are that attest to your family's appreciation of diversity. If you feel you would like to strengthen this commitment, consider some of the following suggestions:

- Every month or so, make an ethnic meal or go to a local ethnic restaurant. With your family, discuss the contributions of the ethnic group from whom this food comes.

- Obtain recordings of music from other cultures and ethnic groups. Your community library may have such recordings on a lending basis. Play the recordings for your family and discuss the people and culture from which the music came. Note the similarities and differences between music from this cultural or ethnic group and your own.

- Foster multicultural awareness by presenting children with literature that portrays persons of other cultures in a strong and positive light. For example, read to or with children *The Story of Harriet Tubman* by Rae Bains (Dial, 1991) to offer a positive African-American heroine, or read *Sacajawea: A Native American Heroine* by Martha Bryant (Council for Indian Education, 1989) to expose children to a strong Native American historical figure. (See Chapter 10 for additional suggestions.)

- Rent videos on some aspect of another ethnic group and, as a family, discuss what you have seen and learned. Your local video store or community library can provide many excellent selections on what is currently available.

- Occasionally take your family to religious services that are attended by persons from a cultural or ethnic background different from your family's, e.g., a Southern Baptist service, a Jewish synagogue, or a Baha'i fireside.

- Decorate your home with artwork from different cultures, races, and ethnic groups. The artwork need not be expensive; local libraries or art museums often have lending collections from which you can choose, and local community colleges or universities may feature the work of art students at a very reasonable price. These art pieces can be used as a focal point for passing on beliefs and values about diversity and appreciation for other cultures.

- Explore becoming part of a foreign or domestic exchange program. Although the ideal situation for positive attitude formations would be for families to live in fully integrated communities where children have opportunities to interact with people of various racial and cultural groups, many neighborhoods are not integrated. Exchange programs provide another way to introduce children to people of other ethnic groups. A good resource is the American Intercultural Student Exchange, 7720 Herschel Avenue, LaJolla, CA 92037 (phone: 619-459-9761).

- Find out about the holidays, festivals, and religious celebrations of other cultural and ethnic groups. Find out when they take place and explore with your children the background and significance of each. A good place to start might be the following holidays:

HOLIDAY	DESCRIPTION
Chinese New Year (*Chinese, Vietnamese*)	An important Chinese holiday that includes festivals, parades, costumes, and the exchange of gifts and food.
Ch'usok (*Korean*)	A harvest moon festival where Korean families gather for large feasts and visit the graves of their ancestors in order to give thanks.
Cinco de Mayo (*Hispanic*)	A celebration of Hispanic American culture, honoring the Mexicans' desire to be free from foreign invaders, as well commemorating the defeat of Emperor Maximillian's army in Mexico in 1867.
Durga Puja (*Hindu*)	A ten-day period set aside by Hindus to honor the Divine Mother, who is regarded as the Sustainer of Life.
Eld ul-Fitr, sometimes called Hari Raya Ruasa (*Islamic*)	An Islamic fasting event celebrated at the end of Ramadan during which participants wear new clothes, pray, and recite verses from the Quran.

HOLIDAY	DESCRIPTION
Loy Krathong (*Thai*)	The Thai Festival of Lights in which candles are floated along rivers and canals throughout the country.
Native American Heritage Month (*Native American*)	A month-long tribute to the history and contributions of Native Americans.
O-Bon (*Japanese*)	The Japanese Feast of Fortune celebration, providing a time to commemorate one's ancestors.

Monitoring Attitudes Developed Outside of the Home

The media messages—from television, movies, books, even some curricular material in schools—about people of various racial, cultural, and ethnic groups are disturbing. Not so long ago, the overwhelming message was that white western cultures must be vastly superior to all others, for it was the dominant culture to be seen on the media. This message continues, though to a lesser extent, today. Additionally, unfortunate stereotypes—"Blacks are lazy"; "Asians are overly ambitious"; "Native Americans have problems with liquor"—are perpetuated not only through the cultural media but also by toys, decorations, costumes, jokes, as well as off-hand remarks heard on a daily basis. These false stereotypical messages are harmful in many ways:

- They promote misinformation about entire groups of people.

- They damage the self-image of entire groups of people who are the victims of such messages.

- They are too often used to justify keeping people in subordinate positions and, thus, to bolster racism and prejudice.

While we as parents may be doing everything in our power to teach our children to honor differences and embrace diversity, we must also be attuned to these stereotypical messages generated outside of our homes. Our responsibility must extend to knowing what our children are learning about racial and cultural issues in school, in church, at other clubs and civic organizations, and through the friends they make. When we are uncomfortable with any outside influences on our children's understanding of race, culture, and ethnicity, we must quickly act to bring about a positive change. Following are some things you can do about this:

- Through family discussion, find out what your children believe to be true about persons from other races, cultures, and ethnic backgrounds. Do not be surprised by any unfortunate stereotypical messages they may have acquired from the media, from other children, or from other outside sources, but at the same time, do not be afraid to immediately correct any false misconceptions and prejudices.

- Visit your children's school and find out how the curriculum deals with issues of diversity and racism. Compare the school's curriculum with some of the suggestions offered in this chapter. If there are important issues that are not being addressed or not being addressed strongly enough, or if stereotypical messages are being conveyed, make an appointment to see the principal of the school to voice your concerns.

- Try to determine what is being taught about race, racism, and diversity of cultures and ethnic backgrounds in your children's religious education, if they attend a Sunday school or other religious study classes. If you are not satisfied with how these critical issues are being addressed, discuss your feelings with the head of the religious institution or the director of the program or school.

- As your children grow older, involve them in projects that contribute to ridding the world of prejudice while promoting unity in diversity. Combine your efforts with those of other families who are working to instill positive racial and cultural values and beliefs in their children. An ideal project for families interested in racial and cultural harmony is "The Activism 2000 Project for Kids," which was created to help young people engage in social and political activities that can lead to a more peaceful world. This clearinghouse offers free information, advice, strategies, and tactics that show children (and their parents) how to effectively get involved with policy makers to help solve current problems (drunk drivers, hate crimes, gun-control needs, environmental abuses, etc.) in your community and the larger world. This "democracy drop-out prevention program," as the founders of the project call it, is appropriate for children of all ages. Interested parents may contact:

> The Activism 2000 Project
> P. O. Box E
> Kensington, MD 20895
> Phone: 1-800-KID-POWER

Following is an activity you can do with your children to sensitize them to the feelings of people from other races or cultures by helping them "tune in" to the feelings of fear, anger, and frustration of limited English-speaking children or children who have just arrived in this country.

"Not Understanding Can Be Frustrating"

Supplies needed: foreign language book or article

1. Invite your children to listen as you read a passage in an unfamiliar language. (You need only to be able to read the passage phonetically.)

2. Read the words without inflection, without showing any pictures, or in any other way giving your children ideas about the content of the words.

3. Afterward, ask your children how they felt when they could not understand what you were reading.

4. Discuss with your children how this is similar to what any child feels when he or she must suddenly live in a culture with an unfamiliar language.

5. Ask your children to brainstorm some ways in which they might be helpful to a child who is new to the culture or does not speak English.

Here are some additional suggestions you can use to help your children be sensitive to other races and cultures:

- With your children, find magazine or book illustrations of a child from another cultural group, e.g., Southeast Asian, Latino, or Native American. Invite your children to describe the feelings (loneliness, curiosity, possible rejection, hopefulness, happiness, or joy) they see in the pictures of this child. You might also suggest that your children role play meeting the pictured child.

- Ask your children to imagine how they might feel if, for some reason, all children with blue eyes (or whatever color eyes your children have) were to have fewer privileges and rights than children with brown eyes. Would this be fair? Invite your children to give their reasons. Talk with your children about how this situation compares with the barriers faced daily by people of color.

- Ask your children why they think some children tease others; discuss some of the reasons for teasing. Have your children draw sketches of imaginary situations in which people have kept the peace with others who come from backgrounds different from theirs. Ask your children to enumerate some problems that might occur at school or at play when children from different cultures misunderstand one another. Help them to brainstorm some ways that such problems could be resolved through peacekeeping.

- Ask your children what part the following people play in keeping peace: children, parents, the government, police officers, teachers, churches.

Embracing Diversity

Most of what has been discussed so far in this chapter has concerned ways to involve children with diverse people and to help children become aware of their ability to affect positive change. One additional way we can influence our children's attitudes toward diversity is the most direct and possibly the most positive of all—through a family vision statement.

A vision statement that professes your family's views on racial and cultural harmony may be one of the greatest gifts you can give your family. It is a clear way of communicating your values and attitudes to your children in a forthright manner, and it is a concrete way of helping your children understand that change in the world has its first steps in the home. A family vision statement may take many forms: It can be an affirmation, a poem, a chant, a prayer, a ritual, a song, or some other form of creative expression. Some families may choose to use more than one form of expression so that all family members, regardless of age, can relate to the statement. Younger children, for example, might understand the concept best when it is made into a song or even a game. Parents can orchestrate the vision statement so that all family members can contribute their own ideas to the final product.

The following activity provides some suggestions for helping your family create their own vision statement.

 "A Family

Vision Statement"

Supplies needed: paper
                                 writing utensils
                                 other creative materials as desired

1. At a Family Peace Meeting (see Chapter 3), discuss the idea of creating a family vision statement for embracing diversity. Help all family members brainstorm their ideas about other cultures, races, and ethnic backgrounds. Allow each family member to contribute something to the statement.

2. Talk to your children about the significance of a vision statement for the entire family. Let them know they are free to share the statement with people they know so their friends will be aware of your family's beliefs and attitudes about race, cultures, and diversity.

3. Be ready to continually revise the vision statement. As your children internalize the statement and compare it with their growing experiences with the world, they will have more ideas to add. Every so often, revisit the statement and encourage family members to offer their new thoughts and ideas.

4. Decorate, as desired, and display the family vision statement in a very prominent place where all family members and visitors can see it. Recite it on a regular basis. Invite your children to memorize it and share what it means to them.

Using these guidelines, one family brainstormed their ideas and, over the course of several Family Peace Meeting sessions, formed them into the following Vision Statement:

One Family's Vision Statement
We believe that human beings are like flowers in a garden. Like those flowers, there are many different colors, shapes, sizes, and varieties of people. Like flowers, each human being is unique, special, and different from any other. And just as we appreciate the different flowers, so too, we appreciate the differences in each member of our family, and the differences of the human beings of the world. We honor people of different colors, with different customs, habits, and beliefs. We encourage each other to love all our brothers and sisters regardless of skin color, way of life, or spiritual faith. We ALL work together for a more peaceful world.

A Closing Word about Racial and Cultural Attitudes

The pervasive disease of prejudice and the fear of differences add to the pain and suffering in the world. In order to create a more peaceful world, we must work to eradicate this debilitating disease by first encouraging our children to respect their own heritage as a way toward developing a respect for the heritage of other people. If our children, the leaders of tomorrow, can be taught to be sensitive to the authentic human values and the cultural contributions of each group of people whom they encounter, then they can look toward the future with hope for a more peaceful world.

7 SEX-ROLE STEREOTYPES

Creating Peaceful Gender Concepts

"Consider a son reared and trained twenty years by a devoted mother. . . . Having brought him through dangers and difficulties to the age of maturity, how agonizing then to sacrifice him upon the battlefield! Therefore, the mothers will not sanction war nor be satisfied with it. So it will come to pass that when women participate full and equally in the affairs of the world . . . war will cease; for woman will be the obstacle and hindrance to it."
—'Ab du'l-Baha, *The Promulgation of Universal Peace*

Trucks Are to Cuddle

Like many parents of our generation, my husband and I have been committed to raising our child without the barriers of traditional gender stereotypes that restrict possibilities for both girls and boys. We have been careful to give our daughter toy cars, fire engines, and erector sets, along with dolls and cooking sets. Yet, tiptoeing into my daughter's room one afternoon, I had the surprise of discovering Chrissy tucking her favorite red truck into her doll's crib with the gentle admonition, "There, there . . . go to sleep now, baby!" I walked away chuckling and shaking my head—and also questioning whether the nurturing role is not simply determined at birth. If it is not, when and how *do* children acquire their notions of what is appropriate behavior for their gender?

The old adage "actions speak louder than words" is never more true than when it applies to the transmission of values to children. We need especially to be aware of this in everyday circumstances around the home. It is critical to look at how our domestic actions affect our children's perceptions about what might be considered appropriate and inappropriate behavior for either gender. With this in mind, the following list of questions is offered to help you take a closer look at possible manifestations of sex-role stereotyping, particularly in the division of labor, in your own household.

TUNING IN
How Much Sex-Role Stereotyping
Is There in Your House?

PARENTING

1. Who comforts your children when they have been hurt?

2. Who reads to your children at bedtime?

3. Who listens to school/interpersonal problems of your children?

4. Who takes care of your children when they are ill at home?

5. Who takes your children to medical appointments?

6. Who goes to parent-teacher meetings?

7. Who selects your children's clothes?

8. Who drives your children to rehearsals, sports activities, girl scouts, friends' houses, etc.?

9. Who disciplines your children?

10. Who gets your children up and ready for school in the morning?

11. Who attends your children's sports events and/or recitals?

12. Who plans parties for your children?

ROUTINE CHORES

1. Who changes the diapers?

2. Who takes the garbage out?

3. Who mends the clothing?

4. Who does the laundry?

5. Who cooks the meals?

6. Who handles the correspondence?

7. Who does the cleaning?

8. Who does the dishes?

9. Who does the grocery shopping?

10. Who arranges for babysitters? Household repair work?

11. Who fixes broken appliances?

12. Who does electrical repairs?

13. Who fixes leaky faucets, toilets, etc.?

14. Who maintains the car(s)?

15. Who fixes broken toys?

HOUSEHOLD BUDGETING

1. Who determines how money will be spent?

2. Who pays the bills?

3. Who prepares the taxes?

4. Who earns the money?

5. Who balances the checkbook?

6. Who does the banking?

7. Who gives your children their allowance?

MISCELLANEOUS

1. Who cares for the pets?

2. Who selects your automobile?

3. Who does outdoor activities with your children?

4. Who coaches your children's sports teams?

5. Who does the yard work?

Gender Stereotypes

In considering the issue of sex-role stereotyping, it may be helpful to offer a definition. "Sex-role stereotyping" refers to misconceptions or oversimplifications about traits, behaviors, or characteristics based solely upon a person's gender. Sex-role stereotypes are an oppressive legacy to offer our children and one that does significant damage to all of us. It is not only that these attitudes are based on misconceptions that makes them harmful; it is also that these same misconceptions later cause our daughters, in particular, to feel less important than their male counterparts and keep them from reaching their true potential in the world.

When we confront the sex-role stereotypes in our culture—starting with the messages our children receive at home—we offer our children the opportunity to:

- realize that their hobbies and career choices are in no way limited by their gender

- know that their gender in no way hampers the kind of person they wish to become

- become conscious of the forces in society that may try to limit and oppress them

- know that they are strong enough to challenge these forces

- become aware of what they can do to change the current attitudes about males and females in our society

Family Sex-Role Models

Take a look at the questionnaire you completed at the outset of this chapter. You may find (as I did) that there are some traditional stereotypical sex-role behaviors in your family. It certainly is not uncommon, for example, for a woman to be doing all the cooking and household chores, while the man is earning and managing the money and doing all the repair work. Are we inadvertently providing poor role models for our children if we find that we have fallen into these time-honored molds?

Not necessarily. Traditional sex roles and behaviors are not in and of themselves "wrong." There is certainly no right or wrong way to divide up the labor in a household. But you do need to consider the following four factors carefully when determining whether the current division is working well for your family:

- *time*

In circumstances where one spouse has a significantly more demanding job or career, in terms of time and flexibility, than the other spouse (whether male or female), the spouse with more time at home, may find it necessary to assume a disproportionate share of the household and parenting chores.

- *skills*

It sometimes happens that one partner has more of a "knack" for a specific skill, such as money management or cooking, or has had training or education in a particular area. That person may wish to take on that particular responsibility. This arrangement might also be the most efficient.

- *level of enjoyment*

This is usually the area requiring the most compromise, but two adults are sometimes able to work it out so that each can take on tasks that they tend to enjoy (e.g., planning parties or doing yard work) and avoid the chores they really detest (e.g., balancing the checkbook). Of course, in most situations compromise will have to be made. More than likely both adults will still need to assume some tasks that they do not particularly like and, in some cases, a few of the least appealing chores may have to be shared or rotated.

- *comfort level with change*

Often sex-role behavior patterns, in regard to household chores for example, are established early on in a relationship, according to the patterns that were observed in the families of both partners, with little thought or discussion. But if one partner, for whatever reason, becomes dissatisfied with the way the chores have been previously distributed, it is then necessary to discuss the need for some change. Though always difficult, change may be harder for some than others. Some spouses may be more resistant, and their feelings, too, must be respected.

Sensitivity and a deep level of communication are crucial when dealing with issues that touch our very core, our identity, our sense of who we are. Any discussion of sex-role stereotyping means that the adults in the family must be willing to listen very carefully to the way each other is feeling. They also need to spend the time it takes to work out new patterns that are acceptable to both partners and with which they can support one another harmoniously, particularly in the areas of:

- encouraging gender equity at home
- changing gender perceptions at home

Encouraging Gender Equity at Home

When it comes to modeling gender equity, probably the most important issue in the household division of labor is how nurturing and care-giving tasks (cooking and laundry especially) are divided. These tasks can easily be perceived by the children as "serving" tasks. Therefore, to avoid having children believe that it is the exclusive job of women to serve others, it is a good idea for the male role model in the family to take at least some of the serving roles.

However, if your comfort level with a traditional sex-role division of labor in your household is high, and you do not want to make any changes, there is still good news: There are ways you can maintain the status quo while you are raising your children to feel comfortable with more gender-free distribution of tasks. All children, male or female, can be taught the serving skills—such as cooking, cleaning, and doing the laundry—by the parent who usually does them. As children get proficient at doing them, these tasks can be shifted from the parent who ordinarily does them and rotated equitably among the children. In this way the serving skills will begin to lose their specific gender definition. Similarly, both girls and boys should be taught how to fix a bicycle, change a tire, pound a nail, and mow the lawn, as well as how to sew a button on a shirt. Such deliberate training in all survival skills for both genders will most assuredly help to raise a new generation of independent human beings who may not feel "locked into" predefined sex roles.

Changing Gender Perceptions at Home

In the safety of their families, children can be taught directly—and through modeling—that their hobbies, abilities, and eventual career choices are not limited by sex-role stereotypes. However, an equally challenging task is to let children know there are many diverse kinds of families who may not be anything like the stereotypical sitcom families on television but who are also loving and caring, and should be considered positive role models.

It may be helpful here to discuss what exactly constitutes a "family." If we as parents would agree to broaden the term to include any group of individuals who are bound together by a deep caring and commitment to each other and to any children involved, then our children could be more open to recognizing and appreciating diverse families. Do your children know any nontraditional families, with or without children? Discuss what traits your children observe that define such groupings as a family. When families who are different from your family grouping are highlighted in the news, magazines, or other media, bring them to your children's attention and consider with your children what makes these families *family*.

Additionally, we can guide our children to the important realization that human beings in our culture are at liberty to make the decision *not* to marry or *not* to have children while still leading perfectly happy and fulfilling lives. To reinforce this idea, expose your children to a wide variety of single adults who have chosen not to marry, or for whom marriage was not an option, as well as adult couples who have chosen not to raise a family, so your children will realize that these are viable options open to all people.

The following activity may help you reinforce the idea that there are many diverse ways to be a family and that chores within a family need not be assigned according to gender.

"Differing Families, Differing Roles"

Supplies needed: paper, writing utensils
an assortment of puppets, dolls,
    or paper dolls representing people
    of all ages and races

1. Gather all family members together around a table or on the floor.

2. Discuss the idea of what constitutes a family. Guide your children away from the notion that a family must always have a mother, father, and children, and toward the concept of family as a group of people who care about each other, support one another, and are committed to each other.

3. Invite your children to help you make a list of all chores that any family would have to perform. Write these chores on small slips of paper.

4. Provide your children with an assortment of puppets or dolls or paper dolls. Encourage them to experiment or play with various groupings of people. For each grouping your children create:

- Ask your children, "Could this be a family? Why or why not?" Encourage them to base their decisions on the commitment of each person in the group to one another or on other family characteristics you have discussed.

- Direct your children to select the "chore slips" one at a time and assign each chore to one of the family members. Ask your children for their reasons for each assignment. Discuss any stereotypical reasoning they might give, such as, "The mother cooks because women are better at it."

Cultural Sex Roles

Sociologists are aware that children learn about the sex-role behavior expected of them very early, usually during the first year of their lives and long before they have entered school. While there is little evidence for genetically-determined behavior differences, we do know that how one "should" behave according to one's gender is actually "taught" through subtle parental patterns that we rarely think about, such as the rougher physical play that boy babies are subjected to compared with the more delicate handling and coddling that girl babies often experience. Even though we may not do so consciously, we may expect female babies to be quieter and more passive, while encouraging male babies to be more aggressive, even boisterous. Later in a child's life, parents and teachers often encourage certain traditional sex-role behaviors through their own modeling of gender-appropriate behavior, or by subtly squelching any behavior they may see as inappropriate to the gender of the child.

Recently I visited a kindergarten class and could not help but notice the big differences in dress between the little girls and the little boys. While the girls were mostly dressed in pretty or color-coordinated outfits of pastel shades, the boys tended to have on sturdy jeans, tee-shirts, and tennis shoes; the girls were apparently dressed to look "cute" and feminine and were clearly expected to stay clean, while the boys were dressed for rough-and-tumble play.

While such benign differences in treatment and dress may not seem cause for any great alarm, our lives and the lives of our children are very much influenced by the cultural attitudes and practices that later consign men and women to very restrictive roles and set up policies and structures to keep them in those roles.

In the 1800s, women and girls were fighting for their voting rights, but today the serious battles focus around other opportunities for females. Happily, not only women but men too have often committed their words and their actions to gender equality because they also want freedom from traditionally stereotypical (and sometimes demeaning) sex roles. Men, too, realize that such freedom is essential for *everyone*—not just women and girls—to co-exist in a peaceful world.

Yet disturbing cultural sex-role messages still abound; we are confronted by them on an almost daily basis. How can these messages be challenged and changed? What can and do we want to do to turn things around? As parents, it is important to look at how negative messages are perpetuated in four areas in particular:

- school environment
- access to physical activities
- artistic and intellectual pursuits
- media messages

School Environment

It is important to visit your children's school(s) to determine the answers to the following questions. Ask the appropriate educational representatives and visit your children's classroom(s) to find out firsthand:

- Do teachers attempt to avoid imposing sex-role expectations, such as "girls are neat, quiet, and obedient" while "boys are noisy and practical-jokers"?

- In class, do teachers call on boys more often than girls? Do they allow boys to shout out answers but reprimand girls for doing so?

- For hands-on activities, such as science experiments done in small groups, do girls have equal roles in the manipulating of the materials or are they relegated to recording the progress of the group?

- Are girls encouraged in math, science, and industrial arts, and boys in art, music, literature, and home economics?

- Are curricular materials screened before purchase for sex-role stereotypes, omissions of the contributions of women, and gender-based distortions?

- When ideal instructional materials are not available, do teachers point out and discuss blatant examples of sex-role stereotypes in the existing materials?

- How do teachers refer to nontraditional families?

- Do teachers avoid making assumptions that every child lives with a mother and father, and openly affirm diverse family groups?

- Do guidance counselors encourage female students to seek careers that fit their potential, rather than encouraging them to pursue more traditionally-accepted fields?

If answers to the above questions show limited sensitivity or awareness to the issue of gender stereotypes, you can press for policy change, starting with diplomatic discussion with teachers and/or the principal of the school, and following up with letters to the school board offering positive suggestions for change.

To assure you receive a fair hearing, it is sometimes helpful first to be involved in some of the "mundane" tasks that are frequently solicited from parents, such as volunteering to monitor the school cafeteria, offering to be the PTA membership chair, etc. Establishing yourself as a concerned citizen in this way will make future suggestions from you more likely to fall upon receptive ears.

Access to Physical Activities

Many physical activities that children enjoy—such as football, gymnastics, and ballet—often fall into sex-prohibitive categories for either boys or girls. I, for example, remember that the only physical activity open to me was to become a cheerleader. Cheerleaders could not actually play, but they could "encourage" the boys on to victory! Years later, when it was possible to make the girls' basketball team in school, the message was and is still sent that the boys' team was more important: They got the practice times they wanted in the gym and played their games first; the girls took what was left and played last. The boys had a coach, but the girls had a classroom teacher who "filled in" as a coach.

Unfortunately, there is still a tendency to steer boys into sports activities, like football or soccer, while directing girls toward ballet, gymnastics, or cheerleading. It will be a great day when children are able to choose a physical activity on the basis of their interests and aptitudes rather than what society dictates is appropriate! Certainly matters have improved: Girls are much freer to participate in a variety of sports than they have been in the past. However, there is still much room for improvement in the area of athletics for girls, both in terms of society's attitudes and institutional policies, such as the inequitable allotment of money to women's athletics in universities, to name just one example. Change is possible, starting at the family level. Here are some suggestions:

- Encourage both the boys and girls in your family to swim, jump rope, climb trees, throw a ball, and develop other basic physical abilities.

- Reconsider your gift-giving practices with regard to sex-role stereotypes. Instead of a jewelry-making kit, might your daughter appreciate a new basketball or a baseball glove?

- Contact your local high school and find out how much money is spent on both boys' and girls' sports. Ask for the reasoning if the girls' programs receive less funding. Write to the school board asking that any inequalities be rectified. Discuss the issue with friends and ask them to also write letters to the board. Encourage your children to write letters to the local newspaper telling why they think such inequalities are unfair and how the policies will affect them personally.

Artistic and Intellectual Pursuits

Artistic and intellectual areas also need to be examined carefully for gender stereotyping. Do we as parents encourage our sons as much as our daughters in developing their abilities in painting, poetry, drama, music? Are we as supportive of our daughters in vigorous academic pursuits, such as science, politics, and economics, as we are of our sons? Do we find ourselves more patient in our explanations of how things work or why the deficit is a problem when we talk to our sons than with our daughters? Do only our sons end up with chemistry sets or Legos? And do only our daughters receive piano or flute lessons? These areas are rife with stereotypes, and it is so very unfortunate. Who knows how many potentially gifted ballet dancers have been denied to the world because the boys were led to believe that the study of ballet is for "sissies"? Who knows how many potentially brilliant scientists or presidents were lost to us because girls were convinced that these fields were not open to them!

Media Messages

Most messages from the media about what it means to be a man or a women are less than positive. Some underlying themes culled from recent advertisements include:

A woman is:
- an object, often in skimpy attire, that sells cars and other items
- rarely capable of logical thinking
- very concerned about having a spotless kitchen
- obsessed with her hair, clothes, make-up, skin, etc.
- excessively sentimental and emotional
- physically inferior to a man

A man is:
- obsessed with competing and winning at everything
- overly concerned with material possessions
- likely to settle an argument with fists, a gun, a knife, or a bomb
- resistant to intimacy and commitment in a relationship; "tough"
- domineering in relationships with women
- practical and logical in his thinking

While it is true that magazines, newspapers, comic strips, and television programs continue to portray these traditionally stereotypical characters and situations, it is also true that the media are beginning to reflect an evolving awareness of the myriad of possibilities in gender roles and behaviors for both girls and boys, men and women. However, the media is not apt to change quickly enough. Therefore, we as parents need to find ways to counter its potent force. One effective way to refute negative advertisement is increase your children's awareness of the inaccuracies and inequities portrayed by television ads. The following activity is designed to help you to do just that.

"Television Logging"

Supplies needed: television
                   paper, writing utensils

1. As a family, select one week during which you will monitor the TV shows watched specifically to observe sex-role stereotypical characters and behavior.

2. Decide on what shows you will watch so that they are appropriate for all members of the family so all can participate.

3. Go over the following questions with your children, making sure they understand what to look for:

   • Is there a proportionate number of male and female characters in the show?

   • How does the proportion of exceptionally attractive women compare with the number of equally attractive men?

   • What are the occupations of the women and men in the show?

   • How often are diverse families depicted?

   • How many times does a man solve a problem for a woman? How many times does a woman solve a problem for a man? In each case, are the problems physical, academic, or interpersonal?

   • How often is a man depicted using violence to solve a problem?

   • How often is a woman shown in sexually provocative attire? (This includes advertisements, too!)

4. Provide paper for each family member to keep a "television log" of what the family watches. Ask your children to write down the name of each show watched and the answers to the above questions, as best they can. (If you have younger children, you may want to volunteer to be their "scribe" as you watch the shows with them.)

5. At the end of the week, gather as a family to review the results. Use your findings to stimulate discussion with your children about how men and women are portrayed in the media.

6. If, after reviewing your television logs, your family decides that certain favorite shows offer unfavorable images of men, women, and diverse

family groups, your family may decide to take the most powerful step of all: Register your displeasure by turning off the TV the next time the offending programs are on.

Encouraging Positive Qualities in All Children

In addition to looking at sex-role stereotypes about what boys and girls can *do*, we also need to look at our cultures'—and our own—stereotypes for what boys and girls can *be*. Obviously, the kinds of men and women our children grow up to be is a vastly more important issue than whether or not they grow up skilled at playing the piano or adept at fixing a broken bicycle. But unfortunate sex-role stereotypes are also linked to many important internal qualities. For example, boys are often considered to be assertive, logical in their thinking, and strong, decisive leaders. Girls, on the other hand, are generally considered to be the peacemakers, to be caring, intuitive, nurturing, and sensitive to the feelings of others. *All* of the these qualities are necessary and valuable in *all* of us, and all these traits need to be very deliberately encouraged in both boys and girls.

The development of these qualities can be encouraged through a wide range of toys and play activities, as well as through a host of school activities, but probably the most effective encouragement of positive human qualities happens through parental modeling. For example, a strong mother who is not afraid to express her opinions, who participates in sports according to her own interests, who pumps gas or hammers a nail for herself speaks volumes to her children about gender roles without ever having uttered a word. Similarly, a father who is openly affectionate with his children, who demonstrates how to peacefully settle an argument, who listens carefully to the feelings of children, who shows an interest in the arts helps to break down the prevalent notions of what men and women "should" and "should not" be.

To reinforce these important concepts, you may want to cut out or photocopy and post the set of reminders, "I Am Unique," on page 141. Encourage your children to say them often, almost as mantras, to help instill the belief that they are in no way limited by sex-role stereotypes or any other societal bias. To help your children appreciate the diversity of human beings and to help erase stereotypes and boundaries, try the following activity with your family.

"We Are All

Valuable"

Supplies needed: paper, writing/coloring utensils

1. With the entire family, discuss the statement "I am unique and valuable." Ask every family member what they think makes a person "unique" and "valuable."

2. Then ask your children to consider:

   • What does physical strength or size have to do with being unique or valuable?

   • Which is more important to being unique and valuable: what is on the inside or what is on the outside?

   • How should someone who is unique and valuable behave toward someone who is being shunned by others?

   • What responsibilities do "unique" and "valuable" people have for keeping the peace?

3. After discussing the above questions, ask your children to write down some important reasons why they consider themselves unique and valuable. (If your children are younger, you may want to suggest that they draw some pictures of what makes them unique and valuable.)

4. Ask your children to share what they think makes each member of your family unique and valuable.

Especially for Parents of Daughters

Though this chapter has focused on how sex-role stereotypes are detrimental to *both* males and females, the truth is, a major share of oppression is shouldered by girls and women. To assure that your bright, confident young daughter(s) will grow up to become a woman who is sure of herself and able and willing to lend her voice to a world that will desperately need her opinions and ideas, here are some special suggestions to parents of daughters:

   • If your daughter is quiet, be sure she is encouraged to contribute to dinner-table conversation and other discussions. It is amazing how many dinner conversations are dominated by sons!

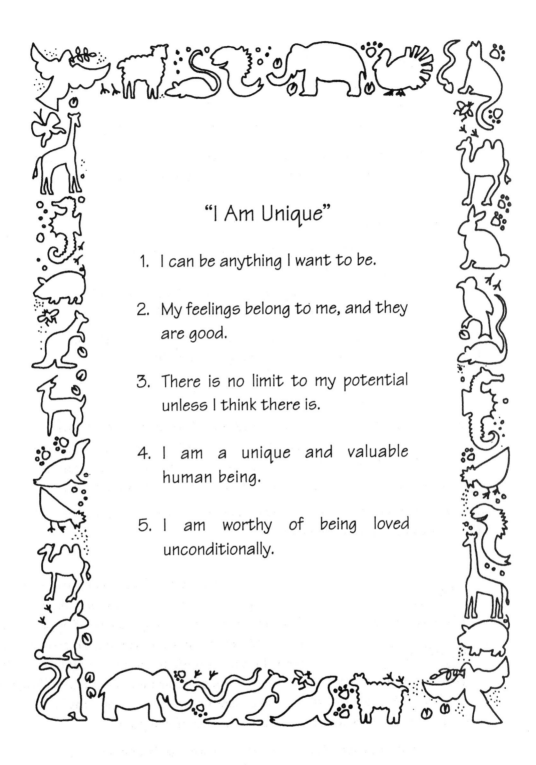

"I Am Unique"

1. I can be anything I want to be.

2. My feelings belong to me, and they are good.

3. There is no limit to my potential unless I think there is.

4. I am a unique and valuable human being.

5. I am worthy of being loved unconditionally.

RAISING PEACEFUL CHILDREN IN A VIOLENT WORLD

- Reward and compliment the academic achievements of your daughter and discuss with her how these successes can lead to future successes in a career.

- Downplay the importance of outward appearances with your daughter. Unwittingly, parents (and friends and relatives) often praise their daughter's dress, neatness, and physical attributes, causing a girl to begin to believe her appearance is her most salient feature.

- Enroll your daughter in some single-sex activities, such as girl-scouting or Camp Fire Girls. If finances permit, you may want to consider sending your daughter to an all-girls' school. In co-educational classes, research shows that girls learn to be spectators while the boys are encouraged to be the "doers." In single-sex situations, girls have many more opportunities to assume leadership roles.

What If Children Have Questions about Their Sexual Identity?

While our daughters often have a difficult time coping with the limited expectations society holds for them, children who have questions about their sexual identity have perhaps an even lonelier road to travel. It is critical that boys and girls who have anxieties about sexual identity be given an outlet in which to share their questions and fears without concern that they will be negatively evaluated or that they are disappointing—or even shocking—their parents. If you feel you may have difficulty in being a sounding board for your child's feelings about his or her emerging sexuality, seek out a empathic pastor, teacher, counselor, or friend who can listen and provide support for your child. If your child is actively questioning his or her gender identity, or is experiencing a burgeoning awareness that their gender orientation does not match that of their peers, you can help most by offering assurance of unconditional love and support—commodities that are rightfully taken for granted by most children but that are too often withdrawn by hurting parents who have difficulty coping with the fear that their child may be formulating a clear preference for those of the same sex.

It is important to provide support early. Homosexual adults often report that vague feelings of attraction for those of the same sex surfaced early—in some cases, even before they entered school. The grim statistic reported by Parents and Friends of Gays and Lesbians International

(PFLAG), that the suicide rate among homosexual young people is four times greater than for heterosexuals of the same age, underscores the injurious impact of these feelings on a young person's sense of self-worth.

Additionally, if your child is feeling "out of step" with others, he or she may especially need strategies to peacefully deflect teasing or physical abuse from persons who are fearful of what they do not understand. Your child will need to learn not only how to counteract ignorance and scorn but also how to educate others in a positive way. The peacekeeping suggestions given in Chapter 4, "Ten Responses to Potentially Violent Situations," may be particularly important.

There are also several things that you as a parent can do to help yourself. You may want to start by getting more information: Research the latest findings on homosexuality. The information you find may be invaluable in helping you better understand your child's feelings. You may progress through several stages of feelings as you respond to your child and consider your options. You may want to seek some counseling, both for you and your child. At some point, you may also want to find out what other parents experience. Your local chapter of Parents and Friends of Gays and Lesbians can be a source of affirmation and information. There you may find that other parents share similar feelings of fear or anger or concern and can offer support. Above all, do not blame yourself. Your child's sexual orientation does not reflect your abilities as a parent or the choices you made when raising your children.

Finally, remember that if your child has taken the risk of being open with you about anxieties about sexual orientation, he or she has also taken the risk of being alienated and rejected. This is the very time when your compassion, support, and empathy are most critical.

A Closing Word about Sex-Role Stereotypes

All of us long for a day when children will be free to be whoever they want to be without having to squelch their bright expectations when those expectations do not conform to what some arbitrary definition of maleness or femaleness dictates. We long for the day when children grow up to be aware of their own sex-stereotyped behavior and beliefs and, then, with intentional control and action, work to change their thinking. And finally—perhaps most importantly—we long for a day when sensitive men and women will work alongside one another, cooperatively seeking a more sane and peaceful world.

SECTION II

PEACEFUL ENTERTAINMENT

8

TIPS

FOR

TELEVISION

Co-Existing with the Tube

"Society attacks early, when the individual is most helpless."
—B. F. Skinner, *Notebooks*

Taming the TV

"Please . . . can I stay up with you?"

Late on a Friday night my six-year-old niece stood in her flower-print nightgown, pleading. She had returned from an afternoon and early evening of playtime at a friend's house. Now she wanted to stay up with her aunt.

"Why do you want to do that?" her mother asked.

The little girl replied, "I can't sleep."

"What's REALLY the matter?" asked her mom.

"Wellll . . . I keep thinking about what I saw on TV at Janice's house."

"What did you watch?"

"Uh, some people got killed on TV," she said. "I saw blood and axes. I didn't want to watch, but I kinda wanted to be scared. Janice does it all the time."

"I used to want to stay up, too," I told my niece, "especially when I felt scared."

Both the girl's mother and I talked with her further to help her recognize her feelings and to offer ways to help her feel peaceful and safe. We felt she needed extra support for the transitional period between watching "scary television" away from home and "coming home." We engaged the young girl in some activities we hoped would extinguish her newly-acquired fears and anxieties and would rebuild a haven of peace for her for the evening.

We decided to start the evening over again. First, we invited the six-year-old to select a pair of her mother's pajamas that would be fun to wear, as well as a "dress-up" way to help her sleep through the night. We suggested that she select any lamp in the house to plug in her room for a night light. Then we gave her a choice of having a warm shower or a bath filled with bubbles. After her relaxing bath, the three of us snuggled together on the living room sofa and told the girl's favorite bedtime story with gusto, using many exaggerated hand movements and different silly voices for the characters. Then, the girl selected a favorite music tape, and we listened together as we treated ourselves to several cups of hot cocoa. Creating a cozy atmosphere, we plumped a pillow behind the girl and rumpled a blanket around her on the sofa, tucking her in between us. We each sat beside her as we told more stories, this time humorous tales about family members, each one beginning, "Do you remember the funny time when . . . ?" Finally, we watched as she nodded and drifted off to sleep—a successful conclusion to "starting the evening over." Another battle with the effects of television violence had just barely been won.

Television is an all-too-pervasive force in our society. Though sometimes we might wish TV would go away, it is clear that TV is a part of our children's lives, and it is not going to disappear.

It might be helpful to consider the television viewing habits of your family as a basis for considering the pros and cons of this omnipresent medium.

TUNING IN
How Is TV Handled in Your Home?

1. How many hours per week do the adults in your family spend watching television?

2. Do the adults in your family often watch shows that depict scenes of violence? Give examples.

3. How many hours per week do your children spend watching television? What are your reasons?

4. How much violence do you think your children see on television?

5. Does an adult monitor what your children watch on television and discuss the contents with them? Give examples.

6. Do you believe violence on television has a negative effect on children? What are your reasons?

7. How do you feel your views on television viewing affect your children's peacemaking attitudes?

8. If you believe violence on television has a negative effect on children, how do you try to mitigate the effect?

What's the Fuss about Television?

Dr. Spock once wrote that he would not read even mildly cruel stories to young children or let them see even slightly disturbing programs on television. This was not just to keep them from being frightened but also to keep them from becoming tolerant of violence. He said there are plenty of life experiences that inevitably disturb children (and adults, too) without our creating them unnecessarily.[1] If you are concerned about the amount of violence on television, this chapter can help you co-exist with television peacefully and offer you a choice of alternative activities for your children.

---

1   *Dr. Spock's Baby & Child Care.*

In our experience as parents who support television nonviolence, my husband and I found that the censoring approach of limiting the hours of watching TV worked for a while, but we still felt we were losing the battle against TV violence. Just when we thought we might be winning over the shooting, stabbing, raping scenes in the programs shown on our local stations, more stations would come on the air. We knew we could not monitor every single show on every channel or turn off every violent scene used as an advertisement for an upcoming show. We also did not want to wrap our child in cotton batting to protect her. Gradually, we realized we were part of a growing group of concerned people who believe the hundreds of studies indicating that the mayhem and murder on TV can encourage aggression and violent behavior in children. Recently, as parents against television violence, we have received some hope and support through the following:

- the Television Violence Act of 1990 and the Children's Television Act of 1990, which requires networks to provide *educational* programs

- the twenty-year actions by members of the National Parents-Teachers Association (PTA) researching violence on TV, lobbying against it, and printing material on concerns about violence (The National PTA is currently joining forces with the Center for Media Education to monitor compliance with the Children's Television Act and to work with stations to improve programs aimed at children.)

- the voluntary meetings by network executives and others to determine how to reduce the level of violence in shows

- the organization of the National Council for Families & Television, which explores the effect of violent TV programming on children specifically and on everyone else in general

- a national conference on "Television and Preparation of the Mind for Learning" by America's Department of Health and Human Services

- the success of parents teaching children to fight back intellectually at television violence and teaching their children "television literacy"

When Your Children Are Charmed by a Flickering TV Set

When you find that your children are charmed only by the flickering television set, there are two major areas of concern: the long-term effect of television violence on your children, and on other more active and wholesome pursuits that your children may be missing out on while sitting entranced in front of the TV set. Television can create and deliver a sensory experience that is almost total for young children. Watching TV takes no personal involvement on the children's part. It is all done for them in a total and often passive experience. What can a parent do to refute the power of the tube? We already know that TV is a powerful attraction, with its fanciful characters and situations. Yet we also know that fantasy is important in our children's' lives. Fantasy on TV can be a child's way of working out fears and distressful dilemmas. Consider the child who feels powerless. Perhaps the child feels small in the big world of adults. Fantasy through TV may help the child face these feelings of powerlessness through his or her imagination and through the playfulness of fantasy rather than be overwhelmed by the feelings.

You can neutralize the addiction of TV through various strategies designed to combat the addictive lure. For example, books with fanciful stories, read aloud to your children, will enable them not only to experience fantasy but also to have many imaginative firsthand experiences. Your children can come to realize that books can be just as fulfilling as television. As a parent interested in television literacy, consider also these suggestions:

- set limits
- make choices
- watch with your children
- talk with your children
- make changes
- be active

Set Limits

Start by placing some limits on your children's TV viewing hours. When children of preschool or kindergarten age become interested in a TV program, suggest one-half hour a day for the viewing time. Provide alternative activities that will interest them. If your older children are already watching two to four hours of television a day, you may want to reduce the viewing time *gradually* until you are down to no more than one hour a day.

Make Choices

While your children are very young, choose the programs on TV for them. When they start first grade, begin to have family meetings to agree together which programs will be watched. When they begin second grade, the pressure of other children and what they watch on TV and what TV characters they talk about will affect what your children want to watch. When you reach a time when you are saying, "No," while your children are arguing, "But I *want* to!" help them understand what concerns you and why you disagree, giving your reasons about the particular program.

Watch with Your Children

Watch your children's favorite television programs whenever you can. Plan to see, at least one time, every program your children watch and get a feeling for what your children enjoy. Do you like the programs? Does anything about them concern you? What values are presented by the shows? Are the programs exhibiting values similar to the ones you are trying to instill in your children?

Talk with Your Children

Make comments about what your children are watching, about what you think is worthwhile and wholesome, and what you think is negative and destructive. Tell your children your reasons. For example, when their favorite cartoon character is hitting another, do not excuse this as "slapstick comedy," but use the action as a chance to talk about why hitting others is not the way to solve a problem and discuss alternative ways to resolve the situation.

Make Changes

When necessary, take steps to change your children's viewing habits. With TV violence on the increase, more than ever you may want to regulate how much television your children watch and what kind of programs they see: Just count the violent acts yourself. Are there REALLY about 5 violent acts an hour during adult prime-time? Are there REALLY about 26 violent acts per hour in children's cartoons, as the National Council for Families and Television has recently suggested? If what your children watch *does* contain these violent acts, select some more positive programs, with their input.

Be socially active about what your children are watching. To educate your children about your family's values, talk to them about the programs they are seeing. Turn off what you do not like. Join your local PTA group and become active and help monitor violence, including your local station's compliance with the Children's Television Act. With other interested parents, work with local TV stations to improve the programs aimed at children. With your children, write a letter together to a local station and tell them that you "can't turn on what isn't there." Ask for:

- programs without violence

- programs with reduced violent acts that also show the *consequences* of such acts

- travelogues

- programs that show respect and interest in the cultural heritage of all people

- programs that show America's history and gender-positive and multicultural contributions

- programs that teach beginning reading, writing, and arithmetic

- programs that will help teen-agers get jobs by offering bulletin boards of local job openings, information about interviewing for jobs, ideas for starting small businesses; and by teaching skills such as computer word processing, typing, and car repair

- programs that will help young people begin checking accounts, invest their money wisely, and fill out their first income tax forms

- programs that will help us all be better world citizens, by focusing on the world's music, literature, artistic treasures, and people's achievements in caring for the environment

If you are interested in some organizations and publishers concerned about violence in television, you can contact any or all of the following:

- California Newsreel
  149 Ninth St., Suite 420
  San Francisco, CA 94103

  Offers a video series for parents and teachers, *On Television: A Three-Part Video Series*: "Teach the Children," "Public Trust or Private Property," and "The Violence Factor."

- Center for Media Education
  1012 Heather Ave.
  Takoma Park, MD 20912
  Offers material about its two ongoing projects, "The Future of TV" and "The Campaign for Kids' TV."

- National Parents-Teachers Association
  c/o National PTA Orders
  P. O. Box 88873
  Chicago, IL 60680
  Offers material about "Television and Your Family."

- Train of Thought Publishing
  P. O. Box 311
  Redmond, WA 98073-0311
  Offers manual for parents and teachers titled *Television and the Lives of Our Children.*

Helping Your Children Feel Safe

Television violence can cause aggressive behavior and reinforce values that teach children that aggression can resolve conflicts. As President Clinton recently lamented, television too often "romanticizes" violence and too rarely shows the pain and suffering that it causes. In a study of TV violence done by the American Psychological Association, researchers found that the average child in the United States watched 8,000 murders and saw more than 100,000 other acts of violence on television before finishing elementary school.[2] To compound the problem, special effects can make the violence children see on television appear exceptionally realistic. Some producers feel they must push for more and more violence to add excitement to their shows. When your children cannot forget a scary TV program, you may need to take direct steps to help them feel safe. Among the most important steps you can take are the following:

- avoid violent shows
- talk about fears
- look for the source of fears
- clarify confusing portrayals of "good" and "bad"

---

2 Reported in the *Sacramento Bee*, January 13, 1994.

Avoid Violent Shows

The most direct step is a preventative one: Avoid exposing your children to programs with violence. Select carefully what your children watch on TV. An overload of violence may cause your children to be so saturated with violence that they become desensitized to it. Seeing too much violence can "numb" them to the cruelty and horror of violent acts.

You may soon receive technological assistance in defusing TV violence. A newly marketed device called Intelevision contains a micro-chip called a C-Chip ("C" for "choice") that will allow you to block programs you feel contain too much violence. Although certain cable companies already allow parents to block out an entire channel, the Intelevision will offer a new measure of precision, allowing you to block specific programs at the specific times you choose.

Talk about Fears

Get an idea about what frightens your children. Spending time with them can take the form of relaxing and enjoyable moments, but it can also be a time for you to offer reassurance. If you are open and honest with them about what frightens *you*—on television, in fiction, in a nightmare, or in real life—they will see that it is normal and acceptable to have fears. Your children may then be more likely to open up and talk about what is scary for them. Talking about fear helps to defuse it.

Look for the Source of Fears

Often what children fear on television is a projection of what they fear in real life. Help your children take on the very thing that terrifies them. If, for example, your child is upset by a television program showing a small child getting beaten up by a bully, it is possible he or she is experiencing, or is worried about, the same situation. Use the fictionalized scenario to discuss your child's feelings about the violent situation. Suggest ways the television character might peacefully cope with the problem, soliciting input from your child.

Clarify Confusing Portrayals of "Good" and "Bad"

Help your children look for good and bad in *all* characters. Remind your children there is always potential for human goodness in others. You may need to point out, however, that it is not always possible to distinguish the "good guys" from the "bad guys" on TV by who carries a gun. On TV, it is not only the "bad guys" who wield weapons. The "good guys"—police officers, detectives, vigilantes, and private citizens with permits—are often shown acting violently. Unfortunately, the inference is that illegal means can justify the ends—at least in the hazy world of television. It is easy for children to become confused, and they may benefit from some parental explanation.

Alternatives for Family Viewing

Most parents have found themselves saying, at one point or another, "Why can't TV script writers come up with some nice, wholesome family stories like they used to?" Those of us who grew up with "Leave It to Beaver" may wonder why there needs to be such a depressing parade of drug scenes, nudity, and rough language on television, let alone the violence. We may long for stories that would help us build peaceful characters in our children. There *are* alternatives available.

One family I know has traded in standard television fare for selected videos. They liked the idea of being able to choose entertainment for their family instead of having it foisted upon them by indifferent programming directors. The family started out with the so-called "funny family films," such as "Home Alone II" and "Kindergarten Kop." Disillusionment came swiftly when they witnessed the prankish violence and disrespect for authority in the first film and the blatant sex outside of marriage in the second. So much for the "funny family films," they decided.

This family then bypassed the current films touted for children and began resurrecting the old, time-honored classics, such as the collection of Disney classic films, the great musicals such as "The Sound of Music" and "Fiddler on the Roof," and some award-winners such as "Gone with the Wind" and "Lilies of the Field." As they revisited these films, the parents were delighted at how much the whole family enjoyed the entertainment and were amazed at how wholesome, interesting, and educational many of the themes were. Their children often begged to see their favorites again and again, and the parents (for once) had absolutely no qualms about agreeing to their request. I have recently come upon another alternate solution to the proscribed television fare in the form of a company called "Feature Films for Families, Inc.,"[3] which offers films that focus on moral values, faith, courage,

---

3   You can obtain a catalog from Feature Films for Families, Inc., by calling their toll-free number: 1-800-347-2833.

and adventure. Their catalog assures viewers that none of their selections contain obscenities, profanity, or violence, and it provides plot summaries to help parents in making film choices. In addition, the "Parent's Guide" printed on each video box can be used to help stimulate family discussions, offering questions such as, "Why do you think Scott gave Pete his bike?" and "Does doing what's right always bring immediate results that we can see?" It is possible to cut down, or even eliminate, regular television programs and commercial "funny family films" by acquiring a library of these edifying videos. Some sample selections of videos include:

- "The Butter Cream Gang" is a film about growing up in a small town and learning to love unconditionally, even though the heart is aching.

- "Space Camp" tells the story of a group of teen-agers who attend summer camp at the NASA space program. They go aboard the Atlantis space shuttle during an engine test, and the space craft is accidentally launched. It takes the group's combined efforts, courage, and trust to bring the youngsters and the spacecraft safely back to Earth.

- "Miracle at Moreaux" focuses on three Jewish children who flee Nazi-occupied France in 1943 to find refuge in a Catholic school run by a nun, who helps the children to reach the border and freedom.

- "In Your Wildest Dreams" portrays an eighteen-year-old who becomes a stock market millionaire while completing a computer school assignment. With help from his family and girlfriend, he struggles to handle this windfall with honesty and integrity.

A Strategy to Eliminate Television: One Woman's Story

There is one other dealing-with-television strategy you might want to consider: the total elimination of the television habit. Weaning families off the tube is very difficult. Author Marie Winn has named television the "plug-in drug" because it is so addictive.[4] Once children start watching regularly, it is extremely hard to break the habit.

---

4   See book listings on page 159.

When the daughter of one of my friends was a toddler, the child routinely watched the morning session of "Mr. Rogers' Neighborhood" and "Sesame Street." The child's mother, Elva, would turn on the television and race to her desk, frantic to get in an hour-and-a-half of work while her daughter was occupied by TV. Quite often Elva would put tapes of the same shows on again in the afternoon so she could get supper cooked and the house tidied "in peace." She depended on these slots of time and planned her days around them, as many parents of small children often do.

By the time Elva's daughter was six, the child was turning the television on whenever she liked, demanding to be passively entertained. The child had become a television junky, and her mother realized she was a co-conspirator. Elva decided to reorder her priorities.

She looked carefully at the patterns of her family relationships and determined that television had begun to dominate their lives. She looked ahead and foresaw the issue only getting worse as her daughter got older. Reminding herself of the mounting arguments against television, she tried to envision the greater richness, vibrancy, and depth of family life possible once her family members got over their dependence on television. Strengthened in her commitment to limit TV viewing, she decided first to eliminate the afternoon session. She did not announce the plan; instead, Elva scheduled a series of afternoon activities she knew her daughter would enjoy. When the child asked to watch a favorite program, Elva told her that, instead, they would be doing some enjoyable activities that afternoon. The two visited a children's museum, walked down to the river and fed the ducks, and invited a friend over to bake gingerbread cookies. The transition went fairly smoothly, although it took a lot of work at the beginning when Elva had to plan diversions and also free herself from her other obligations so that she could spend the quality time with her daughter in the afternoons. Gradually, the planned diversions were withdrawn, as Elva encouraged her child to discover creative ways to amuse herself. Elva went through the same process with other television viewing sessions that were "prime time" for her child, and within six months television was totally gone from their lives.

It has been three years since Elva unplugged the TV, and she reveals that the benefits have been overwhelming. Her testimony compares favorably with that of many other parents, some of whom have stopped TV "cold turkey." When television disappears as an option, children quickly discover how to fill up their days with more constructive, active activities. Forced to become self-reliant, they become inventive creators of the adventures of their own lives. Instead of watching an animated version of

Cinderella, for example, they may delve into the dress-up box and *become* Cinderella—or the tiny mice or the handsome prince or the mean stepmother. When they are tired or bored, instead of zoning out in front of the tube, they may quietly read a book, put together a jigsaw puzzle, or just lie in the grass, peacefully contemplating the cloud formations. Thus, children learn that they are responsible for themselves; that they can fill their days with interesting, useful activities; and that they can entertain themselves when they are bored, calm themselves when they are frazzled, and divert themselves when they are restless. With these important abilities, they can go forward into more peaceful lives, having developed the inner resources to help them on their journey.

If you are interested in exploring the possibility of eliminating television from your family life, here are four books designed to help:

- *Four Arguments for the Elimination of Television* by Jerry Mander. New York: William Morrow, 1990.

- *The Plug-In Drug and Unplugging the Plug-In Drug* by Marie Winn. New York: Viking/Penguin, 1985.

- *Amusing Ourselves to Death* by Neil Postman. New York: Viking, 1990.

- *Who's Bringing Them Up?* by Martin Lange. Gloucester, England: Hawthorne Press, 1981.

A Closing Word about Television

Most parents worry about the amount of television their children watch. Many recent books have warned about the dangers of excessive television viewing, especially when what is viewed is violent and when the viewers are impressionable young children. The pervasiveness of violent behavior on TV has been proven to have a carry-over effect into attitude formation about conflict resolution and even war. If children are being conditioned by TV to accept violent behavior, the inevitable result is that they will be less likely to question violence as a means of settling conflicts.

As parents in an increasingly volatile world, we may wish we could return to an earlier time when life seemed more simple and innocent for children. Since that is not possible, we need to do all we can to preserve our children's right to a peaceful childhood. Careful monitoring of television is one way to protect that right.

9 TOYS

AND

GAMES

Fostering Peace through Play

> "Children are not born knowing the many opportunities that are theirs for the taking. Someone who *does* know must tell them."
> —Ruth Hill Viguers, in "Ruth Hill Viguers: A Reader's Tribute," *The Horn Book Magazine*

"You GOT Me!" Recently I was walking my dog in the park near my home when I observed two little boys playing an animated game of "Soldier." They were "shooting" one another with toy guns that looked so realistic, a chill ran down my spine as I watched them.

"Ker pow! Ker POW!!" cried one little boy, leaping from the jungle gym to the sand box, his tiny fingers on the trigger.

"Aaahgh! You GOT me!" came the reply, as the other youngster performed a dramatically protracted death scene I felt quite certain was for my benefit. Well, I was "impressed," all right.

Strolling back home, I could not stop my mind from mulling over the mock violence. I pondered: Is there a real connection between toys and behavior? Or are children's playthings merely a harmless reflection of the society in which we live? While family, friends, school, and religious groups undoubtedly have the most significant roles in influencing youngsters, I mused, children *are* part of their environment. Part of that environment, I reasoned further, is the toys and games with which they are intensely involved on a daily basis. Logically, then, toys and games could influence who will be the peacemakers and who will be the peacebreakers in future generations.

For you to consider this important issue, it may be helpful to assess what kinds of toys and games are in your home and just how your children play with them, using the following questionnaire.

TUNING IN
What Toys and Games Are Popular in Your Home?

1. What kinds of toys and games are in your home?

2. When your children play games, how many times are the participants laughing with, and not at, one another?

3. What are your children's moods and feelings when they are playing with their games and toys?

4. Do the toys your children play with teach them problem-solving or logical thinking? How?

5. What percentage of your children's toys reflect violent acts or violent people?

6. How do you feel your views on entertainment, and the toys and games that you select for your children, affect their peacemaking attitudes?

7. In what ways do you think toys affect your children's behavior?

Toys Related to Violent Actions	It happened in New York, but it could have occurred anywhere: thirteen-year-old Nicholas Heyward, Jr., toting an eighteen-inch toy gun, was shot and killed by a police officer who thought the eighth-grader's play weapon was real. The hapless victim was "just playing."

Several weeks later, at least two major toy retailers responded to this and other similar incidents by announcing that they would stop selling realistic-looking toy guns in their stores. If this seems like a victory, it may be; but it is only a drop in the bucket. There is still an enormous emphasis in toy stores on toys related to aggression, killing, and war. The next time you visit a toy store, count the number of toys that are directly or indirectly related to violent behavior. What you will find is a frightening testimonial about the very violent world in which our children are growing up.

Toy manufacturers often use television commercials and advertisements, especially during Saturday morning cartoons, to tout their latest products. Unfortunately, some of children's very favorite television characters have been neatly packaged into these toys. If the television show and its major characters have a violent stance, then the toys are designed so that children can imitate the character's aggressive, and sometimes violent, behavior.

Is it possible that the most warlike of these toys can lead to later violent actions and lifestyles? Every child who plays with a GI Joe may not grow up to be a career soldier, of course, any more than every child who plays with a doctor's kit will grow up to be a doctor. But a steady diet of toys designed so children can pretend they are fighting or participating in wars surely sends them a clear message that such behavior is tolerated, if not condoned, by the adults who have purchased the toys.

Of late, video games have been used to depict especially graphic acts of violence and vicious assaults against women. Many child psychologists are especially concerned with this form of entertainment because of the total involvement required of participants; while violent scenes on television may be viewed passively or somewhat dispassionately, the very nature of interactive video games insists that the players put themselves actively in the role of "perpetrator." When the perpetrator is simply playing tennis, loading boxes on trucks, or climbing vines, such play can be harmless and perhaps even challenging, but when the perpetrator is asked to kill the opponent using martial arts, to cut out a victim's heart, or to render a women helpless, the cumulative effects on a young person can only be imagined.

If you are concerned about the prevalence of violent toys in your children's life, there is good news! Children can still have a very rich and creative fantasy life without violent toys and games. Following are some suggestions to bring peaceful alternatives into your home:
- choose your young children's toys
- watch your children at play
- make clear comments about toys and advertising

Choose Your Young Children's Toys

Carefully select toys that will teach your young children about the world around them in positive and peaceful ways. As they get older, there will be more pressure to have what other children have and want, or to have the toys advertised on TV. More than likely, a time will come when they will be enamored by a toy or game that you feel will instigate aggressive behavior or foster values at odds with your own. This would be a good time to discuss the toy at a Family Peace Meeting. Talk with your children about what the toy is supposed to be used for and how it might be contradictory to what your family believes. Examine the toy with your children so you can demonstrate what there is about it that has influenced your negative feelings. Finally, offer alternative toys or games that are as similar to the original as possible, but without the violent connotations and possible repercussions.

Watch Your Children at Play

Parents trying to raise peaceful children often tell me that, while they would never allow guns or other violent toys in their homes, their youngsters have created toy weaponry out of everything from play blow dryers to building blocks to twigs. One bewildered parent lamented that her son had fashioned a toy gun out of a piece of toast! This is more than likely just creative play, and as the gun will not last any longer than the toast, I tell the parents not to worry. But it is important, in general, to watch *how* your children play, even with "peaceful" toys. Particularly when children are playing together, you could steer them toward cooperative rather than competitive games. Check to see that, when they are using their toys and games, there is much positive talking and laughing, rather than anger and tears. And any games or toys that require one child to touch a child in a way that is not gentle should be actively discouraged.

Make Clear Comments about Toys and Advertising

Make clear comments to your children about what you find offensive and what you find positive and constructive in toys. Explain how your evaluation is based upon your values. If the toys or games in question are being touted by a TV commercial, talk to your children about why the toys are being advertised and what manipulative advertising techniques are being used to sell the toys.

For older children, discuss the following advertising techniques used in commercials and then, with your children, look for examples of these techniques in current commercials:

- *magic*
  Some commercials advertise that when a toy or game is played with, magical things happen, such as being transported into a fantasy land. Children often do not realize the magic is only in the commercial.

- *favorite characters*
  Favorite cartoon characters, or actors from children's favorite shows, are used to pitch toys and games. Cartoon characters, of course, cannot like or dislike anything because they are not real. And actors are just that—actors. They are paid to say what they say and may not even like the product.

- *size and sound distortions*
  In the world of commercials, dolls appear to be lifesize, and trucks and cars make realistic sounds that children believe will accompany the toy. This, of course, is not usually true.

- *lots of happy friends*
  Commercials show toys and games being enjoyed by a group of animated boys and girls, thus making children believe they will never be lonely if they have this toy or game.

Often when children are aware of these misleading advertisement techniques and realize that someone is trying to manipulate them, they become much less susceptible to commercials and begin to think more critically.

Alternatives to Violent Toys and Games

The violence-addicted world in which we live seems to be intent upon insisting that our children grow up desensitized to, and tolerant of, violence. As peace-loving parents, we may often feel like wringing our hands when children's toys and games are designed to rob them of their innocence and potential for becoming peaceful adults. Fortunately, questionable toys and games are not the only ones available for our children. There are also many toys, games, and activities on the market that are very wholesome and provide a stimulus for positive play, an appreciation for beauty in the world, as well as a reverence for peace and cooperation.

The next few pages explore the following peaceful alternatives to violent toys and games:

- re-discovering wholesome toys
- selecting age-appropriate nonviolent toys
- choosing computer software

Re-Discovering Wholesome Toys

We can say "no" to violence by filling our children's lives with toys and games that will not only nurture peacefulness in them but also attract them and hold their interest. Many alternatives to violent toys and games are offered in the following list:

- airplanes (wooden or electric)
- baking sets
- beads and bead kits
- beeswax for modeling shapes
- bird-watching kits (binoculars, minicamera, bird identification cards)
- board games, such as checkers, Parcheesi, and chess
- butterfly-collecting kits
- candle-making kits
- chalk
- chemistry sets
- clay
- coin- and stamp-collecting kits
- colored pencils
- construction paper
- cooking sets
- costumes
- craft books and supplies
- crayons
- dolls
- doll houses
- dominoes
- erector sets
- face-painting kits
- finger-paints
- finger puppets
- flower-pressing kits
- flower-card kits
- Frisbees

- garden tools
- giant inflatable balls
- gift baskets to make
- glider kits
- greeting-card kits
- guide books for making animal shadow shapes
- hat collection for make-believe
- hobby horses
- holiday ornament kits
- insect specimen kits
- jumbo jacks
- jumbo marbles
- jump rope and jumping rhymes
- kites
- knitting sets
- knot-making kits
- lanyard ropes
- looms
- magician's kits
- marionettes
- microscopes
- musical instruments
- music boxes
- objects to juggle
- origami kits
- paint brushes
- paper-making kits
- pickup sticks
- picnic sets
- pioneer logs and block sets
- playing cards
- pocket magnifying glasses
- pogo sticks
- potholder looms
- pottery wheels
- prisms
- puppets and puppet theaters
- puzzles
- sand box toys (shovel, pail, sieve, etc.)
- sock-monkey doll kits
- song books
- star kits with plastic globe and stars that glow
- stickers and sticker-collecting books
- stilts
- stone sculpture kits
- string and string games kits
- tape recorders
- tapes[1]
- tea sets
- telescopes
- tie-dye kits
- sailboats
- watercolors and other paints
- wood-burning kits
- wreath-making kits
- writing pens (try felt tips with assorted aromas)
- yo-yo's

Selecting Age-Appropriate Nonviolent Toys

If you are not sure which of the above toys would be developmentally appropriate for your particular youngsters, the following rough "rule of thumb" may be helpful:

---

[1] My family is a big fan of Red Grammer's "Teaching Peace" tape, available from Smilin' Atcha Music, P.O. Box 446, Chester, NY 10918.

- *newborns, up to age 1*

  Select brightly colored toys of varying textures, or toys that make soothing noises, such as music mobiles or rattles. Soft dolls or animals are always good and, for baby who is sitting up, blocks, nesting cups, or sturdy (cloth or cardboard) picture books are appropriate.

- *toddlers, ages 1 to 3*

  Toddlers enjoy toys that encourage active physical play, such as beach balls, toy wagons, and tricycles. Toys that encourage make-believe are also good, such as dolls, play furniture, and play food. Toddlers also love to sort and fit toys, blocks, simple puzzles and tend to enjoy musical instruments.

- *preschoolers, ages 3 to 5*

  Children this age love to pretend, so consider toys that imitate the world around them, such as toy farms, gas stations, or a circus or puppet theater. Transportation, too, is fascinating to children of this age, so trucks, cars, planes, and trains are excellent selections. Also, to activate their burgeoning intellect, also include word and memory games, construction sets, simple art materials, books, and tapes.

- *grade-school children, ages 6 to 9*

  Toys can help hone skills and thus build self-confidence at this age, so look for models, science, art or craft kits, board games, and table-top sports games. For active play, think about sleds, skates, pogo sticks, scooters, bicycles, and other sports equipment. Solitary play is still important at this age, so encourage it with miniature villages, doll houses, and pop-up books.

- *older children, ages 9 to 12*

  At this age, children are beginning to develop life-long interests, so encourage hobbies and crafts, advanced construction sets, as well as science sets concerned with chemistry, astronomy, or biology. Books and tapes are ideal choices for this age group, as are painting, sculpting, and models for the artistically inclined. Do not forget computer programs if you own a personal computer. (See the section on "Choosing Computer Software," page 169.)

- *adolescents*

  After about the age of twelve or so, children's tastes begin to resemble more closely those of adult's. Board and computer games are still popular, as are additions to budding collections, such as stamps, cars, trains, coins, dolls, and so forth.

In your search for nonviolent toys and games, there are many to choose from, and a good number of those listed above need not be expensive. In addition, you might want to explore the following resources:

- Dr. Toy's 100 Best Children's Products
  Institute for Childhood Resources
  220 Montgomery Street, #2811
  San Francisco, CA 94104
  415-864-1169
  (Send a self-addressed, stamped envelope.)

- The Nature Company
  P.O. Box 188
  Florence, KY 41022
  606-342-7200

- Hearth Song
  156 N. Main Street
  Sebastopol, CA 95472
  707-829-0944

- Chinaberry Book Service
  2780 Via Orange Way, Suite B
  Spring Valley, CA 91978
  800-776-2242

- The Smithsonian Institute
  Department 0006
  Washington, D.C. 20073-0006
  202-357-1300

Choosing Computer Software

One source of entertainment for children today is available on the personal computer, which is more and more finding its way into the homes of American families. A problem can occur when children are more computer-literate than their parents (this is certainly the case in *my* home!). Therefore, it may be helpful to take a look at the sometimes overwhelming world of computer software to see what we as parents should know to ensure that what we are buying is not only wholesome and constructive but also appropriate to the developmental level of our children. Here are some suggestions you may find helpful:

- Talk to your children's teachers. Discuss your values and ask the teachers to shed some light on your youngsters' abilities so you can buy programs that will stimulate your children's' interests and provide assistance in subject matter as well. Additionally, find out which programs are being used at school. These programs are likely to have passed stringent standards for quality. If you have the same programs at home, your children will be receiving reinforcement in their school work.

- Be alert to software programs touted by famous heroes or television characters your children like. Because obtaining the rights to these characters is often expensive for the computer company, the programs may be less focused and not as well produced as products that do not use famous characters.

- Look for programs that involve children's active participation toward a meaningful, constructive goal. A good program requires your children's constant input—choosing ideas and paths to take, constructing scenarios—so that they are not simply observing passively. Also look for programs that offer a variety of skill levels or scenarios so your children can "grow" with the program and not become bored by it.

- Choose programs that stimulate creativity and critical thinking. There are many programs that invite children to choose how a story will play itself out, and there are also many high-quality drawing and painting programs that allow children to express their artistic abilities. Programs for music allow children to write their own original songs. Finally, some of the new "desktop publishing" programs allow children to create stories, book reports, and even their own family newspapers.

In addition to creative toys and games you can purchase or make, there are many activities your children can do alone, with other children, or with your entire family in lieu of playing with violent toys and games. The following list of activities may stimulate your thinking. While some of these activities cost money, many of them simply require time and an imaginative spirit.

- go fishing with your children
- bake cookies
- stroll along a trail together in a nearby nature area
- invite your children's friends to your home for a read-aloud session
- start a children's cake-decorating class
- check out the local art museum or science center with your children
- take your children to the local library
- go to storytellings put on by a local Storyteller's Guild
- explore the constellations together (an astronomy book from the library can help you explore)
- have a marathon Parcheesi game (the winner can be excused from chores for a day)
- jump in the fall leaves together
- enroll your children in gymnastics or other sports
- go bicycling together and take turns choosing the route
- feed the squirrels in the local park together
- keep a journal with your children and take turns writing to one another in it
- volunteer the entire family to help out in a soup kitchen, a homeless shelter, or a nursing home
- take your children to the ballet, symphony, or theater
- take a ride together out into the country
- build a tree house together
- go sledding or tobogganing in the winter time
- have a picnic lunch in the park or your backyard
- go window shopping with your children
- check with a local music store about music lessons for the entire family
- go horseback riding
- take up bird watching as a family (the local Audubon Society can get you started)

- tell cumulative stories to one another (one person begins and then turns it over to the next person)
- consider a fitness program for the entire family at the local YMCA
- take your children to a naturalist program sponsored by a local zoo, park, or nature area
- give each other foot massages
- play a game of catch in the park
- take turns reading to one another
- lie on the grass and watch the clouds; see what the cloud formations remind you of

The alternative toys and activities suggested in this chapter may have created a distinct feeling of dejá vù for you. Many of these toys, games, and activities are those that we parents loved as children and the very same ones that even our grandparents may have enjoyed! It is often true that we are so eager to give our children all the things we did not have, or could not afford, that we sometimes forget to give them the wonderfully rich things we *did* have: family discussions, reunions, picnic, long walks, games, traditions, and lots of working and playing together—with considerably less distraction from video games, "boom boxes," channel-changers, or noisy battle-related playthings. While we sometimes feel our children are more "sophisticated" than we were, we need to keep in mind that wholesome, stimulating play and activity will *never* go out of style.

A Closing Word about Toys and Games

There is no compelling evidence to suggest that the occasional playing of cops and robbers or elaborate war games will harm our children or cause them to grow up to be violent adults; however, there are a myriad of positive entertainment choices that can fill children's limited recreational time with wonder and joy. If *all* of our children's formative years were spent with these creative and often thought-provoking alternatives, who knows? We just might raise a new generation of human beings who would prefer to consider the constellations rather than wage a war.

10 PEACEFUL LITERATURE

Finding Role Models for Peace in Children's Books

"Books enable readers to realize their humanity while delighting in the souls of all."
—Bernice E. Cullinan, editor, *Children's Literature in the Reading Program*

"Tell Me a Story"

"But, Mom, WHY can't we EACH have a story?" asked my friend Susan's eight-year-old son, Seth, who was squirming slightly in his rumpled pajamas. He sat on one side of his mother on the overstuffed sofa while his nightgowned sister, Kim, age six, sat on the other.

"Not tonight," the bespectacled mother said, recognizing her son's problem. Sometimes she read or told a story that would appeal to both an eight-year-old boy and a six-year-old girl, as well as promote peacekeeping ways for her children, but tonight she was reading one of Kim's favorites.

As a way to keep their attention, Susan often inserted the names of her children in the stories, so she continued, "As I was saying, Seth, the older brother, was VERY angry at his little sister, Kim."

As she turned another page in the story, Kim interrupted with her six-year-old 'flash news bulletin' about the story character: "But Kim didn't mean to do it."

Seth showed his annoyance at his sister's interruption with a grimace on his face: "Yes, she did."

Kim, fumbling with the buttons on her nightgown, instantly became protective of her namesake story character: "No, she didn't."

At this, Seth shot back:" Yes, she did." He folded his arms resolutely.

Drawing their attention back to the story, Susan continued: "He was angry at his little sister because he THOUGHT she let his pet turtle get away. Let's listen and find out how he makes up with her later."

This scene was typical of most evenings. Susan would read or tell her children a story related to peacekeeping, including stories about family relations, nonstereotypical roles for girls and boy, and stories sensitive to the values and cultural contributions of diverse groups of people. These nightly bedtime stories were her way of developing an intimate feeling of "family" and promoting peacekeeping and other values her family treasured. Seth and Kim were encouraged to insert "bulletins" aloud during the story so they could play back and forth with each other's thoughts. The storytime also gave Susan a chance to be emotionally and intellectually close to her children on a daily basis and an opportunity to insert her own reflections as different story characters acted through the book's events.

If you, too, spend quality time reading with your children, you may want to think about the following questions that concern the books you select.

TUNING IN
What Do You Read to Your Children?

1. What are the cultural role models in the stories you read to your children or they select to read?

2. Describe the themes of the current books your children are reading. Are they peaceful? Violent? Cooperative? Competitive?

3. Are females in your children's books pictured in active or passive ways? Describe their portrayal in a favorite book.

4. How often are males seen showing emotion in the stories your family reads together?

5. How often are females and persons from other races and cultures shown in positions of authority in your children's books?

6. How often are males and females shown being mutually supportive of one another in your children's books?

7. Is generic male terminology avoided, e.g., using something other than "he" as a pronoun applied to both genders, in your children's books?

8. How many of your children's books are written/edited/ illustrated by females or persons of color?

9. How do you think the children's literature you and your children read affects their peacekeeping attitudes?

10. What are the values of the heroes and heroines in the books you and your children select?

Benefiting from Books

If you want your children to be "book-wise" (and not "book-naive," that is, someone who has never listened to children's stories read by an adult), you are probably already engaging in bibliotherapy in your family: the use of books to help your children better understand themselves, others, and the problems of everyday life. Bibliotherapy is not new; it is a practice that dates back to the time of Aristotle around 384-322 B.C. In ancient Greece the libraries were inscribed with the prescriptive words "The Medicine Chest for the Soul," and many parents still turn to this literary medicine today.

Carefully selected children's stories offer many advantages to the reading family. Documented studies have presented a wide range of effects and benefits of children's literature:

- Books nurture children's personalities.

- Books show respect for others when free and liberated nonstereotypical story characters are presented.

- Books bring the richness of contributions of people from different racial, ethnic, and cultural groups into your home.

- The supportive, familiar assurance of reading prepares your children for the times when family members or friends will have "bad moments" together.

- Books provide role models for peaceful interactions of fictional friends, nuclear family, and extended family.

- Books help you develop your children's perceptions of what goes on in the world and whets their interest to participate in it.

- Books emphasize the value of being sensitive to others.

- Books have the power to change negative attitudes into positive ones.

- Books help children understand themselves and others better.

- Books provide children not only with an opportunity to reflect on the actions taken by story characters but also to continue to imagine alternative actions that might be taken.

- Books can help children peacefully resolve, or at least better understand, problems before they are met in real life.

- Books provide an expanded setting for problem-solving; there is no "reading referee" who might react negatively to children's actions, comments, and decisions.

- Books with strong fictional characters help children learn coping skills.

- Books foster children's general development, especially their intelligence, codes of conduct, and values.

- Books help children deal with anxieties when they can see fictional characters conquering *their* fears.

- Books can provide fictional confrontations that allow children to exercise the peacemaking skills necessary for facing confrontational situations in real life.

All this supports a conclusion that the careful use of children's stories can assist in developing peacemaking behaviors as children grow and develop into positive peacekeepers.

Selecting Books

At the same time books are helping your children achieve reading fluency or providing entertainment, they can also be providing valuable and worthwhile peacekeeping experiences. As you share books, you will be helping your children not only to learn the value and enjoyment of books but also to appreciate the peacemakers in the stories. You will want to look for stories that have useful and appealing ways of solving problems nonviolently. To help you in selecting books that will assist your children in growing toward being peacemakers, here are some things to keep in mind:

- Start with your knowledge of what your children *need* to further develop their peacekeeping behaviors.

- Look for books with free and liberated nonstereotypical characters (e.g., males who are sensitive; females who are strong).

- Look for books with characters sensitive to others and who pay deserved tribute to people from different races, cultures, and income groups.

- Search for books that have stories that will address your children's peacekeeping interests.

- Look for book characters (people, animals, etc.) who strive for peace with others.

- Look for story heroes and heroines that match your children's drive for self-esteem and autonomy in life.

- Introduce your children to stories that have main characters who are involved in the process of keeping the peace when they are caught in various situations that could escalate and lead to violent actions.

- Find book characters who act in situations where peace is valued and violence is not.

- Look for story characters who have personalities with courage, compassion, love, and who demonstrate reconciliatory behaviors.

Beyond Reading

Once you have selected a story, pre-read the book to yourself before reading it aloud to your children. Then plan to do more than just read the words on the pages. Gather your young children to you closely and hold the book so they can see the pictures while listening and imagining. Focus on your children's interest in the story and keep the narrative flowing along with your reading gusto, when it is appropriate. It does not matter if you miss some of the exact words. If your children become restless, read with more enthusiasm or find a more interesting book. Use all of your parental powers of persuasion to wake up the peace awareness in your children, as you discuss what the characters did that was positive, or how your children would have responded in the same situation. Remember that when you read aloud, you are showing your children you respect them as an audience. You are also using a strong parental asset: your experience with books and with the world. You can show your children how the two can go hand-in-hand to help them grow and develop as peacekeepers.

To effectively enhance children's stories further, set the stage for reading in a comfortable way. Make the story a "lap story" with your child on your lap. Or make the story a "love hands" story by holding hands during the reading. Or turn the story into a "hug-a-story" format by giving hugs before, during, and after the reading. You can help get your young children "into" peacekeeping stories by letting them "read" the pictures to you from the book. (You might even try this with your older children!) Acknowledge their efforts to "read" with expression and show the proper "surprise"; support their efforts. A child's ability to tell the story from the pictures is, coincidentally, one of the greatest predictors of later reading success.

To further enhance your children's listening and reading about peacekeepers, consider ways in which you can help them emulate vicariously the peacekeeping models in the stories:

- Retell a story through dramatic play to allow your children, for a while, to be transformed into a fictional character who embodies peacemaking behaviors.

- Act out a brief skit of one of the scenes in the books.

- Stop the story at a critical point and ask your children to suggest one or more endings—alternative ways to peacefully solve the problem.

- With your children, act out the ending(s) they have suggested; then sit together and talk about other nonviolent alternatives.

- Have a follow-up discussion to show your children that there is value in solving problems in peaceful ways and that they, like the book characters, can become peacekeepers and promote nonviolence through their individual actions.

- With your children, write a telegram, postcard, or letter to a family member or a friend to encourage that person to read a particular book about a character who solved a difficult problem without resorting to violence; loan the book along with the message.

Books that Embrace Racial and Cultural Diversity

While we once might have expected to live in a relatively homogeneous neighborhood, a family can now look forward to their children interacting in a heterogeneous community with many citizens—young and old—who have a diverse set of racial, cultural, and ethnic backgrounds. Each person, in the neighborhood and at school, is a unique individual with a unique history and stories to tell. Through carefully selected children's books, you can demonstrate your conviction that every individual is good and worthwhile. When you introduce your children to stories that have as their main focus characters who are models in the process of overcoming cultural stereotypes and presenting positive multicultural concepts, you will be enriching your children's multicultural view and their potential as peacekeeping human beings.

If children's stories about the peaceful behaviors of diverse people can affect the peace-wiseness of a child, then you as a parent can look for peaceful book characters who will positively affect your children's understanding of cultural stereotypes and help them learn peacekeeping behaviors. Look for these important features in the stories you select:

- books that will help your children celebrate multiethnic diversity

- characters that will help your children develop further understanding about people from diverse races and cultures

- role models from different cultural groups who will help your children overcome ethnic stereotypes

- role models from different cultural groups who have used peaceful behavior to overcome violence and make valuable contributions toward peace

There are many stories to chose from about the peacekeeping ways of girls and boys from many cultures. The following suggestions may help you get started. Fur further suggestions, see Appendix B (page 236).

Celebrating Multiethnic Diversity

Everyone Cooks Rice by Norah Dooley (Carolrhoda, 1991)
In the story Carrie searches for her younger brother, Anthony, among her multicultural friends in the neighborhood. As she goes from house to house, she samples every family's dinner, and one night, it seems that everyone is cooking rice. By the time Carrie finds Anthony, she has sampled rice dishes beginning with Mrs. D's "Black-eyed Peas and Rice" and ending with Mrs. Hua's "Tofu with Vegetables."

Activity:
Review the recipes for nine different rice dishes that are included at the back of the book. Select one that you and your children can cook together. Have fun as you follow the simple directions for one of the special rice dishes that Carrie sampled in her diverse neighborhood.

Understanding Children in Diverse Cultures and Backgrounds

Cinderella
Introduce the story of *Cinderella* in various versions from different countries. Point out that children in other countries may know the familiar story in a different form. Select one or more of the following versions. Read each variation aloud with your children and take some time to determine what you can find out about the culture from the illustrations and the text of the story.

MULTICULTURAL VARIATIONS OF CINDERELLA:

- AFRICA: *Mufaro's Beautiful Daughters* by John Steptoe (Lothrop, Lee and Shepard, 1982)
- AFRICA: *The Talking Eggs* by Robert D. San Souci (Dial, 1989)
- CHINA: *Yeh Shen: A Cinderella Story from China* by Ai-Lang Louie (Philomel, 1982)
- EGYPT: *The Egyptian Cinderella* by Shirley Climo (Crowell, 1989)
- SOUTHERN UNITED STATES: *Moss Gown* by William Hooks (Houghton Mifflin, 1990)
- VIETNAM: *In the Land of Small Dragon* by Ann Nolan Clark (Viking, 1979)

Activity:

After reading various versions of the *Cinderella* story from different cultures, discuss with your children how each Cinderella character was able to cope with difficult problems. Ask them the following questions:

- How did the young woman in this story persevere?
- How did she overcome obstacles?
- How did she solve problems?
- How did she manage to stay peaceful within herself?
- How were the Cinderella characters alike, although they were from different cultures?

The Devil's Arithmetic by Jane Yolen (Viking/Kestrel, 1988)

This is a story of time travel in which Hannah, tired of hearing her Jewish relatives talk about the Holocaust, wants to be somewhere else RIGHT NOW. Her wish is granted when she steps out into the building hallway and travels through time into a small village in Nazi-occupied Poland. She becomes the villager Chaya, whose name means "Life," and as "Chaya" she experiences the Holocaust. On a cattle car with her family and friends, she is branded, stripped, and shaved at the concentration camp. When Hannah finds herself once again traveling through time back to her family's apartment, she appreciates her relatives for who they are and what they know.

Activity:

(This activity is especially helpful with older children.) Encourage your children to think of extended family members, what they do, and what they know. Discuss what your children know and add information where you can—especially information about any contributions made by these family members to the community. Next, lead your children into talking about the ways in which they can show appreciation for these family members. Discuss why showing appreciation is a peacekeeping approach within your family.

Overcoming Racial and Cultural Stereotypes

Florence Griffith Joyner: Dazzling Olympian by Nathan Aaseng (Lerner, 1989)
This is the story of a girl who was encouraged by her mother to develop her special talents, whatever they might be. Dee Dee, as Florence was called, had a talent for independence early, and she could go without speaking for days when she felt like it. Her special athletic ability was discovered when she was quite young: She was a very fast runner and won her first track competition when she was only seven! "Flo Jo," as she is sometimes called today, is known around the world for her athletic ability at running. She has won many medals at the Olympics for excelling at track competitions.

Activity:

After reading this story with your children, talk about ways Florence Griffith Joyner was not afraid to be someone special, even when she was a small girl. Talk about how your children are special. Help them see that "special" can mean many things: being helpful, kind, compassionate, sensitive, knowing when to say "no," as well as doing your best when drawing, playing sports, reading, or engaged in other activities. Have your children name some of the ways in which they are special. Write their ideas on a sheet of paper. Then invite them to draw a picture or write a story about how Dee Dee was special when she was a child.

My Mother the Mail Carrier/Mi Mama La Cartera by Inez Maury (Feminist Press, 1976)

This is a bilingual book that describes Lupita's mother: She is brave, strong, and a good cook; she loves outings and likes her work, carrying mail. Her daughter, Lupita, wants to be a jockey when she grows up. She wants a nonstereotypical occupation and, like her mother who enjoys her work, Lupita knows she will like her work too—being a jockey!

Activity:

With your children, look in the newspaper for articles about jobs people do. Point out nonstereotypical jobs and discuss the extent to which the culture you live in might affect a job sought by a person of a particular racial or ethnic background. Further, discuss with your children whether they think there should be any limits to the jobs that people can do. Discuss the abilities or talents your children thinks a person needs to do his or her job.

Recognizing Multicultural Role Models in Peacekeeping

Gandhi's Story by Shakuntala Masani (Henry Z. Walck, 1950)

This is the story of the life of one of India's great leaders and one of the greatest peaceloving figures in history. It is told in a simple, direct style that makes wonderful reading for you and your children. Beginning with a description of Ghandi as a shy but lively boy in his small Indian town, the story traces his studies in England, his crusading for human rights in South Africa, and finally, his emergence as a revered pacifist leader in India. It seems that the author, Shakuntla Masani, knew Gandhi well and writes of him with the highest personal reverence and affection. As a model for peacemaking, Gandhi's life was a testament to the idea of change through peaceful resistance, and his life story can be an inspiration for your children about ways to effect change peacefully.

Activity:

Discuss with your children Gandhi's method of resisting one's opponents peacefully and its name, "Satyagraha." "Satya" means "truth" and "graha" means "firmness," and the two words together, "satyagraha," suggest that the most peaceful way to resolve a conflict is to adhere tenaciously to the truth. Ask your children to think of a time when they were in an argument with someone else but knew that they were telling the truth when the other child in the argument was not. Invite your children to think out loud about how this scene might have been carried out more peacefully if they had used Gandhi's "satyagraha" to resolve the disagreement.

Pocahontas: Powhatan Peacemaker by Anne Holler (Chelsea, 1993)
This book emphasizes peacekeeping in the portrayal of Pocahontas' life and her major role in helping the English settlers survive at Jamestown. It also portrays the life of the Algonquin people who settled on the coastal lowlands in present-day Virginia, as well as the history of the white settlement. In marrying an Englishman, Pocahontas defied her own people and suffered from the very people she had helped settle in this "new land." But she was an important peacemaker as she tried to build a bridge between two different cultures.

Activity:
Read Holler's story aloud to your children. Then, read aloud portions from *When the Great Canoes Came* by Mary Clifford (Pelican, 1993) for the Native People's point of view about Pocahontas and the English settlers in Virginia. Talk with your children about the similarities and differences between Pocahontas as a peacekeeper in the two stories. Ask your children to discuss, from their of view, the correctness/incorrectness of Pocahontas's actions when she defied the ways of her own people and how she was a peacemaker.

Books that Present Nonstereotypic Women and Men/ Girls and Boys in All Cultures

The books children read exert a good deal of influence over how they perceive sex roles and behaviors. Finding nonstereotypic models in children's literature has not always been easy or, depending on where one looked, possible. However, in recent years publishers of basal readers and children's library books have become increasingly aware of the influence stories can have on children, and they have responded by correcting some of the discrepant roles and stereotypic portrayals of females and males. This improved representation, in terms of balance of number of male and female characters, has been the beginning of righting the wrongs in children's books.

Although these changes have been encouraging, we as parents still need to examine not only basal and supplementary books in our schools, but also other children's literature for stereotypic content that demeans, leaves out, or misrepresents whole groups of people, especially females and minorities. It is our responsibility to replace sexist stories with stories that are enhancing to nonstereotypic gender roles. This first step in taking corrective action is to review your children's reading materials *before* presenting them to your children. Look especially for the following important features:

- *desirable traits*
  Do the portrayals of females and males have predominantly desirable personality traits?

- *contributions*
  Do the stories present the contributions to society of females and males as peacekeepers?

Evaluating children's books by these two features will help your selection become a powerful tool in your efforts to correct imbalances and misrepresentations in gender expectations to which your children might be subjected.

The following books present desirable traits and important contributions of males and females from a wide variety of different cultural groups. (For further suggestions, see Appendix B.) Such books will help your children to form a more positive vision of people who may be different from them.

Barbara Jordan: The Great Lady from Texas by Naurice Roberts (Children's Press, 1984)

Barbara Jordan's family was black and poor, living in the South when there was much racial prejudice. Barbara knew that to get ahead in life, she would have to be well-educated. Barbara became a lawyer so she could help change the laws that had hurt her and other African-American people. She was also elected as a Texas Senator. She then worked to end segregation laws in the very places where they were made.

Activity:
After reading the book, discuss with your children the person who inspired Barbara Jordan's decision to become a lawyer and why being a lawyer was especially important to her. Ask your children to think about a person they know, have seen on television, or have read about who would be a good "role model." Ask them to share their ideas about what kind of a person makes a good role model and how the jobs they do help them influence others in a positive way.

Samantha Smith: A Journey for Peace by Anne Galichich (Dillon Press, 1987). Samantha Smith decided to do something about the frightening situation between the United States and what was then the Soviet Union. In 1982 she wrote to Yuri Andropov, the new Soviet leader, about her concerns. Samantha was only ten years old at the time. She soon learned that her letter had been printed on the front page of *Pravda*, the most important newspaper of the Soviet Union. She then received a letter from Andropov himself, beginning an important relationship between herself, her home town in Maine, and the Soviet Union, a country whose children also wanted peace.

Activity:
Discuss with your children how Samantha, even though she was a little girl, made a difference. Ask your children what problems they see that need to be solved in America today. Have them try an experiment to see which of our leaders will respond to a letter about their concerns about peace. Guide them in writing and sending a letter. Help them understand that *every* person has a responsibility to inform the people we elect to office about what we are thinking, even if we do not receive a reply.

Books that Counter TV Violence with Peacekeeping Role Models

Books can be a primary source in helping you win out over the violence of television, video games, and movies. Once your children begin to know that they will not be bored when you read aloud, and they begin to experience that your facial expressions and voice changes can be as compelling as the TV screen (or video games or movies), they will relax with you. Then you can guide them away from Power Rangers and violent cartoon characters and into realms of new interests in stories or poems. You can choose realms that are peaceful, compassionate, sensitive, nurturing, and perhaps, uniquely intriguing. The more your children use their imaginations—what Shakespeare called the "mind's eye"—during storytime, the more the spell of the flickering screen will be broken. As you awaken your children's ability to listen to stories, they will want more and more. You will not only be weaning them from addictive television but you will also be teaching them to love books. And you will have begun to counter the effect of TV violence on their thinking, conscience, and problem-solving behaviors.

To grow in peacekeeping behaviors, children also need to have a perspective on the pain and suffering of others when violence occurs. Especially when read aloud, well-written books can help your children become aware of the resulting harmful effects of needless violent acts. This awareness will be in sharp contrast to TV's focus on fast actions, fast-moving violence—never on the human suffering that results from the violent actions. When your children read about a book character who shows concern and compassion for others who have suffered from violent acts, they will gain new perspective, understanding, and empathy.

To foster peaceful ways, choose books that feature the following important characteristics of peaceful behavior:

- collaboration and cooperation among friends and family members

- the value of friendship among people who are different from each other

- trust and respect for people who are different from one another

- appreciation for the unique traits of all people

At times, you may want to turn to the stories you know best—the classic stories you heard as a child. What are some of the peaceful characteristics of the heroes and heroines in the tales you know? What are some of the stories by the Grimm brothers that you liked? Dip into your past and select the stories you loved and want to share with your child. You will also find that contemporary authors write realistically about peace, peaceful behaviors, and peacekeepers, as well as violence and the human suffering it causes. Here are a few suggestions; also refer to Appendix B for additional listings.

FOR VERY YOUNG CHILDREN

The Bouncing Dinosaur by Ann Nolan Clark (Farrar, 1990)
> A tale of a unique friendship. Boris, a bouncing dinosaur, befriends animals who are quite different from him—a monkey and a rabbit.

Baby Kermit and the Dinosaur by Victoria Holt (Random House, 1987)
> Another story about an unusual friendship in which a toy dinosaur comes to life and is a hero when it rescues Baby Piggy from a dangerous situation.

Activity:
> For each of the above stories, you could talk to your children about what makes a good friend. Ask them to discuss why they think a monkey and a rabbit might be considered "unusual" friends, or why people might be surprised when a dinosaur rescues a pig. Give your children crayons and paper and ask them to draw a picture of two friends who are quite different. Then ask them to explain what the friends are doing and why they like each other despite their differences.

FOR CHILDREN AGES 5 TO 8

Farmer Schultz's Ducks by Colin Thiele (Harper, 1988)
> Family members collaborate to find a solution to Farmer Schultz's problem: His duck pond is across the street from his farm, and the increased traffic makes the trip to the water too dangerous for the wandering ducks. The family realizes that something has to be done to care for the ducks, and during a family meeting, each member offers an alternative that shows they care about the small creatures.

Activity:
> After reading this story to your children, discuss the peaceful alternatives the family used to solve Farmer Schultz's problem. Ask your children which alternatives they think would work best for the ducks and encourage them to give their reasons. Invite them to create new ways for Farmer Schultz to solve his problem with the ducks.

Always and Forever Friends by David Adler (Clarion, 1988)
> A girl named Wendy finds a "best" friend who turns out to be Honor, an African-American child of a biracial marriage.

Mrs. Abercorn and the Bunce Boys by Janice Fosburgh (FourWinds, 1986)
> Mrs. Abercorn, an energetic woman who befriends two young brothers, helps them discover the value of friendship and trusting in others.

> *Activity:*
> For either of the above stories, help your children act out the initiation of the friendships described in the books. Have them then help you create a list of why the two sets of friendships might grow and thrive. Ask them how they would respond to other children who are critical of friendships they have developed.

"Golden Oldies"

While there is a longer list of children's books about peacekeepers in Appendix B, the following book list features some of the "golden oldies" that have been used by parents over the years to neutralize and counter the effect of violence. These stories have a special emphasis on peaceful ways and present different approaches for resolving conflict in nonviolent ways. Perhaps you read some of them or listened to them read aloud when you were a child.

FOR CHILDREN AGES 5 TO 8

PEACE IN THE FAMILY

Awful Evelina by Susan Beth Pfeffer (Albert Whitman, 1979)
> Meredith is dreading going with her family to visit her aunt, uncle, and cousin because her cousin Evelina always hits her and steps on her toes. The grown-ups do not seem to notice. This time is different: The two girls have a wonderful time playing together.

Bad Luck Tony by Dennis B. Fradin (Prentice-Hall, 1978)
> Tony is eager to develop a positive relationship with his grandfather, although the last time he saw his grandfather, Tony was a baby.

Bad Boy, Good Boy by Marie Hall Ets (Thomas Y. Crowell, 1967)
> A little boy, Roberto, who speaks only Spanish, gets confused and feels isolated. When he learns to speak English, his father becomes proud of him, and he becomes proud of himself.

Let's Be Enemies by Janice May Udry (Harper & Row, 1969)
> When children in the same family get angry and jealous, their parents help them find realistic and peaceful ways of resolving their problems.

Potatoes, Potatoes by Anita Lobel (Harper & Row, 1967)
> Two brothers are on opposite sides of a battle, and they conclude there is "no gain for the pain" in violence when they realize they are fighting on their own potato field.

Ramona and Her Father by Beverly Cleary (Morrow, 1977)
> When Ramona is in second grade, Father loses his job, and Mother begins to work full-time. Father, worried and irritable, looks after Ramona after school. After Christmas, Father announces his new job.

The Repair of Uncle Toe by Kay Chorao (Farrar, Straus & Giroux, 1972)
> A man and his nephew resolve their differences in a most unusual way.

To Hilda for Helping by Margot Tomes (Farrar, Straus & Giroux, 1977)
> Hilda, a cooperative and helpful little girl, receives a tin-can top medal from her father for helping set the table at night. Her sister, Gladys, becomes extremely jealous of Hilda's medal.

William's Doll by Charlotte Zolotow (Harper & Row, 1972)
> William's father, brother, and male friends are upset when he wants a doll to play with. William's friends and his brother call him a "sissy," but he is defended by his peacekeeping grandmother, who explains that William can practice for the time when he becomes a father himself.

PEACE WITH FRIENDS

Bang, Bang, You're Dead by Louise Fitzhugh and Sandra Scoppettone (Harper & Row, 1969)

> A group of children at play begin a "make-believe" battle, but their behavior becomes more and more aggressive and hurts others.

Goggles! by Ezra Jack Keats (Macmillan, 1969)

> Two young black boys in the inner city, Peter and Archie, find a pair of motorcycle goggles near their hideout in a deserted lot. They creatively avoid a conflict with three older bullies who want the goggles.

The Hating Book by Charlotte Zolotow (Harper & Row, 1969)

> This narrative helps children cope with their anger by examining the fact that we all have likes and dislikes, and they are part of what makes us "unique."

I'm Not Oscar's Friend Anymore by Marjorie Weinman Sharmat (Dutton, 1975)

> Oscar's "former friend" tells the reader that Oscar used to be his friend, but then Oscar said something "very fresh to him" and he said "something fresh right back." Then, Oscar escalated the situation and said something FURTHER in return. Soon, the two weren't friends anymore. When the "former friend" finally calls Oscar, he finds that Oscar has forgotten all about the fight.

Joshua's Day by Sandra I. Surowiecki (Lollipop Power, 1977)

> When Joshua has problems and conflicts that make him angry, his daycare teacher and his mother help him find peaceful ways to solve the problems.

A Letter to Amy by Ezra Jack Keats (Harper & Row, 1968)

> Peter wants to invite Amy, who is special to him, to his birthday party, even though he knows his friends will make fun of her because she is a girl. When Amy arrives, he doesn't even blink when the other boys say, "A girl—ugh!"

Rosie and Michael by Judith Viorst (Atheneum, 1974)

> Rosie likes Michael when he's "dopey, not just when he's smart." And Michael likes Rosie when she's "grouchy and not just when she's nice." Their true friendship overcomes all problems.

Run Away Home by Dorothy Halle Selligman (Golden Gate Junior Books, 1969)

>One day everything goes wrong for Billy, and he decides to run away. When he goes down the street, he meets many of his friends who tell him that they've all run away at one time or another, too. Suddenly, Billy can't remember what he was upset about, and he goes home.

FOR CHILDREN AGE 9 AND OLDER

PEACE IN THE FAMILY

Henry Three by Joseph Krumgold (Atheneum, 1967)

>When Henry's parents decide to build an atomic bomb shelter in their backyard, Henry is ridiculed and rejected by some of the others in his neighborhood.

The Perilous Road by William O. Steele (Harcourt, Brace Jovanovich, 1958)

>During the Civil War, eleven-year-old Chris experiences the pain and suffering of battle and tries to rescue his brother, a Union soldier, from a Confederate ambush.

Thee, Hannah by Marguerite De Angeli (Doubleday, 1940)

>Hannah, the daughter in a Quaker family, stops her rebellion and learns to appreciate the gentle ways of the Quaker beliefs.

Tree of Freedom by Rebecca Caudill (Viking, 1949)

>Stephanie takes an apple seed with her when her family flees the troubles of the Revolutionary War, and she plants and cares for it until it grows into a "tree of freedom."

White Archer: An Eskimo Legend by James A. Houston (Harcourt Brace Jovanovich, 1971)

>When he suffers the loss of his parents and sister, Kungo decides to take revenge but later experiences a change of heart and decides not to avenge them.

PEACE WITH FRIENDS

Adam and the Golden Cock by Alice Dalgliesh (Scribner's, 1939)
    In 1780 during America's revolutionary days, Adam, knowing
his family are Whigs, experiences the meaning of loyalty and
friendship when he realizes his friend is from a Tory family.

Bread and Butter Indian by Anne Colver (Holt, Rinehart and Winston, 1970)
    During America's Revolutionary time period, Barbara gives her
bread and butter to an Indian boy, and he becomes her friend.

The Tamarack Tree by Betty Underwood (Houghton Mifflin, 1971)
    In Connecticut in the 1830s, a white girl becomes friends with
an African-American girl, despite the community's hostility
toward African Americans.

PEACE IN THE COMMUNITY

The Liberation of Clementine Tipton by Jane Flory (Houghton Mifflin, 1974)
    In 1876 during the Centennial Celebration, Clementine starts
her own peaceful revolution by thinking for herself.

The Little Fishes by Eric Haugaard (Houghton Mifflin, 1967)
    Set in Naples in World War II, a twelve-year-old orphan develops
compassion as he begins to understand the belligerent people
around him.

One Day for Peace by Alexander Crosby (Little, Brown, 1972)
    A girl organizes a peace march in her town to speak out against
the death of her friend in Vietnam.

Peace Is an Adventure by Emery Kelen (Meredith, 1967)
    Brief stories about different employees of the United Nations
who work for peace around the world.

We Shall Live in Peace by Deloris Harrison (Hawthorne, 1968)
    Portrays Martin Luther King's nonviolent ideas.

A Closing Word about Books

It is an exciting notion that children's books have the power to change children's attitudes. Children's stories with strong yet peaceful characters provide an alternative to TV violence and can foster the development of peacemaking behaviors. Carefully selected stories from children's literature stimulate a child's mind *actively*, counteracting the mind-numbing *passive* stance children assume when watching TV or movies. Additionally, selecting books with positive sex-role models and models from different racial and multicultural groups can provide children with insight into the ways fictional characters respond to violence, show compassion for the suffering of others, and face problems courageously and peacefully in their own lives. By actively presenting peaceful behaviors through the use of children's books that are nonstereotyped and that present positive images of diverse races, cultures, and gender roles, parents and children will take a vicarious "giant step" toward living peacefully in a violent world.

SECTION III

PEACEFUL
RELATIONSHIPS

11 EXPANDING PEACE AT HOME

Celebrating Family Relationships

"Domestic peace! Best joy of earth, when shall we all
thy value learn?"
—Anne Brontë, *Domestic Peace*

A Classic Standoff

It was a warm, sunny afternoon in May several years ago, and I had just settled myself into my favorite lounge chair in the backyard and was looking forward to the peace of relaxing and reading a magazine. Alas, I soon realized I had company.

"I want it!" declared five-year old Gavin.

"Nuh-uh!" retorted Chrissy, eighteen months younger and half his size.

There on the patio a classic standoff unfurled: Gavin on the seat of the children's dump truck with Chrissy perched defiantly upon the truck's shovel, which was straining beneath her weight.

My initial reaction was anger at this disruption of my precious quiet moments. I wanted to grab the dump truck away from them, drag both children into the house, and put them in "time out." Fortunately, a higher grace intervened. I was able to recall our family's decision to work at mutual problem-solving and help the children to resolve their conflicts as much as possible.

After listening to a few minutes of their yelling and crying, I decided the two were at an impasse. I intervened:

"Doesn't seem like either of you is getting to have fun playing with the dump truck. Are you happy about that?"

Both shook their heads vehemently, indicating they were not.

"What do you suppose you could do that would make you both a bit happier?" I asked hopefully.

Both children squirmed uncomfortably, looking longingly at the dump truck. Finally, Gavin responded, "Well, we could take turns. Each of us could play with the truck for ten minutes." (This had been the solution to a previous impasse.) I congratulated Gavin on his problem-solving idea and volunteered to tell them when the ten minutes were up. Chrissy offered to let Gavin go first.

I smiled and said to myself, "Yes! It really can work!" I was reminded once again that when we remember to give our children a chance, they very often to rise to the occasion of becoming peacekeepers, even when they are very young.

There is much that we as parents can do to teach our children peace as a process—starting with showing them how to look inside themselves and be peaceful and accepting of what they see. As they establish peaceful selves, they can be open to peace with their siblings and other family members. When they have a strong and peaceful internal foundation upon which to build, they can practice peace in school and in the community. The natural evolution of such a process is that children with a peaceful orientation feel compelled to share their liberating state of being with everyone, everywhere in the world. The progression unfolds as a flower unfolds: A peaceful self leads to a conscience—and a consciousness—toward others.

This chapter provides a wide range of practical activities you can use to help strengthen this peaceful progression in your children.

| Peace | A peaceful attitude toward life is quite naturally germinated in a peaceful home and nurtured by peaceful role models. |
| Within | However, there are specific ideas you can introduce to your children to expedite the acquisition of a peacemaking |

attitude. The following activities can help children focus on what is good and peaceful in their current lives. By concentrating on the positive, yet accepting—and sometimes working to change the less-than-positive—children can develop a more peaceful way of viewing the world.

"My Peaceful Neighborhood" (all ages)

Supplies needed: none

1. Explain to your children that sometimes we are so close to our own home, neighborhood, and surroundings we fail to appreciate the wonderful things that we have; therefore, we do not feel as peaceful as we could.

2. Have your children close their eyes while you lead them through an imaginary walk around their neighborhood. Help them visualize a favorite tree, a favorite park or building, a stream or lake, a bush in the yard, birds they have heard, flowers they have smelled, or other features of their environment that make them feel happy. If you happen not to live in a particularly peaceful neighborhood, concentrate on small spots of peace—for example, flowers someone has put in the window, smells of something baking, a place between buildings where the sun feels warm. Even in the most unlikely places, peaceful oases can be found.

3. Ask your children to open their eyes and retrace their journey orally, sharing the things that help them feel especially at peace.

"Peace through Change" (all ages)

Supplies needed: paper
writing utensils

In order to be peaceful within, and to grow up to be peaceful adults, children can learn to expend their energies on the things they can change and not to feel guilty about those things that are beyond their control.

1. Read the "Serenity Prayer" to your children:

> *God grant me the serenity to accept the things I cannot change;*
> *courage to change the things I can;*
> *and wisdom to know the difference.*

Discuss the meaning of the prayer with them.

2. Make two columns on a sheet of paper. On top of one column, write "Things I CAN Change" and on the top of the other column write "Things I CAN'T Change."

3. Help your children think of items for each column from their own lives.

4. Ask them where they think they should focus their energies—on the first or the second column? What are their reasons?

5. Focusing on column one, "Things I CAN Change," ask your children to list some positive things they can do to make these changes happen, such as cleaning up the house, helping raise money for the homeless, writing letters to city council members, etc. Invite younger children to draw a picture in response to one thing they feel *they* could do to change things for the better.

"The Ideal Family" (up to age 8)

Supplies needed: colored construction paper
scissors
felt-tip pens
glue or paste

Sometimes, through television or other media, children have an idealized vision of the way their home lives—and other family members—should be. Because reality, in most cases, differs markedly from this dream, children can feel cheated and thus find it difficult to feel peaceful inside.

1. Ask your children to describe what they think an "ideal" family should be like.

2. Determine, if possible, where their notions come from. If they are basing their ideas on television families, discuss why TV families so often appear "perfect." If they are comparing your family to those of their friends', ask them if they suppose the friends' families are always as perfect as the friends makes them appear.

3. Encourage your children to consider what is wonderful about *your* family life—even though it may fall short of an ideal.

4. Invite your children to write something positive about their family life on strips cut from colored construction paper. Possibilities include friendship

with a brother or sister, family pets, special birthday traditions, favorite family foods, the atmosphere at home, the family's concern when someone is hurting, etc.

5. Paste or glue the paper links together into a chain. Put the chain on display where visitors can see it. Invite your children to tell visitors what the term "family" means to them.

6. Add to the chain by encouraging your children to be on the alert for other wonderful features of your family.

 "Dialogue

Notebooks" (age 9 and older)

Supplies needed: notebook for each child
                  writing utensils

1. Discuss with your children the idea that writing down feelings—good and bad—is often a way to help us accept our feelings in a more peaceful way.

2. Give each child a notebook and invite them to decorate the cover of their notebooks as they wish.

3. Explain that they can use their notebooks to carry on a conversation with you. They may write about ANYTHING they are feeling, saying as much or as little as they want to share. Tell them you will respond without evaluation (this is extremely critical!) in the margins.

> For example, Tanya writes, "Sandra [her sister] always gets to go with Dad to the store on business trips. He likes Sandra better than me." Her mother responds by validating Tanya's feelings and then suggesting a peaceful avenue for change: "I'm sorry you feel that way, Tanya. That must be making you sad. Could you talk to Dad about the way you are feeling?"

4. For children who resist writing, suggest that they write only three words—any three words—that tell how they are feeling. You can then write comments or questions in the margins about these words, such as, "Oh, I see you're feeling sad. Is that because your friend Gus moved away? That must have been difficult for you."

"Dealing with Angry Feelings" (up to age 8)

Supplies needed: none

All people have negative thoughts and angry feelings on occasion. It is up to us as parents to teach our children that such feelings are "normal," *and* it is important to teach them to respond to these feelings in ways that are not hurtful to others.

1. Ask your children to share a recent angry feeling they have had. What did they do about their anger?

2. Brainstorm together some positive, nonharmful actions that could be taken to release anger. For example:

   • take a long walk or run around the block

   • go out into the woods and scream at the top of your lungs

   • have a pillow "fight"

   • write down your feelings in a letter to yourself

3. Discuss with your children how they think these positive releases of angry feelings compare with the ways they have responded in the past.

Optional:

Suggest that your children role play the situation they described of feeling angry. Have them prepare two role plays—the first with a hurtful reaction, and the second with one of the positive releases they just brainstormed. Discuss the differences between the two role plays, both in terms of how your children felt and how the recipient of their anger might have felt.

Increasing Peace among Sisters and Brothers

The incessant squabbling between brothers and sisters is legendary, and the underlying reasons for it fill many volumes of psychology texts and parenting books. While the bond between siblings in later life is often—remarkably—one of the strongest of human ties, when growing up in the close proximity of most households, siblings often take each other for granted and fail to show the same courtesy that might be afforded their friends or relatives of the same age.

The following activities are designed so you can help your children appreciate their relationships with their siblings and help them consider how unkind words and thoughtless behavior might make others feel.

 "If I Didn't Have a Sibling . . ." (age 9 and older)

Supplies needed: If It Weren't for You
                  by Charlotte Zolotow
                  (Harper & Row, 1966)
                  paper
                  writing utensils

Children often have ambivalent feelings about their brother(s) or sister(s), and they need to know that such feelings are normal; every relationship has moments of positive and negative feelings.

1. Read the story *If It Weren't for You* aloud to your children. (The story starts with a young girl's musings about all the things she could do if her little brother were not around, but ends with the girl admitting she would miss lots of good times, too.)

2. Ask your children if they have ever felt like the girl in the story about their own brother(s) or sister(s). Invite them to share specific incidents.

3. Encourage each of your children to write or tell a story about their own sibling(s), starting with, "If it weren't for you . . ."

4. Then ask them to add an equal number of "But if it weren't for you . . ." lines to express the *positive* dimensions that their sibling(s) add to their lives.

 "Feathers in the Wind" (up to age 8)

Supplies needed: small feathers
                  fan (optional)

1. Explain to your children how words can be like "feathers in the wind": They float and twirl, and it is impossible to predict where or how they will land.

2. Take small feathers and, by having your children blow them or by using a fan, move the feathers around the room.

3. Invite your children to pretend that each feather is a compliment or a kind word said to a brother or sister. Ask them how they think these words would be received by the person to whom they are directed.

4. Change the directions, this time asking your children to pretend each feather is a hurtful remark made toward a brother or sister. Ask them how they think these words would be received.

5. Ask your children how *they* feel when they receive a compliment or a positive remark and how this feeling differs from when they receive a complaint or a hurtful remark.

6. Give your children some time to practice giving compliments to their sibling(s), encouraging them to visualize feathers each time.

 "Word

Power" (all ages)

Supplies needed: colored construction paper
                       scissors
                       felt-tip pens

Children need to understand that words are very powerful and that, even when they do not feel like it, they can control the words they use to keep peace with sisters and brothers.

1. Remind your children of the well-known rhyme:

> *Sticks and stones can break my bones,*
> *but names can never hurt me.*

Discuss how this may or may not be true, how words *can* hurt us, how sometimes people hurt each other intentionally, or how sometimes words come out the wrong way. Discuss how words can also heal and help situations, when someone apologizes or shows acceptance of us even when we make mistakes.

2. To help your children think of some positive ways they can respond to siblings when they are being teased or taunted, have them role play some positive responses to the following situations:

- You take the last cookie, and your brother/sister calls you "greedy" and makes pig noises.

- You are having difficulty explaining your feelings, and your brother/sister mocks your lack of ability to find the right words.

- You are wearing a new tee-shirt; your brother/sister tells you it is ugly.

3. Make up a stack of "word power awards." These "awards" can be made of construction paper, cut into any shapes, that say something along the lines of, "This award is for using words in a positive way." When anyone in the family hears a family member using words to praise, compliment, or solve a difficult situation in a positive way, invite them to issue a word power award to that person.

Restoring Peace between Children and Parents

In any family there are times when the communication between parent(s) and children breaks down. Sometimes resentments build up and mushroom because they have not been talked through. Other times, we parents become so preoccupied with the demands of everyday life that the crucial sharing of what is going on in our children's lives takes a back seat to seemingly more pressing problems. Moreover, there are times when, although there are no particular problems in communication, we neglect to tell our children how much we appreciate them for who they *are*.

The activities that follow provide ways for you to give your children an opportunity to talk with you about what is happening in their lives, how they are feeling about any- and everything, and allow you to tell them just how wonderful you think they are.

"Talk n' Walk" (all ages)

Supplies needed: none

Sometimes, when communication appears to have broken down between a parent and a child, it is helpful to leave the usual scene of the conflict.

1. Invite your child to go on a "talk n' walk," although you need not give your child any specific agenda or goal about communicating.

2. Take a relaxing stroll around the neighborhood, pointing out any gifts of nature that might attract your attention—an unusual bird, a chattering squirrel, or an ant hill will do for a neutral conversation.

3. Practice being comfortable with silence. As you tune in to the rhythms of nature, your child will more than likely be amenable to talking with you about what is going on in his or her mind.

4. Listen! You may find that just listening at these times opens the lines of communication in new ways. Instead of evaluating what your child is saying, merely paraphrase his or her feelings.

> For example, when Chrissy says, "Those boys down the street are so immature! They never let us play basketball with them, just because we're *girls*!," mother replies, "I guess it makes you angry when the boys won't let you play with them. They don't know what a good player you are!"

"When Adults Have Problems" (age 9 and older)

Supplies needed: none

All parents worry that discord between adults will confuse and/or frighten their children. While this may be true at times, *some* conflict is inevitable in any relationship, and children may need strategies to help them to feel less anxious when adults have problems.

1. Explain to your children that, although the adults in the family may be having conflicts with one another, they are working to solve these conflicts peacefully.

2. Take steps to do the following:

   - *diminish guilt*
     Tell your children, "This problem is not your responsibility. Nothing you have done has caused this problem."

   - *stress open communication*
     Tell your children, "It is okay to talk to us about the problem or how you feel about it."

- *invite questions*

  Tell your children, "Feel free to ask questions if there is something you don't understand or something that worries you about the problem."

"Look in the Mirror" (up to age 8)

Supplies needed: small hand mirror

It is sometimes surprising when we as parents realize that our children are not aware of how truly precious and beautiful we think they are! Children simply cannot receive too much affirmation from the adults who love them.

1. Hold a small hand mirror in front of your face with the mirror side facing outward.

2. Invite your children to come up one at a time to the mirror and say, "Mirror, mirror, in front of me, tell me all the wonderful things you see!"

3. Speaking for the mirror, tell your children something that is wonderful about them, paying particular attention to behavior, feelings, and other traits that the mirror cannot really "see." (This mirror is not interested in physical beauty!)

4. Repeat the procedure often, letting your children know just how wonderful you think they are.

Celebrating Peace with the Whole Family

Psychologists tell us that when behavior is recognized and rewarded, there is a greater chance that it will be repeated. With this in mind, we can enhance our children's peacekeeping efforts by taking note of them and celebrating them as they occur. The following activities have been created to help you show appreciation for your children's positive peacemaking actions among family members.

"A Peace Medal" (up to age 8)

Supplies needed:
- tops of yogurt cartons or cottage cheese cartons
- colored construction paper
- scissors
- glue or paste
- felt-tip pens
- safety pins

Positive reinforcement goes a long way toward instilling values of peace and harmony in our children. A concrete way to reward especially peaceful attitudes and behavior is with a "peace medal."

1. Discuss with your children the idea that they are special and can help to keep peace in their own unique ways.

2. Have each of your children share a recent time when they have helped to keep the peace. Invite them to recount the situation and what actions they took.

3. With glue or paste, adhere a circle cut from construction paper to cover the yogurt or cottage cheese container tops. With colorful pens or markers, write the words "To ____[name]____ for helping to keep the peace in the family by ____[action]_____."

4. Glue some more construction paper to the backs of the container tops. Attach a safety pin to the back of each to create a "medal."

5. Ceremoniously award the medals to your children, reinforcing their peaceful deeds.

"Family Peace Day" (all ages)

Supplies needed: varies

A wonderful way to characterize your family's beliefs about the importance of peace is through a Family Peace Day. Friends, neighbors, and extended family could be invited in an open house arrangement, or the festivities could be limited to just the immediate family. Here are some possible Family Peace Day activities:

- Read original stories about ways members of your family have helped keep peace.
- Create and display posters and charts that have a "Peace in the Family" theme.
- Write, plan, and perform brief skits related to peacekeeping.
- Collect poems about peace and read them aloud, accompanied by peaceful music selected by family members.
- Make a diorama (a "shoe box" scene) of your family engaging in a favorite peaceful activity.
- Select songs promoting peace and have a family sing-a-long.
- Paint and display a mural showing peaceful scenes from your family life.
- Prepare food from many different ethnic groups to symbolize your family's appreciation for other cultures.

"Family Peace Notes" (age 9 and older)

Supplies needed: empty tissue box (decoration optional)
paper
writing utensils

Sometimes praise is more concrete and more easily savored when it is written down to be read and reread by the recipient.

1. Use an old tissue box to create a "mailbox" that can be used for intra-family messages.

2. Explain to family members that the box is to be used to give special recognition to the peaceful gestures and peace-promoting activities of family members.

3. Invite family members to be on the lookout for peacekeeping behavior within the family. Have them record and offer praise and appreciation for such behavior on a note addressed to the family member who performed the act.

4. Once a week, during Family Share Time (FST) (see page 45) or during some other family time, distribute the positive peace notes to family members.

Practicing Peace in the Extended Family

Some of the first peacekeeping problems your children encounter may involve relatives, who may not share the same habits, interests, and values as your nuclear family. The following activities can help your children consider ways to interact peacefully with extended family members, as well as foster their appreciation for older relatives, such as grandparents.

"Tolerance with Cousins" (age 9 and older)

Supplies needed: paper
                     writing utensils

1. Discuss with your children the meaning of the word "tolerance" and explain why this concept is important in dealing with family members. Ask them if they have ever been in a position with their cousins, or other relatives, where they disagreed with the person but tried to "tolerate" the person's words or behavior.

2. Make two lists on a sheet of paper, one headed "Tolerant" and the other "Intolerant." Describe a variety of hypothetical behaviors by cousins and ask your children to decide whether they would tolerate the behavior or NOT tolerate the behavior. (You can use the scenarios below or describe others that your children have experienced). Ask your children their reasons. Some examples:

   • your cousin likes country music and you like only reggae

   • your cousin sulks if she doesn't win when you play board games

   • your cousin tells you a joke that has decidedly racist overtones

   • your cousin talks with his mouth full

   • your cousin pulls the chair out from under you when you are trying to sit down

3. Discuss with your children how they might respond to the incidents that they would tolerate, and also how they could handle incidents that they would NOT tolerate because they were unsafe or they are contrary to your family's values.

"The Way It Was" (up to age 8)

Supplies needed: paper
                    writing utensils
                    tape recorder and blank tape (optional)

One way to foster closer relationships with grandparents is to encourage your children to listen to their grandparents' stories of "the way it was in the old days."

1. Invite your children to choose a grandparent (or other elderly relative) close enough to visit, if possible. Or select someone your children could speak with on the telephone.

2. Help your children create a list of questions to ask the person, such as:

   • What was the most peaceful event in your life when you were my age?

   • What things in your life were more peaceful than they are now?

   • What were your favorite "peaceful" things to do?

   • How did you help to keep peace in your family? In the world?

   • What peaceful things do you miss most about those days?

3. Have your children record the answers or write them on paper and share the information at the next family gathering.

4. With the whole family, discuss the value of the peaceful recollections of the grandparents.

5. Ask your children to share the most interesting thing they learned. Ask them how they feel the interview changed their relationship with the elderly relative.

"Peaceful Acceptance
of Relatives" (age 9 and older)

Supplies needed: paper
                    writing utensils

1. Invite your children to consider that, just as each family member is unique and is accepted for who they are, so must each extended family member be accepted for who they are.

2. Discuss with your children how different people have different attitudes, behaviors, habits, likes, and dislikes. While these may deviate from your family's ways, they need to be respected and understood.

3. Make a list of extended family members and assist your children in describing some of the unique habits of each, like this:

Name	Unique Habits (examples)	Peaceful ways to deal with these habits
aunt(s)	smokes	Ask her to please smoke outside.
uncle(s)	teases	Tell him how you feel.
grandmother	hates noise	Try to be quieter.
grandfather	interrupts	Ask permission to finish your thought.
cousin(s)	brags	Ignore it.

4. Discuss a variety of peaceful ways for dealing with the differences of these extended family members, especially when the behavior causes difficulties.

A Closing Word about Peace at Home

As parents, we have all felt, at times, that parenting children is a bit like being next to a grindstone. Whether it grinds us down or polishes us depends on the "peaceful foundation" we have developed—and the wide range of peacekeeping activities we have at our beck and call for our family. The activities offered in this chapter are beginning steps toward "polishing" unique and original peacekeeping characteristics in us and in our children, who will become—we can hope—the "peacekeeping generation."

12 EXPANDING PEACE BEYOND THE FAMILY

Toward a Global Vision

"Ultimately, we have just one moral duty: to reclaim large areas of peace in ourselves, and to reflect it toward others. And the more peace there is in us, the more peace there will be in our troubled world."
—Etty Hillesum, *An Interrupted Life: The Diaries of Etty Hillesum, 1941-43*

Tomorrow's Global Village

It is becoming increasingly clear that people on Earth have a genuine interdependence upon one another for basic survival. The concept of a "global village" is a reality, for example, in the food we eat: It is planted and harvested in one part of the world and shipped by truck, plane, or train for sale to consumers who live great distances from the place of origin. The global village is also evident when a strike in one industry or part of the country prevents the availability of goods in another; when a debilitating Florida hurricane or a persistent California drought results in the Midwest paying higher prices for produce; or when children suffer because of air, water, or land pollution caused by oil spills, chemical waste, or carelessness, or nuclear testing in other parts of the globe.

There are also areas of our lives where global interdependence may not be so readily apparent: Few of us in the United States, for example, are subjected to the sight of children dying of malnutrition on a daily basis or come face-to-face with the abject poverty of a subsistence laborer who toils in the fields to bring sugar, grapes, or lettuce to our tables. And not many of us know personally the feeling of despair that accompanies an inability to provide for the basic needs of our children. Yet there are signs, even if not so obvious, of our tremendous interdependence, beginning in our immediate neighborhoods, schools, and local communities.

When others in the world are suffering, it affects all of us. How can we help our children recognize, without being overwhelmed, the hurting all around us—not only at a distance but also in our own communities? How do we help ourselves and our children respond to pain, stand for justice, and fight oppression in our society? How do we translate the peacemaking skills practiced in our homes into peacemaking in our schools and neighborhoods and the world? How can we teach our children that making changes for peace in the global world begins with taking responsibility for the small acts of peace we can do on a local scale? How do we come to understand in a real way that we do indeed live in a global village where events in one part of the globe impact all of us, no matter where we reside?

The ideas and activities presented in this final chapter are offered to assist you as a parent in enabling your children to be informed and responsible decision-makers as they prepare to become peacemaking citizens and the leaders of tomorrow's global village.

Competition versus Cooperation

An atmosphere of winning, competing to be "first" or "the best," permeates the fabric of our lives—from school sports, to city elections, to business profit ventures, to our country's political and social systems. Indeed, capitalism thrives on such competitive attitudes! This competitiveness fosters a mentality that suggests we should always be "number one" and acquire the most valuable, high style, and topnotch possessions—whether they be mega-houses, designer clothes, expensive jewelry, or the latest model cars.

Even our choice of language reflects our competitiveness. We tend to call ourselves "we," and label others who are different in some way from those in our particular group as "they." Too often the "we's" of our society have control over the "they's" in order to win or succeed. And, invariably, the color, age, religion, sex, nationality, or economic status of the "they's" differ markedly from our own. In the constant struggle to come out ahead, the stakes are infinitely higher in the global game: Winning becomes equal to survival. Control is often exercised in decisions about production, distribution, and access to food, land, and other natural resources. Power is exercised in decisions concerning trade, transportation, health care, education, and the free flow of information. We compete with other peoples for the raw materials with which to manufacture our clothing, shelter, and our impressive collection of consumer goods . . . and to fulfill our massive energy needs as well as our continued reproduction of weapon systems. Too often rivalry begins to border on unfriendliness and then develops into open hostility. Indeed, one dictionary definition of competition is "warfare." In this competitive environment, it is difficult to engender an attitude that focuses on cooperation between individuals, groups, or nations. In a world of limited resources, this competitiveness can be destructive to the development of caring and sharing relationships based upon respect for the uniqueness of human beings and a celebration of the rainbow of differences that exists in humanity.

Learning to work together toward a common goal is essential if we are to achieve either our personal or societal goals of creating a more peaceful, humane earth. There is no doubt that this is the largest challenge we face in our families today as we enter the twenty-first century.

Families Working for Peace

Recognition of the pain and brokenness in the world, accepting that we share a common bond and common goals with the entire global village, must be translated for our children into positive action in order for a peaceful change to occur. Our children need to be reminded, in a variety of ways, that even the tiniest step toward a cooperative, peaceful solution is far better than merely recognizing the pain of others and doing nothing at all. There are several different forms of peacemaking we can utilize:

- peacemaking by example
- peacemaking through direct service
- peacemaking via advocacy
- peacemaking by empowerment

Peacemaking by Example

Many of us make this world a better place by our very existence, without even realizing the impact we are making: We promote peace by example. As we live peacefully—in our inner beings, our spiritual lives, family lives, and the kindly ways we interact with others in our daily routines—and as we guide our children to do the same, we become peacekeeping models. As we discover constructive outlets for our own anger, bad moods, and resentments, we learn to solve conflicts in ways that help all participants to feel satisfied. As we acquire strategies to deal with potentially violent situations, problems can, if not be resolved, at least be diffused. As we are courageous enough to intervene when friends speak out or act out against people they do not understand, we help to curb the epidemic of racism, sexism, and all the other biases and "isms" that permeate our hurting world.

Peacemaking through Direct Service

Many of us respond to human need with direct and immediate actions. Families carry cards, games, toys, books, and flowers to children in hospitals and read aloud to the elderly in nursing homes. Families deliver baskets of food and clothing to needy people and send money to organizations abroad. Families send blankets, medicines, and money to aid victims of wars, earthquakes, floods, hurricanes, and other disasters. Families participate in school clean-up days. This direct service is an important and valuable form of active peacemaking, and through such charitable deeds, we are showing our children how to bring a glimmer of hope to troubled people at home and in other lands.

But a question arises: Does direct action change lives permanently? When the food basket is empty and the flowers are wilted, what then happens to the poor and the elderly? Does giving make any lasting difference in the lives of the recipients? Of course, direct service toward others graphically illustrates a family's belief that sharing is the highest form of cooperation and peacemaking. But we also need to help our children become aware of two other forms of peacemaking that are less frequently employed. The tools of *advocacy* and *empowerment* enable us to offer service that continues to make a difference over a long period of time.

Peacemaking via Advocacy

There is an old adage that says if you give a man a fish, he will eat for a day, but if you teach him *how* to fish, he will eat for a lifetime. "Giving a fish" is the model for direct service, and there are certainly times when such an act is the most appropriate and could mean the actual survival of a person. But advocacy suggests going one step further to ensure that legal fishing rights exist for every person, so that the man (woman, child) can catch his or her own fish.

Advocacy most often focuses on effecting change in unjust or ineffective rules, customs, or laws. "Bread for the World," for example, attempts to influence legislative practices that control the production and distribution of food for people. Advocacy can also mean standing with and speaking out for other people on their behalf.

Advocacy can take many different forms, among them working and speaking out for a variety of people's issues and needs. Advocacy can mean speaking out on accessibility for the physically challenged, and equal treatment for both girls and boys of all cultures and linguistic groups in our schools. Advocacy can mean working for funding for safe energy alternatives and the civil rights of minority groups. Advocacy can be both speaking out and working for the rights of children, the elderly, farm workers, the homeless, battered women, gays, students, and any other disenfranchised people. Advocacy is speaking and doing.

Peacemaking by Empowerment

To follow through with the fishing metaphor, if advocacy is what ensures a person the *right* to fish, then empowerment is what ensures the person also has the *means* with which to fish: a fishing pole, a source for fish, and the necessary fishing skills. Empowerment enables people to act on their own behalf. If advocacy is speaking out on behalf of others, empowerment is what makes it possible for people to speak out for themselves. Empowerment happens when people have access to the skills, tools, and information that allow them to help themselves. Empowerment enables people to make their own decisions about events and conflicts that affect their lives. Empowerment also seeks to find ways of creating a relationship between the receiver and the giver that suggests, "You are an important, valuable, and capable human being." We can do this by affirming the receiver and actively showing an appreciation of the differences between us. When we affirm people, we are empowering them to believe in themselves.

At times, direct service can be a form of empowerment, as when our basket of food includes a warm expression of caring that enhances the receiver's self-worth. Other forms of action that lead to empowerment include working cooperatively in organizations such as social and legislative action groups, food co-ops, neighborhood block clubs, and special projects for people in need, the homeless, abused children, battered women, or the elderly.

Choosing a Form of Action

Which types of action your family decides to take depends upon the specific needs in your school and community, on the current events in the nation and in other countries, as well as the age, ability levels, and interests of your children. Our challenge as parents is to help our children discern what they are capable of doing and which type of action would be the most effective at any given time. As a family, members can gather to discuss:

- How can we find out what assistance is wanted or needed?

- What is already being done about it?

- How can we best use our resources and energy to be part of the solution?

- How can we help by being peaceful examples?

Direct service would be quite appropriate in an emergency. For example, as flood and hurricane victims begin to rebuild their lives, your family may choose to respond by offering gifts of goods, clothing, or physical labor. Or, in situations where you want to encourage others to work for peace, you might choose to serve through advocacy, using such means as personal speeches or informal conversations, bumper stickers, or letters to officials. Advocacy can be carried one step further toward empowerment. When, for example, your family helps raise funds for resources such as tools, supplies, or people with special skills in the areas of medicine, agriculture, or education, you are helping the recipients become empowered to take direct responsibility for their own lives. Similarly, when your family supports a neighborhood food club, health clinic, or library literacy tutoring program, your children are learning that they as individuals have the ability to become involved in events that empower the lives of others. The beautiful irony of empowerment is that it is not only the receiver who is empowered. Children, as contributors, also become empowered because they learn they can have a direct impact!

Activities to Expand Peace Beyond the Family

To continue to build a sense of hope for peace in today's broken and hurting world, our children need to learn by practice that they *can* make a difference in the world by actively working toward peace. An ability to care—to experience pangs of conscience for the misfortunes of others—can be the factor that changes them from observers to effective activists.

As our children begin to take steps toward world peace, however, we need to help them guard against discouragement and disillusionment: They cannot change the world in "ten easy steps." Being a part of the global peace effort means beginning to work toward peace in barely discernible ways—by affecting what is immediately needing positive change in their school, neighborhood, or community.

Following is a collection of activities to help your children practice peacekeeping beyond the family, either through setting an example of peaceful living, offering direct service, working for advocacy, or helping to empower others.

Encouraging Peace at School and with Friends

"School Survey" (age 9 and older)

Supplies needed: paper
                     writing utensils

Your children can be examples of peacemakers by providing evidence that all children are fundamentally the same, even though they may look different and speak another language.

1. Help your children make up a survey form that asks the students in their school, "What makes you feel peaceful?"

2. Assist your children, as necessary, in getting permission to conduct the survey, classifying the results, and making a report.

3. Discuss with your children:

   • Are sixth graders' answers different from second graders'? If so, how?

- Are girls' answers different from boys'? If so, how?

- Do children from other countries feel differently about peace? If so, how?

- How many answers to the survey were basically the same?

- What conclusions can you draw from this survey?

4. Encourage your children to write up the results of the survey for the school newspaper or newsletter. Suggest that they include their own ideas about how the information might affect the way students behave toward one another.

"Feelings that Promote Peace" (age 9 and older)

Supplies needed: paper
                  writing utensils

1. Talk with your children about a time when they felt someone was making fun of them because they were the only boy, the only girl, the only tall child, the only Native American, etc., at a party or other event.

2. Ask your children to think of some words that could be used to describe how they felt. Have them write the words on a sheet of paper and label the page, "Feelings that could cause conflict."

3. Invite your children to participate in the following role play: One child arrives at a birthday party and finds out he or she is the only boy or girl invited. Another child (or you) plays the role of someone at the party who tries to do and say things to make the first child feel welcomed and "at peace."

4. With your children, elicit additional words to describe how the person being welcomed in such a warm way might feel. Have your children write these words on another sheet of paper and label this page, "Feelings that could bring peace."

5. Repeat the role play, this time trading roles. Discuss ways your children could help others feel peaceful in different situations.

"Let Me Introduce Myself" (all ages)

Supplies needed: none

One way children can set a peaceful example is to practice extending friendship to other children.

1. Encourage your children to go up to a child they do not know at lunch or recess and say, "Hi!"

2. Set up some role plays with your children in which they can practice introducing themselves. Suggest such techniques as asking the new child's name and which classroom he or she is in.

3. Suggest that your children try to enlist their friends to make the same friendly overtures.

4. For shy children, or those who communicate better in writing, encourage them to create a card that simply says, "Hi!" Have them deliver the card to a new student in school or one whom they have not met.

5. After your children have had a chance to try out some introductions at school, discuss the reactions and the feelings of both the giver and the receiver.

"A Friendship Map" (up to age 8)

Supplies needed: paper
writing utensils

"Friendship" is an abstract concept for young children, and they often use the term lightly. Help them to consider the term more carefully by creating a word "map" that describes friendship.

1. Ask your children to brainstorm some ideas to answer the question, "What IS friendship?"

2. Ask them to think of some words to describe what friendship is LIKE.

3. Ask them to offer some words that tell what friendship is NOT like.

4. Ask them to offer some examples of friends and tell how each friend fits the description of friendship. Arrange these answers in the following format:

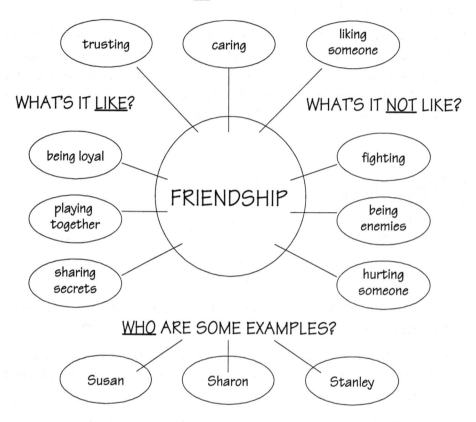

WHAT **IS** FRIENDSHIP?

trusting

caring

liking someone

WHAT'S IT **LIKE?**

being loyal

playing together

sharing secrets

FRIENDSHIP

WHAT'S IT **NOT** LIKE?

fighting

being enemies

hurting someone

WHO ARE SOME EXAMPLES?

Susan

Sharon

Stanley

"Competing
with Friends" (up to age 8)

Supplies needed: none

Although many schools are moving away from competition and attempting to move toward cooperative grouping, children still inevitably have to face competition with friends at school.

1. Discuss with your children how they feel about winning and losing.

2. Ask them to share a time when they had to compete against a friend. Ask them how they felt. Ask if the competition hurt the friendship. Explore their reasoning.

3. Have your children help you list some qualities of good winners and good losers.

4. Brainstorm together some ways these qualities could help a situation when your children have to compete against other children with whom they wish to remain friends.

5. Encourage your children to consider a different way of thinking about competition: Instead of "winning" and "losing," shift their focus to "achieving" and "learning." Discuss with them the importance of learning something new and gaining satisfaction from having taken a risk, even when the attempt does not lead to a victory.

"Friends or Enemies?" (age 9 and older)

Supplies needed: paper
writing utensils

1. Talk with your children about their understandings of the meanings of the terms "friend" and "enemy."

2. Ask them to think of a time from their own experience when a friendship suddenly went "sour," when they became enemies with someone who had once been a good friend.

   • Why did the former friend suddenly become an enemy?

   • What events led to the ending of the friendship?

3. Ask them if they have feelings of regret because of things that they failed to say or do.

4. Invite them to write a letter of apology to the former friend, expressing their regrets about the break up, or ending of, the friendship and what they wished they might have done differently.

5. After a period of time, check back with your children to discuss the outcomes of the letters. What did they learn about friendships that soured? What did they learn about the power of a sincere apology?

"Growing a

Peaceful Heart" (age 9 and older)

Supplies needed: varies, depending on what community help
your children decide to offer

1. Ask your children to consider the idea that one of the most profound ways they can affect world peace is by reaching out to others. Explain to them that, when they do this, they are figuratively "growing a new heart."

2. Discuss with your children what they think is meant by the phrase "growing a new heart."

3. Ask them to think of times in their own lives when, through caring about others, helping someone overcome sorrow, or resolving conflict in a peaceful way they felt themselves "growing a new heart."

4. Brainstorm some other ways they could "grow a new heart" by reaching out to others in their neighborhood or community. You might want to suggest some of the following possibilities:

   • Once a week be a "goodwill person" in your neighborhood. Go around to people you know, exchange kind words, and see if there are things you could do to help out.

   • Stop in at a retirement or nursing home in your neighborhood. Offer to help write a letter for someone who has difficulty writing by hand, read an article, or simply chat with senior citizens who rarely have visitors.

   • Organize a Clean-Up-Our-Street day where your children and their friends pick up litter, trim shrubs, and paint (if appropriate).

   • Start a Gang-Awareness Campaign and have discussions with your children about ways they might be able to dissuade prospective members from joining gangs by reaching out in friendship.

"Helping in the Community" (age 9 and older)

Supplies needed: local newspaper
varies, depending on community projects
your children decide to undertake

You can help your children get involved with your community by heightening their awareness about community needs.

1. Scan the local paper with your children to discover local needs and problems. Is there a creek that needs to become free of pollution? Does a lake's shore need a planting of young trees for fish hatchlings to swim under? Does litter on a street need to be swept up or graffiti removed from buildings? What needs to be done?

2. As a long term project, have your children consider taking on one of the following projects:

   • Take a walk around the neighborhood and identify any minor problems that need attention, such as a sidewalk damaged to the point where is could cause injury. Write a letter to the appropriate city official asking for repairs.

   • Introduce yourself to an elderly resident in the neighborhood. Ask the resident what his or her needs or wants are. Make plans to assist the older person weekly with errands, yard work, or any odd jobs that need doing.

   • Determine the ethnic background of the people living in your neighborhood. Create a poster called "Living Together in Our Neighborhood." On the poster, draw a map and identify the houses of the neighbors on your street. Offer several positive comments about each one. Copy the poster and distribute it to any neighbors who would like one.

"Giving to Charity" (up to age 8)

Supplies needed: varies, depending on the fund-raising project your children decide to organize

1. Discuss with your children the meaning of the word "charity." Ask them if they think everyone in their community has enough food to eat, warm clothes to wear, and sufficient shelter.

2. Suggest to your children that they become involved in a charity fund-raiser. Explain that you will help them organize it and do some of the work, and that the money raised will go to help some community people who are in need.

3. Share ideas about ways your children and willing friends might make money. Some suggestions include:

   - a neighborhood garage sale
   - a carnival with games and prizes
   - a bake sale
   - a car wash
   - a can or paper recycling collection
   - a lemonade stand

4. Have your children and the other participants decide upon a neighborhood organization that would best utilize the funds they raise. The following are possibilities:

   - a homeless shelter
   - a soup kitchen
   - a local hospital
   - a local hospice
   - a local library

"Citizens of the Earth" (up to age 8)

Supplies needed: paper (optional)
writing/coloring utensils (optional)

1. Discuss with your children the idea that each human being is responsible for all the things on the planet earth.

2. Brainstorm with your children some ideas they may have about how they could contribute to peace on earth—both now, as children, and later, as adults.

3. Ask them to draw a picture, or write or tell a short story, about what their life might be like in a peaceful future.

4. As they share their pictures or stories, ask them to offer some ideas about what they might be doing now to help the future be peaceful.

"Peacekeeping Heroes and Heroines" (age 9 and older)

Supplies needed: paper
writing utensils
stamped envelope
biographies of peacekeepers
    (see list below and Appendix B)

1. Point out to your children that almost everyone has some kind of a reputation, and that reputations may differ in different situations, ranging from home, school, in the neighborhood, in gangs or clubs, or with friends. People may behave one way with one set of people and another way with another set of people who have different interests, values, and goals.

2. Ask your children to discuss the following questions:

   • How does someone get a "peaceful" reputation?

- How might someone change a reputation that is NOT peaceful?

- What are the reputations of some of the friends and community members you admire?

3. Encourage your children to write a letter to someone they consider "peaceful," letting the person know what it is they admire.

4. Have your children read biographies about peacemakers in the world and tell other family members what they have learned about the peaceful endeavors of such peacekeeping heroes and heroines as:

- Nelson Mandela

- Golda Meir

- Mahatma Gandhi

- Dr. Martin Luther King, Jr.

- Hanan Ashrawi

- Anwar Sadat

- Jimmy Carter

- Mother Teresa

- Reverend Tutu

 "Being Aware

of the World!" (age 9 and older)

Supplies needed: daily newspaper or weekly news magazine

You can develop and heighten your children's awareness by reviewing war-ravaged situations that are the daily life for children like themselves.

1. Have family members take turns scanning daily newspapers or magazines for events of peace, war, or other human drama happening in all parts of the world.

2. At the dinner table or during Family Sharing Time (FST) (see page 45), ask one family member to read and summarize a particular event.

3. Ask other family members to take turns describing their feelings about the event and possible ways they feel they could get involved (such as sending blankets to flood victims or creating a congratulatory card for persons signing a peace accord).

4. Encourage the family member who has contributed the information about the event to have the "last word." This person may choose to summarize what other family members have said, or share his or her personal reactions to the event as well as what he or she might want to do about it.

"What Can <u>We</u> Do about It?" (up to age 8)

Supplies needed: varies, depending on the projects you and your children decide to do

1. Ask your children to tell about one thing going on in the world that makes it a less-than-peaceful place.

2. Help them brainstorm some things they could do about a world problem. Here are some possibilities:

   - Create a bike fender sticker or a car bumper sticker asking for peace.

   - Write a letter to the editor of a national newspaper describing your family's longing for peace.

   - Join in a peace vigil, march, or parade.

   - Make peace buttons to wear and distribute.

   - Create a banner that reads, "Every family in America has its own ways of being peaceful. Here are ours: _____ ." Display the banner in a prominent place.

   - Make and distribute peace posters to be displayed in the front windows of houses.

A Closing Word about Peace in the World

Parents often ask me, "Isn't all this 'save the world through peacekeeping stuff' a little bit heavy for kids? Aren't you asking us to subject our children to aspects of reality they aren't emotionally or intellectually ready to handle?"

My answer is that the world needs young people to be hopeful *and* that hope needs to be rooted in reality. Children need to know that, difficult as it is, change is possible and that they can help to bring about change.

Similarly, they need to learn how to deal with situations calling for change, as well as how to manage peaceful conflict resolution. While I do not recommend overloading youngsters with social problems, I *do* believe we can help them learn to deal more effectively with the real world that surrounds them. When a "real world" focus is integrated into other, lighter dimensions of childhood and wholesome family life, then children will not grow up warped and cynical, but rather creative, capable, and caring—truly confident that they can make the world a more peaceful place.

O O O

"No more Wars, no more bloodshed.
Peace unto you. Shalom, Shallam, forever."

—Menachem Begin,
on signing the Egyptian-Israeli Peace Treaty,
Washington, D.C., March 16, 1979

AFTERWORD

Can we really raise peaceful children in this violent world?

I believe we can.

Because human beings cause violence, human beings can also put an end to it. Imagine a world where harsh words, unkind deeds, or violent actions were eliminated. If that were so, violence in families, fighting in schools, shootings in the streets, and wars in the world would be ended. Just like that.

Stopping violence is not that simple, of course; important changes in the world seldom are. But stopping violence is possible. And the consequence, if we do not find a way to create a generation of peacemakers to end it, will be the destruction of this wonderful planet and all of humankind.

Creating a generation of peacemakers means we will have to be more understanding and respectful of people who are different from us. We will have to work harder at disciplining with love and respect. We will have to help our children become engaged with constructive forms of entertainment. We will need to do all we can to see they grow up in families who love, affirm, and peacefully communicate with them.

We CAN make a difference in the way we handle conflict. We CAN practice resolving problems more effectively. We CAN teach our children to understand and respect the rights of others and to be peace-loving human beings. We CAN make a difference now—and for tomorrow—for ourselves, our family, our community, and the world.

APPENDIX A

Further Readings for Parents

Azerrad, J. *Anyone Can Have a Happy Child: The Simple Secret of Positive Parenting.* New York: M. Evans, 1980.

Berman, S., and P. LarFarge, eds. *Promising Practices in Teaching Social Responsibility.* Albany, NY: State University of New York Press, 1993.

Bettelheim, B. *A Good Enough Parent: A Book on Child-Rearing.* New York: Random House, 1987.

Bloch, D. *Positive Self-Talk for Children: Teaching Self-Esteem through Affirmations.* New York: Bantam, 1993.

Boice, J. L. *The Art of Daily Activism.* Oakland, CA: Winghow Press, 1992.

Capa, R. *Children of War, Children of Peace.* Photos by Robert Capa. Edited by Cornell Capa and Richard Whelan. Boston: Little, Brown, 1991.

Carmichael, C. *Non-sexist Childraising.* Boston: Beacon Press, 1977.

Cecil, N. L., and P. L. Roberts. *Developing Resiliency through Children's Literature.* Jefferson, NC: McFarland & Co., 1992.

Clarke, J. I. *Self-Esteem: A Family Affair.* Minneapolis: Winston Press, 1978.

Crary, E. *Kids Can Cooperate: A Practical Guide to Teaching Problem Solving.* Seattle: Parenting Press, 1984.

Drew, N. *Learning the Skills of Peacemaking: An Activity Guide for Elementary-Age Children on Communicating, Cooperating, and Resolving Conflict.* Menlo Park, CA: Jalmar Press, 1987.

Edelman, M. W. *The Measure of Our Success: A Letter to My Children and Yours.* Boston: Beacon Press, 1992.

Elwood, R. S. *Many People, Many Faiths: An Introduction to the Religious Life of Humankind.* Englewood Cliffs, NJ: Prentice-Hall, 1987.

Faber, A., and E. Mazlish. *How to Talk So Kids Will Listen and Listen So Kids Will Talk.* New York: Avon, 1980.

Firestone, R. *Compassionate Child-Rearing: An In-Depth Approach to Optimal Parenting.* New York: Insight Books, 1990.

Fraiburg, S. H. *The Magic Years: Understanding and Handling the Problems of Early Childhood.* New York: Charles Scribner's Sons, 1959.

Friedman, B., and C. Brooks, eds. *On Base! The Step-by-Step Self-Esteem Program for Children from Birth to 18.* Kansas City, MO: Westport, 1990.

Fugitt, E. D. *"He Hit Me Back First!" Creative Visualization Activities for Parenting and Teaching.* Rolling Hills Estates, CA: Jalmar Publishers, 1983.

Glenn, S. *Raising Self-Reliant Children in a Self-Indulgent World.* Rocklin, CA: Prima Publishing & Communication, 1985.

Gore, T. *Raising PG Kids in an X-Rated Society.* Nashville: Abingdon Press, 1987.

Grammer, K., and R. Grammer. *The Teaching Peace Songbook and Teaching Guide.* New York: Smilin' Atcha Music, Inc., 1993.

Greenspan, S. *Playground Politics: Understanding the Emotional Life of Your School-Age Child.* Reading, MA: Addison-Wesley, 1993.

Grevon, P. J. *Spare the Child: The Religious Roots of Punishment and the Psychological Impact of Physical Abuse.* New York: Knopf, 1991.

Haessly, J. *Peacemaking: Family Activities for Justice and Peace.* New York: Paulist Press, 1980.

Halpern, H. M. *Cutting Loose: An Adult Guide to Coming to Terms with Your Parents.* New York: Bantam Books, 1978.

Hamburg, D. A. *Today's Children: Creating a Future for a Generation in Crisis.* New York: Time Books, 1992.

Harris, J. *You and Your Child's Self-Esteem: Building for the Future.* New York: Carroll & Graf Publishers, 1989.

Hopkins, S., and J. Winters. *Discover the World: Empowering Children to Value Themselves, Others, and the Earth.* Philadelphia: New Society Publishers, 1990.

Hopson, D. P. *Raising the Rainbow Generation: Teaching Your Children to Be Successful in a Multicultural Society.* New York: Simon & Schuster, 1993.

Hopson, D. S., and D. Powell-Hopson. *Different and Wonderful: Raising Black Children in a Race-Conscious Society.* New York: Prentice-Hall, 1990.

Johnson, D. W., and R. T. Johnson. *Teaching Students to Be Peacemakers.* Edina, MN: Interaction Book Co., 1991.

Kennedy, M., and J. S. King. *The Single-Parent Family: Living Happily in a Changing World.* New York: Crown Trade Paperbacks, 1994.

Kozol, J. *Savage Inequalities: Children in America's Schools.* New York: Crown Publishers, 1991.

Leach, P. *Children First: What Our Society Must Do—and Is Not Doing—For Our Children Today.* New York: Random House, 1994.

Lickona, T. *Raising Good Children: Helping Your Child through the Stages of Moral Development.* New York: Bantam Books, 1983.

Luck, K. L. *52 Ways to Nurture Your Child's Natural Abilities.* Nashville: Oliver-Nelson, 1994.

MacKay, M. et al. *When Anger Hurts.* Oakland, CA: New Harbinger, 1989.

McGinnis, K., and J. McGinnis. *Parenting for Peace and Justice.* New York: Orbis Books, 1983.

McGinnis, K., and B. Oehlberg. *Starting Out Right: Nurturing Young Children as Peacemakers.* Oak Park, IL: Meyer-Stone Books, 1988.

McKissack, P., and F. McKissack. *Taking a Stand Against Racism and Racial Discrimination.* New York: Franklin Watts, 1990.

McMahon, T., ed. *It Works for Us! Proven Child-Care Tips from Experienced Parents across the Country.* New York: Pocket Books, 1993.

Merritt, J. *Empowering Children.* Portland, OR: Parenting Resources, 1988.

Merritt, J. *A Parent's Primer.* Portland, OR: Parenting Resources, 1989.

Middleton-Moz, J. *Children of Trauma.* Deerfield Beach, FL: Health Communications, Inc., 1989.

Miedzian, M. *Boys Will Be Boys: Breaking the Link between Masculinity and Violence.* New York: Doubleday, 1991.

Miller, A. *Prisoners of Childhood.* New York: Basic Books, 1981.

Miller, A. *For Your Own Good: Hidden Cruelty in Child Rearing and Roots of Violence.* New York: Farrar, Straus & Giroux, 1983.

Minuchin, S. *Family Kaleidoscope.* Cambridge, MA: Harvard University Press, 1984.

Neff, L. *One of a Kind: Making the Most of Your Child's Uniqueness.* Portland, OR: Multnomah Press, 1988.

Nelson, J. *Positive Discipline for Single Parents: A Practical Guide to Raising Children Who Are Responsible, Respectful, and Resourceful.* Rocklin, CA: Prima Publishers, 1994.

Patterson, J., and P. Kim. *The Day America Told the Truth.* New York: Prentice-Hall, 1991.

Petepiece, T. G. *Caring and Capable Kids: Developing Pro-Social and Peacemaking Skills Grades 3-6.* Spring Valley, CA: Magic Circle Publishing, 1988.

Ring, E. *Teaching Ethnic and Gender Awareness.* Dubuque, IA: Kendall/Hunt, 1990.

Roberts, P. L., and N. L. Cecil. *Developing Multicultural Awareness through Children's Literature.* Jefferson, NC: McFarland & Co., 1993.

Roberts, P. L., and N. L. Cecil. *Gender Positive! Modifying Gender Stereotypes through Children's Literature.* Jefferson, NC: McFarland & Co., 1993.

Rochman, H. *Against Borders: Promoting Books for a Multicultural World.* New York: HarperCollins, 1993.

Rosenbluth, V. *Keeping Family Stories Alive: A Creative Guide to Taping Our Family Life and Lore.* Point Roberts, WA: Hartley & Marks, 1990.

Schulman, M. *Bringing Up a Moral Child: A New Approach to Teaching your Child to Be Kind, Just, and Responsible.* Reading, MA: Addison-Wesley, 1985.

Shure, M. B. *Raising a Thinking Child: Help Your Young Child to Resolve Everyday Conflicts and Get Along with Others.* New York: H. Holt, 1994.

Sinetar, M. *Human Rights for Children.* Alameda, CA: Hunter House, 1992.

Sears, W., and M. Sears. *The Discipline Book: Everything You Need to Know to Have a Better-Behaved Child–From Birth to Age Ten.* New York: Little, Brown and Co., 1995.

Sloane, H. *The Good Kid Book: How to Solve the Most Common Behavior Problems.* Champaign, IL: Research Press, 1988.

Webster-Doyle, T. *Why Is Everybody Always Picking on Me? A Special Curriculum for Young People to Help Them Cope with Bullying.* New York: Atrium Society, 1994.

West, C. *Race Matters.* Boston, MA: Beacon Press, 1993.

Whitfield, C. L. *Healing the Child Within.* Pompano Beach, FL: Health Communications, Inc., 1987.

Wichert, S. *Keeping the Peace: Practicing Cooperation and Conflict Resolution with Preschoolers.* Philadelphia: New Society Publishers, 1989.

Yawkey, T. D. *Caring: Activities to Teach the Young Child to Care for Others.* Englewood Cliffs, NJ: Prentice-Hall, 1982.

Zimmerman, R. *What Can I Do to Make a Difference? A Positive Action Sourcebook.* New York: Penguin Books, 1991.

APPENDIX B

Further Readings for Children

BIOGRAPHIES

FOR CHILDREN UP TO AGE 8

Accorsi, William. *My Name Is Pocahontas*. New York: Holiday House, 1992.

> The story of Princess Pocahontas, beginning with her childhood, and telling of her friendship with John Smith and marriage to John Rolfe.

Adler, David A. *A Picture Book of Abraham Lincoln*. Illustrated by John Wallner and Alexandra Wallner. New York: Holiday House, 1989.

> Facts about Lincoln's personality woven together with his desire for knowledge and his directness in solving problems.

Adler, Davis A. *A Picture Book of Simon Bolivar*. Illustrated by Robert Casilla. New York: Holiday House, 1992.

> The story of Bolivar, beginning with his boyhood and his tutor, and concluding with his achievements in adulthood.

Bains, Rae. *Harriet Tubman: The Road to Freedom*. Illustrated by Larry Johnson. Mawah, NJ: Troll, 1982.

> The story of Tubman, who did much to bring more peaceful times to her people by helping others escape from their slavery and opening schools for freed slaves in North Carolina.

Greene, Carol. *Robert E. Lee: Leader in War and Peace*. Illustrated by author. Chicago: Children's Press, 1989.

> A story about Lee's family, early life and education in Virginia, with some background about slavery and the Civil War Years.

Greenfield, Eloise. *Rosa Parks*. Illustrated by Eric Marlow. New York: Thomas Y. Crowell, 1973.

> The story of Parks, a woman who hated the special rules by which black people were forced to live.

Gross, Ruth Belov. *True Stories about Abraham Lincoln*. Illustrated by Jill Kastner. New York: Lothrop, Lee & Shepard, 1990.

> A series of brief stories that portray different aspects of Lincoln's early years and his later life.

Lee, Betsy. *Mother Teresa: Caring for God's Children*. Minneapolis: Dillon Press, 1983.

> The story of a Yugoslavian girl named Agnes Gonxha Bojaxhiu, whom we now know as Mother Teresa.

Smith, Kathie Billingslea. *Harriet Tubman.* Illustrated by James Seward. New York: Messner, 1989.

> The story of Tubman, who was a field worker and led more than three-hundred slaves to freedom, thus earning her the name of "Moses." During the War between the States, she was a cook, servant, spy, and scout for the Union Army.

Stevens, Bryna. *Deborah Sampson Goes to War.* Illustrated by Florence Hill. Minneapolis: Carolrhoda, 1984.

> The story of Sampson, who fought as a soldier in the American Revolution even though she was a young woman disguised as a man, and suffered many illnesses and injuries.

FOR CHILDREN AGE 9 AND OLDER

Brandenburg, Aliki. *A Weed Is a Flower.* Illustrated by author. New York: Simon & Schuster, 1965, 1968.

> A story of George Washington Carver, with information about his birth, early childhood, and adult life.

Bryant, Martha F. *Sacajawea: A Native American Heroine.* Billings, MO: Council for Indian Education, 1989.

> The story of the life of Sacajawea, the Shoshone Indian girl best known for her part in guiding the Lewis and Clark Expedition.

Chang, Ina. *A Separate Battle: Women and the Civil War.* New York: Lodestar, 1991.

> Multiple stories about women during the Civil War who faced prejudice and poor treatment by men as they showed their strong spirits and assisted in the war effort.

Clayton, Ed. *Martin Luther King: The Peaceful Warrior.* Illustrated by David Hodges. New York: Archway, 1968.

> The story of Martin Luther King, Jr., who dreamed of a career helping people.

Crofford, Emily. *Healing Warrior: A Story about Sister Elizabeth Kenny.* Illustrated by Steve Michaels. Minneapolis: Carolrhoda, 1989.

> The story of an Australian nurse who developed the "Sister Kenny" method of treatment for polio.

Duran, Gloria. *Malinche, Slave Princess of Cortez.* Hamden, CT: Linnet/Shoe String Press, 1992.

> The story of the Aztec princess Malinche who was given in slavery to Cortez and who also was an interpreter during the Spanish conquest of Mexico.

Ghermann, Beverly. *Sandra Day O'Connor: Justice for All.* Illustrated by Robert Marsheris. New York: Viking, 1991.

> The story of an influential, controversial woman who was the first woman Supreme Court Justice.

Giff, Patricia Reilly. *Mother Teresa: Sister to the Poor.* Illustrated by Ted Lewin. New York: Viking Kestrel, 1986.

> The story of Agnes Bojaxhiu, who was born in Skopje in the early 1900s, joined the Sisters of Soreto, went to India, and became Sister Teresa.

Greene, Carol. *Desmond Tutu: Bishop of Peace.* Chicago: Children's Press, 1986.

> The story of Nobel Peace Prize winner Tutu, who was born in South Africa, became a teacher and later a priest, and instituted many peaceful methods to change the politics of his country.

Greene, Carol. *Indira Nehru Gandhi: Ruler of India.* Chicago: Children's Press, 1985.

> The story of Indira Gandhi, who helped her father in his work for India's freedom, was elected as prime minister, and became a powerful world leader.

Holbrook, Stewart. *America's Ethan Allen*. Illustrated by Lynd Ward. Boston: Houghton Mifflin, 1949.

> The story of Ethan Allen, who went to the Continental Congress to ask that Vermont be admitted to the Confederation. When his correspondence with a British commander was discovered, he was accused of treason, but his guilt was never proven.

Meltzer, Milton. *Benjamin Franklin: The New American*. Illustrated by author. New York: Franklin Watts, 1988.

> The story of Franklin as a multifaceted person who had both strengths and weaknesses.

Meltzer, Milton. *Betty Friedan: A Vote for Women's Rights*. Illustrated by Stephen Marchesi. New York: Viking Penguin, 1985.

> The story of Betty Friedan, a remarkable woman who spearheaded the women's movement, documenting her life from childhood as an awkward, plain-looking Jewish loner, to her current career as author.

Reit, Seymour. *Behind Rebel Lines: The Incredible Story of Emma Edmonds, Civil War Spy*. New York: Harcourt, 1988.

> The story a woman who posed as a man (one of four hundred women) to fight in the civil war.

Stanley, Diane, and Peter Vennema. *Shaka: King of the Zulus*. Illustrated by Diane Stanley. New York: Morrow Junior Books, 1988.

> The story of Shaka, who had no help in developing his nation but who became known as a fighter, ruler, and leader of a vast army.

Wepman, Dennis. *Jomo Kenyatta*. New York: Chelsea House Publishers, 1985.

> The story of East African Jomo Kenyatta, who vowed that he would lead the Kenya people out of the abject poverty and exploitation to which the British white people had subjected them.

Uchida, Yoshiko. *The Invisible Thread*. New York: Messner, 1992.

> The author's story about her happy childhood, her father's success in business in American and their rich, happy life—in contrast with her later years spent in internment and her experience during World War II in the Japanese-American concentration camp.

FOR CHILDREN UP TO AGE 8

Ada, Alma Flor. *The Gold Coin*. New York: Atheneum, 1991.

Juan is a thief who considers his fortune made until he spies a woman holding a gold coin, telling herself that she must be the richest person in the world. Every place Juan goes, he discovers that the woman, Dona Josefa, has just helped someone in need and is on her way to help someone else.

Bottner, Barbara. *Bootsie Barker Bites*. Illustrated by Peggy Rathman. New York: Putnam, 1992.

Because their mothers are friends, the tyrant Bootsie and the unnamed narrator are thrown together. However, the narrator decides to beat bully Bootsie at her own game and she succeeds.

Gackenbach, Dick. *Claude Has a Picnic*. Illustrated by author. New York: Clarion, 1993.

Claude, a basset hound, discovers that all of his human neighbors have a problem about something. No one is feeling peaceful, but wise Claude helps out and becomes a goodwill canine ambassador.

Hoffman, Mary. *Amazing Grace*. Illustrated by Caroline Binch. New York: Dial, 1991.

When the class plans to produce *Peter Pan*, Grace wants the lead but hears a peer say she can't because she's a girl and because she's black. At home, her mother and grandmother help her achieve a peaceful state of mind and tell her she can be anything she wants to be if she puts her mind to it.

Hurwitz, Johanna. *E is for Elisa*. Illustrated by Lillian Hoban. New York: Morrow, 1991.

Eight-year-old Russell, who is in the Cub Scouts and goes to cookouts, promises never to tease four-year-old Elisa again.

Hutchins, Pat. *My Best Friend*. Illustrated by author. New York: Greenwillow, 1993.

Two girls are best friends yet are decidedly different. One can button her clothes, climb, jump and run with ease, while the other cannot do these things as well. However, at night, when the wind blows the bedroom curtains and frightens them, it is the "cannot" girl who is brave and uses her common sense to calm them both.

Kinsey-Warnock, Natalie, and Helen Kinsey. *The Bear that Heard Crying*. New York: Cobblehill, 1992.

Three-year-old Sarah Whitcher gets lost in the woods near her home in New Hampshire in 1783. This is a story based on true events experienced by the author's ancestors.

Lester, Helen & Munsinger, Lynn. *Pookins Gets Her Way*. Illustrated by authors. Boston, MA: Houghton Mifflin, 1987.

Pookins, a young child, always gets her way. However, she learns that getting everything she wants does not always make her happy.

Lystad, Mary. *The New Boy*. Illustrated by Emily McCully. New York: Crown, 1973.

When a new boy moves in across the street, all young George can see are the boy's nerdy clothes and big glasses. George is not sure he wants to play with this child, but his father urges him to befriend the new boy.

MacDonald, Maryann. *Rosie Runs Away*. Illustrated by Melissa Sweet. New York: Atheneum, 1990.

Rose is feeling very frustrated: She wants to bake with Mama, but Mama is too busy caring for Rosie's little brother, Mat.

McDonald, Megan. *The Potato Man*. Illustrated by Ted Lewin. New York: Watts, 1991.

"Abba no potata man," is what Mr. Angelo, the potato man, calls out, and he becomes the object of the boys' pranks in the neighborhood. As Mr. Angelo wins the pranksters over with his gentleness and understanding, some of them show compassion, understanding, and remorse for their acts.

Martin, Jane Read, and Patricia Marx. *Now Everybody Really Hates Me*. San Francisco: HarperCollins, 1993.

After Patty Jane is sent to her room as the consequence for hitting her brother, she decides never to leave, and her imagination takes her on hilarious adventures in her bedroom.

Mendez, Phil. *The Black Snowman*. Illustrated by Carole Byard. New York: Scholastic, 1989.

When young Jacob Miller says, "I hate being black" to his mother, his brother cajoles him into making a snowman that they dress in a kente clothe—brightly colored material that brought magic to the Ashanti people before they were sold to slavery.

Merriam, Eve. *Fighting Words*. Illustrated by David Small. New York: Morrow, 1992.

Dale and Leda are "good" enemies and are envious of what each other has. Ready to do battle, they meet halfway between their two homes and fight with insults as they chase each other through the streets after which they shake hands and praise one another on their "good fight" and promise to meet again to fight with the power of their words.

Milgram, Mary. *Brothers Are All the Same*. Illustrated by Rosemarie Hausherr. New York: E. P. Dutton, 1978.

Nina, Kim, and Joshie are all members of the same family, but Joshie is the only one who was adopted. The girls think Joshie is their brother, the same way any brother would be, but the boy next door disagrees.

Mills, Claudia. *A Visit to Amy-Claire*. Illustrated by Sheila Hamanaka. New York: Macmillan, 1992.

Rachel, a young Asian American, looks forward to a visit with her older cousin, Amy-Claire, but once there, she is jealous and feels isolated. However, Rachel sorts out her feelings of rivalry with her cousin.

Polacco, Patricia. *Chicken Sunday*. Illustrated by author. New York: Philomel, 1992.

A store owner accuses three children of pelting his shop with eggs. To make peace with him, they prepare a gift of hand-dyed eggs in the Russian style taught to the author by her grandmother.

Polushkin, Maria. *Baby Brother Blues.* Illustrated by Ellen Weiss. New York: Bradbury Press.

A classic story of sibling rivalry in which a little girl cannot believe how silly and messy her new baby brother is. And yet everybody—her parents, grandparents, friends, aunts, and uncles—makes a fuss over him and thinks he is adorable.

Ransom, Candice F. *Shooting Star Summer.* Illustrated by Karen Milone. New York: Caroline House/Bonds Mills Press, 1992.

When Cousin Shannon visits for two weeks, the (unnamed) narrator loses her hostility, and the two find out they have a lot in common.

Raschka, Chris. *Yo! Yes?* Illustrated by author. New York: Orchard, 1993.

Meeting on the street, two boys talk to one another and start a friendship. Their conversation consists of brief exchanges, such as, "What's up?" "Not much." "Why?" "No fun." "Oh?" "No friends." They agree to be friends and close the deal by jumping up in the air and yelling, "Yow!"

Schreier, Joshua. *Hank's Work.* Illustrated by author. New York: Dutton, 1993.

Dad yells at Hank when Hank messes up the worktable. Hank stomps off to his room and, with his acid-green crayon, draws a monster who comes to "life" and tells Hank's dad, "Shhh, don't yell!" and gives out frightening roars.

Sharmat, Marjorie Weinman. Sometimes Mama and Papa Fight. Illustrated by Kay Choran. New York: Harper & Row, 1980.

When Kevin's mother and father argue, he doesn't understand why he can't tell them, "Stop this instant!" just as they tell *him* when he and his sister fight. The story makes the point that grownups sometimes have disagreements that can be resolved peacefully.

Sharmat, Marjorie Weinman. *Thornton the Worrier.* Illustrated by Kay Chorao. New York: Holiday House, 1978.

Thornton, who is not a very peaceful person, worries about bad weather, mosquito bites, enemies, fleas, toothaches—everything. He is "so busy worrying, he has no time for his favorite television program."

Vigna, Judith. *Nobody Wants a Nuclear War.* Illustrated by author. Niles, IL: Albert Whitman, 1986.

In this technological-age story, a young girl is afraid there might be a nuclear war and she will never get to grow up. Her mother reassures her that grown-ups all over the world will never stop looking for ways to prevent nuclear war.

Weiss, Nicki. *Battle Day at Camp Delmont.* Illustrated by author. New York: Greenwillow, 1985.

Everything is fine at Camp Delmont until the sports competitions on Battle Day, when best friends Sally and Maude find themselves on opposite sides.

Weiss, Nicki. *A Family Story.* Illustrated by author. New York: Greenwillow, 1987.

Rachel and her younger sister, Annie, have a special bond between them that continues as they grow up. Portrays how love continues as family relationships grow and change.

Weiss, Sally. *Maude and Sally.* New York: Greenwillow, 1983.

Maude and Sally are best friends, and they do everything together, fantasizing that they would be twins if ". . . you were a little taller and I were a little shorter." Their happy friendship runs into problems when Sally goes away to summer camp for six weeks and develops new friendships.

Williams, Karen Lynn. *Galimoto*. Illustrated by Catherine Stock. New York: Lothrop, Lee & Shepard, 1990.

In a small African village, seven-year-old Kondi goes on a peaceful search to get some wire to make a toy. He gets what he needs from other children and adults by using gentle powers of persuasion. His nonagressive manner is rewarded when he has all that he needs to create the special toy—a "galimoto."

FOR CHILDREN AGE 9 AND OLDER

Byars, Betsy. *Summer of the Swans*. Illustrated by Ted Conis. New York: Viking, 1970.

As Sara, a painfully self-absorbed child, attempts to find her missing brother, Charlie, she begins to develop a more accepting attitude toward the things she cannot change, while beginning to appreciate the positive relationships in her life.

Ferguson, Alane. *Cricket and the Crackerbox Kid*. New York: Bradbury, 1990.

Cricket, a lonely only child of affluent parents, stays on the fringes of school cliques, realizing it is social suicide to be friends with young people from poorer neighborhoods. A new boy in her class is assigned to be her partner for a school project. Though he is poor, the two become friends.

Fox, Paula. *The Village by the Sea*. New York: Orchard Books/Watts, 1988.

In the beginning of the story, Emma is clearly an unfortunate victim of circumstances. When she stops angry and defensive, and

begins to understand her irrational aunt's feelings, her compassion allows her to reach out and change her situation in a positive way.

Haven, Susan. *Is It Them or Is It Me?* New York: Putnam, 1990.

As Molly copes with adolescence and forgives friends and enemies, there is considerable humor in her first detention, her first romance, and her first experience with conflict resolution.

Myers, Walter Dean. *The Mouse Rap*. New York: Harper & Row, 1990.

In Harlem, fourteen-year-old, quick-thinking, fast-talking Frederick Douglas is "The Mouse," a kid who loves basketball—and gets reacquainted with his once-estranged father.

Nelson, Theresa. *And One for All*. New York: Orchard Books, 1989.

Three friends in high school suffer tensions in their male/female friendships. When Wing joins the Marines, knowing he will be sent to Vietnam, Sam gets deeply involved in the peace movement, and Geraldine, Wing's sister, falls in love with Sam.

Paterson, Katherine. *Bridge to Terabithia*. Illustrated by Donna Diamond. New York: Harper & Row, 1977.

In rural Virginia, ten-year-old Jess Aarons forms an unlikely friendship with Leslie Burke, a little girl whose family has left the city for a better way of life. The two create Terabithia, a secret kingdom in the woods where magical, beautiful things happen.

Pfeffer, Susan Beth. *Courage, Dana.* New York: Delacorte Press, 1983.

Dana is a self-effacing twelve-year-old who inadvertently becomes a local heroine when she rushes into traffic to save a little child's life.

Radley, Gail. *The Golden Days.* New York: Macmillan, 1991.

Both eleven-year-old Cory, a foster home runaway, and elderly Carlotta, a nursing home runaway, are brought together and have similar needs for love, acceptance, and something they call their "golden days of freedom."

Rochman, Hazel, and Darlene Z. McCampbell. *Who Do You Think You Are? Stories of Friends and Enemies.* Boston, MA: Joy St./Little Brown, 1993.

Teen-agers from various ethnic groups are featured in this collection of sensitive stories by North American authors such as Maya Angelou, Richard Peck, John Updike, and others.

Rylant, Cynthia. *A Kindness.* New York: Orchard, 1988.

A fifteen-year-old boy learns new feelings of love after he explores his feelings when his single mother becomes pregnant and keeps the baby.

Slepian, Jan. *Risk n' Roses.* New York: Philomel, 1990.

Skip, a new girl in a new neighborhood, wants to be accepted into Jean Persico's gang. Each member must meet a challenge, a tormenting act, devised by Persico, but Skip stops being mesmerized by Persico and decides to go her own way more peacefully.

Snyder, Silpha Keatley. *Libby on Wednesday.* New York: Delacorte, 1990.

Libby goes to public middle school where she feels she is superior to her classmates because she has been educated at home, while they feel she is socially inferior to them. In a writer's club, all learn of the serious problems of others in the world.

Stopl, Hans. *The Golden Bird.* Illustrated by Lidia Postma. New York: Dial, 1990.

Hospitalized with cancer, eleven-year-old Daniel receives daily messages from a Golden bird that enable him to discuss his impending death with his mother and others peacefully, with love and honesty.

Strachan, Ian. *The Flawed Glass.* New York: Little, Brown, 1990.

On an island off Scotland, Shona MacLeod and her family face dangerous poachers and are involved in a conflict with the new American owner of the island. Shona, physically handicapped, is a peacekeeper who becomes friends with Carl, the owner's son.

Vogel, Ilse-Margaret. *My Twin Sister Erika.* New York: Harper & Row, 1976.

Inge tells how she and her twin sister, Erika, struggle with friends and family who constantly compare them or confuse them with each other.

Zolotow, Charlotte. *If You Listen.* New York: Harper & Row, 1987.

Pre-teen Lia rarely sees her wealthy father and realizes her mother is taking too many pills. When they arrive at their country home for the summer, Lia makes friends with a girl named Sue Ellen with whom Lia shares confidences and a growing friendship.

FOR CHILDREN UP TO AGE 8

Birdseye, Tom. *Waiting for Baby*. Illustrated by Loren Leedy. New York: Holiday House, 1991.

A small boy waits for his baby sister to be born, and he thinks of all the special things they will do together.

Brenner, Barbara. *Wagon Wheels*. Illustrated by author. I CAN READ series. New York: Harper & Row, 1978.

Based upon a true story taken from the diaries of a family of black settlers in the pioneer days of the 1870s, the Muldie boys and their father travel over the arduous Kansas trail in covered wagons while fighting prejudice because of their skin color.

Coerr, Eleanor. *Chang's Paper Pony*. Illustrated by Deborah Kogan Ray. New York: Harper & Row, 1988.

In California during the gold rush days, Chang is lonely and asks his grandfather if he can have a pony, but he realizes their poverty and knows there is no way they can afford one. When Chang finds some gold nuggets in the cracks of the floorboards in Big Pete's cabin, he gives the nuggets to Big Pete and in return, Big Pete surprises him with a pony.

Coerr, Eleanor. *The Josefina Story Quilt*. Illustrated by Bruce Degen. New York: Harper & Row, 1986.

In the 1850s, Faith's family is traveling to California in a covered wagon with her pet hen, Josefina, who causes trouble but redeems herself when her cackles warn the family of robbers in their wagon.

McAllister, Angela. *The Battle of Sir Cob and Sir Filbert*. Illustrated by author. New York: Clarkson Potter/Crow, 1992.

Two knights, Sir Cob and Sir Filbert, who each want more room, fight for their castles with twangsuckers and pikeypokes. When the two finally discover that their castles have been destroyed, they decide to build another castle together and become friends.

Rylant, Cynthia. *When I Was Young in the Mountains*. Illustrated by Diane Goode. New York: E.P. Dutton, 1984.

A young girl describes her happy years growing up in the Appalachian mountains of Virginia.

Stevenson, James. *Don't You Know There's a War On?* New York: Greenwillow, 1992.

A a ten-year-old boy is left at home in 1942 while his father and brother go to fight in World War II. Includes a rare glimpse into a life full of spies, heroes, and ration books.

Wilder, Laura Ingalls. *Little House in the Big Woods*. New York: Harper, 1952.

The story of Wilder's early childhood in a log cabin on the edge of the Big Woods in Wisconsin, for she is "Laura" of the story.

FOR CHILDREN AGE 9 AND OLDER

Avi. *The True Confession of Charlotte Doyle*. New York: Orchard Books, 1990.

Courageous Charlotte is a thirteen-year-old, nineteenth century young lady from an upper-class family, who finds herself, accidentally on purpose, on a ship crossing the Atlantic during a mutinous three-month crossing.

Coerr, Eleanor. *Sadako and the Thousand Paper Cranes*. Illustrated by Ronald Himler. New York: Putnam, 1977.

In Hiroshima, Japan, Sadako Sasaki was two when a bomb destroyed her city, and ten years later she discovers she has cancer, the "A-Bomb disease." In her remaining months, Sadako uses her hands to fold bits of paper into origami cranes, believing the legend that if you fold one thousand paper cranes, the gods will make you well.

Bergman, Tamar. *The Boy from Over There*. Translated from Hebrew by Hillel Halkin. Boston: Houghton Mifflin, 1988.

On a kibbutz in a children's house in 1947, several children wait for their families. Rami's father returns with Avramik, the boy from "over there" where the war is being waged, who copes with the taunts and teasing by others.

Blos, Joan. *A Gathering of Days: A New England Girl's Journal, 1830-1832*. New York: Charles Scribner's Sons, 1979.

Thirteen-year-old Catherine Cabot Hall searches for peace in her life and writes in her diary about things that touch her daily: being in charge of the household; caring for her eight-year-old sister, Mattie, and her father since her mother died; and her days at school.

De Angeli, Marguerite. *The Door in the Wall*. New York: Doubleday, 1949.

Robin, a young boy, is crippled by a strange disease, and he goes to live with the monks when the Black Plague hits London. With perseverance and the help of the monks, he learns to become independent and develop his abilities, and he is able to save the town where his parents live.

De Jong, Meindert. *The House of Sixty Fathers*. Illustrated by Maurice Sendak. New York: Harper, 1956.

Small Tien Pao helps a wounded American airman. Later, when both are found by Chinese guerrillas, Tien is taken to Hengyang where the Japanese are still fighting. Sixty American soldiers help him to look for his family.

Fleischman, Sid. *The Whipping Boy*. Illustrated by Peter Sis. New York: Greenwillow, 1986.

Jemmy has been plucked from the streets to serve as the spoiled Prince's "whipping boy" who would take punishments in lieu of the Prince, as it was forbidden to spank the heir to the throne. Jemmy and the Prince decide to run away together but find themselves kidnapped by notorious villains. Jemmy's quick thinking allows the two to escape.

Forbes, Esther. *Johnny Tremain*. Illustrated by Lynd Ward. Boston: Houghton Mifflin, 1943.

Johnny, an apprentice to Paul Revere, becomes involved with the Revolutionary war, the activities for the Committee for Public Safety, and the first battle of the Revolution at Lexington and Concord.

Goldin, Barbara Diamond. *Cakes and Miracles: A Purim Tale*. Illustrated by Erika Weihs. New York: Viking, 1991.

In the late 1900s, Hershel, blinded by illness, uses his mother's dough to sculpt unusual cookies in shapes of the images he sees in his mind and helps his mother sell them for Purim.

Heide, Florence Parry, and Judith Heide Gilliland. *Sami and the Time of the Troubles*. New York: Clarion, 1992.

Ten-year-old Sami and his sister Leila are like children everywhere, except that they are living in places where violence has become the accepted way of resolving differences.

Hunt, Irene. *Across Five Aprils*. Chicago: Follett, 1964.

In the Civil War, nine-year-old Jethro Creighton, a southern Illinois farm boy, sees his brothers divided on the issue of freeing slaves.

Hurwitz, Johanna. *The Rabbi's Girls*. Illustrated by Pamela Johnson. New York: Morrow, 1982.

Courageous Carrie, one of six daughters of Rabbi Levin, tells her account of a stressful year in the life of her family.

Murphy, Jim. *The Long Road to Gettysburg*. New York: Clarion, 1992.

In Civil War times, nineteen-year-old Lieutenant John Dooley and seventeen-year-old Union Army Corporal Thomas Galway face one another at Pickett's Charge.

O'Dell, Scott, and Elizabeth Hall. *Thunder Rolling in the Mountains*. New York: Houghton Mifflin, 1992.

During the horrible winter of 1977, the Nez Perce Nation of the Wallowa Valley in Oregon flee the U.S. Army troops, who are forcing them to move to a reservation in Montana. Based on eyewitness accounts and recollections of survivors.

FANCIFUL STORIES

FOR CHILDREN UP TO AGE 8

Greenfield, Eloise. *Grandmama's Joy*. Illustrated by Carole Byard. New York: William Collins, 1980.

When Rhondy asks if she is still her grandmama's joy, grandmama replies, "You'll always be my joy." Rhondy realizes that enormous peacefulness is made possible by a stable, constant relationship with a loving human being.

Mayer, Mercer. *There's an Alligator Under My Bed*. New York: Dial, 1987.

A little boy has a problem: He is the only one who sees the alligator under his bed. He realizes he will have to take matters into his own hands.

Priceman, Marjorie. *Friend or Frog*. Boston: Houghton Mifflin, 1989.

A young girl has a frog named Hilton, who is ". . . green and spotted, which is unusual for a friend but attractive in a frog."

Wolf, Winfried. *The Dream Tree*. Illustrated by Manfried Shluter. Translated by Anthea Bell. New York: North-South Books, 1987.

When he is trying to sleep, Michael is pestered by witches, ghosts, and giants. He takes control of his life and banishes his fears by sending them all away to a tiny desert island in the sea.

Grifalconi, Arin. *The Village of Round and Square Houses*. Boston: Little, Brown, 1986.

Demonstrating that it is sometimes peaceful to be away from the people you love, the women of the village decide they enjoy being together to talk, laugh, and sing in the round houses, and the men become used to relaxing in their own place in the square houses.

Hooks, William H. *The Ballad of Belle Dorcas*. Illustrated by Brian Pinkney. New York: Knopf, 1990.

Brave Belle Dorcas of the Gullah people is a "free-issue" person, the child of a slave master and a slave woman. Though free-issue people generally married other free-issue persons to take advantage of the relative freedom, Belle Dorcas loves Joshua and no one else will do.

Kimmell, Eric. *Herschel and the Hanukkah Goblins*. Illustrated by Trina Schart Hyman. New York: Holiday House, 1985.

Herschel of Ostropol is looking forward to reaching the next village on his journey so that he may celebrate Hanukkah with the villagers. He is disappointed to find they are *not* celebrating Hanukkah because they are afraid of a band of goblins that haunt the synagogue.

L'Engle, Madeleine. *An Acceptable Time*. New York: Farrar, Straus & Giroux, 1989.

Meg's teen-age daughter, Polly, travels back in time three thousand years. In this prehistoric period, she finds herself in an unusually peaceful land with a tranquil Native American tribe, the "People of the Wind." Polly gains great wisdom and faces the dilemma of staying in that time period or going back to her own troubles in the turbulent present.

Rodda, Emily. *The Pigs Are Flying*. New York: Greenwillow, 1986.

Rachel has been ill for several days, and she is getting bored. She wishes something would happen and it does: She finds herself in a strange land where it rains pigs, and the intensity of a storm is measured in UEFs—"unexpected event factors." Rachel is bewildered by this strange world, but she fights back her tears and figures out a way to return to her family, whom she suddenly appreciates enormously.

Davol, Marguerite W. *Black, White Just Right!* Chicago: Albert Whitman, 1993.

A contemporary interracial family is depicted in everyday situations to show children how similar all families really are.

Dwight, Laura. *We Can Do It!* New York: Checkerboard Press, 1989.

Highlights five "special" ethnically diverse young children and what they are able to do. Includes photographs of the children.

Groffe, Toni. *War and Peace.* East Jordan, MI: Child's Play, 1992.

Discusses the ravages of war and the beauty of peace in clear language and beautiful pictures young children can understand.

Mizumura, Kazure. *If I Built a Village . . .* Illustrated by author. New York: Crowell, 1971.

Through whimiscal, poetic text, the author shares her vision of what an ideal village might be like. Her ink-and-wash drawings and joyous watercolor paintings show how an environment can be naturally beautiful if it is cared for.

Scholes, Katherine. *Peace Begins with You.* Illustrated by Robert Ingpen. San Francisco: Sierra Club Books, 1989.

Beginning on a personal level, this book looks at why people's needs and wants do not always fit together easily and how this can cause conflict. Includes ways in which conflicts can be resolved peacefully, ending with national and international ways to protect peace.

INDEX

* Family Activities are shown in italics; Family Posters are capitalized.

NANCY LEE CECIL, PH.D., is the author of *Teaching to the Heart, Freedom Fighters*, and eight other books about literacy instruction, as well as co-author with Patricia L. Roberts of *Developing Resiliency through Children's Literature*. Nancy has also written over two dozen professional articles that have been published in such journals as *The Reading Teacher* and *Reading Improvement*.

Dr. Cecil earned her doctorate in education from the University of Buffalo and is currently a professor of education at California State University, Sacramento. She also has had a rich background teaching in public elementary schools in upstate New York, the inner city of Savannah, Georgia, and the U.S. Virgin Islands. As a local, national, and international speaker, she offers workshops on peaceful parenting techniques and lectures on affective issues in literacy.

Nancy shares her life with her husband, Gary, her daughter, Christina, and assorted animals. In her leisure time, she enjoys reading, traveling, and long walks with her family. The Cecils reside in Carmichael, California.

ROMANTIC ART

ROMANTIC ART

MARCEL BRION

64 color plates, 166 monochrome plates

McGRAW-HILL BOOK COMPANY, INC.

New York   Toronto   London

© THAMES AND HUDSON LTD 1960

TEXT PRINTED BY JOH. ENSCHEDÉ EN ZONEN HAARLEM HOLLAND

MONOCHROME ILLUSTRATIONS PRINTED BY BRAUN ET CIE MULHOUSE FRANCE

COLOUR ILLUSTRATIONS PRINTED BY W S COWELL LTD IPSWICH ENGLAND

ART AND COLOURED PAPERS SUPPLIED BY FRANK GRUNFELD LTD LONDON

BOUND BY VAN RIJMENAM N.V. THE HAGUE HOLLAND
LIBRARY OF CONGRESS CATALOG NUMBER 60-12761

07910

CONTENTS

All the measurements in this book are given in centimetres, followed by inches in brackets. Height precedes width.

INTRODUCTION

ROMANTICISM is not one of those aesthetic phenomena which can be neatly allocated to a particular period or country. On the contrary: it is a way of looking at things, a certain vision, which is found, whether simultaneously or not, in the most widely different spheres of art, philosophy, music and poetry. It even affects such seemingly objective studies as science and sociology and Romantic art bears the marks of its contacts with the society of the day, both that part of society which accepted it and that part which rejected it. Any attempt to define it by merely contrasting it with Classicism, its traditional 'opposite', results in arbitrary, artificial and negative conclusions. But even in itself, without recourse to external comparisons, the collection of forms and ideas lumped together as 'Romanticism' is equally difficult to reduce to a convenient formula. Its principal elements are fairly easy to define: restlessness, yearning, the idea of growth, self-identification with nature, infinite distance, solitude, the tragedy of existence and the inaccessibility of the ideal; but all these are variously combined and mingled, of various origins and tending in various directions.

Actual works of art speak more eloquently than definitions. One can learn more about the nature and essence of Romanticism from a Schumann symphony, a Caspar David Friedrich landscape or *Childe Harold's Pilgrimage* than from any scholarly disquisition on the subject. Nor does Romanticism reveal itself if approached dialectically or by reasoning; only through an immediate and total communion with its spirit can one penetrate to its real depths. It is useless to attempt to decide with absolute certainty whether this or that artist is a Romantic or not. Chronological classifications are completely inapposite in a matter so much less cut-and-dried than the art-historians would like to believe. When did Romanticism begin and end? This question could only be asked by someone ignorant of the complexity and extent of the problem and it can only be answered by an appeal to the inquirer's own sensibility, by requiring him to note what painting and music arouse in him the excitement, nostalgia and disquiet indissolubly linked with the Romantic sensibility.

For, in fact, Romanticism is a constant of the human mind which repeatedly comes to the surface at given stages in the history of art and civilization whenever circumstances favour its resurgence and return to dominance. It is one of the stages through which the human mind inevitably passes, and its repeated outbreaks show

how much dreams and nostalgia, horror of the finite and longing for the infinite are natural to man, offering an ideal, a self-projection to the painter, the musician and the poet—a concept which extends far beyond aesthetics alone.

It is possible to see Romanticism as only another facet of Baroque, and the Romantic spirit at its most characteristic as merely a prolongation of the Baroque spirit, but this thesis raises numerous problems and implications which cannot be discussed here. Nevertheless it is confirmed by the fact that Rococo, the 'bridge' between Baroque and Romanticism, itself seems to contain a modified version of the Romantic sensibility. It is above all the most Baroque heroes—Don Juan, Hamlet, Faust, Don Quixote—whom Romantic artists choose to portray, feeling themselves to be intimately related to these great symbols of the human dilemma.

That there is a strong connection between Baroque and Romanticism can only be denied by those who understand neither the one nor the other. It has been forcibly demonstrated by Eugenio d'Ors, the great Spanish aesthetician, who considers Romanticism a branch of Baroque and has gone so far as to invent a graphic new name for it, the '*barohus romanticus*'.

This brilliant theory has contributed much to a more accurate evaluation of Baroque art and indeed to the new concept of Baroque in general which has become current within the past few decades—probably one of the more useful achievements of modern art-history. The term 'Baroque' had long been used as a pejorative epithet, signifying all that was ridiculous, exaggerated and extravagant, just as 'Gothic' had been for the men of the 17th or 18th century a synonym for 'barbarianism'.

Those who base their calculations on chronology, dividing off father from son, elder brother from younger brother, would deny all Romanticism to such artists as Mozart or Watteau, on the grounds that they belong to either the Rococo or the Classical period, according to which particular system one cares to adopt. But the variations of human genius cannot be pigeon-holed in this way; it is ridiculous to suppose that a certain outlook, a certain artistic temperament began and ended on given dates, like the pheasant season. If we accept that Rembrandt, El Greco and Rubens belong to a sort of early Romanticism, a 'first edition' of the Romanticism which was to flourish in the 19th century, we are suggesting (with ruinous effect to the time classification) that there could have been Romantics in the Baroque period. Nevertheless one could make out a case for the Romanticism of Baldung Grien, Grünewald, Dürer, Magnasco, Monsù Desiderio and Valdés Leal and it would not be impossible to postulate an 'eternal Romanticism' with equivalents in non-European art.

But extending the field of vision always involves a risk of losing sight of the target itself. One has no alternative but to focus on certain artists in particular if one is to give them any detailed attention, and as the larger number of Romantic artists reached the peak of brilliance in the period from about 1750 to 1850, this is the obvious period to select. It would be most interesting to trace the currents, visible or concealed, which led up to this golden age of Romantic forms and ideas and continued after its subsidence, but such explorations are beyond the scope of this book.

From the foregoing it will have emerged that hard-and-fast distinctions between pre-Romantics, proto-Romantics and precursors of Romanticism are entirely inapposite; there is no point in discussing which of Brahms and Chopin is the more Romantic or maintaining that the *Embarquement pour Cythère* cannot be Romantic because *The Death of Sardanapalus* cannot be anything else.

Where France is concerned, we may accept the judgment of Delécluze who said of the artistic movement fermenting around him: 'Those who call themselves "Romantics" differ so much in their opinions, follow principles so contradictory, that it is impossible to extract one central idea from all this chaos. I myself have given up trying to understand it.' Similarly Paul Valéry urged that it was wrong to try to provide a single absolute solution for a problem which did not admit of such a solution. And he added: 'One would have to have lost all ability to reason closely to attempt to define Romanticism.' Goethe provides us with an excellent example of an artist who remained Romantic by temperament to the end of his life yet whose desire for Classicism governed and controlled his natural impulses and instincts, creating a harmonious alliance between the two elements.

Every textbook quotes Goethe's apparently decisive and unequivocal rejection of Romanticism. Pushed to the end of his tether by importunate questions, he said: 'I call what is healthy Classical and what is unhealthy Romantic.' Undoubtedly the greatest of all the authentically Romantic creations, in painting, music and poetry, attain to a majesty and perfection which may well be called 'Classical', but today this term is used in a much wider, more supple sense than was current in the 18th or 19th century. Today we would hardly accept the basic, inherent opposition postulated by the critics of those days and expressed here by Goethe.

To take his judgment literally would be to accept as valid an arbitrary, brutal, over-simple dictum which almost certainly did not represent his true opinion or, at any rate, the whole of it. It is possible to agree with him if he was simply distinguishing between the healthier side of Romanticism—in which it approached Classicism (which for him meant health)—and the morbid side, which represented a corruption of Romanticism.

In reality, however, it is over-simplifying Romanticism to think of it as a single phenomenon, for its different aspects in different countries, the widely differentiated Romanticisms of, say, England, France and Italy, can hardly be grouped under one heading. To take landscape-painting alone: only by a wilful forcing of analogy and comparison can the painters of the Posillipo School, the Barbizon School, and Caspar David Friedrich of Pommerania be put into a single category; nevertheless they are all Romantic, even if in different ways and for different reasons.

One can only venture (without claiming to reach absolute truth) on an approach equally uncontaminated by traditional prejudices and opinions and by hasty or bold generalizations. This approach would consist of an examination and comparison not only of the artists generally acknowledged to be 'Romantic', but also of those who are linked with Romanticism either by their feeling, their technique or their aspirations and restlessness.

The common characteristics of European Romanticism, irregularly scattered through the different countries of the Continent and assuming different guises in each of them, are revealed in a sentence from Baudelaire's *Aesthetic Curiosities*. He too attempted to devise a definition valid for all the different branches and not merely for isolated cases. He says: 'The word Romanticism means modern art—that is, intimacy, spirituality, aspiration for the infinite expressed with all the means open to the arts.' This definition is completed by Delacroix' statement in his *Journal*: 'If by Romanticism is meant the free manifestation of one's personal impressions I am a Romantic, and not only that, but I was a Romantic at the age of fifteen.' By using Delacroix' and Baudelaire's words as a key to the cryptogram of 19th-century art, we arrive at a fairly clear impression of certain valid *leitmotifs*.

In insisting on the force of personal impression, Delacroix is carrying to extremes the autonomy of individuality, the rights of personality, in opposition to the universal feeling and passions demanded by Classicism; to a certain extent he is anticipating and giving in advance a justification for Impressionism. The Romantic outlook is largely made up of sensibility, always allowed to predominate over reason, a spirit of revolt affecting the relationship of man to society and extending to pictorial, literary and musical techniques, criticism of divine and human laws and rebellion against the established social order. To these are added a stormy longing for independence, for no other compulsion but those of the instincts and passions. This is the mental make-up which gives its characteristic bias to Romantic aesthetics. The establishment of new links between man and the universe, communion with nature, the newly discovered possibility of becoming friends with things that had previously been objects of terror—night, the deep, dreams and the infinite—all these add to artists' capacity for feeling and demand new means of expression.

These last are manifested both in purely original creations, in the supremacy of painting over all the other arts, and in the re-evaluation of old artistic forms, unjustly forgotten or despised.

In his longing for 'distance', both material and spiritual, the Romantic artist discovered the unknown marvels of the Orient and returned to a typically Romantic Middle Ages, magnified and embellished by his nostalgia for 'the past': these desires for both novelty and 'olde-worldliness' are not contradictory, for they are both forms of 'distance'.

It was one of Romanticism's prime ambitions to produce the 'total work of art', that is, a work which should appeal simultaneously to all the senses, to sensibility, the emotions and the intelligence. This vague conception of 'the work of art of the future' is common, in its different acceptations, to both Philipp Otto Runge and Richard Wagner, for instance; it demands that everything should appeal to all the perceptions, should be accepted simultaneously as music, poetry and visual art. This voracious appetite for totality is in fact one of the essential elements of the Romantic spirit with its assumption that emotion is incomplete unless it is aroused by all the senses, even if, on occasion, it does not achieve its aim.

'The man that hath no music in himself ... is fit for treasons, stratagems, and spoils ... let no such man be trusted,' said Shakespeare, the greatest inspiration of Romantic painters and musicians; they were quick to understand this attitude and found in it the justification for their own sensibility. Walter Pater discovered in Baroque and that part of the Renaissance which is already Baroque (Giorgione, for instance) one of the basic laws of the Romantic code, that a work of art is more perfect the closer it comes to music. Poetry itself enlarges and renders more subtle its means of expression the more it approaches music, as in Keats, Shelley, Nerval, Hoffmann's *Kater Murr* and Jean Paul's *Flegeljahre*. And, of course, the reverse was equally true. Composers did their best to 'widen the scope of music' by introducing all kinds of non-musical elements—painting, literature and even philosophy. One has only to think of typical 19th-century programme music, Lisztian tone poems or Mendelssohnian evocations of Fingal's Cave or Shakespeare's Athens.

To get the most out of a Romantic picture, to appreciate to the full its complexity, it is not enough merely to note its pictorial qualities. The reason why Romantic painting has become largely foreign, even sometimes unintelligible, to us of the present day, is precisely this: that whereas Romanticism encouraged non-visual qualities, we, since Impressionism, have condemned everything that is 'literary' or 'anecdotal', everything that is not pure painting.

It is a serious mistake to ask *how* a given work was painted and not *why*—a mistake which obscures the work's essential nature. Materials and technique, paint and brushwork take up so much of our critics' attention that they have none left over for deeper, more secret qualities, for the poetic and musical elements so inextricably interlinked with the pictorial element in, for instance, the works of the German Romantics.

For more than a century, everything in a picture which is not pure painting has been stigmatized as 'literary'; it is, perhaps, one of the greatest merits of the Surrealists that they laid stress on the 'subject' again, in complete opposition to the current trend. It would be absurd to look for nothing in a picture beyond the way the story is told; because art-critics were not interested in the stories told, they also came to ignore the poetic content of Romantic pictures by means of which artists attempted to stimulate the emotions.

It is normal, and probably salutary, for an excess in one direction to provoke, as a reaction, an excess in another; one can understand how an overriding preoccupation with subject-matter should be succeeded by an immovable proscription of subject-matter as such. And, in a way, one can account for the present equivocal position whereby Delacroix is appreciated only for his 'painterliness', setting aside all the other qualities of his pictures—his powerful imagination, art of telling a dramatic story, feeling for construction, skill in evoking a supernatural atmosphere—just as Caspar David Friedrich is reproached with not having essentially modified painting techniques—brushwork, materials, etc.—which are, after all, nothing more than means to an end.

For the Romantics, the pictorial element never became an end in itself; the painter continued to appeal to those parts of the mind which are not stimulated only by the visual and tactile, but also by intense human feeling. The aim of the Romantic picture was to portray the human animal in his nostalgia, restlessness, and a confused mixture of aspirations and melancholy, and to mirror the emotions aroused in the spectator; it was to be poetry and music as well as painting, both in subject and treatment. Consequently it demands great sympathy on the part of the spectator and, where we of the present day are concerned, a revision of our ideas as to aesthetic merits.

The late eighteenth century saw the beginning of the full expression of Romanticism which continued far into the nineteenth century. But the spirit of Romanticism has been with us at least since the Renaissance. Immediately following this Introduction, under the heading 'Forerunners of Romanticism', eight paintings by masters of earlier periods are reproduced, in which the Romantic mood is the principal content. They serve as evidence of man's inherent romanticism and as a prelude to the Romantic Age.

I · FORERUNNERS OF ROMANTICISM

I · GIORGIO DA CASTELFRANCO, known as GIORGIONE c. 1476–1510

Giorgione was probably born at Castelfranco in about 1476 and may well have studied with Girolamo da Treviso in that town, before working in the best-known Venetian workshops—those of Gentile Bellini, Carpaccio, Alvise Vivarini and Lazaro Bastiani. He painted the frescoes in the Fondaco dei Tedeschi at Venice which have since disappeared, but there is some doubt as to which paintings should be attributed to him. *La Tempesta* is one of the few which are certainly by his hand; Antonio Michiel relates that he saw it in 1530 in the palace of Gabriele Vendramin. In Vendramin's Collection this mysterious composition was known as *Mercury and Isis,* and art-historians have long debated the problem of its true subject. Various hypotheses have been put forward but the picture's most striking qualities are its Romantic atmosphere, the sustained harmony of the landscape and the enigmatic relationship between the figures and the background. His attitude towards the elements—a devout, almost religious awe—marks Giorgione out as one of the precursors, if not creators, of the Romantic landscapes. He died of the plague on 25 October, 1510.

La Tempesta

78 × 72 (30¾ × 28⅜). Gallerie dell'Accademia, Venice

II ALBRECHT ALTDORFER c. 1480–1538

Born at Regensburg, Altdorfer belonged to the so-called Danube School which exerted a considerable influence on 16th century German landscape painting. He was one of the first to give an important place to realistic depictions of various aspects of nature. With him landscape ceases to be only symbolic or decorative and becomes one of the main components of the cosmic emotion which the artist attempts to express. In *The Battle of Alexander,* Altdorfer uses the precision and delicacy of a miniaturist to convey the details of the armour and accessories of this crowd of figures engaging in mortal combat. The most strikingly 'modern' part of the composition is the huge landscape showing an expanse of sea and mountain stretching away to infinity. Altdorfer shows here an early version of the pathetic fallacy, in which the struggle of the sun with the clouds runs parallel with the struggle of man against man and underlines the 'sun-god' nature of Alexander, contrasting with his enemy, symbolized by the darkness; at the same time, the limitless extent of the landscape suggests the limitless conquests of the Macedonian King who aspired to be master of the whole universe. In his conception of huge ambition coupled with a passionate feeling for 'distance', Altdorfer is revealed as one of the best examples of the 'Romantic constant', one of the essential characteristics of German art.

Detail from *The Battle of Alexander*

1529. Limewood. 401 × 305 (158 × 120) Alte Pinakothek, Munich

III ALBRECHT DÜRER 1471–1528

Born in Nuremburg, Dürer began working with his father, a goldsmith. Later he travelled round Germany, visiting Colmar, Strasbourg, Basle, Augsburg and Ulm, and studying the techniques and æsthetic aims of the great contemporary masters. He also paid two visits to Italy, staying for long periods in Venice, and spent some time in the Netherlands. Of all his contemporaries he had the closest and most fertile contacts with the best artists of his day. He established a link between the traditions of the Middle Ages and the new ideas of the Renaissance, while, with his passionate championship of the individual and tragic attitude to life, he looks forward to the coming Baroque, which may be called a 'first edition' of Romanticism. His watercolour drawing of the *Virgin with Animals* dates from the beginning of his artistic maturity. Although the painter was probably not aware of it, his Virgin is a direct descendant of the Mediterranean mother-goddess, the Magna Mater or Mother of the Animals presiding over all creation who is to be found both in archaic Greece and Mesopotamia.

Virgin with Animals

c. 1503. Pen and watercolour. 32.1 × 24.3 (12⅝ × 9½) Albertina, Vienna

IV DOMENICO THEOTOCOPOULI,
known as EL GRECO 1548–1614

Born in Crete, El Greco moved while still young to Venice where he worked in the circles of Titian, Veronese and Tintoretto. Later he settled in Toledo where he died in 1614.

Landscape of Toledo dates from the final period of El Greco's life and is characteristic of the way in which he was capable of expressing his dramatic feeling in a simple landscape as freely as in a scene of religious ecstasy or martyrdom. The harsh, violent appearance of the Castille town he had made his home is rendered with a tragic force, underlined by the hot, oppressive intensity of his greens, blues and greys. Dramatic in itself, the landscape becomes even more so through the Romantic clouds brooding sinisterly over the scene, the tense, almost unbearable, silence before the storm. The construction of the landscape, whose elements seem to mingle like metals in an alloy, has certain affinities with some works by Cézanne, particularly in the so-called Gardanne period when he built up individual forms to make a coherent structure. But here the objects and town seem about to dissolve, to be disrupted and transformed by the violence of their inner fire, almost as though they were being subjected to some form of alchemy; the architecture has become pure drama.

Landscape of Toledo

121 × 106 (45⅝ × 41¾) Metropolitan Museum, New York

V MICHELANGELO MERISI, known as CARAVAGGIO 1573–1610

Considered to have been the creator of Italian Baroque realism, which flourished in Bologna, Rome and Naples, Caravaggio saturated homely scenes, or subjects taken from the life of Christ or the saints, with enormous dramatic intensity. Though refusing to idealize figures or objects and painting with almost banal naturalism, he imbues them with a spirit of holiness so that supernatural overtones are given to apparently commonplace scenes. *The Supper at Emmaus* in the National Gallery provides us with a fine illustration of what may be called his 'super-naturalism'— his way of showing the brief movements of the soul beneath its heavy encasing of flesh. The movement of Christ's hands above this almost illusionist still-life introduces the very spirit of the miracle into a scene which in itself is entirely without nobility or mystery.

The Supper at Emmaus

c. 1605. 139 × 195 (55 × 77½) National Gallery, London

VI REMBRANDT HARMENSZ van RYN 1606–69

Rembrandt's landscapes exert an extraordinary fascination on account of their mixture of imagination and observed reality. It was his habit to make notes in ink or walnut-stain on the scenes he saw during his walks, and then to reconstruct in his studio a scene which was, at one and the same time, a reflection of his own spirit and of the spirit of the real landscape whose elements he rearranged to suit his own purposes. In fact, what distinguishes Rembrandt from the other Dutch landscape painters of the day is the fact that his landscapes are, essentially, pure creation, lyrical and passionate inventions deriving from musical as well as pictorial sources, rather than objective 'slices of life'. These are the pictures which inspire critics to talk of Rembrandt's 'fantastic realism', another way of describing his 17th-century 'Romanticism'.

Landscape with Obelisk

1638. Wood. 55 × 71 (21⅝ × 28) Isabella Stewart Gardner Museum, Boston

VII JACOB van RUISDAEL 1628–82

There are two versions of Ruisdael's *Jewish Cemetery,* one in the Gemäldegalerie, Dresden, and the one illustrated, both dating from roughly the same period. Ruisdael himself was the most illustrious member of a family of painters from Haarlem, and he exerted a tremendous influence on the evolution of Dutch landscape painting. Both pictures derive from a pen drawing from nature now in the Teyler Museum, at Haarlem. This was purely objective, but the painted versions are Romantically transmuted into an evocation of an almost supernatural atmosphere; regardless of their true position, Ruisdael groups together all the objects with the most emotional impact—the tombs, the trees twisted by the storm, the ruined church, the rainbow emerging over the wood—and arranges them with the virtuosity of Romantics like Joseph Anton Koch or Caspar David Friedrich. The result is a symphony in form and colour, so orchestrated as to create a dramatic mood, and so planned as to acquire the force of an anguished and mysterious *memento mori.*

The Jewish Cemetery

c. 1660. 42 × 89 (56 × 74) Detroit Institute of Arts

VIII ANTOINE WATTEAU 1684–1721

Of the two versions of *L'Embarquement pour Cythère*—the second, painted for Jean de Julienne and bought by Frederick II, is at Charlottenburg—this one best expresses the Romantic character of a painter in whom, as in Mozart, Rococo visibly develops into Romanticism. Watteau may have borrowed his subject from Rubens' *Gardens of Love* but he charged it with a dramatic fire quite absent from the Antwerp master's work. The moving splendour of this sunset over a park already succumbing to autumn underlines the melancholy mood of an allegory in which there is more sadness than pleasure, more despair than enthusiasm. For Watteau's disenchanted heroes Cythera is the isle of the dead rather than the isle of love, isle of a peace untroubled by both tragedy and joy. The Charlottenburg version is probably a picture of a stage scene; Watteau sometimes 'immortalized' various very popular operas or plays for the delight of enthusiasts. The Louvre picture no longer shows any traces of its origin; the music in which the whole composition is bathed comes from the subtle orchestration of forms and colours, forms which are solid without being massive and colours which are transparent, composed of light. Here Watteau's genius reached its height in the portrayal of a world both real and imaginary, where man is truly 'such stuff as dreams are made on'.

L'Embarquement pour Cythère

1717. 128 × 193 (50⅜ × 76) Musée du Louvre, Paris

II ARCHITECTURE AND SCULPTURE

ROMANTIC ARCHITECTURE is not a style; it is, even more obviously than in the other arts, a combination of many styles. Yet it would be wrong to accuse the Romantic Age of eclecticism pure and simple. Whatever it borrowed it transformed and used in new contexts, and the result is an architecture with a definite flavour of its own. Contemplating its buildings today, we can see that the contrast between Neo-Classicism and Medievalism was more apparent than real: both were the outcome of the same longing for the past, particularly for the remote sources of man's history, united with an urge to return to nature.

In their search for images to express this longing, architects went further afield than they had ever done before. Romanesque and Byzantine could claim to be part of the European tradition, but Chinese, Arabic, Egyptian and Indian were purely exotic. It is true that *chinoiserie* had been a fashion in the 18th century, but it was always used simply as decoration, never as a structural style. Only after the breakdown of the academic tradition in architecture which had lasted from the Renaissance well into the 18th century did it become possible to erect whole buildings in a style completely outside the tradition. Such examples, however, were always extreme. In general, architects worked in one or more of three styles: (1) Neo-Gothic, (2) Neo-Classical and (3) 'revolutionary'. We may conveniently deal with the last of these before discussing the other two.

The name 'revolutionary' has been applied to a group of French architects, of whom the leaders were Ledoux (1736–1806), Lequeu (1758–c. 1824) and Boullée (1728–1799), who consciously set out to create a new style, totally different from anything that had hitherto been seen. Their experiments resulted in some interesting buildings; for instance the beautiful and striking Chaux salt-works, the 'ideal city' designed by Ledoux. This was exceptional in that it was actually built—most of their designs remained on paper. In their restlessness, their taste for excess and their romantic discontent, they were true innovators, but their vision was too bold and their standards too uncompromising for them to attract disciples.

The movement leading to Neo-Gothic began in different ways in different countries. In England it was as much *survival* as *revival*. Gothic was so much a part of the landscape and of national sentiment that it was long considered the best style for churches and 'temples of learning'—that is colleges and universities. Consequently a sort of ecclesiastical and academic Gothic had continued to hold its sway even during the 17th and 18th centuries. At the same time, however, it began to be consciously enjoyed for its historical associations. The dawning of a new approach to architecture is to be found in the imitation ruins and 'follies' of the English landscape garden and in the early 'Gothick' houses of dilletanti such as Walpole. Respect for the past and an insistence on archaeological accuracy later served to damp down the vital spirit that might have made Neo-Gothic a really new art. The care and exactitude with which architects like Pugin and Scott copied medieval buildings stifled the imagination and eventually deprived their works of the 'romantic mood' that had been the original motive of their creation.

The process can easily be recognized by comparing the generation of architects working before 1825 with those that came later. No one could mistake buildings like William Adam's (1688–1748) Castle of Douglas or Robert Morris's Inverary Castle (the first fruits of Neo-Gothic in Scotland) or George Dance the Younger's (1741–1825) work on St Bartholomew the Great, London, for authentic Gothic manor-houses and churches. These architects aimed only at resuscitating medieval forms that were capable of harmonizing with the 'modern spirit'; they were not producing copies. But with the advent of Augustus Welby Pugin (1812–1852) the subject assumed a more doctrinaire significance. It now grew to be a matter of religious conviction with Pusey and the Ecclesiological Society strongly ranged on the side of Gothic. It was said that 'men over sixty remain faithful to Palladio, but those under sixty have declared for Gothic.' Pugin himself was converted to Roman Catholicism out of love for the Middle Ages, and built the church of St Augustine, Ramsgate, at his own cost. He was also interested in the symbolism of Gothic, and in 1833 published a defence of Gothic, as the only Christian architecture. This became the Bible of his disciples and his two principal imitators, Sir George Gilbert Scott (1811–1878), known as 'the greatest Goth in Europe', and Sir Charles Barry (1796–1863) who with Pugin's aid rebuilt the Houses of Parliament in the purest Perpendicular style.

In Germany the background of taste was somewhat different. Goethe in his youth had hailed Gothic as the form of architecture expressing lofty aspirations and the longing for the infinite. (In later life, under the influence of Winckelmann, he came to set a higher value on the opposite qualities—calm, simplicity and reason.) Political conditions also played their part.

The Middle Ages had been proposed as the ideal for the younger generation by Wackenroder, then by the Boisserée brothers and Goethe, and in 1828 Dürer's tercentenary celebrations set a triumphant seal on the resurrection of Gothic. But despite efforts by architects to revive and rejuvenate their borrowings from the past, the contributions to Romantic art made by such men as Georg Möller, K. von Heideloff, Schwechten, Ziebland, and K. Rösner produce only an artificial, cold effect, sometimes rather grandiose but lacking in all true originality. And yet the Germans had always remained genuinely attached to the Middle Ages, as they had never been attached to Classicism, an import from abroad which had never been thoroughly assimilated. Consequently the Gothic style was taken up with great enthusiasm as the emblem of a nationalist revival, of a new patriotic spirit, and of a new German unity.

Karl Friedrich Schinkel (1781–1841), an apparently paradoxical figure who progressed like Goethe from Gothic to Classicism, began by making designs on medieval patterns as for the Neue Petrikirche and the Mausoleum of Queen Elizabeth at Berlin and ended with pastiches of the Propylaea of the Acropolis. Although he had never been to Greece he nevertheless aspired to introduce the styles of Antiquity into the German architecture of his day despite the fact that he had previously worked hard, with a passion clearly visible in his pictures, for a revival of Gothic. During a visit to Italy (1803–1805), he was mainly attracted by 'Venetian Gothic', the 'Saracenic' monuments of Sicily and Milan cathedral. His stage designs, too, created a new medieval Germany, a fitting background for the *Sturm und Drang*

ETIENNE-LOUIS BOULLÉE 1728–99
Boullée was the oldest of the three French architects (the others being Ledoux and Lequeu) who broke with the Baroque tradition and invented new forms largely based on elementary geometrical shapes. The intention was to give expression to poetry and ideas in architecture.

1 *Entrance to a Cemetery*
Bibliothèque Nationale (Cabinet des Estampes), Paris.

CLAUDE-NICOLAS LEDOUX 1736–1806
Ledoux is the best known of this group (Ledoux, Boullée, Lequeu) since he was the only one whose architectural dreams were in part actually realized in the 'Ideal City' of Chaux. His theories and projects were published in *L'Architecture considerée sous le rapport de l'art, des mœurs et de la législation* (Paris, 1804) from which these two illustrations are taken. All his works aim at expressing definite ideas; in the Memorial this is obvious, but even in a functional building like the House of the Surveyor, the gushing water forced through a man-made arch is meant to express the victory of man over nature.

2 *Memorial in Honour of Womankind*

6 *House of the Surveyor of the Loue*

LAURENT (A. L. THOMAS) VAUDOYER 1756–1846
Vaudoyer was a pupil of Peyre. He won the *Prix de Rome* and spent several years there, followed by a highly successful career in Paris. This house was designed while he was in Rome; in it he uses the old symbolic device of a starry dome to represent heaven and the universe, supporting it on a ring of Doric columns, the earliest of the Greek orders. The illustration comes from *Annales du Musée*, Vol. II, 1802, plate 64, by C. P. Landon.

3 *Design for the House of a Cosmopolitan, Rome*

JEAN JACQUES LEQUEU 1758–1825
Lequeu was a highly imaginative architect, whose projects were indeed sometimes so fantastic that they could never have been put into practice. The tendency is poetic, often with a touch of the macabre. He drew inspiration from the most exotic and varied styles—Gothic, Chinese, Indian, Egyptian—yet, as this design shows, his architecture remained programmatic. The illustration comes from Lequeu, *Traité de l'Architecture Civile*.

4 *Monument to the Sovereignty of the People, An I de la République*
Bibliothèque Nationale (Cabinet des Estampes), Paris.

PIERRE-JULES DELESPINE or DELEPINE 1756–1825
Delespine was a pupil of M. J. Peyre and himself became a teacher at the Ecole des Beaux-Arts. He built several houses in the Rue de Rivoli, and also some commercial buildings such as a covered market. But he too was under the spell of programmatic architecture and in this design for a tomb of Isaac Newton he attempted to give expression to the physicist's achievements in a hemispherical dome, which is not only a perfect mathematical form but also fittingly expresses eternity and peace. In his own words: 'L'Académie propose un tombeau en l'honneur de Newton. Ce monument élevé a la gloire du plus grand genie doit moins respirer la magnificence que la grandeur imposante et la noble simplicité. Il sera possible de faire pressentir par une allégorie ingénieuse et analogue aux écrits du grand Newton a quel usage peut être destiné le monument qu'on propose.' The illustration is from a coloured engraving in *Prix d'Architecture* (1779–87).

5 *Design for the Tomb of Isaac Newton*

1

2

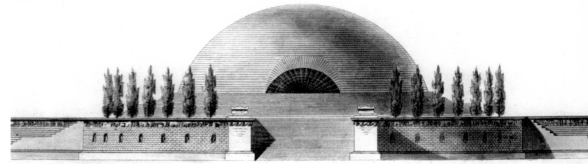

5

3

4

6

7

9

10

8

11

JAMES WYATT 1747-1813

Wyatt was an architect of great brilliance and versatility who could, and did, produce designs in either Classical, Gothic or Romano-Byzantine styles. His most outstanding and daring composition was Fonthill Abbey (1795 to 1807) which he built for the eccentric William Beckford. The octagonal tower collapsed in 1825 and the building has since been entirely demolished. Ashridge, his other great house, built for the Earl of Bridgewater, is still standing. It was begun in 1806 and finished in 1817 by Sir Jeffrey Wyattville, Wyatt's nephew. The picture of Fonthill Abbey is taken from J. P. Neale's *Views of the Seats of Noblemen and Gentlemen* and that of Ashridge from a drawing of 1813 by J. Buckler.

7 *Ashridge, Staircase Hall*

Royal Institute of British Architects.

10 *Fonthill Abbey*

CHRISTIAN JANK, EDUARD RIEDEL, GEORG DOLMAN and JULIUS HOFFMANN

The original idea for Neuschwanstein came from King Ludwig II of Bavaria, an eccentric monarch with a mania for building. The design was the work of Jank, a stage designer, and it was built, under the supervision of Riedel, Dolman and Hoffmann between 1869 and 1886. With its romantic situation, its ramparts and its towers, the principal one 197 feet high, the castle is a greatly exaggerated replica of a medieval stronghold, with a certain resemblance to the Wartburg. The interior is full of allusions to the Middle Ages, but it has a certain coolness and lack of sentimentality which indicates the approaching end of the Romantic Movement.

8 *Schloss Neuschwanstein*

HORACE WALPOLE 1717-97 and WILLIAM ROBINSON c. 1720-75

Robinson was the professional architect who supervised the actual construction of Strawberry Hill, but the conception and most of the design came from Horace Walpole and his dilettante friends. The style is 'Rococo-Gothic', the Gothic forms being used playfully, without any insistence on historical accuracy. The earlier part of the house was built between 1749 and 1754 as the centre of a landscape garden; the tower dates from 1759.

9 *Strawberry Hill*

KARL FRIEDRICH SCHINKEL 1781-1841

Schinkel received his architectural training from Friedrich Gilly. He is usually remembered as a Neo-Classicist, but he also had strong Romantic leanings, which found expression in the castles and country houses that he built for the Prussian nobility and the royal family. These are usually set in the picturesque surroundings of an 'English' landscape garden, and in their castellated style show the influence of the English Gothic revival. Schinkel had visited England in 1826. Schloss Babelsberg was designed in 1834.

11 *Schloss Babelsberg*

drama, while he composed a wealth of variations on the imaginary Egypt of Mozart's *Magic Flute*.

Despite his love and admiration for Gothic Schinkel made practically no attempt to use it for buildings. It was not that he thought it unsuitable but merely that he would have encountered practical difficulties which he imagined to be insurmountable. He maintained that the technique and tectonics of the medieval masters had been completely forgotten and it was this conviction which led him to work in a Neo-Greek style that was easier to design and carry out. The German inferiority complex with regard to authentic Gothic also accounts for the hesitation, groping and inhibitions which for so long prevented the completion of Cologne Cathedral; the more these Romantic architects admired Gothic the less they felt able to reproduce it fittingly. The Greeks, on the other hand, inspired them with no such feelings. Schinkel's Classicism was Greek, not Roman. The longing for Greek harmony led him into this direction. Perhaps he saw in Greek architecture the very elements of construction—the carrying vertical members upon which were laid the horizontal architraves; after all, he had said 'Die Architektur ist die Fortsetzung der Natur in ihrer konstruktiven Tätigkeit' (Architecture is the continuation of nature in her constructive activity). He considered it as the task of man to follow up nature (die Natur weiter zu bilden). Thus here again one must notice the desire to go back to nature, to work in close contact with her.

In France, yet other factors come into play. Here where the national temperament was as favourable to Classicism as to Gothic, the return to the Middle Ages was chiefly significant in its sentimental, political (the Middle Ages stood for the monarchy . . .), and archaeological connotations and was founded on a just evaluation of the aesthetic, technical and functional excellence of Gothic. In general the architects who 'built medievally' had previously restored churches damaged by age or the hand of man; the work of Debret on St Denis, d'Alavoine on Rouen and Duban on the Ste Chapelle had been pure reconstruction, but the style attained a creative level in the building of Ste Clotilde by Gau (1790-1853) in 1846, the Paris Hôtel de Ville by Codde and Lesueur, the Library of Ste Geneviève by Labrouste (1801-1875) and the Château de Pierrefonds, St Denis, Vézelay and Carcassonne etc., by Viollet-le-Duc (1814-1879). It was hard to distinguish copies from new inventions; the copiers made a virtue of eschewing all novelty, but by using the new iron construction techniques they were able to give an added *élan* to Gothic. Sometimes restoration and original work mingled, as in the designs of Viollet-le-Duc, who combined a pious wish to restore the original in an authentic manner with an imaginative, very personal liberty of interpretation which occasionally led him, in his idealization and worship of everything medieval, to be more Gothic than the Goths. However, his many restorations are no contribution to 19th-century architecture; they rather represent a diminution of authenticity.

The fashion for Gothic was attacked in France, however, more fiercely than in the other countries of Europe. Some of its opponents were supporters of Neo-Classicism, others were simply men who objected to the sterility of artificially reviving defunct forms; this resistance and opposition occur even in writers as Romantic as Lamartine and Michelet. In 1832 Lamartine wrote to Victor Hugo: 'Gothic is beautiful but it lacks order and light, the two basic principles for all creations which are to endure.' Probably the uses and abuses of Gothic in middle-class villas, with their crenellated towers, look-outs, spires and ogival windows provoked a reaction even in enthusiasts; in other words, they turned against Gothic because of the absurd distortions it was made to undergo. This is what Michelet meant when he declared that Gothic was a failure: 'In the name of history we protest. This heap of stones has nothing to do with history.' But despite such reactions Neo-Gothic architecture continued to flourish, and its vogue did not come to an end. During the single year 1852 two hundred Neo-Gothic churches were erected in France.

LEOPOLD EIDLITZ 1823–1908

Eidlitz was born in Prague and was one of the many European architects born and trained in Europe who went to the United States. He designed Iranistan in 1847–8 in an Indo-Moorish style for the circus magnate P. T. Barnum, who had been travelling in Europe and returned with designs and drawings from which he built another Brighton Pavilion in America. Eidlitz's work, however, is truer to its Indian sources than was Nash's.

12 *Iranistan, near Bridgeport, Connecticut*

JEAN LOUIS DESPREZ 1743–1804

Desprez was born in France, but spent most of his life in Sweden, where he designed several buildings, notably Castle Haga and the Mausoleum of Linnæus. He is more important, however, as a painter and engraver than as an architect. His work includes stage-designs, landscapes and imaginary scenes. This illustration shows his interest, which he shared with many of the Romantics, in the Egyptian style, which seemed to combine for them the macabre, the eternal, the majestic and the exotic. In his architectural drawings the influence of Piranesi is apparent, but Desprez was in general much more whimsical and Romantic.

13 *Design for a Tomb*

WILLIAM PORDEN c. 1755–1822
and **JOHN NASH** 1752–1835

The 'Indian' style, though part of the tendency towards the exotic, never became as popular as the other Oriental styles. At Brighton the so-called 'stables', now the Dome, were built for the Prince of Wales by William Porden in 1803. After 1815 Nash enlarged the pavilion, using the Indian motifs more freely and achieving an altogether more fantastic effect.

14 *Brighton Pavilion*

Probably by GIUSEPPE PATRICOLA
(active first half of 19th century)

This villa was commissioned in 1799 by King Ferdinand IV and Queen Maria Carolina after their flight from Naples. The designer was probably Patricola, an architect from Palermo about whom very little is known, but it is attributed by some to G. Maroriglia. The house, in spite of its name, is a mixture of several diverse styles, including Chinese, Turkish and—especially in the colour scheme of the decoration—Roman Pompeii, then in process of excavation. Yet the building as a whole has a Rococo lightness that makes it seem closer to Strawberry Hill than to the Brighton Pavilion.

15 *Palazzo Cinese, near Palermo*

MAURO TESI 1730–66

Tesi was not an architect but a painter and engraver of architectural subjects; he was chiefly active in Bologna, where he decorated many churches and palaces. His series of aquatints, *Raccolta di Disegni Originali di Mauro Tesi* (Bologna, 1787), from which this illustration is taken, contains theatrical designs, ideas for tombs, etc. He was particularly interested in ancient Egyptian art, and made many designs in this manner.

16 *Sepulchral Chamber*

M DE MONVILLE

Le Désert de Retz near Chambourcy was an estate owned by M de Monville who in 1771, probably with the help of Hubert Robert, laid out the gardens in the English landscape style, with numerous 'follies' and architectural fantasies. The house is built in the shape of an enormous fluted Greek column in ruins, thus combining the Romantic love of ruins with nostalgia for early Greek art. In the grounds are Gothic and Chinese buildings and an ice-house in the form of an Egyptian pyramid. The engravings are from G. L. le Rouge, *Jardins Anglo-Chinois*, Paris, 1774–89.

17, 18 *Interior and exterior of the house of M de Monville, Le Désert de Retz*

JOHN NASH 1752–1835

The great Regency architect, who in his streets and terraces contributed so much to the Neo-Classical character of London, was at the same time ready to design 'Picturesque' buildings in any of the revived styles. Blaise Hamlet (1811) is a group of small rural cottages, reminiscent of the Middle Ages, intended to evoke a primitive simplicity.

19 *Diamond Cottage, Blaise Hamlet, near Bristol*

A. J. DAVIS 1803–92

Davis worked in a fairly broad Neo-Classical manner, ranging from Greek revival to a sort of Italian Renaissance style which he called 'Tuscan'. In particular he was active in promoting the 'Picturesque', which became an important movement in America only in the 1830's. Blithewood (1834), a 'Gothic' house with gables and a tower is set in a typically 'Picturesque' landscape garden. The Gatehouse, as well as the Rustic Lodge for Llewellyn Park (c. 1852–70), is built in the rural cottage style, which Davis liked immensely and applied to many of his smaller houses. The pictures are taken from lithographs in the Metropolitan Museum, New York.

20 *Rustic Lodge, Llewellyn Park, West Orange, N.J.*

22 *Blithewood, Robert Donaldson Estate, Fishkill, N.Y.*

KARL FRIEDRICH SCHINKEL 1781–1841

The grounds of Muskau were laid out by its owner, Prince Pückler, on the model of the landscape gardens of England, where he had travelled widely. In 1834 he published a book on the subject, with illustrations by the painter W. Schirmer of the Muskau house and park: *Andeutungen über Landschaftsgärtnerei*, Stuttgart, 1834 (the illustration shown here is plate 10). Schinkel erected several small buildings from 1822 onwards, but the castle itself, which he also designed, was never built. Friedrich Förster said, however, that to walk through the gardens of Muskau was like walking through a picture-gallery full of paintings by Claude, Poussin and Ruisdael.

21 *View of the Castle at Muskau*

12

15

13

14

16

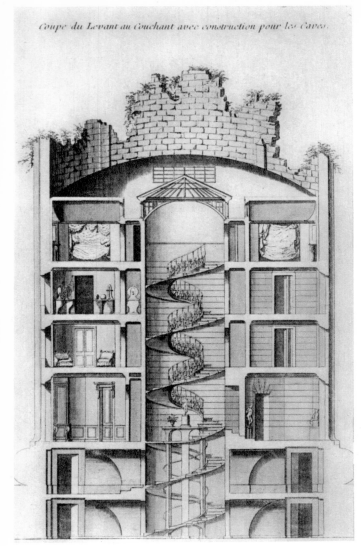

Coupe du Levant au Couchant avec construction pour les Caves.

17

19

20

18

21

22

25

23

26

24

27

30

28

31

29

32

UNKNOWN ARCHITECT

In the third quarter of the 18th century the estate was 'improved' by the then owner, Sir Harry Englefield. In 1798 it was bought by the Duke of Marlborough and it is to him that it owed the 'peculiar character of varied loveliness and splendid decoration' for which it was noted. It abounded in rustic buildings, and showed vividly the Romantic longing for nature and desire to return to rural simplicity. The illustration is taken from Mrs Hofland, *Descriptive Account of the Mansions and Gardens of White Knights*, illustrated by T. C. Hofland (London, 1819).

23 *'Round Seat' from White Knights, near Reading*

CHARLES HAMILTON

The gardens of Pains Hill were 'improved' by their owner Charles Hamilton from 1750 onwards and are an excellent example of the 'Picturesque' landscape garden, of which few survive. This type of garden, modelled on the paintings of Claude, Salvator Rosa and Gaspar Poussin, is the most characteristic English contribution to the arts of the 18th century and, as the 'English Garden', has spread all over Europe. Pains Hill, like other such gardens, is carefully laid out, though it looks so natural, every clump of trees carefully planted and spaced. Such gardens are usually dotted with summer-houses in various styles, Gothic, Grecian, Chinese, etc.

24 *Pains Hill, Cobham, Surrey*

WILLIAM CHAMBERS 1723–96

This great and important architect is known mainly for his Neo-Classical buildings, such as Somerset House. There was, however, another more exotic side to his imagination. In 1757 he brought out *Designs for Chinese Buildings,* and in Kew Gardens he designed not only the pagoda shown here but a Roman arch, a mosque and a classical temple, thus creating a sort of world in miniature not unlike the one that Hadrian had in his villa at Tivoli. The illustration comes from his *Plans of the Gardens and Buildings at Kew in Surrey*, 1763.

25 *Chinese Pagoda, Kew Gardens*

F. J. BELANGER 1744–1818

Buildings that were designed as part of an English landscape garden had to conform to the standards of the 'Picturesque', as does this 'folie' built by Belanger for M de Saint-James between 1782 and 1787. The Romantic passion for the primitive is given expression in the combination of wild nature and very early architecture. For temples the Doric order was considered the most suitable since it was the earliest of the Greek orders and therefore most in keeping with nature. The rustic vault formed of unhewn stones is also characteristic of the current attempt to avoid all artificiality.

26 *Folie de Saint-James*

GIOVANNI BATTISTA PIRANESI 1720–78

Piranesi was a practising architect, but his buildings were insignificant compared with his achievements as an engraver. He was born in Venice and later moved to Rome, where he was fascinated by the surviving monuments, succeeding wonderfully in conveying their grandeur and ruined magnificence. Their high vaults, arches, columns and piers provide the inspiration for many of his own inventions. The *Carceri* (c. 1745, reworked 1761) are full of imaginative fantasy, conveying an effect of sinister gloom with great dramatic power.

27 *Etching from the 'Carceri'*

KARL FRIEDRICH SCHINKEL 1781–1841

Schinkel was a stage designer before becoming an architect, and until 1815 worked almost exclusively for the theatre. Possibly he was drawn to it by his early love of painting, but the scope it gave to the poetic imagination no doubt attracted him also. The fairy tale setting of *Ondine* and the medieval atmosphere of Kleist's play exactly suited his romantic spirit. The illustrations shown here are taken from *Sammlung von Theater-Dekorationen erfunden von Schinkel:* published in Potsdam in 1849.
Ondine plate 12, *Kätchen von Heilbronn* plate 11.

28 *Stage Design for 'Kätchen von Heilbronn'*

32 *Stage Design for 'Ondine'*

J. M. GANDY 1771–1843

Born in England, Gandy was trained as an architect and made an extensive Italian tour which came to a sudden end in 1798. His architectural practice was always modest, and he is chiefly known as the assistant and draughtsman of Sir John Soane, whose works he portrayed in rather grandiose watercolours. He also made drawings for vast imaginary buildings which he could have had no hope of ever seeing actually built, and has for this reason been called 'the English Piranesi'. The illustration shown here is one of a series of watercolours.

29 *Design for an Imperial Palace*

Royal Institute of British Architects, London

HUBERT ROBERT 1773–1808, attributed to

Robert began as a sculptor, but in later life worked only as a painter and draughtsman. Like most of his contemporaries he went on the grand tour to Italy and was so fascinated by the country that he stayed there many years, drawing and sketching the Italian landscape, its ruins and ancient remains, its gardens and fountains, avenues and statues. In the company of the painter Fragonard and the dilettante Abbé St Non he travelled to Naples and Sicily. St Non later published an account of this tour under the title *Voyage Pittoresque de Naples et de Sicile*. In 1765 Robert returned to France, but continued to paint mostly the same subjects, basing them on his earlier sketches.

30 *Ruins in a Landscape*

Royal Institute of British Architects, London

H. CUTHBERT active 1852–77

Cuthbert was a stage designer who worked in London at Covent Garden, Drury Lane and the Princess's Theatre. He is known to have designed the sets for several of Charles Kean's Shakespearean productions, including *King John* (1852), *Macbeth* (1853) and *Hamlet* (1858). This illustration shows the courtyard of Elsinore (*Hamlet,* Act I, Scenes 1 and 4). Cuthbert was undoubtedly of great help to Kean in conveying the atmosphere of the plays and in achieving historical accuracy.

31 *Stage Design for 'Hamlet'*

Victoria and Albert Museum, London

The European 'resurrection' of Gothic may be at least partly accounted for as a nostalgic return to art-forms long forgotten or rejected—one facet of the subsurgence of national feeling after its long sleep throughout the 18th century. But these explanations are by no means applicable to the United States which had no such past, no roots from which this revival could have sprung. Why should a new country, inhabited by a new people, enthusiastically take up the models offered by European Gothic, instead of creating its own forms and style? The answer is that before breeding its own architects America remained an offspring of Europe, and it was Englishmen such as Latrobe (1764–1820) or Frenchmen such as Godefroy (1789–1833) who introduced Romanticism into the New World.

Neo-Classicism had its partisans too and Latrobe himself was broad-minded enough to put forward two suggestions, one Classical, one Neo-Gothic, in the 1805 competition for the Cathedral of Baltimore. In preference to unity of style American architects strove towards an eclecticism of greater or lesser extravagance, the most characteristic products being Nutt's Folly by Samuel Sloan or Trollope's Folly in which Classical, Gothic, Turkish and Venetian styles all rub shoulders together. On the other hand the medieval churches of Upjohn (1802–1878) and Ishiel Town (1784–1844) are timid and unoriginal pastiches, for reasons similar to those which enervated Ste Clotilde in Paris and the Neo-Romanesque churches which sprang up all over Germany under Wilhelm I; in general, however, the Americans were less interested in archaeology than European architects. Their originality is seen less in completely creative works than in amalgams of styles by no means obviously akin, as in the villas built by Town and Davis (1803–1892) between 1830 and 1850.

One of the reasons why Gothic was bound, of necessity, to survive in America was that, as in England, it had always been associated with religion and education, as being the ecclesiastical and academic style *par excellence*. But from churches and universities artificial medievalism passed on to purely functional buildings. There may have been a certain justification for modelling the Smithsonian Institute (1852, Robert Dale Owen, Robert Mills, James Renwick) on an Anglo-Norman fortress, for constructing a new Westminster Abbey in Yale (1840, Town and Davis) and for sprinkling the Wadsworth Athenaeum at Hartford with square towers and Tudor windows, all these buildings coming perhaps under the heading of 'academic Gothic'. But that the Boston railway station should have been built in 1847 as a Rhenish castle complete with keep and watchtower seems merely absurd. However, it is a measure of the intense fascination exercised by Gothic at this time, even on the pioneers of the New World.

SCULPTURE

ART-CRITICS, probably influenced by the categorical condemnations of two such eminent Romantics as Théophile Gautier and Madame de Staël, tend to be unjustly severe on Romantic sculpture. Gautier maintained that 'of all the arts the one which lends itself least to Romantic expression is certainly sculpture. It seems to have reached its definitive form in Antiquity. Every sculptor is of necessity Classical; at bottom he is always an adherent of the Religion of Olympus.' For her part Madame de Staël perceived an inherent incompatibility between sculpture, which she called a pagan art, and painting, the Christian art *par excellence*.

It is, of course, true that sculptors received a long-lasting impetus from Neo-Classicism, particularly in France and England; in funerary art, however, the

THOMAS BANKS 1735–1805

It was in Rome, where he lived for seven years and met Fuseli, David and Wright, that Banks executed this group of *Thetis and her Nymphs,* in which Rococo merges into Romanticism. He was a man of vast culture whose aim was to equal Greek sculpture; moreover he was one of the most active exponents of the 'Gothic Revival', cultivating a synthesis of Classicism and Romanticism which can be seen in all his works.

33 *Thetis and her Nymphs Consoling Achilles*

1778. Marble bas-relief, oval.
91.5 × 119.8 × 9 (36 × 46¼ × 3¾)
Victoria and Albert Museum, London

JEAN BERNARD DUSEIGNEUR,
known as JEHAN 1808–66

Duseigneur was fêted by his contemporaries as the 'Victor Hugo of Sculpture'. Unfortunately his fame was confined to most limited Romantic circles and he had to sacrifice his standards in order to make a living; he ended his life as a most conventional sculptor, executing official commissions. His *Orlando Furioso* belongs to his best period and is his masterpiece.

34 *Orlando Furioso*

1867 (the plaster model dates from 1831). Bronze
130 × 146 (51¼ × 57½)
Musée du Louvre, Paris

HIRAM POWERS 1805–73

This sculptor belonged to a group of American artists who frequently sought inspiration and guidance in Italy; Henry James called them 'the white marmorean flock'. Powers was still strongly attracted by the academic tradition and use of mythology, but he was equally inclined towards a forceful, direct realism. Before becoming a maker of wax models for the Dorfeille Museum he had been a shop assistant. He went to Italy in 1837 and stayed there till his death.

35 *Proserpine*

Marble. h. 50 (19½)
Collection of the Newark Museum, Newark, New Jersey

WILLIAM WETMORE STORY 1819–95

Like Powers, Story lived in Italy, where he was friendly with Robert Browning; he worked in Rome and Florence, producing a very large number of busts and statues in a rather cold, but sometimes energetic, style.

36 *Venus*

1864. Marble. h. 100 (39½)
Museum of Fine Arts, Boston

33

35

34

36

37

38

39

40

41

BENGT ERLAND FOGELBERG 1786–1854

After studying in Stockholm, Fogelberg lived first in Paris and then in Italy among the circle surrounding Thorwaldsen. As a result he became one of the motive forces behind the artistic revival in Sweden with its resurrection of Gothic and the ancient Scandinavian gods. Nevertheless his mythological lyricism is restrained by a sort of Classical 'temperance'.

37 *The God Thor*

Plaster. h. 67 (26⅜)
Nationalmuseum, Stockholm
Study for the large statue of Thor executed in Rome in 1840

WILLIAM RIMMER 1816–1879

A doctor and enthusiastic anatomist, Rimmer dissected numerous corpses before applying this knowledge to sculpture. His realism was so exact that when his *Gladiator* was exhibited in 1861 the critics thought that he had taken casts from a living model. He also sculpted directly in granite in a similar style.

38 *Female Head*

Marble. h. 48.5 (19″)
Corcoran Gallery of Arts, Washington

FRANÇOIS RUDE 1784–1855

Rude's idealistic and Republican opinions are reflected in his work. He refused to go to Italy for fear that it would contaminate his taut, vigorous realism with its academicism. The subject of this monument was given him by the commanding officer of the grenadiers of the Imperial Guard who had commissioned it, but refused it as unacceptable when it was finished.

39 *The Imperial Eagle Watching over Napoleon*

1845. Bronze. 29×54×29 (11⅜×21¼×11⅜)
Musée des Beaux Arts, Dijon

ANTOINE AUGUSTIN (AUGUSTE) PRÉAULT 1810–79

By temperament violent and given to excess, drawn towards the 'infinite', Préault produced works of a tragic and cruel character which were rejected by Salons and Academies alike. His life was passed in extreme, and often bitter, solitude; like Pierre Puget, he thirsted for 'large works' to the extent of longing to 'sculpt mountains'.

40 *Massacre*

1834. Bronze bas-relief. 109×140 (43×55½)
Musée de Chartres

FÉLICIE DE FAUVEAU 1799–86

Two passions dominated Félicie de Fauveau's life: sculpture and politics. She was a fervent Royalist and took part in the machinations of the Vendée. She remained single in order to devote herself to her art, but this art, which she had intended to be 'monumental', remains distinctly 'troubadour' in its tendencies and is weighted down with a wealth of anecdotal details. Her sculpture reflects a nostalgic, distorted Medievalism.

41 *Queen Christine of Sweden Refusing to Spare her Equerry Monaldeschi*

Haut-relief in terra cotta and coloured plaster 34×54 (13⅜×21¼)
Musée de Louviers

monument to Nelson in St Paul's by John Flaxman (1755–1826) and the tomb of Sir Eyre Coote at Westminster by Thomas Banks (1735–1805) bear witness to the birth of a new spirit which shines through their dry Canovan style. In line with the tradition whereby England, incapable of breeding her own sculptors, borrowed them from Italy, Holland or France, 'English' sculpture since the Renaissance had been represented by such men as Torrigiani, Le Sueur, Grinling Gibbons and Roubiliac. Authentic Britons such as Nollekens, Wilton and Bacon continued to produce scholarly but self-inhibiting imitations of classical models.

There is more originality in certain Germans—Gottfried Schadow (1764–1850), Christian Rauch (1777–1857), Ernst Rietschel (1804–1861); but even their Romanticism falls far short of that of their painter-compatriots and one looks in vain for a sculptor-genius comparable with Friedrich or Runge. France, on the other hand, produced Romantic works of real originality and vigour. Despite resistance from public taste, schools and academies (which remained pugnaciously Classical) and the selection committees of the *salons* which refused to exhibit these revolutionaries, the first half of the 19th century saw the rise of a number of important sculptors as Romantic in spirit and expression as the poet Hugo or the painter Delacroix. It is true that they were influenced by poetry and painting; their outlook was contaminated by a certain 'pictorialism' and they deliberately turned their backs on pure sculpture. But their works provided a welcome reaction against the all-pervading 'pretty little' statuettes in biscuit porcelain or bronze which filled French interiors of the day.

In the very efforts of the Romantic sculptors to obtain effects apparently possible only in painting, one senses a salutary attempt to broaden the scope of sculpture. The fantastic bas-reliefs of Antonin Moine (1796-1849) are wholly un-sculptural; *Goblins Abroad* (1831, Musée des Beaux-Arts, Rouen), *Gnomes Fighting* (1835), *Witches' Sabbath* (1833), the favourite themes of an artist who felt so foreign to his age that in 1849 he killed himself in order to escape from it—these subjects call to mind the engravings of Louis Boulanger, Devéria or Gustave Courbet. Unlike Moine, Félicie de Fauveau (1799–1886) enjoyed a long life and lasting success despite the extravagance of the composition which won her fame, a *Monument to Dante* covered with columns, rosettes, ridge ornaments, gargoyles, spires, and symbolic or allegorical ornaments which would take a volume to describe: the 'monument' itself was hardly more than 6 ft 6 ins tall.

Jehan Duseigneur (1808–1866) was a likeable man whose work, like his clothes— he always wore a velvet doublet—contained a curious mixture of serious Romanticism and 'troubadour' tinkerings. 'Troubadour' was the epithet given to a sort of bastard Gothic in which the monumental was reduced to a minute scale, serious emotion became affectation and sentiment slid into sentimentality. Unfortunately Duseigneur had more ambition than talent, more dreams than ability to realize them. His most genuine and vigorous work is the *Orlando Furioso* of 1831, now in the Louvre.

A more interesting artist, making no concessions to the artificiality which was often a feature of Romantic sculpture, Antoine Augustin Préault (1810–1879) was sombre and violent by nature and attempted to make his works express his rather revolutionary social ideas. In opposition to the spirit of the age, which favoured miniature statuettes, knick-knacks and curios, so that even large-scale works were often treated with an attention to minute detail and cultivation of the picturesque which reduced them to the level of toys, Préault's passion for all that was large-scale and monumental was such that mountains would have provided him with the ideal sculptural subject. His *Slaughter* in the Museum at Chartres is characteristic of the ideals of an artist who could say: 'Not for me the finite but the infinite', and who was spurred on by an ambition to enclose the limitless forms of the soul within visible bounds.

François Rude (1784–1855) was as powerful as Préault but less of a visionary; his Napoleonic, social lyricism is both simple and robust. At his best with the visible and tangible, he felt ill at ease with products of the imagination and his *Napoleon Awakening to Immortality* in the Louvre is clumsy and awkward. But his attempt to combine inexpressible dreams with plastic reality made him the direct precursor of Auguste Rodin (1840–1917) whose Post-Romantic *Monument to Work* and *Gate of Hell* (1880–1917, Musée Rodin, Paris), both saturated with 'literary' qualities, are reminiscent of the sociological Romanticism already strongly expressed by Graillon, the poet of the humble and oppressed.

Since Classical Rome, sculpture had hardly ever been used as a weapon of satire. It was left to two Romantics, Jean Pierre Dantan (1800–1869) and Honoré Daumier (1808–1879), to restore the statuette to its position in the political satirist's arsenal. During the same period Antoine Louis Barye (1796–1875) gave a transfusion of Orientalism (to be discussed later at greater length) to animal sculpture. At the other end of the scale David d'Angers (1788–1856) was practising a theatrical species of Realism while James Pradier (1792–1852) is notable only for the superficial grace of his work. Barye is a true Romantic in the hectic honesty of his animals, shown at the crucial moments of battles or death-scenes; he depicted Romantic struggles between an elephant and a tiger, a lion and a snake and was criticized by David for 'not conceiving his animals philosophically'. A careful observer of nature, like his pupil Julie Charpentier, Barye showed his animal models as heroes of a dramatic epic of super-real dimensions.

ENGLISH ROMANTIC PAINTING grew out of a far-reaching transformation of the English feeling for nature. From now on Nature was to be shown without artifice, without 'literary' programme; in it the Romantics sought only the poetry of truth. Though some artists still went to Italy to perform the traditional 'grand tour', others repudiated this time-honoured obligation and almost all found their chief inspiration in the English landscape, an inexhaustible source of artistic interest and joy, of pure delight for the heart and the senses. Moreover English Romanticism drew added sustenance from supernatural, irrational, fantastic and fairy-tale qualities which are a constant of the British character and from its inbred saturation with the poetry of Milton, Shakespeare and the Bible; to these were added Macpherson's Ossian as soon as that famous literary hoax was published, and Percy's gloomy *Reliques*.

Thus two elements of equal importance, a genuine, immediate and sincere appreciation of nature and a translation, often unconscious, of literary into pictorial poetry, combined to mould the personality of the first Romantics, in particular William Blake, John Martin and John Flaxman. (Although the stated ambition of the last-named was to be a Classical painter, his vibrant compositions after Dante and Aeschylus are in a graphic Romantic style comparable with that of Carstens.) The example and teaching of Fuseli, the Swiss artist living in England, also gave a strong impetus to English Romanticism.

When William Blake (1757-1827) said 'the world of imagination is the world of eternity', he was in effect defining the essential character of both his art and himself. For him there was indeed no barrier between truth and illusion, experience and invention, nature and super-nature. He was on familiar visiting terms with the characters of the Bible; King David made a habit of coming in through his window, he was once present at the funeral of a fairy and on another occasion, to his horror and disgust, a ghost appeared to him. Both as a man and as an artist ('the supreme man is the artist, the prophet is the man of imagination') he was convinced of the integral unity of a universe from which he banished all intellectually created distinctions between true and false. But as well as being a visionary he was a skilful, zealous, even passionate technician; he invented a new engraving technique for use in his own books so that the illustrations and poems could make up an organic and visual whole. He also experimented with numerous media, from smooth-flowing watercolour to a thick, almost granular paste, claiming that some of the formulae were dictated to him by angels or prophets of Israel.

Throughout his life he was an avid reader of Chaucer, Milton and the Bible and a disciple of Boehme, Swedenborg and Paracelsus; ten years before his death he learned Italian in order to be able to read Dante in the original. If he was totally inexperienced and unqualified in the practical affairs of life, not to say abnormal in his efforts to adapt himself to them, it was because his whole attention was claimed by the invisible and the imaginary. His kingdom began where other men's ends; it is easy to see why he was misunderstood, left almost destitute and, thanks to his moody character, almost without protectors and friends.

The most striking quality of his art is its deep, essential honesty, the perfect objectivity with which he portrays his inspired fantasy. Blake's figures have a classical beauty close to those of Carstens and Flaxman, a purity of line reminiscent of Ingres. Profound mysteries are brought out into the bright light of day, without disguise, without chiaroscuro; Blake had the courage to approach the most intimidating aspects of the supernatural with the simplicity of a child. Convinced of the absolute reality of his visions, which to him represented 'the truth', he portrayed them in a pictorial idiom which Raphael or Michelangelo would have recognized as valid. There is nothing in common between his style and that of Odilon Redon, for instance, which he would have considered to disguise the truth rather than reveal it; his angels communicating with mankind take on the sinuous grace of Prud'hon's girl-figures. Occasionally his pictures are reminiscent of Botticelli's drawings illustrating the *Divina Commedia* and his *Satan Watching Adam and Eve* (1808, Museum of Fine Arts, Boston) calls to mind the idyllic idealism of Philipp Otto Runge's *The Times of Day*, e.g. *Morning* (Kunsthalle, Hamburg).

The figures themselves may be cold and static but this is offset by the extraordinary movement which runs through the compositions as a whole; the play of curves and balancing counter-curves in the rapid passages of his undulating forms almost succeeds in conveying cosmic energy itself; each stroke has an autonomous vitality, at once supple and tender like a musical phrase. Thus he manages to maintain a balance between the text of his poems, pulsating with a Biblical lyricism, often emphatic, rhetorical and weighted down with obscure symbols, and their translucent visual version, mostly achieved with superb economy of means and often reduced to a magnificent interplay of pure lines.

In this Blake somewhat resembled John Martin (1789–1854) although Martin was prevented from attaining a classical balance by the taste for excess which gives an overtone of extraordinary fantasy to his paintings, mezzotints and illustrations to *Paradise Lost*; the last-named are the only works of his generally known since his pictures are not easily accessible. Particularly attracted towards representations of the bizarre and extraordinary, which he brought to a strange but fascinating perfection, Martin specialized in apocalyptic visions, whether taken from real episodes of ancient history, as in *Marius Meditating on the Ruins of Carthage* and *Sadak in Search of the Waters of Oblivion* (1812, Southampton Art Gallery) or from the Miltonic struggle between the legions of the damned and the angels. As he portrays them the endless halls of Lucifer's subterranean palace have the same architecture as the colonnades of Carthage; in both the architectural perspectives are set in a gloomy vastness lit by thousands of candles and fade mysteriously away into the distance. His hell is a labyrinth of grottoes illuminated by murky lights, of rocky vaults extending beyond the scope of the eye, of seas whose waves leap up to extraordinary heights. Giant candelabra light up Dante's '*città dolente*', which sometimes resembles a monstrous stage peopled by hordes of demons. There is a striking contrast between these chasms where space closes in on itself like a huge shell and the broad landscapes, bathed in sunlight, of the Earthly Paradise where walk the Chosen. Although the antique nudity of his handsome Satan wearing a Greek soldier's helmet makes one think of the Classical heroes of Flaxman or

GEORGE ROMNEY 1734–1802

His reputation as a portraitist should not obscure the fact that Romney also produced dramatic compositions, generally taken from Shakespeare and Milton. His Romanticism is marked by a strong tendency towards the supernatural and fantastic.

1 *Nature Unveiling Herself to Shakespeare*

1786. Pen and wash. 25.7×40 (10⅛×15¾)
Royal Institution of Cornwall, Truro

ALEXANDER RUNCIMAN 1736–85

The son of a Scottish architect, Runciman was strongly influenced by the Italians, Michelangelo and the Mannerists. He was a friend of Fuseli and owed his celebrity principally to his Ossianic Cupola for Penicuik House, no longer in existence.

2 *Fingal Engaging the Spirit of Loda*

Pen and wash. 41.2×52 (16¼×21½)
National Gallery of Scotland, Edinburgh

SIR JOHN EVERETT MILLAIS 1829–96

With Rossetti and Holman Hunt, Millais founded the Pre-Raphaelite Brotherhood in 1848. Known principally for his portraits and genre paintings, he was one of the staunchest advocates of the return to the simplicity and sincerity of the primitives for which all the Pre-Raphaelites yearned.

3 Study for *The Flood*

1849/50. Pencil, pen and wash.
24×41.6 (9½×16⅜)
British Museum, London

WILLIAM BLAKE see p. 74

4 Study for *America*

c. 1793. Pen and ink lightly touched with watercolour.
29.3×17 (11⅝×6⅝)
British Museum, London

DANTE GABRIEL ROSSETTI p. 86

5 Illustration to Poe's *The Raven*

1846. Pencil, pen and brown ink. 33.6×22.8 (13¼×9)
Charles Alexander Monro Collection, England

1

4

2

3

5

6

7

8

9

10

Fuseli's Nibelungen, the fallen angel's wild, desperate eyes are typically Miltonic and Romantic.

As aforesaid, Milton and Shakespeare were the strongest literary influences on the English Romantic painters. George Romney (1734–1802) the great portraitist, depicted Milton after his blindness, dictating his poems to his daughters, but in general it was Shakespeare who provided the richest sources of material. *King Lear in the Storm* (1767, National Gallery of Scotland) by John Runciman (1744–1768) is one of the best examples of this pictorial Shakespearianism, but it can be found to an equal extent in painters as un-English as Delacroix, Carstens, Koch and Fuseli. Richard Westall (1765–1836) and H. Cuthbert (worked 1858–1877) also based their best works on the great Elizabethan dramatist and derived their most brilliant inspirations from him. However Richard Parkes Bonington (1801–1828), much admired by the French, on whom, as one of the most discerning and refined landscapists of the period, he had a profound influence, derived only a sort of 'troubadour' grace from this Shakespearianism, while, as a history painter, Bonington went for preference to episodes from the Renaissance or Middle Ages for inspiration. David Scott (1806–1849) revealed a serious, dramatic strength, particularly in his grim picture of the Russians burying their dead.

John Copley (1737–1815) and Benjamin West (1738–1820), both outstanding history painters, belong to American rather than English art but John Hamilton Mortimer's (1741–1779) *Hercules Killing the Hydra*, William Etty's (1787–1849) *Hero Expiring on the Body of Leander* (Coll. Mrs E. J. Britton) and Benjamin Haydon's (1786–1846) pictures, appreciated in his day and still much discussed, are significant minor Romantic works, although it would be wrong to judge them on the highest level. Joseph Wright, known as Wright of Derby (1734–1797) belongs perhaps more to the 18th century than to Romanticism, although his *Virgil's Tomb by Moonlight* (1779, Coll. Colonel Crompton-Inglefield) is in the true Romantic spirit.

More interesting and less well known are the animal portraitists. Animal portraiture had begun to flourish in the 17th or 18th centuries due to the famous English love of dogs and horses, and Francis Barlow (1626–1702), James Seymour (1702–1752) and John Wootton (c. 1686–1765) are justly admired; but only Romanticism could produce truly excellent horse-painters like Sawrey Gilpin (1733–1807) and James Ward (1769–1859), and at least one genius in this field: George Stubbs (1724–1806).

Stubbs wrote two learned technical works on the anatomy of the horse and the comparative anatomy of man and animals, worked as an engraver and was employed by Josiah Wedgwood to make enamelled pottery plaques. His vision of the animal world was essentially dramatic, like that of Delacroix, Géricault and Barye after him, and like Goya, Gros and Fuseli, he was struck by the 'magical nature' of the horse, by its almost supernatural mystery which made it something akin to a god in Germanic mythology. His masterpiece is the series of three pictures representing a fight between a horse and a lion which he is said to have painted after being present at a similar fight during a visit to Morocco in 1755. The last of the three was copied by Géricault. The most striking is in the Walker Art Gallery, Liverpool: in a landscape of rocky gorges half plunged in darkness— harmonizing magnificently with the fear and anguish of the main protagonist— appears the horse, a luminous white, like a sun-creature, while the lion, crouched in the half-darkness from which he is about to spring, gives the impression of being an agent of the night, terrifying, and hellish. Seeing him the horse rears and snorts, gripped by a sort of sacred terror. The contrast between the horse's dazzling whiteness, balanced by the silvery pearl of a cloud in the sky, and the darkness symbolizing death, gives this scene a tragic emphasis rarely equalled in Romantic painting. Even Delacroix' *Sardanapalus*, with its horses being sacrificed by black slaves, fails to reveal the 'personality' of the animals with anything like the same power. The twitch of the horse's skin, his tautened muscles, his mane tossed by the wind and eyes full of anguish, recall the beautiful horses of Baldung Grien's engravings or the soldier's palfrey in Dürer's *Knight, Death and the Devil*. Another remarkable work by Stubbs is his enigmatic picture of two monkeys, *A Baboon and an Albino Macaque Monkey* (c. 1770, Royal College of Surgeons of England). Here his aim seems to have been to catch the moment where animal nature approaches very near to that of human beings, where the attitudes and movements of the monkeys are 'almost human'. In this picture Stubbs, guided almost by Poe's feeling for the grotesque, achieves something less trivial than animal-painting, something more like an invasion of the mysterious territory of the subconscious. However, Ward almost rivals him with his pathetic pictures of *A Horse Fighting a Boa* (1803, Private Collection) and *The Fall of Phaeton* (Lord Camrose Collection), both infused with an extraordinary wildness of spirit.

The two most important influences on English landscape painting were, on the one hand, the landscape itself with its distinctive features, and, on the other, a sort of cult of Claude Lorrain practised by English art-lovers. Probably they would not have become so passionately enamoured of this painter had they not detected in him a sensibility similar to their own, a conception of the sublime and the pictorially beautiful which had already exercised a profound influence on garden design, before ever being applied to painting. The truly Romantic musicality of Claude's paintings and the way his landscapes float in a supernatural atmosphere, so that one can almost feel the presence of the gods—all this is allied to Shaftesbury's philosophical theories which caused the 18th century to push the metaphysical idea of a pantheist universe to the point where it became a positive deification of nature. In addition, Berkeley's 'practical dream' had called in question the reality of matter and of experience. England had never felt strongly, innately sympathetic towards the artificiality of Neo-Classicism, which even in its hey-day had failed to take root and was now outmoded. The 'picturesque' was far more accessible and more admired than aesthetic perfection and it fostered a whole generation of landscape gardeners creating Romantic 'follies' for gentlemen's parks, lovers of Neo-Gothic who expanded their architectural fantasies and archaeological paradoxes to fit the scale of buildings like Fonthill and Strawberry Hill, castle-size and extravagant both in their conception and in their form. Price's definition of the picturesque as 'roughness, irregularity, continual variation of forms, colours, light and sound' throws an interesting light on the innate English taste for fantasy, instinct—for nonsense, even—a by-product of the spirit of liberty, of autonomy that makes every Englishman sufficient unto himself.

It is very interesting to examine to what extent and by what means Claude's works in English collections inspired the first landscape-gardeners to revolt against formal gardens and topiary, with their shaped bushes and straight walks. Almost certainly Chambers, Kent, Lancelot Brown, Whately and their non-professional disciples Walpole, Hamilton and Lyttelton detected a harmonious mixture of sublime and picturesque elements in Claude's pictures. Even when Richard Wilson (1714–1782), a Welshman who remained unknown to the wider public and misunderstood by art lovers, was painting the country round Rome he brought to his work an English nostalgia which cast a curiously Anglo-Saxon veil over the Italian scene. On his return to England, on the other hand, he grafted an Italian atmosphere on to the English scene. However, it is clearly the memory of Claude's powerful and harmonious organization which helps him to organize and reconcile these anglicisms and italianisms.

Edward Calvert (1799–1883), a friend of Palmer who attempted a metaphysical interpretation of the English landscape, and Francis Danby (1793–1861) who was for a time John Martin's rival in the so-called 'fantastic genre', are good examples of this assimilation, at a deep level, of objective nature, everyday scenes, and influences from earlier Continental artists; the two sides counterbalance each other, whereas a too exclusive attachment to French or Italian technique would probably have tied down these English artists to a servile and sterile imitation of the past.

Even when Nature is the only inspiration of the English landscapists, their way of looking at it is clearly related to Claude and they still, during the early period at least, prefer views which have something in common with the beauty portrayed by him. In making it a condition of the bequest of his pictures that one of his landscapes should be exhibited between two pictures by Claude, Turner indicated how much creative impulse he had derived from the example of the painter with whom he felt such a strong affinity.

Although the English landscape in general becomes, like a Claude picture, a composition in which the real is organised in a poetic and musical fashion, there are two quite separate methods of achieving this. Adherents of the first merely detected and reproduced the poetic reality within the objective appearance of the scene: this school included the early English Romantics Richard Wilson, John Crome, known as Old Crome, and the Norwich School which derived from him. The second group envisaged landscape as fantastic-pathetic creation, either interpreted or wholly imagined. It included men of very different temperaments and talents—Gainsborough and Palmer, Constable and Turner. With the first group the accent is on objectivity; with the second the vision is so subjective that sometimes, with Turner, it almost turns into a kind of unreality or abstraction, and the actual subject of the picture either disappears or becomes unimportant.

Old Crome (1768–1821) probably had more in common, both aesthetically and temperamentally, with the Dutch painters than with Claude, but the example of Ruisdael and Hobbema helped him to find himself and his best works are, of course, those which are most characteristic of himself alone, for example *The Poringland Oak* (c. 1818, National Gallery, London) or *Moonrise on the Marshes of the Yare* (c. 1808, National Gallery, London). These pictures have a quality absent in Wilson although the latter's *Cader Idris* (c. 1774, National Gallery, London) attains to an impressive grandeur which always escapes the more familiar style of Crome. It is easy to understand why Constable said that Wilson's landscapes dwelt in his mind like 'delicious dreams'.

The early Romantics first declared their independence of Italianism by completely eliminating historical or mythological characters or replacing them with English peasants and countryfolk. The few figures from the *Odyssey* and *Aeneid* retained by Turner merely served to intensify his own Romanticism by grafting on to it a certain Romantic vision of antiquity. Wilson had himself observed (and in this was supported by Reynolds) that only an unreal landscape could contain unreal characters.

But one is bound to ask: 'What is reality?' for artists seem to have envisaged it and expressed it in so many different ways. At first sight it would seem that Thomas Gainsborough (1727–1788) submitted his landscapes to the same process of idealization as his portraits; he starts by observing objectively, then looks for the essence of the thing observed (the view or the face) and finally saturates the whole picture with a romantic, dreamy, melancholic or pathetic atmosphere characteristic of his own temperament. He casts a fairy-like grace over the figures, transforming them into something 'rich and strange', simultaneously aristocratic, lyrical and Romantic. But when he set about composing a landscape picture he was not in fact content with merely seeking after nature; he constructed it according to synthetic hallucinatory techniques of the same kind as those advocated by Leonardo da Vinci, the Chinese painters and Hokusaï. Reynolds writes that he saw in Gainsborough's studio curious models made with blades of grass, lumps of moss, twigs, pebbles and pieces of looking-glass; with the aid of these models, which probably gave an initial impulse to his imagination, Gainsborough *invented* his landscapes.

This strange means of stimulating the creative faculty—for it is perfectly clear that Gainsborough was not content with merely enlarging or copying his models— has something in common with the process of poetic inspiration. It never distracted

Gainsborough from real nature, because a sort of two-way exchange between real and created nature grew up. The more one studies Gainsborough's pictures the more one appreciates the quality of beauty which he transferred, exalting it in the process, from the 'subject' to the canvas.

This whole process of transmutation and exaltation is typically Romantic. Both *The Harvest Wagon* (1771, Barber Institute, Birmingham) and *The Bridge* (c. 1777, National Gallery, London) start from an 'impression', a 'feeling', but these are developed and amplified; in recalling the emotion originally aroused by the natural scene the minute components of the model are transfigured into elemental powers. The painted landscape vibrates with a deeper resonance and the little toy figures Gainsborough had placed on the model in the positions they would occupy in the picture take on a magical life.

The superiority of Gainsborough's figures to the animals in James Ward's (1769–1859) pictures is immediately obvious, although Ward was a brilliant, forceful colourist, justly admired by Géricault. He had a feeling for the earth; his palette contained warm, rich reds and luscious greens and he cast over the whole of his canvases a pale golden light with a sumptuous sheen. His sensuality was shared by William Etty (1787–1849), particularly in the latter's passionate nudes, realistic, often a little heavy, but always with a fine healthy relish that sometimes escapes Thomas Stothard (1755–1834). On the other hand, few could rival Stothard in his manner of transplanting classical or mythological figures into a typical, fresh English park (*The Greek Vintage*, c. 1821, *Nymphs Discover Narcissus*, c. 1793, both in the Tate Gallery, London). His figures have the 'fashionable' grace and elegance, sometimes inclining to affectation, of the ladies painted by Gainsborough.

It was no accident that John Constable (1776-1837) became a landscape-painter. After a long struggle with his father who refused to let him take up the hazardous career of an artist, he finally wrung from him the concession that he might paint portraits—the branch of the profession considered by the family to be the most lucrative and possibly also the most honourable. And it was indeed his portraits which gained him the admiration of his contemporaries; they did not know what to think of his landscapes. Nevertheless he was destined to become the supreme portraitist of the English scene, in both its humbler and its more majestic aspects. He was particularly anxious to add nothing beyond what could be seen: 'The landscape-painter,' he wrote, 'must walk in the fields with a humble mind. No arrogant man was ever permitted to see nature in all her beauty.' Remote from academic formulae, convinced that the artist should confine himself to 'the close and continual observance of nature', careful not to overlook the slightest puff of wind wafting a cloud, the smallest play of light on a leaf, he focussed his gaze on all his surroundings with enormous intensity. The idea that only certain aspects of nature were beautiful was rejected; all was grist to his mill, since all could be metamorphosed by the enchantment of light and shade. Sky, trees, water—he concentrated on them the passionate attention of one who knows that no single sight can ever be recaptured. Deeply conscious of the mutability of the world, he proclaimed: 'No two days nor even two hours are alike; neither were there ever two leaves of a tree alike since the creation of the world.' The man who is convinced that each instant, each morsel, of nature is unique, would indeed be a fool to deprive himself of the joy of capturing as many as he can.

This attitude involves a certain inward struggle, visible in Constable's sketches, whose rapid execution in short, precise, essential strokes, aims to capture a particular moment and, despite the fleetingness of time, to capture it in all its fullness. For the same reason there is a vast difference between his sketches and finished pictures. If one examines the two versions of *The Hay Wain* (1821, National Gallery, London), *Salisbury Cathedral* (1823, Sketch: Guildhall Art Gallery, London. Picture: Coll. Lord Ashton of Hyde) or *The Leaping Horse* (1825, Sketch: Victoria and Albert Museum, London. Picture: Royal Academy, London), one sees that in each case

JOHN MARTIN see p. 72

11 Detail from *The Last Man*

1833. Watercolour. 47.6 × 74 (18¾ × 27¾)
Laing Art Gallery, Newcastle-upon-Tyne

12 *Manfred on the Jungfrau*

1837. Watercolour. 38 × 53.9 (15 × 21¼)
City Museum and Art Gallery, Birmingham.
The subject is taken from Byron's *Manfred*

THOMAS GIRTIN see p. 63

13 Subject from *Ossian*

Pencil and grey wash on buff paper. 27.3 × 41.2 (10¾ × 16¼)
D. L. T. Oppé and Miss A. L. T. Oppé Collection, England

ALEXANDER COZENS 1717–86
Cozens, born in Russia, is one of the richest and most varied figures of English proto-Romanticism. From his friendship with Beckford he derived a penchant for fantasy, and his landscapes are bathed in a sort of enigmatic mystery, even when they are taken from nature and of a realistic character. He died in Rome.

14 *The Cloud*

Grey and black wash on toned paper. 21.5 × 31.7 (8½ × 12½).
D. L. T. Oppé and Miss A. L. T. Oppé Collection, England

11

12

13

14

15

16

17

18

19

20

JOSEPH MALLORD WILLIAM TURNER see p. 82

15 *The Mer de Glace, Chamonix with Blair's Hut*

1802. Pencil and watercolour over pencil on grey paper.
31.4×47.3 (12⅜×18⅝)
British Museum, London

JOHN SELL COTMAN 1782–1842
Cotman is considered, along with Girtin and Turner, one
of the 'founders' of the English watercolour. For some time
he shared the fame of the two aforementioned painters.
His works are among the first to express the graceful
English landscape with fitting sensitivity. The fluidity of his
colour and delicacy of his light gave his pictures a
rare charm.

16 *Croyland Abbey*

1804. Watercolour. 29.5×53.7 (11⅝×21½)
British Museum, London

RICHARD PARKES BONINGTON 1801–28
Although he died at a very early age, Bonington exerted a
considerable influence on other artists, particularly the
French Romantics. After studying with Gros, he worked in
Delacroix' studio. His landscapes and historical scenes have
an outstanding freshness and vivacity.

17 *The Castelbarco Tomb, Verona*

1827. Watercolour. 19×13.3 (7½×5¼)
Museum and Art Gallery, Nottingham

RICHARD WILSON 1714–82
After studying with Wright and practising as a portraitist
in London, Wilson went to Italy and took up landscape
painting with Zuccarelli and Joseph Vernet. He was a solitary
man, a great lover of nature; although certain memories of
Italy can be traced in his pictures, he may almost be called the
creator of the English landscape.

18 *Grotto*

White and black chalk on light brown paper.
16.6×21.3 (6½×8½)
British Museum, London

JOHN CONSTABLE see p. 78

19 *Night Scene: Building and Trees*

c. 1830–6. Sepia and grey wash. 18.7×22.8 (7⅜×9)
Victoria and Albert Museum, London

FRANCIS DANBY 1793–1861
Danby, an Irishman, attempted to rival John Martin in fantasy
and Turner in watercolour technique, but his most personal
and original works are those in which he expresses the
sincere emotions of a truly Romantic spirit with an almost
naive simplicity.

20 *Romantic Woodland*

1825. Watercolour. 19×24.6 (7½×9¾)
D. L. T. Oppé and Miss A. L. T. Oppé Collection, England

the 'sketch' is no rough preliminary, it is a finished work, whole and complete in
itself, the equivalent of the final picture in the artist's eyes—perhaps even superior
to the final picture, because it contains the initial emotion which gradually fades
away the more it is worked over. Thus the freedom of the sketch, still glowing
with the intoxication of a communion with nature which the art-lover of the day
could hardly share is replaced in the final version, to be bought eventually by the
art-lover, by a classic perfection, sometimes even a rather cold formalism: the fire
of the sketch has been surrounded with a guard and prudently damped down.

Even the rhythms change: the violent currents, internal and external, always
in a state of creation, as it were, turn into a calm, grandiose monumentality. When,
as in his *Hadleigh Castle* (1829, National Gallery, London), he painted the bitter
solitudes of a haunted castle abandoned to ruin in a landscape devastated by a
storm, the critics raised an outcry. For here objective vision verged on visionary
creation and on distinctly Romantic fantasy, and Constable found himself faced
with scornful incomprehension.

Even Ruskin had not grasped the quite individual quality of Constable's trans-
figuring vision; he maintained that the artist saw no more of the landscape than
could be seen 'by an intelligent fawn and blackbird'. Constable had attempted to
explain his aesthetic outlook in his *Lectures on Art*, published between 1833 and 1836,
and in the preface to his collection of engravings, *English Landscape*, in 1830 but he
was too modest to be able to explain the true nature of his genius, or perhaps he
was merely incapable of doing so, remote as he was from all aesthetic theory. In all
sincerity he attributed the merit of his works to the things portrayed and judged
himself superior to others of his day or earlier only in having seen and expressed
what they could not or would not acknowledge.

Constable wrote of aiming at 'light—dews—breezes—bloom—and freshness;
not one of which has yet been perfected on the canvas by any painter in the world'.
This reveals pride as well as humility, and a feeling for the true value of things; if
it is unjust to the Dutch painters before him who had already discovered that 'the
sky is the keynote, the standard of scale, the chief organ of sentiment', it shows
that he considered himself mainly as an interpreter. In worshipping light, the ever-
changing factor which changes all things, he had made the crucial observation that
light is not colourless or transparent but, on the contrary, a substance in itself, a
real substance. And in divining the material quality of light he was enabled to paint
the material quality of mist and to give his skies the value of a compact, rather
than a fluid, element. The typical dampness in the air which hangs over the English
scene became almost tangible; well may Fuseli have remarked that on seeing a
Constable picture he felt like calling for his greatcoat and umbrella. This irritable
slightly spiteful quip of Fuseli's contains a good deal of truth and it is no paradox
to call it one of the finest compliments ever addressed to Constable.

If one compares it with Constable's descriptions of Turner's paintings as 'golden
visions' which, however, 'one would like to live and die with' it is easy to understand the different meanings that can be attached to light and atmosphere. For
Constable these are two opposing material forces; the artists's task is to reconcile
them and make them harmonize, giving each an equal energy and substance.

From *Malvern Hall* (1809, National Gallery, London) onwards we see the
treatment of space truly characteristic of Constable; it is not the immense extent
of the scene which counts, as in this picture or the *Dell in Helmingham Park* (1830,
Tate Gallery, London), but the density of space, every particle vibrating with energy.
The artist almost seems to have foreseen modern scientific theories on the nature
of light, for it acquires an autonomous power, a value in itself. It is because light
is life itself, an element among elements, and because he was the first to see this and
express it with such vigour and certainty that Constable represents one of the
highest and purest peaks of Romantic art and that his pictures, exhibited in Paris
in 1824, proselytized French painters with all the success of a new gospel.

In the year before Constable's birth in Suffolk, Joseph Mallord William Turner (1775-1851) was born at a London barber's, near Covent Garden. At a very early age, Turner was apprenticed to an engraver, and began by drawing fine, Romantic scenes of Gothic abbey ruins—Tintern Abbey, Malmesbury Abbey, etc.—becoming interested in the architectural problems they presented. More receptive to the poetry of these ruins than Constable, who declared that 'the feelings which guided their inventors are unknown to us' and opposed everything Neo-Medieval because 'a new Gothic building is in reality little less absurd than a new ruin', Turner early steeped himself in the rich melancholy of these spires and vaults patterning the sky with their delicate ogives. He also cultivated a taste for Claude who inspired his large compositions on Classical subjects, his *Appulia in Search of Appulus* (1814, Tate Gallery, London), *Dido Building Carthage* (1815, National Gallery, London), *Dido and Aeneas* (1814, Tate Gallery, London), *Aeneas with the Sybil* (c. 1800, Tate Gallery, London), *Agrippina Landing with the Ashes of Germanicus* (1839, Tate Gallery, London) and whose sunsets over the sea, sumptuous lines of columns and archways opening on to the shore he frequently imitated.

The word 'imitated' is not really correct, for in fact Claude's pictures helped him to find his own style. Even when dealing with Italian scenes actually painted in the Roman *campagna* during his first visit, he recreated them along lines suggested by his own poetic temperament. Although he studied the geological character of a region in great detail, with a materialistic fervour and care which enchanted Ruskin, and examined scientifically the nature of rocks and trees, he lacked Constable's humility; he recomposed the elements of a landscape with a freedom that shows that the picture in his mind's eye mattered more to him than the objects seen with his physical eye.

His forms became less and less material, shedding weight and opacity to become the 'golden visions' which fascinated Constable, despite his different aesthetic outlook, until they lost all substance and dissolved into iridescent mists, sheets of rain sparkling in the sun, as in the well-known *Rain, Steam and Speed* (1844, National Gallery, London) or the *Steamer in a Snowstorm* (1842, National Gallery, London). Turner's stay in Venice in c. 1835 confirmed him in this tendency—already begun with *Sun Rising through Vapour* of 1807 (National Gallery, London)—and in the philosophy of creative illusion. Little remains of reality in these festivals of light over the canals, where earth, water, sky and atmosphere are all reduced to a pearly haze.

Naturally enough Turner increasingly used watercolour, the lightest, subtlest, most transparent medium, to convey these mélanges of illusion and reality. Of his hundreds of watercolours many are studies from nature but most represent his efforts to capture his dreams, the imaginary landscapes of his mind. Only watercolour, which does not thicken light or add weight to the atmosphere, was capable of portraying the magical universe in which the artist lived, although he also tried to translate it into verses (mostly clumsy) which he appended to some of his pictures. He also had certain didactic ambitions, revealed principally in his *Liber Studiorum* which he composed over a period of twelve years on the model of Claude's *Liber Veritatis*; and Ruskin admired the large number of symbols and allegorical meanings in his work (Ruskin claimed that every part of the monster in *Apollo Killing the Python,* 1811, Tate Gallery, London, had some mythological significance). But he was above all the poet of light, the man who blended into a single indissoluble chord the world of reality and the world of appearances. His work constitutes an innocent but bitter struggle between matter and mind and Ruskin attributed both his failings and his errors to his lack of faith and despair.

In other words, whereas Constable attained the immanent but made no attempt to progress beyond it, Turner stubbornly pursued the transcendent. If for Constable light has ceased to be a property of objects and become an object in itself, Turner wants matter to dissolve in the light with which he floods it and to be only a state, a condition of the existence of light . . . In this sense light is spirit—formative and animating spirit—and it is easy to understand how the outcome of Turner's evolution, very like Cézanne's, should have been that he reduced forms and substances to series of coloured vibrations.

Watercolour had become the favourite technique of many English painters; they appreciated the spontaneity, immediacy and freshness of execution which it encouraged, or rather necessitated, since with watercolour retouching is impossible. The poetic genius of Keats and Shelley had its pictorial overtones; through the medium of watercolour, pictures became pure poetry, as Constable wrote of John Cozens (1752–1799) who he thought was 'the greatest genius who ever painted landscapes'. A friend of William Beckford, owner of Fonthill and author of *Vathek*, Cozens travelled with him in Italy. He studied with his own father, Alexander Cozens, who had published a work entitled *New Method of Assisting the Invention in Drawing Original Compositions of Landscape* which contained several formulae like those used by Gainsborough. Thomas Girtin (1775–1802) was a friend of Turner, who said of him that if Girtin had not died so young (at twenty-seven), he (Turner) would never have achieved any outstanding success, since Girtin's genius was far greater than his own. He managed to reconcile the poetry of watercolour with the solid substance of the material portrayed which, in his painting, did not melt away into light but acquired an even greater reality. David Cox (1783–1859) was originally a stage designer in Birmingham and even in his watercolours, sometimes treated like backcloths (e.g. *The Terrace of Haddon Hall*, 1849, Ashmolean Museum, Oxford), there remains a certain graceful artificiality.

John Sell Cotman (1782–1842) produced oil paintings with a rare quality of dramatic nobility (*The Wagon*, 1828, Castle Museum, Norwich; *After the Storm*, 1825, Private Collection, Norwich). His watercolours date mostly from his youth and he seems to have abandoned this mode of expression when he was about thirty. John Varley (1778–1842) was a friend of Blake's and teacher of Samuel Palmer. By contrast with Girtin and Cozens he may seem a minor figure; he was, however, a skilful teacher, although he erred on the side of virtuosity and his sensibility became rather rusty in the course of his purely technical researches.

If one may speak of a Romanticism of transcendence in connection with the watercolourists, the Romanticism of Samuel Palmer (1805–1881), the visionary naturalist, is an expression of the magic in matter itself, the mystery of the immanent. Samuel Palmer went much further than Constable in giving landscape a curious autonomy, although he almost always added to it animals or men working in the fields. His Baptist upbringing, the influence of Blake, to whom he turned *via* Linnell, his admiration for Claude, his long walks at night in fields and woods— all contributed to this intuitive feeling towards pantheistic mysteries. A precocious boy, he exhibited three landscapes at the Royal Academy when he was hardly fourteen, but his temperament was not academic. Longus, discovered in his father's bookshop at Stoke Newington, had implanted in him the ideal of an idyllic Greece; and the Michelangelism of George Richmond, traces of which remain in his *Creation of Light* (1826), prepared him to experience and express the English scene as a dream.

The Harvest Moon (1835), *Coming from Evening Church* (1830, both Tate Gallery, London), and the *Pastoral Scene* (1834, Ashmolean Museum, Oxford) transport the spectator into an unreal atmosphere or, it would perhaps be better to say, make him feel a different reality from the normal one. The very original technique used by Palmer—a mixture of oil paint and tempera—gives the pictures a singular *texture*, which appears thick and clotted without losing any of its transparency. Unlike those artists who pride themselves on faithfully portraying a particular landscape, he moves in an imaginary world where the 'other face of the reality of matter' reveals itself in serene intimacy and the broad, deep breathing of the landscape throws up great harmonic waves of a new and moving beauty. The words 'reality' and 'illusion' lose their ordinary meaning when one speaks of Palmer's pictures; only the enigmatic vocabulary of the subconscious is fit to express the waking dream in which Palmer drifts through the meadows and copses of an English village.

English Romanticism began to draw to a close as talents became smaller and outlooks more conformist; the great schools of portraiture and landscape painting gradually declined until they were replaced by the genre scenes of Wilkie and Mulready. But there is something typically Romantic about the foundation of the Pre-Raphaelite Brotherhood in 1848, eleven years after Constable's death; if, that is, one accepts as Romantic the desire to abandon one's own age on the grounds that it is mediocre and commonplace instead of attempting to transform it and give it back its past glory. William Holman Hunt (1827–1910), Dante Gabriel Rossetti (1828–1882) and Edward Burne-Jones (1833–1898) had found inspiration from the same source as the Nazarenes; taking refuge in a foreign country and period, they fled to Renaissance Italy for their artistic and intellectual sustenance.

Although sharing their Romantic nostalgia they lack the intense communion with nature which sustained Constable, Friedrich and Rousseau. Moreover, they seem to have been completely ignorant of the fact that while they were demanding an artificial, deliberately archaic aesthetic standard, the great Samuel Palmer had painted his finest pictures with a true 'supernaturalism of nature' which they would never have attained, weighed down as they were with theory and precept. Nevertheless there is something sincere and noble, and hence Romantic, in their revolt against the materialism and machinery-worship of the Industrial Age. Ruskin was of the opinion that the Pre-Raphaelites, with their dreams of a far-off world of beauty where all was purity, simplicity, poetic grace and dreamy voluptuousness, had founded the 'noblest school of art we have seen in the past three centuries'. William Morris (1834–1896) was more successful in his nostalgia, exercised mainly in the field of decoration; he combined Gothic elements with elements of folk art.

Beside Burne-Jones' pallid angels and Rossetti's pensive beauties there is something refreshing about Madox Brown's (1821–1893) robust realism, although the quality of the painting always remains subordinate to the subject. Visual and pictorial feeling are less important than the story being told. Constable and Turner have no successors; in confining themselves to the past the Pre-Raphaelites condemned themselves to an even narrower academism than that of the Nazarenes, in that it was even more systematic and deliberate. Only George Frederick Watts (1817–1904) contributed an element of novelty, although his art too was heavily contaminated by literary overtones. However, despite an excess of symbolism, ideology and 'grand ideas' not absolutely necessary for good pictures, he succeeded in being more truly dramatic, more genuinely poetic, than the other painters of his day, always excepting Samuel Palmer, who is in a class of his own.

The Aesthetic Movement, super-refined, uncommitted to the point of deliberate decadence, to which Walter Pater and Oscar Wilde belonged in the sphere of literature, Burne-Jones and Rossetti in the sphere of painting, was a kind of extension of English Romanticism, just as in France Odilon Redon and the Symbolists represented a kind of extension of French Romanticism. In 1821 Constable had said that thirty years later there would be no more English art, and it was exactly thirty years later that Turner died, although Palmer lived on for another thirty years and Whistler took up where the preceding generation had left off. In the interval Romanticism had said all that it had to say; the Pre-Raphaelites cultivated an ideal whose life-blood had dried up and which turned too much towards the past to provide nourishment for the future. Perhaps in perfecting their various modes of expression Blake, Constable, Turner and Palmer had made further development impossible, not only for their own contemporaries, but also for the immediate future.

SAMUEL PALMER see p. 76

21 *Cornfield by Moonlight with the Evening Star*

Watercolour, gouache and pen. 19.4×29.7 (7¾×11¾).
Sir Kenneth Clark Collection, England

22 *The Valley of Vision*

c. 1828. Pen and wash, heightened with white
28.1×66 (11⅛×26)
L. G. Duke Collection, England

21

22

23

24

25

26

27

GEORGE STUBBS see p. 68

23 *Owl*

1800. Pencil. 39×26.2 (15¾×10⅜).
Free Public Library, Worcester, U.S.A.

24 *Flayed Horse*

c. 1776. Black chalk. 36.2×19.7 (14¼×7¾)
Royal Academy of Arts, London

JOHN HAMILTON MORTIMER 1741–79
Mortimer heralded the advent of Romanticism with his
taste for excess and violence, his use of subjects from
Shakespeare, witchcraft, folk-lore, etc., and his break away
from the academic outlook.

25 *Orchestra of Demons*

Pen and ink. 15.6×21.6 (6½×8½)
British Museum, London

JOHN VARLEY 1778–1842
Varley founded the Old Watercolour Society and exerted
a considerable influence on the English painting of the day,
indirectly affecting even such men as David Cox, Samuel
Palmer and John Linnell.

26 *Cader Idris*

c. 1803. Watercolour. 28.5×44.4 (11¼×17½)
City Museum and Art Gallery, Hereford

THOMAS GIRTIN 1775–1802
Turner, who was a great admirer of Girtin and had learned
much from him, was convinced that if Girtin had lived, he,
Turner, could never have attained celebrity. Girtin did in
fact discover new ways of enriching watercolour and
added a new 'dimension' to the medium which was to
become one of the best vehicles for Romantic feeling.

27 *Bolton Abbey*

1800. Watercolour. 32.3×47.5 (12¾×18¾)
City Art Gallery, Leeds

IX JAMES WARD 1769–1859

Ward began as an engraver, studying under J. R. Smith and his brother William Ward. His first paintings were influenced by the rural sentimental manner of his brother-in-law, George Morland. In 1800 the Agricultural Society commissioned him to paint the various species of cattle, sheep and pigs of Great Britain; this collection of animal portraits was a financial failure but established Ward's reputation as an animal painter. Between 1815 and 1821 he devoted a long period to an immense composition showing the Battle of Waterloo. Ward was a believer in the apocalyptic doctrines of Edward Irving and admired Blake and Fuseli; his own pictures are often suffused with a powerful apocalyptic feeling and he never began to paint without previous meditation and prayer. Within his realism there is a strong element of lyricism and poetry.

Regent's Park: Cattle Piece

1807. 73 × 117 (28¾ × 46) Tate Gallery, London

X JOSEPH WRIGHT, known as Wright of Derby 1734–97

Wright began by studying portrait painting and became most successful in this
sphere. Josiah Wedgwood, for whom he collected material in Italy, held him to be
one of the greatest painters of the age. The first English painter to become interested
in the spirit of the Industrial Revolution, he painted forges, foundries and scientific
experiments not only for their documentary value but also for their striking effects
of light, which he reproduced with much originality. This picture of a family
making an experiment with an air-pump is a good example of his tastes. The
children's distress at seeing the dead bird is reminiscent of Greuze, while the force
with which each character is individualized and the strange beauty of the light-
effects give the homely scene an air of fantasy, almost of religious feeling which
reminds us that to the 18th century science still wore a mystical aspect.

Experiment with an Air-pump

1768. 183 × 244 (72 × 96) Tate Gallery, London

XI GEORGE STUBBS 1724–1806

A Baboon and an Albino Macaque Monkey combines all Stubbs' qualities—the documentary scientific interest he attached to animal painting, his anatomical knowledge, the truth of the surrounding atmosphere in which he placed his 'models', and, in addition, a truly 'psychological' approach to animal painting. It shows moreover with what originality he approached these scientific subjects. He was obviously not only concerned to differentiate the two species of monkey by their zoological characteristics: he gave each a distinct personality, all the more fascinating in that these animals are not very remote from the human race. The dark background against which the two strangely melancholy figures are placed shows up the warm, supple softness of their coats, giving the whiteness of the Albino a mysterious brilliance. The picture was commissioned by John Hunter, a surgeon and anatomist who made a remarkable collection of animal pictures which were to illustrate his revolutionary theories on physiology. Stubbs painted a series of portraits of rhinoceroses, monkeys, tigers and panthers for him.

A Baboon and an Albino Macaque Monkey

Millboard. 69.8 × 99.1 (27½ × 39) Royal College of Surgeons of England (Hunterian Collection), London

XII GEORGE STUBBS

Stubbs, the finest of the English animal painters, was also a capable scientist; he published at least one book (on the anatomy of the horse) which still remains a standard work. Wedgwood also commissioned him to produce designs for his porcelain vases. His favourite subjects were taken from rural life and hunting, but he was also interested in wild animals. He painted three versions of the *White Horse frightened by a Lion,* one of which (that in the Louvre) was copied by Géricault. In this picture documentary accuracy is raised to the level of dramatic emotion. No other painters have rivalled Stubbs in portraying the strange soul of the horse, its enigmatic reactions, and (in this case) the almost supernatural atmosphere surrounding the 'noble creature' in the light, in contrast with the wild beast emerging out of the darkness.

White Horse frightened by a Lion

1770. 101.6 × 127.6 (40 × 50¼) Walker Art Gallery, Liverpool

XIII THOMAS GAINSBOROUGH 1727–88

Gainsborough, the son of a Suffolk cloth merchant, was trained in London from 1740 under the influence of Gravelot, but he was more enthusiastic about the Dutch masters of the 17th century. Fortunately his love for the English countryside urged him to apply his sensitive and eloquent talents to the familiar beauty of his native Suffolk. His passion for truth did not inhibit him from clothing the objective reality of the creatures and things he saw with a poetic feeling, particularly in the 'fancy pictures' of the latter part of his life. He was able to portray the intimate harmony between the souls of the landscape and the figures in it with marvellous felicity. Landscape is no longer mere background but the source of living emotion.

If the Romanticism of a work like *The Morning Walk* is not immediately obvious, it nevertheless forms a link between the 'pre-Romantic' 18th century and the spirit of full-blown Romanticism of the first half of the 19th. This picture is all refinement of form and delicacy of sentiment. A pair of happy lovers are walking in one of the parks in which art and nature combine to produce the 'picturesque' quality so dear to the period. No extravagant passion disturbs the serenity of their happiness, the delicate harmony of the blues, greens and greys is exquisitely fresh and the charm of the work is only heightened by its (apparent) air of incompleteness.

The Morning Walk

236 × 178 (93 × 70) National Gallery, London

XIV JOHN MARTIN 1789–1854

This visionary artist who painted numerous fantasy pictures and illustrations of a rare, sombre beauty for Milton's *Paradise Lost,* started as a painter in enamel colours for a porcelain manufacturer. But Turner's pictures and the *Eidophousikon* of De Loutherbourg inspired him with a profound and genuine sense of the supernatural which is revealed in his pictures and engravings. He also used curious effects of light with good results.

Of all Martin's works *Sadak in search of the Waters of Oblivion* is the most accomplished and successful; it is really only part of a larger composition which has unfortunately been lost. The theme is taken from a Persian legend, the story of the noble Sadak and the djinn Alfakin. The contrast between the small size of the figure and the barren immensity of the rocky isle where the djinn had promised that he would find the waters of oblivion is brought out with passionate vehemence and dynamism. Its stormy atmosphere and the oppressive arrogance of the figure are reminiscent of Lucifer in Milton's epic. The play of light on the bare stone has a fierce splendour.

Sadak in search of the Waters of Oblivion

1812. 76.2 × 62.4 (30 × 25) Southampton Art Gallery

XV WILLIAM BLAKE 1757–1827

Blake is the Romantic artist *par excellence;* not only is his work inspired by the supernatural and fantastic but his whole life was dominated by these elements. Many of his paintings represent his 'visions', characters from the Bible, from history or from fairy tales whom he 'saw'. His poetry and painting have exactly the same feeling—speak, as it were, with one voice—and, by means of his invention whereby he could engrave text and illustrations on the same plate, he managed to achieve a remarkable unity between them. He was completely indifferent to the material side of life and lived only for the things of the spirit. The Bible, Milton's poems and the *Divina Commedia* were his favourite reading matter and he made several attempts to illustrate the latter. Despite the fact that his artistic outlook is far removed from that of 14th century Florence, he penetrates to the depths of Dante's mind, theological world and symbols.

Blake's spiritual aspirations were, strangely enough, linked to a sort of cult of innocent nudity; more than once friends visiting his house found him and his wife completely naked 'and they were not ashamed'. The body admittedly hides the soul's full light but Blake, instead of minimizing it, sought to make it transparent. Watercolour was better able than oil-painting to show 'sublimated' flesh, capable of being seen through like crystal. The sculpturally solid nudes in the picture illustrated, draped in almost invisible veils, retain their impressive monumentality while allowing the light of the spirit to pour out all around them. The colour symbolism and mystical meaning of the iridescences are particularly interesting in this picture, since they come very close to Dante's theology and æsthetic code.

Dante meeting Beatrice in Paradise

1824. Watercolour. 94 × 133 (37 × 52½) Tate Gallery, London

P.g Canto 29 & 30

XVI SAMUEL PALMER 1805–81

Palmer was chiefly influenced by Fuseli and Blake, to whom he was introduced by John Linnell. Blake attracted him particularly because he too was a mystic and interested in exploring the supernatural; he was also a student of Jakob Boehme and the German mystics. Nevertheless he took his subjects from the everyday life of the English countryside which he portrayed with the affection of a Virgil, concentrating on the work of countrymen and the progress of the seasons. To express his feeling for nature he elaborated a very individual technique, combining oil-tempera and watercolour painting and adding thick layers of varnish which give many of his pictures the depth and lustre of lacquer. In his compositions, figures and objects are often tumultuously heaped up, with an effect which is moving rather than clumsy, since it is clearly dictated by a desire to obtain effects like those of his favourite poets, Coleridge and Wordsworth. But his way of expressing his feelings for the mystery, perhaps even the terror, of nature, is his alone. In particular, he reached new heights in depicting the secret majesty of the night and dusk and the emotions they aroused in him. Palmer reveals the supernatural elements inherent in nature itself and lifts them on to the plane of a magical communion with landscape. His *Coming from Evening Church*, with its mountains blanched by moonlight and its long line of churchgoers straggling along the valley, seems to say that there is no substantial difference, and perhaps no difference in essence, between man and inanimate objects.

Coming from Evening Church

1830. 31 × 20 (12 × 7½) Tate Gallery, London

XVII JOHN CONSTABLE 1776–1837

Constable's education came from nature rather than the Royal Academy where he studied from 1796. He identified himself with the English countryside to the point where he was able to express its innermost and most secret life. Hedges, trees, brooks and meadowlands all stimulated him, awoke an echo in his own soul. For him it was never necessary to people the landscape with mythological or classical figures in order to fill it with a godlike presence. His manner of painting changed as he became more and more concerned with the expression of feeling in his landscapes, and less dominated by the influence of Claude and Ruisdael. Without ever cultivating a 'Romanticism' which was very remote from his character and temperament, his work became more and more saturated with increasingly tragic feeling. Owing to the enthusiasm aroused in France by the 1824 exhibition of English landscapes, Constable was adopted as the high priest of Romanticism, which he neither knew nor believed in. He aimed only to be a faithful mirror of nature and it was in spite of himself that he became its inspired mouthpiece. His rich, warm manner conveyed every least variation in light, the play of clouds, reflections in water, stormy skies, thick black forests and mellow golden cornfields. Towards the end of his career, after a lifetime of research into technique, his brush is sensitive enough to convey every gradation of his moods.

Dedham Mill

c. 1819. 53.5 × 76 (21 × 30¼) Tate Gallery, London

XVIII JOHN CONSTABLE

Constable's seascapes, unlike those by Turner, are not lyrical transcriptions of nature stirred by a drama created by the painter, but sober, sensitive representations of objective fact. His Romanticism is seen most clearly in his pictures of fields and woods with which he was more familiar and could enter into closer communion. The things which made most impression on him—glistening grass, dewy hedges, the sun playing through the leaves of a tree, the solid yet pliant earth beneath the feet of the walker—all these were missing from the 'mighty monster'. But although Constable may not always have grasped and conveyed the half-demoniac, half-divine qualities of the sea, he at least revealed an element of beauty in it which few painters before him had achieved. For this he had recourse to the method of form- and colour-analysis which he had devised for landscape painting.

Weymouth Bay

53 × 75 (21 × 29½) National Gallery, London

XIX JOHN CONSTABLE

The title of the *Marine Parade and Chain Pier, Brighton* is somewhat misleading; its subject is not so much the sea and Brighton beach as the clouds, as in a Sung dynasty painting. It is, in fact, one of Constable's most powerful and successful sky-studies. The almost documentary part of the picture—the fishing boats, houses and sails—are endowed with a sort of supernatural life by the sinister, sulphurous sun, struggling through the heavy clouds. While still remaining faithful to reality, always Constable's chief aim, he allows himself great freedom in this depiction of humid air, atmosphere heavy with water, wet wind stinging the cheeks.

Marine Parade and Chain Pier, Brighton

1824. 127 × 185 (50 × 70⅞) Tate Gallery, London

XX JOSEPH MALLORD WILLIAM TURNER 1775–1851

After studying at the schools of the Royal Academy and with Girtin, Turner began work as a watercolourist, later turning to oils. He exhibited throughout his life and his influence on the course of Romanticism in general was immeasurable. His work includes historical and mythological scenes as well as dramatic seascapes and sunsets on an epic scale in which forms and colours are treated with an inexhaustible variety. Towards the end of his life the form in his pictures tended to dissolve into light and movement as if he was trying to make art return to the basic principles of universal creation, to the origin of life itself. So powerful was his imagination that it transformed things seen into a fantasy world with laws and dimensions quite different from those of objective reality. Though *The Shipwreck* is based on a wreck actually seen by Turner, the whole scene is translated into fantasy by the artist's imagination; the waves become the convulsions of a monster animal, its winces and sudden starts, the elements undergo a process of 'divinization' and 'animalization'.

The Shipwreck

c. 1805. 171 × 241 (67½ × 95) Tate Gallery, London

XXI JOSEPH MALLORD WILLIAM TURNER

Turner said that he took the subject of *The Parting of Hero and Leander* 'from the Greek of Musæus'. The story goes that Leander swam the Hellespont every night to see his love, Hero, a priestess of Aphrodite. When returning one night he was swallowed up by the waves and Hero, in complete despair, also drowned herself. Turner retells this sad tale in one of the strange poems with which he often accompanied his pictures. The colour of the composition combines all the darkest and most powerful tones at the painter's command. The structures of the temple of Aphrodite, looming up towards the sky like strange dream-buildings, the sinister darkness of the water brushed by a ray of moonlight, the groups of phantom-like figures representing the souls of the drowned welcoming Leander—all these elements are united in a magnificently subtle and balanced harmony. As yet Turner's forms have not completely dissolved into light; the masses still have their weight and force. Nevertheless his æsthetic ideas and technique are undergoing a radical metamorphosis. Eight years earlier Etty, known and admired by Turner, had exhibited a picture on the same subject at the Royal Academy, but the later work far outstrips it in solemnity and myth-like, supernatural power. This tragic story also aroused Byron's imagination.

The Parting of Hero and Leander

1837. 146×236 (57½×93) Tate Gallery, London

XXII JOSEPH MALLORD WILLIAM TURNER

On hearing that the Houses of Parliament were on fire during the night of 16th October 1834, Turner hurried out to watch; on his return he made several paintings which combine an immediate impression of this tragic event with memories of similar 'previous' tragedies, such as the burning of Troy. Myth and reality were so mingled in his mind that he lent the very real spectacle which he had seen from a crowded Waterloo Bridge the splendour and horror of a cosmic catastrophe. The two paintings he made from his watercolour sketches and memories were exhibited the following year at the Royal Academy. The forms merge in the confusion of leaping flames and nocturnal darkness, and in the more highly coloured parts of the picture, in particular, the luminous impasto seems about to burst into flame itself. The other version which is very different in composition (the bridge and crowd are almost invisible) is in the Cleveland Museum of Art, Ohio.

Burning of the Houses of Parliament

1834. 92.5 × 123 (36½ × 48½) Philadelphia Museum of Art

XXIII JOSEPH MALLORD WILLIAM TURNER

According to the tradition attached to the *Steamer in a Snowstorm,* Turner had himself tied to the mast in order to be better able to watch the snow falling on the ship in which he was travelling. This snowstorm at sea is made up of equal parts of imagination and observation. It is brilliantly executed with a virtuosity seen only in Turner's later works where substance melts away into light, into transparent humidity. Perhaps none of his paintings so fully deserves to be called an 'apocalypse of the heavens', in Ruskin's phrase. Turner's contemporaries were not all able to appreciate the novelty of his art, which was much ahead of its time. One of the critics, composing the traditional report on the Royal Academy exhibition, called this picture 'soapsuds and whitewash'. The great freedom of the brushwork and the circular rhythms show that Turner worked with an independence of treatment and virtuosity of technique almost unique in the period.

Steamer in a Snowstorm

1842. 90 × 120 (35½ × 47½) Tate Gallery, London

XXIV DANTE GABRIEL ROSSETTI 1828–82

The members of the Pre-Raphaelite Brotherhood are Post-Romantics both in their æsthetic code and in what they expected of painting. Rossetti, commonly considered the founder of the movement, was a poet as well as a painter and practised both arts equally. Like the other Pre-Raphaelites and the supporters of the Arts and Crafts movement, he had nothing but scorn for the materialistic, thriving Victorian era and hankered after a past filled with craftsmanship, rustic jollity and general 'beauty' which was largely a figment of his imagination. There are perhaps analogies between the ideals of the Lukasbund of Cornelius and Overbeck and those of the German Nazarenes, but Rossetti's pictorial qualities are finer and his lyrical invention more original.

The Wedding of St George and Princess Sabra

1857. 86 × 86 (34 × 34) Tate Gallery, London

XXV

WILLIAM HOLMAN HUNT
1827–1910

Holman Hunt was, like Rossetti, one of
the Pre-Raphaelites but his style is more
vigorous and virile. In *Claudio and
Isabella,* a subject taken from Shakespeare's
Measure for Measure, he tries to represent
a meeting between two imaginary characters in a realistic, everyday manner.
In this, Holman Hunt was not unlike
Millais and even Egley; he lacked the
poetic drive of Rossetti and Burne-Jones.
On occasion his attempt to 'be true to
life' makes his work prosaic, stiffening
the figures and stultifying any expression
of inner life. If he is a Romantic at all it
is by virtue of his fixed conviction that the
Middle Ages represented a paradise lost.
His melancholy evocation, from the standpoint of the Industrial Era, shows an
idealized past which he loaded with slightly
theatrical beauties in order to escape
from the hard facts of his unsympathetic
surroundings.

Claudio and Isabella

1850. Panel. 77.5 × 45 (30½ × 18)
Tate Gallery, London

IV GERMANY

GERMAN ROMANTICISM sprang from two sources. On the one hand it represented a deliberate revolt against the ideals of the 18th century, artificially imposed by a small élite of thinkers who borrowed their ideas from French rationalism and the Age of Reason. On the other it was directly linked with the tradition of the great German art of the 15th and 16th centuries. The re-discovery of the medieval texts of the *Minnesängers* and the *Nibelungenlied* by Bodmer together with Herder's work on folk poetry, created a new understanding for those masterpieces of 'the past' which the *Aufklärung* had despised or, quite simply, not known. At the same time both artists and thinkers began to experience nature directly, to embark on a scientific-mystical study of the natural elements. Painters read the *Naturphilosophen;* Carl Gustav Carus' pictures, for instance, express their pantheist conception of Mother Nature, of a Nature closely attuned to man's sensibility, just as much as do his philosophical and biological works. Eyes were suddenly opened to the German countryside, to the Rhine, the 'German river' with its castles, cathedrals, and little towns unchanged since the Middle Ages.

Probably no other period in art-history has produced such a close communion of ideas between artists and philosophers. Carus, who managed to be painter, doctor, naturalist and geologist, is, of course, exceptional but the *Weltanschauung* of painters in general shows much in common with that of the philosophers of the period, whether the painters actually studied philosophy or whether these ideas were merely in the air. The letters of Runge and Friedrich show that the 'tellurism' of Dietrich Georg von Kieser, the architectonic approach to the human organism of Giovanni Malfatti, the 'violent' state of nature proclaimed by the Norwegian Henrik Steffens and the *Weltorganismus* of Karl Friedrich Burdach had penetrated into the world of art. Moreover artists probably knew something of the work of Ennemoser and Johannes Carl Passavant and shared Lorenz Oken's view that 'without a philosophy of nature there can be no philosophy of the mind'. It is well known that Dr Malcus, Hoffmann's strange friend, had an enormous influence on the author of the *Tales*.

This common stock of ideas linking artists, poets and scientists and providing the driving impulse for the researches of all three is found in Schelling, to whom the philosophy of nature owed so much, Franz von Baader, Ritter, J. J. Wagner and the mesmerist Eschenmayer. While Novalis was proclaiming that 'the highest philosophy deals with the marriage of nature and mind', Gotthilf Heinrich von Schubert, who wrote on the 'dark side of the natural sciences' in his *History of the Soul* and *Symbolism of Nature,* was combining the 'biosophy' of Ignatius Paul Vital Troxler, the conclusions of Gottfried Reinhold Treviranus on the phenomena and laws of organic matters, the 'symbolism of elements' of Johannes Baptista Friedrich and the 'arithmetic of life' of Wilhelm Butte after Zoroaster . In short, outlooks, both philosophic and aesthetic, underwent a radical transformation, completely disrupting artists' previous notions of the function and meaning of art.

Romanticism brought about a 'medieval mood'. Cologne Cathedral, on which work had continued ever since the Middle Ages and which was now to be finished in the Romantic period, almost seemed to constitute a bridge between the past and the present, besides being a symbol of the enduring vitality of Gothic forms. The Romantics boasted that they were the only true interpreters of Gothic, that they had revived the forms and spirit of medieval art, and Schlegel wrote: 'We really live in the true Middle Ages for these were wrongly interpreted in bygone days.'

Although early German Romanticism repudiated Classicism, it hailed as one of its first masters the Danish painter Jacob Asmus Carstens (1754–1798), to be discussed later, who worked in a sort of Romantic Classicism (or, if you like, Classical Romanticism) along the lines suggested by Wehl in his book on beauty in painting. In an age when there was a close collaboration in art between Copenhagen and Germany, he had a profound effect on German Romanticism. Bonaventura Genelli (1798–1868) who like Carstens aimed to reconcile in his pictures the two arbitrarily contrasted outlooks, Classicism and Romanticism, divided his attention between medieval and Neo-Classical subjects, themes borrowed from Shakespeare, the idol of the German Romantics, and, in a vague way, from Greek mythology.

While the earlier 18th-century German artists had succumbed to the fascination of Italy and France and sought inspiration and teaching at Rome or Paris, the Romantics turned away towards the North. Not only did distinguished teachers like Abildgaard and Jens Juel teach at the Academy of Copenhagen, but, even more important, the physical and spiritual climate of the Scandinavian countries harmonized with the temperament and aspirations of the Germans. Southern German artists in particular went to study in Denmark, turning their backs on Italian lightness and gaiety, French clarity and the sunny, shadowless landscapes which so attracted the Nazarenes. It should be borne in mind, however, that the Lukasbund was founded in Vienna, and passed from thence to Rome.

The fame of the Danish masters attracted Friedrich, Runge, Blechen and Kersting to their studios. The Nordic Michelangelism of Carstens, his violently passionate 'Romantic Classicism', the Ossianic mists, the epic world of the sagas and war-poems common to both Germany and Scandinavia, drew the Germans like iron filings to a magnet and aroused their curiosity and fellow-feeling. Exchanges between Copenhagen on the one side and Hamburg and Dresden on the other became more and more frequent. Dahl, a Norwegian, was very successful in Saxony and largely instrumental in founding the Dresden School; the minor artists—not of course those great masters whose powerful, untameable originality would always save them from the dangers of servile imitation—of Germany and Denmark began to share a sort of common pictorial language.

Peter Cornelius and his friends of the Lukasbund (the 'Guild of St Luke'), also known as the Nazarenes, who took up residence in a deserted monastery near Rome to paint and follow an almost hermit-like way of life, attempted a revival of German medieval religious art, aiming at simplicity of spirit and execution, sobriety of line and colour, an almost naive but ever sincere ingenuousness. It is difficult for us to appreciate to the full the Nazarenes' freshness of feeling, their honest desire to return to the humble but pious aesthetic attitude of the 'primitives' (by which they meant the Italians and Germans of the 15th century, and even

LUDWIG ADRIAN RICHTER   see p. 121

1 *Geneviève de Brabant*

Drawing. 18×27 (7×10½)
Victoria and Albert Museum, London
Probably a sketch for the picture in the Kunsthalle, Hamburg

MORITZ VON SCHWIND   see p. 119

2 *The Spirit of the Mountain*

c. 1846. Pen. 16.7×30.3 (6⅝×11⅞)
Folkwang Museum, Essen
Study for the painting

JULIUS SCHNORR VON CAROLSFELD   see p. 99

3 *Siegfried and Kriemhild*

Pen and ink, pencil and watercolour. 18×22 (7¼×8⅝)
Victoria and Albert Museum, London

MORITZ VON SCHWIND

4 *The Faithful Sister and King's Son*

The drawing is an illustration to a fairy story
Pen. 28.2×21.9 (11⅛×8⅝)
Historisches Stadtmuseum, Munich

JOSEPH ANTON KOCH   see p. 120

5 *Landscape with Hercules at the Crossroads*

Pen and brush, heightened with white
27.4×41.7 (10¾×16⅜)
Folkwang Museum, Essen

1

2

3

4

5

6

7

8

Raphael and Dürer), their effusions of joy bound up with a resolve to make pure art grow out of a pure life. We tend to suspect an affectation of archaism, an attempt to attract notice by rebelling against the art and thought of the recently ended 18th century; but in rejecting the splendour of German Baroque painting as well as Rococo affectations they were as much anti-Baroque as anti-Classical. In reality their 'return to the Middle Ages' was the manifestation of a nostalgia for the past and a whole-hearted desire to use it as a pattern for building the present.

Johann Friedrich Overbeck (1789–1869) voiced the ideals of the brotherhood he founded in Vienna in 1809 (it moved to Rome in the following year) when he described 'the three ways of art' which he had decided to follow: the way of imagination, typified by Michelangelo, the way of beauty, typified by Raphael, the way of nature, typified by Dürer. From 1810 the Convent of S Isidoro became a refuge for German painters who wished to live a religious life and practise a religious art; Overbeck was converted to Catholicism and many followed his example. Under the patronage of the German consul Bartholdy and Prince Massimo they constructed huge groups of murals in which they tried to emulate the great frescopainters of the Italian Renaissance. A number of talented painters gathered round Overbeck and Cornelius: after Wintergerst, Vogel, Hottinger and Sutter, the first founders of the Brotherhood, who were soon eclipsed and forgotten, came certain noteworthy artists—Wilhelm Schadow (1788–1862), Heinrich Maria von Hess (1798–1863), Johann Anton Ramboux (1790–1866), Josef von Führich (1800–1876), Schnorr von Carolsfeld (1794–1872), Carl Philipp Fohr (1795–1818) and Joseph Anton Koch (1768–1839), the 'father of the Romantic landscape'. One of the most engaging of the religious Romantic painters was Maria Alberti (1767–1810) who began in the manner of Pompeo Batoni and ended her days tending typhoid sufferers in a convent in Westphalia. The life and art of Maria Alberti, whose works are rare and little known, represent the type of the true Romantic, both in the freshness and sincerity of her feeling and in her loving-kindness culminating in total self-sacrifice.

Can the Nazarenes really be called Romantics, since their avowed ideal was to imitate the art-forms of the past as closely as possible, changing nothing? Fortunately most of them were too forceful of temperament and original of thought to be content with passively imitating an aesthetic ideal valid for the 16th century but no longer so for the 19th; and at the present time it is, of course, their originality and not their faithfulness to old ideals which most appeals to us. The chief virtue of their works is freshness, of feeling and colour, a dawnlike delicacy and openness of heart and mood. Effortlessly, almost accidentally, they find the way back to medieval simplicity, because they themselves had succeeded in attaining simplicity of spirit and vision. Goethe misjudged them when he said that they 'painted in retrograde, returning to the womb in order to create a new artistic age'. It is true that, technically speaking, the Nazarenes contributed nothing to the progress of modern painting, and that they even attempted to bring it to a complete standstill, but they are nevertheless characteristic of a certain aspect, far from negligible, and indeed very interesting, of nostalgic German Romanticism; out of their movement grew an entirely new way of looking at and reproducing landscape, which the three Olivier brothers—Ferdinand (1785–1841), Heinrich (1783–1848) and Friedrich (1791–1859) —learned from Koch.

It was due to them too that landscape took on a new importance in religious painting. It was no longer enough to set Biblical figures against simple Italian-style backgrounds; now episodes from the Old and New Testaments were subtly blended into the German countryside. The Valley of the Jordan in *The Baptism of Christ* painted by Ferdinand and Heinrich von Olivier between 1808 and 1810 (Wörlitz Church) is as sharply individualistic as if it had been painted in the 16th century by an artist of the Danube School; the groups of angels and spectators are no longer borrowed from Ghirlandaio or Perugino, like those of Overbeck or Cornelius, but

PETER VON CORNELIUS 1783–1867

Cornelius founded the Lukasbund, the precursor of the Nazarene Movement, whose aim was to rediscover the sincere piety, simple realism and freshness of inspiration of the painters of the Middle Ages and Early Renaissance. He decorated the Casino Massimo and the Casa Bartholdy, Rome, with frescoes. Later he went to Munich, where he became principal of the Academy in 1825; he also did frescoes for the churches of that town.

6 *Faust's Walk on Easter Day*

The subject is taken from Part I, Scene 2 of Goethe's play
Pencil. 40×35 (15¾×13¾)
Historisches Stadtmuseum, Munich

KARL FRIEDRICH SCHINKEL 1781–1841

While studying architecture in Berlin, Schinkel taught himself landscape painting. Equally enthusiastic about the Middle Ages and Classical Antiquity, he is a Romantic in his pictures and a Neo-Classical architect; his buildings are often based on Greek temples. He also did stage designs. His best paintings show ideal buildings in imaginary landscapes.

7 *The Castle of the Grail*

Drawing. 28.9×32.1 (11¼×12½)
Wallraf-Richartz Museum, Cologne

CARL PHILIPP FOHR 1795–1818

Like many Romantic artists, Fohr died at a very early age; he was drowned at Rome while crossing the Tiber. A pupil of Koch and Rottmann, he painted few pictures, but his drawings reveal a fresh and robust originality.

8 *Götz von Berlichingen among the Gypsies*

An illustration of Act V of Goethe's famous early drama
Pen and wash. 37.4×47.4 (14¾×18⅝)
Hessisches Landesmuseum, Darmstadt.

treated with the realistic imagination, pictorial vision and animation characteristic of the old masters of Swabia and Franconia.

The seductions of Italy did not lure Franz Pforr, who died in Albano at twenty-four, away from his native German heritage. His *Entry of the Hapsburg Emperor Rudolf II into Basle* (1809–1810, Städelsches Institut, Frankfurt) retains a rustic vigour, an ingenuous, almost naive, depth of feeling and robust naturalism which have nothing in common with the concept of ideal beauty and Gothic Classicism cherished by the Nazarenes, intoxicated as they were by the Italian Renaissance. But the brightest star of the new school was Carl Phillipp Fohr (1795–1818) who drew on the inspiration of both Rome and Florence, only to drown himself in the Tiber at the age of twenty-three; after carefully studying Cranach and Altdorfer, he translated them into a Romantic idiom in his *Return from the Hunt* (Schloss-museum, Darmstadt). Little infected by the contagion of Italianization, he retained a robustness and a sort of bitter feeling for reality which comes out most clearly in his portraits. A German landscape provides the background for the *Vision of St Eustace* (Städelsches Institut, Frankfurt) by Johann David Passavant (1787–1861) who had worked with David and Gros in Paris before settling in the monastery of S Isidoro. Ludwig Sigismund Ruhl (1794–1887), on the other hand, cultivated a more artificial, literary, 'troubadour' style in his *Fair Melusine at her Toilet* (Kunst-halle, Mannheim).

As well as using religious subjects, these painters followed the lines laid down in the poetry of Herder, von Arnim and Brentano, interesting themselves in ancient German folk poetry, *Märchen,* songs, epics and legends. The vanished charm of medieval poetry began to be reborn in paintings and drawings. Pocci, Disteli, Speckter, Neureuther, Moritz von Schwind, and Ludwig Richter never tired of illustrating stories of mermaids, knights and enchanters, the intimate unity of forti-fied towns with watchmen sounding their trumpets from tall watch-towers. In France, fewer towns had retained their medieval appearance under the onslaught of Classicism; but in Germany a large number of authentic medieval towns still existed so that these Gothic backgrounds were not deliberately archaic, artificial reconstructions, but a reflection of original forms which had remained unaltered through the centuries and were still capable of an ever-fresh, ever-fertile grace and beauty.

Alfred Rethel (1816–1859) revived the old theme of the Dance of Death, once a familiar subject in churches and cemeteries and used as the subject of a series by Holbein. Rethel, who painted large historical compositions on the history of Charlemagne (Aachen Cathedral), was haunted by a world of ghosts and skeletons, an increasing obsession which culminated in his losing his reason at the age of thirty-seven. Although he visited Italy twice, in 1844 and 1852, he derived nothing from it except a certain taste for Biblical realism in the manner of Alma Tadema; he was deeply, basically German, like Schnorr von Carolsfeld (1794–1872) who, despite being a Nazarene, no longer modelled himself on Fra Angelico or Raphael but on Dürer, the most German of painters, to whom the Romantics devoted a pious worship and fervent admiration. Despite its slight, superficial Italianism, his *Family of St John visiting the Family of Jesus* (1817, Gemäldegalerie, Dresden) is, both as a whole and in detail, a tribute to the vigour and originality of the German genius.

Antiquarian and archaistic preoccupations were never essential to Romanticism, which, in Germany at least, never had the artificiality which is often found in French Neo-Gothic. There the attachment to the Middle Ages was an organic growth, stimulating a desire to create something new, even if this 'novelty' retained features of the old. German poets and artists were driven on by a nostalgic feeling for the Gothic centuries; as though lured on by a lost paradise, a vanished golden age, when all was strength, joyousness, exaltation, religious fervour, harmony and happiness, they thrust behind them the rationalism of the 18th century which seemed to them to have destroyed all this. In their pictures they attempted to model

FRANZ HORNY 1798–1824

Horny was a friend of Friedrich von Olivier and Schnorr von Carolsfeld and, like them, shared in the group activities of the Nazarenes in Rome. He died at twenty-six in the village of Olevano near Rome, to which he had moved. Horny was a highly talented designer and watercolour painter.

9   *View of Olevano*

Pen and brown ink over red chalk. 53.2 × 37.3 (21 × 14½)
Martin von Wagner Museum, Würzburg

CARL ROTTMANN 1797–1850

Rottmann's taste for 'heroic pastorals' in the style of the Italian Baroque painters and Koch was reinforced by his long visits to the Bavarian mountains. He also travelled in Italy and Greece where he worked on a series of landscapes which absorbed his whole attention until the end of his life.

10   *Italian Landscape*

Pen and ink, pencil and watercolour. 31 × 47 (12⅜ × 18½)
Victoria and Albert Museum, London

LUDWIG VOGEL 1788–1879

Vogel took part in the movement for religious revival in painting taken up by the group of German artists who lived in the Convent of S Isidoro. Later he returned to Switzerland, his native country, took up residence in Zürich and devoted himself henceforth to painting landscapes of his own country.

11   *Portrait of Overbeck*

Pencil and wash. 26 × 15 (10¼ × 5⅞)
Kunsthaus, Zürich

LUDWIG ADRIAN RICHTER

12   *Italian Landscape near Castelgandolfo*

Drawing. 27 × 29 (10¼ × 11½)
Victoria and Albert Museum, London

CASPAR DAVID FRIEDRICH see p. 110

13   *Setting Sun on the Beach, Rügen*

Sepia. 24.8 × 37.7 (9¾ × 14⅞)
Dr Fritz Nathan Collection, Zürich

LUDWIG ADRIAN RICHTER

14   *Rowing Boat on the Lake of St Wolfgang*

1823. Pen, pencil, brown and grey wash. 12.5 × 18.6 (4⅞ × 7⅜)
Winterstein Collection, Munich

EDUARD VON STEINLE 1810–86

A characteristic member of the Austrian Romantic school, Steinle studied under Kupelwieser and then worked in Rome with Cornelius, Overbeck and Führich. He is best known for his engravings, particularly his illustrations to the works of Clemens von Brentano, legends and folk tales.

15   *Little Girl under an Apple-Tree*

1841. Pen. 16.4 × 17 (6½ × 6¾)
Folkwang Museum, Essen

9

11

10

12

13

14

15

16

17

18

19

20

21

22

PHILIPP OTTO RUNGE see p. 105

16 *View of the Alster, Hamburg*

c. 1805. Pencil and gouache. 43.3×31 (17×12¼)
Winterstein Collection, Munich

CASPAR DAVID FRIEDRICH

17 *Rocky Gorge in Saxony*

Sepia. 69.3×49.4 (27¼×19½)
Folkwang Museum, Essen

JULIUS SCHNORR VON CAROLSFELD 1794–1872
After working with the Nazarenes in Rome, he was engaged by
Ludwig I of Bavaria to decorate his castle and the Munich
Residenz. He brought to his historical painting and
illustration a brilliant imagination and an energetic,
colourful lyricism.

18 *Portrait of the Painter Johann Scheffer von Leonhartshoff*

1816. Pencil. 25×20.4 (9¾×8)
Bibliothek der Akademie der Bildenden Künste, Vienna

JOHANN WOLFGANG VON GOETHE 1749–1832
Goethe was always interested in the visual arts, particularly
drawing, for which he evinced a very real talent. The fire
and spirit of this drawing make it easy to understand why
at one time he even wondered whether to devote himself
to painting rather than poetry.

19 *Study of Rocks*

c. 1785. Pen and brown and grey wash. 11×17.1 (4⅜×6⅝)
Winterstein Collection, Munich

FERDINAND VON OLIVIER 1785–1841
Olivier's life was divided between art and diplomatic
missions which often took him abroad. He knew Koch and
was much influenced by him when becoming a member of
the Lukasbund. Towards the end of his life he became
professor of art-history at the Munich Academy.

20 *View of Salzburg*

c. 1818. Pencil heightened with white. 19×31.8 (7½×12½)
Albertina, Vienna

CARL GUSTAV CARUS 1789–1869

21 *Gothic Cathedral Seen through Ruins*

1832. Chalk. 23.7×24.2 (9⅜×9⅝)
Folkwang Museum, Essen

JOHANN ANTON RAMBOUX 1790–1866
Born in Trier, Ramboux worked first with the Lukasbund
in Rome, then with David in Paris, and later in Munich.
He took advantage of his stay in Italy to make watercolour
copies of numerous famous Renaissance paintings, on which
he drew for inspiration in his own pictures.

22 *The Choir of Cologne Cathedral from the South-West*

1844. Pencil and watercolour. 60×107 (23⅝×42⅛)
Stadtmuseum, Cologne

the present on the past, not by artificial imitation but by awakening in themselves
the old spirit which had inspired the old art.

Moritz von Schwind (1804–1871), a Viennese of great charm, preserved a childlike freshness of heart and mind throughout his life; he really believed in the legends
of the forests, the Rhineland, the adventures of knight-errantry. Voluble, prolific,
typifying the axiomatic 'Austrian gaiety' in its most exquisite and subtle form, he
approached the idyllic reality of his *Symphony* (Neue Pinakothek, Munich) with
the same gusto as the imaginary happenings of wizards and fairies in his book
illustrations. Like Eduard Jakob von Steinle (1810–1886), another Viennese, he
recaptured the whimsical gaiety of the student on holiday, of the Renaissance artists
travelling through the beautiful towns of Germany, filled with flowers, music and
goodfellowship. Three fine Romantic engravers, Eugen Napoleon Neureuther
(1806–1882), Ludwig von Maydell (1795–1846) and Ludwig Adrian Richter (1803–
1884) must be mentioned in connection with Schwind and Steinle, although they were
better known as illustrators than as painters. Richter, in particular, conjured up
unforgettable pictures of an ideal Germany, with its cosy half-timbered houses and
forests haunted by eerie gnomes and unicorns. But he also created at least one picture
on an entirely different level from all the rest of his work, as melodious and evocative
as a Schumann symphony; his *River Scene on the Elbe* (1837, Gemäldegalerie, Dresden)
combines all the typical Romantic themes—the rocks crowned with ruins gilded
by the setting sun, the wandering student, the musician, the pair of lovers . . .

Schwind's tender nostalgia, almost painful in its intensity, is transformed into a
form of irony by Karl Spitzweg (1808–1885), a much misunderstood artist who
rediscovered the poetry of Biedermeier Germany, with its touching if unromantic
episodes, and gave it a curious paradoxical beauty compounded of sweetness of
manner and genial mockery. *The Poor Poet* (c. 1835 Neue Pinakothek, Munich) and
The Serenade (Schackgalerie, Munich) are good examples of this mixture of wit and
tenderness which adds a very individual savour to Spitzweg's works. However,
perhaps only a German can appreciate him to the full.

The Tyrolean, Joseph Anton Koch (1768–1839) is an important link in the chain
of development of German Romantic landscape-painting, a halfway house in its
progress from the anecdotal and descriptive to a deep lyricism in which man and
nature share the same emotional world and merge into a single being. Besides painting
a large number of 'heroic pastorals' in the Italian style and religious scenes set
against conventional backgrounds, Koch was the first to see and portray mountains
in a truly modern way. Before going to Rome, where he remained forty-five years,
until the end of his life, he had studied the glaciers and waterfalls of his own region
and the Bernese Oberland with loving attention. A certain clumsiness is visible in
his treatment of these unknown places and in the way he organizes the picture like
a continuous narrative in which the details are arranged, verse by verse, after the
fashion of a poem by Haller or Gessner; but his feeling for nature is sympathetic
and his depiction of it has the accuracy which comes of having actually seen the
objects portrayed and experienced their influence. His *Bernese Landscape* (1817,
Ferdinandeum, Innsbruck) and his famous picture of the *Waterfall of Schmadribach*
began a development which was to culminate in the work of Caspar David Friedrich. If Koch was more often a narrator than a poet, a visualizer than a visionary,
this does not detract from his enormous importance and fundamental influence on
the Nazarenes and a large number of other painters.

Koch's objective, analytical reproduction of nature was not the only approach
of the age; a more Romantic method was described in the following way by Carl
Gustav Carus (1789–1869) in his *Nine Letters on Landscape-Painting*: 'A man contemplating the magnificent unity of a natural landscape becomes aware of his own
smallness and, feeling that everything is a part of God, he loses himself in that
infinity, giving up, in a sense, his individual existence. To be engulfed in this way
is not to be destroyed; it is a gain: what normally one could only perceive with the

spirit almost becomes plain to the physical eye. It becomes convinced of the unity of the infinite universe.'

Each word of this statement should be carefully considered, for it defines the essential tenet of Romantic landscape-painting, with its lofty spiritual mission, its near-mysticism almost more important than its aesthetic function; this pantheistic communion is the privilege of the artist who has become aware of existence and felt the force of the spiritual life 'which links the movements and metamorphoses of external Nature to the variations of feeling within ourselves', as Carus wrote.

Caspar David Friedrich (1774–1840) towers over the other German landscape painters of his day, in that his visionary pantheism found richer and more varied expression. His drawings, models of precision, show that he observed nature with a patient attentiveness, an almost photographic attention to detail, that he attempted to grasp the individuality of each tree, and of each branch of each tree because both the tree and the branch were living creatures; the artist wants from them the secret of the organic structures which create, and maintain life and loves them with a feeling of universal intimacy which does away with all arbitrary distinctions between the *ego* and the *non-ego*. For the Romantic everything became a part of the artist, everything emanated from him and a continual osmosis was established between man, borne away on the tide of universality and that tide itself in which he was absorbed.

In his *Rainbow* (c. 1809, Folkwang Museum, Essen) or his famous *Two Men Gazing at the Moon* (1819, Gemäldegalerie, Dresden) contemplation indeed becomes action; it is a movement of the soul out towards objects which are then assimilated back into the profound personality of the contemplator. When he recommends the artist to 'shut your physical eye and look first at your picture with your spiritual eye, then bring to the light of day what you have seen in the darkness...' he is defining an essentially Romantic process by which the representation of a real, external, objective landscape is simultaneously a transcription of the picture inhabiting the painter's conscious and subconscious mind ... A direct contact, without intermediary, is established between *natura naturans* and *natura naturata*, and the one is so inextricably bound up with the other that it becomes impossible to distinguish the mood of the artist from the external images reproducing that mood. If, on the other hand, the emotion behind the contemplation spontaneously shaped the landscape in the artist's mind's eye to conform with nature, the external image is, of course, also the visual materialization of the artist's mood.

This metaphysical, symbolical content is to be found in nearly all Caspar David Friedrich's pictures, although it is not always deliberately emphasized by the painter. Whether the subject is mountains, creeping up out of the morning mists or sinking into storm-clouds, or the port of Greifswald, whence ships are sailing towards the horizon with the majesty of souls taking wing for the infinite, human destiny is always the indirect subject. For Friedrich, the scope of a landscape was exactly parallelled by the scope of the mind behind it; this feeling for amplitude, for open areas, comes out clearly in his preference for seascapes with only a thin strip of shore to remind one of land, for skies filled with dramatic clouds, for (above all else) the Pomeranian sand-dunes stretching out as far as the horizon, for mountains whose soaring peaks make one think of the quest for the Infinite, as in Chinese paintings. To Friedrich there was an essential conflict between the close forest, pressing down on the individual spirit, suffocating it, and the 'open' world of the sea and the sky. Technically he succeeds in suggesting the presence of the Infinite by means of his fluid, transparent light-touched pictorial style. The figure with his back to the spectator looking into the depths of the background, who recurs in so many of the pictures, is a symbol of the nostalgic longing for 'distance' which tortured Friedrich's lonely, troubled soul.

In his paintings light, too, acquires the function and position of a metaphysical entity, of a spiritual 'illumination' delivering man from the dark prison of his unconscious mind, desires and ambitions. But all these symbols merge in a great

FRIEDRICH OVERBECK 1789–1869
After helping to found the Lukasbund in Vienna in 1809, Overbeck went to Rome where he played a leading part in the growth of the Nazarene Movement. He reacted strongly against the art of the 18th century, aiming to recapture the solid aesthetic and moral virtues of the Middle Ages and to revive religious art which, he held, had degenerated since that period.

23 *The Wise and Foolish Virgins*

Pencil and colour wash. 35.5 (14) in diameter
Original Drawing from the Staatliche Graphische Sammlung, Munich

PHILIPP OTTO RUNGE

24 *Noon*

This is a sketch for the picture of the same title
1803. Pen and wash. 71.7×48 (28¼×19)
Kunsthalle, Hamburg

25 *The Lily of Light*

A study for the larger version of *Morning*
1809. Pencil, black and red chalk. 57.2×41 (22⅜×16⅛)
Wallraf-Richartz Museum, Cologne

JOHANN FRIEDRICH OVERBECK

26 *Joseph Telling his Dreams*

Drawing. 13.7×17.5 (5⅜×6⅞)
Private Collection

23

25

24

26

27

29

28

30

vibrating pantheism, in which Nature is loved for itself, for its basic, elemental power, whose different facets are revealed in its various landscapes and seascapes. Friedrich once said to Peter von Cornelius, when the latter was visiting him, 'God is everywhere, even in a grain of sand'. This communion with the divine which gives his work an intensely religious flavour is revealed in all his subjects: the crucifix on a high mountain of the *Cross in the Mountains* (1808, Gemäldegalerie, Dresden), the *Cross in the Riesengebirge* (Staatliche Museen, Berlin), the ruins of a convent or Gothic cathedral, the infinite expanse of the North Sea, or the dark concentration of a pine-forest. It results, however, not from a deification of Nature or the elements, but from the conception of a universal omnipresent soul which had been shared by the German mystics from Meister Eckhart to Angelus Silesius and Böhme and poets like Novalis and Hölderlin.

Completely indifferent to the opinion held of him by his contemporaries though kind and hospitable to those who visited him, secretly consumed by an ineradicable melancholy which, in his later years, led to insanity, Friedrich dissociated himself from his era and he still remains outside any historical scheme. In his pictures Nature, down to its smallest detail however solid and material, is an all-pervading spirit, and in the same way his influence continued to pervade art long after his own age was past. His gospel was spread abroad not only by his actual pupils, Gerhard von Kügelgen (1772–1820), Ferdinand Hartmann (1774–1842), Georg Friedrich Kersting (1785–1847), who painted a fine portrait of him, and the Riepenhausen brothers; the visionary pantheism of his art lived on in post-Romantics like Marées and Böcklin and, even more distinctly, in the Expressionist landscapes of Heckel, Kirchner and Nolde. Moreover there is hardly a single passage by Friedrich which Paul Klee would not have endorsed.

Two other painters stand out from the great body of German landscapists, by reason of their affinities with the *Naturphilosophen* and the imaginative powers linking them with Friedrich. Both Ernst Ferdinand Oehme (1797–1855) and Carl Blechen (1798–1840) are practically unknown outside Germany. Oehme's *Cathedral in Winter* (Gemäldegalerie, Dresden) combines all the most striking of the typically Romantic themes—Gothic spires and churches, dead trees, snow, the night and curious lights shining behind stained-glass windows. Blechen was the author of a Romantic masterpiece, unfortunately lost in the Glaspalast catastrophe in Munich in 1931: it shows a thunderbolt falling on a vehicle which is shattered in pieces. Just as Delacroix wanted to paint the flash of a sword, so Blechen attempted a concrete picture of a thunderbolt, investing it with a tragic grandeur which gives it the stature of an instrument of divine or infernal fatality.

Blechen had begun as a stage designer under the supervision of Karl Friedrich Schinkel (1781–1841) who was at one and the same time a passionately pro-Classical architect who covered Germany with copies of the Parthenon and the Propylaea, and a violently pro-Gothic painter. His best pictures show medieval townships whose castles brood over the majestic curves of a river and whose skylines are diversified by the spires and bell-turrets of fantastic cathedrals almost unreal in their bizarreries and colossal size and eccentricity. In Schinkel's paintings as in those of Blechen, there is a certain 'theatricality'—if not melodrama—as well as obvious influences taken direct from Romantic plays on medieval subjects; the Romantic poets—Hugo, Clemens von Brentano, etc.—made a great point of faithfully presenting 'local colour' and 'historical atmosphere', without, however, giving up any of their right to liberty of interpretation.

The exceptional beauty of these masterpieces of 'tragic' landscapes should not blind us to the merits of the minor Romantic painters. In Austria, Ferdinand Georg Waldmüller (1793–1865) and Adalbert Stifter (1805–1868), better known as a novelist, produced sensitive, sympathetic interpretations of the gentle country around Vienna; the Prater and Vienna Woods may lack the mysterious majesty of the forests portrayed by Friedrich, Carus, Oehme and Blechen, but on the other

JULIUS SCHNORR VON CAROLSFELD

27 *Study for the Large West Window of St Paul's Cathedral, London*

1862. Pen and ink, pencil and watercolour
85 × 53 (35½ × 21)
Victoria and Albert Museum, London

CARL SPITZWEG see p. 123

28 *The Departure*

Drawing. 22 × 33 (8¾ × 13)
Victoria and Albert Museum, London

JOSEPH ANTON KOCH

29 *Dante and Virgil in the Underworld*

Pen. 37.2 × 30 (14⅝ × 11¾)
Niedersächsische Landesgalerie, Hanover
The subject is a combination of several scenes from Dante's *Inferno*: the embezzlers thrown into the lake of boiling pitch, the Magistrate of Lucca, the appeasement of Malacoda, the Chief of Demons, and the story of Ciampolo of Navarre

LUDWIG ADRIAN RICHTER

30 *Peasants Returning from the Fields*

Drawing. 29 × 17 (11¼ × 6¾)
Victoria and Albert Museum, London

hand the Austrians evince an easy and sometimes moving grace in their depiction of the simple charm of the Biedermeier period in the Hapsburg capital.

Owing to the Romantics' desire to lose themselves in Nature, to sink individuality in the current of cosmic energy, the portrait was of less importance in that era than it had been in the preceding century. But, curiously enough, the more outstanding portraits—those of Erwin Speckter, Victor Emil Janssen, Overbeck and Sigismund Ruhl—reveal an intense interest in the secret, private feelings of the individual. The painter thrusts aside the conventional mask covering his sitter's true features to probe into the disquiet, melancholy and nostalgia which have moulded his face.

The portraits by Philipp Otto Runge (1777–1810) are the most moving: *We Three* (1805) and *The Hülsenbeck Children* (1805–6, Kunsthalle, Hamburg) and his various self-portraits are splendid examples of his powerful yet subtle understanding of the world of the mind as expressed in the face, where it forms a sort of tragic landscape in flesh and bone. Runge was not only a portrait painter; fascinated by the universe as a whole he embarked on a series of huge compositions representing each separate hour of the day; these combine allegorical figures with trees and flowers. He died at the age of thirty-three leaving only sketches for these pictures which he had envisaged as grouped together in some sort of sanctuary dedicated to painting, music and poetry—the 'complete work of art', combining all the media, of which the Romantics so fondly dreamed.

In his tender, delicate work, with its monumental aspirations, contrasts stand out and yet are, paradoxically, blended: his fondness for tiny flowers, and his equal fondness for the vast God-illuminated universe, his longing for the absolute and the Infinite and his study of 'correspondences' by which all forms, colours, sounds, feelings, passions and elements would fit into a single plan of divine perfection . . . As with Jean Paul, the author of *Die Flegeljahre* and *Titan* who had a strong influence on Romantic painting, the sight of natural wonders—a dawn, a sunset, a mighty storm—started up in Runge the mystical transports and ecstasy in which man becomes one with the divinity.

As Romanticism is clearly one of the constants of the German mind and genius from the early Middle Ages onwards, reappearing periodically under different guises but always deriving from the same essential spirit, it is difficult to decide exactly when it appeared or disappeared. Ought one to consider as Romantics or as post-Romantics those artists of the second half of the nineteenth century in whom the Romantic ideal, now in a less pure form, is mingled with other concepts such as Realism or Symbolism—Böcklin, Klinger, Hans von Marées, Anselm Feuerbach? Should Lovis Corinth, for example, be called a master of the modern Romantic landscape?

Perhaps it is best to confine oneself to examining the way in which characteristic Romanticism survived. We see it in the simple tender landscapes of Hans Thoma (1839–1924) and those of Ludwig Richter's pupil Karl Haider (1846–1912), in the romantic, tragic compositions, inspired by Friedrich's pantheistic attitude to nature, of Arnold Böcklin (1827–1901), the Classical scenes with an entirely modern feeling of Anselm Feuerbach (1829–1880), and the fantastic engravings of Max Klinger (1857–1920) who was equally interested in Naturalistic 'slices of life', polychromatic sculpture and the visionary possibilities of etching.

A brief mention must be made of the Swiss Albert Welti (1862–1912) who painted the mountains of his own country peopled with hobgoblins, demons and phantoms, Hans von Marées (1837–1887), whose lyrical evocations of antiquity are bathed in the pantheistic spirit of the ancient German forests, and Giovanni Segantini (1858–1899), the hermit of Maloja for whom mountains were living creatures whose quiet rhythmical breathing could atmost be heard in the silence of midday. For all these, 19th-century ideals yielded new modes of expression, ways of thought and feeling which, although completely different from those of the preceding generation, are no less genuinely Romantic in essence and substance.

XXVI PHILIPP OTTO RUNGE 1777–1810

Runge at the age of eighteen joined the firm of his brother Daniel. Daniel, however, realized that art was Philipp's vocation and made him a regular allowance which enabled him to work as he wanted. He studied painting at Hamburg with Herterich and Hardorff, and then, from 1799 to 1801, at Copenhagen with Jens Juel. Later he went to Dresden, where he became friendly with Ludwig Tieck and Caspar David Friedrich. His ideal was to return to the innocence of childhood, the symbol both of the pure heart and straightforward communion with nature. He would have liked people to look at his pictures to the accompaniment of music and poetry, which he felt would bring out and underline the musical and poetic content of the painting. Unfortunately he died before completing his series of *Hours of the Day* which was to be an allegorical depiction of the cycles of nature, man's life on earth, and his transmutation from matter into spirit. In his pictures each shape, almost each colour, takes on a symbolical meaning.

Rest on the Flight into Egypt

1805–6. 98 × 132 (38½ × 52) Kunsthalle, Hamburg

XXVII CARL PHILIPP FOHR 1795–1818

Born in Heidelberg, Fohr first studied under Friedrich Rottmann and G. W. Issels in his native town and Darmstadt. While attending the Academy at Munich in 1815–6 he became acquainted with the art of the old German masters. In the autumn of 1816 he settled in Rome where he was much influenced by Joseph Anton Koch with whom he came into contact; at the same time he studied the Venetians and visited the Roman *campagna* which enchanted him. Principally he painted at Subiaco and Tivoli, finding in these Italian landscapes a Romantic quality quite different from those of Germany and recalling the character of the medieval and Renaissance paintings so much admired by the Romanized Germans, Nazarenes, and others. His œuvre is one of the best examples of what German Romanticism as a whole owed to Italy—a trend which can be seen in Ramboux, Passavant, Führich and, of course, the Nazarenes and Koch. Fohr was drowned accidentally in the Tiber in 1818 just after finishing a drawing showing Hagen listening to the song of the Daughters of the Rhine.

The poetic composition of this *Romantic Landscape in Italy* recalls Koch's style and his methods of construction; the strolling musicians and pilgrims are necessary for 'local colour'. It was painted in 1817, the year before Fohr's death and shows his art at its height. The feeling of distance, the serene yet powerful harmony of the atmosphere and the Italian gaiety affecting both man and nature admirably reflect the spell which Italy cast over the German painters of the period, giving their art a very individual flavour.

Romantic Landscape in Italy

1817. 133 × 97 (52⅜ × 38⅛) Collection of HRH The Prince of Hesse and the Rhine Collection, Germany

XXVIII CARL BLECHEN 1798–1840

While staying in Rome and particularly during the winter of 1828–9, Blechen painted several views of the gardens of the Villa Borghese whose harmonious groups of trees and beautiful light greatly appealed to him. There is nothing of the Nordic, Medievalist Romanticism of his early years in a composition such as this: Nordic ruins and forests are replaced by a fresh, spontaneous, almost impressionistic, sensitivity. Like the pictures he painted in Naples, Amalfi, Capri, Sorrento and the Roman *campagna,* these Villa Borghese pictures show that Blechen had completely cast off his earlier tragic manner, in which there had still been a certain theatrical quality. The Italian landscape awoke his sense of the beauty of nature, and if he seems less 'Romantic' than in the earlier works, he does at least reveal a modern approach to landscape painting. A number of drawings and watercolours which clearly served as studies for this picture are known.

In the Park of the Villa Borghese

78 × 63 (30¾ × 24¾) Nationalgalerie, Berlin

XXIX CARL BLECHEN

As his family intended him for a business career, Blechen began by qualifying himself for this before beginning to study painting at the Berlin Academy in 1822.

While travelling in the following year he met Johann Christian Dahl and Caspar David Friedrich; the latter clearly inspired the most Romantic, Medievalist and mysterious of his works. Between 1824 and 1827 he worked as a stage designer under Schinkel at the Königstadt theatre, principally devising sets for operas and Romantic dramas. During a two-year visit to Italy he discovered a new world of sunlit, tranquil landscapes, of an easy existence beneath an ever-sunny sky. His art became less monumentally tragic; he learned the value of effects of light on trees, his palette brightened and an almost Impressionist sensitivity came to enliven his canvases. This serene, peaceful harmony was shattered in 1839 by symptoms of madness and he died insane in Berlin at the age of forty-two. *Women Bathing* was the outcome of numerous sketches made in the park of Terni.

Women Bathing in the Park of Terni

1829. 32×24.5 (12⅝×9¾) Kunstmuseum, Düsseldorf

XXX CASPAR DAVID FRIEDRICH 1774–1840

Like the similar picture at Weimar, this is one of numerous attempts by Friedrich to bring out the contrast between the 'infinite landscape' and the smallness of the human individual looking at it. The man in the red jacket and white trousers is said to be Friedrich himself, and he appears minute in comparison with the enormous storm clouds and night sky all round. Man is only an insignificant part of nature as a whole, but he can approach its proportions by his understanding, love and communion with it. The background darkness encircled by the fairylike curve of the rainbow represents the fearsome, mysterious force of the elements. The clouds are admirably painted; they were one of Friedrich's favourite subjects and he allowed no one into his studio when he was painting them: 'I have to give myself up to my surroundings, to be united with my clouds and rocks, in order to be what I am'.

Mountain Landscape with Rainbow

c. 1809. 69.8 × 103 (27½ × 40½) Folkwang Museum, Essen

XXXI CASPAR DAVID FRIEDRICH

Friedrich was born at Greifswald on the Baltic which is the subject of many of his pictures and casts its peculiar shadow over most of them. Up to the age of twenty he was taught by Quistorp in his native town; he then studied for four years at the Copenhagen Academy of Fine Arts which exerted a considerable influence on the development of German Romantic painting in general. In 1798 he left Copenhagen for Dresden where he spent the rest of his life, apart from numerous visits to Greifswald. At Dresden he came into contact with other Romantics, both poets and painters—Kleist, Tieck, Müller, Runge, Olivier and Kersting; he did not meet Goethe until 1810. Dahl was a close friend; in fact the two men shared quarters for the last twenty years of Friedrich's life. In 1805 he was awarded the prize of the Friends of Art, founded by Goethe in Weimar, although Friedrich's art, with its passionate, absolute Romanticism, was directly opposed to all Goethe's æsthetic ideas. In his feeling for a certain 'supernaturalism of landscape' he somewhat resembled Carl Gustav Carus and led the way for a number of German artists, including Oehme, Blechen, Kügelgen and Klinkowström. His melancholy developed into more severe mental troubles towards the end of his life and in 1835 he was paralyzed by an attack. Friedrich wrung the last drop of beauty out of the mystical conception of nature he so often expressed in his writings, in a manner not unlike that of Blake.

The Cross and the Cathedral in the Mountains

c. 1811. 45 × 38 (17¾ × 15) Kunstmuseum, Düsseldorf

XXXII CASPAR DAVID FRIEDRICH

Again and again Friedrich painted pictures showing people looking at the moon through trees (see *Two Men Gazing at the Moon,* in Dresden), but the scene always has a mysterious, sinister character, as if magic were brewing. Instead of taking an obvious pleasure in wide open spaces, as in his landscapes, Friedrich here confines himself to forests of twisted and stunted trees. The moon itself, crowned with a halo of mist, is revealed against a backdrop of misty vapour. The two figures look as if they have climbed the mountain during the night to watch this pallid moon rise and feebly light up the country around and the dark tree-tops. In this composition, akin to the analogous one at Dresden, Friedrich shows how intense his fantasy could be, how sensitive he was to the 'nocturnal face of natural phenomena', in the words of the philosopher von Schubert, and how strongly he could be overwhelmed by supernatural feeling when looking at familiar things and places at unfamiliar moments. The tree, with its exposed roots and stripped branches, seems about to turn into a living monster.

Man and Woman Gazing at the Moon

1819. 35×44 (13¾×17⅜) Nationalgalerie, Berlin

XXXIII CASPAR DAVID FRIEDRICH

Friedrich's biographers trace the origin of *The Wreck of the 'Hope'* to a news item which is said to have had a profound effect on the artist. It is known, too, that he was very moved on one occasion by the sight of the ice breaking up on the Elbe and he never forgot having seen his brother drown in the frozen masses, as a child. On the other hand ships are usually symbols of human life in Friedrich's seascapes: the *Four Ages of Man* in Leipzig is an example of this, as are the many pictures showing ships either leaving the port of Greifswald in the grey brightness of the morning (youth) or returning in the evening, tired and despondent. Friedrich's ships are endowed with a strange living quality, as if for him they were indeed equivalent to human beings by virtue of the profound underlying unity of nature linking inanimate and animate objects together. Thus *The Wreck of the 'Hope'* means the termination of a life, the destruction of hopes and energies, destiny overwhelming the individual and crushing it in its inescapable embrace. This theme so haunted Friedrich that he painted two versions of the wreck and Quandt tells that he planned a third. It was one of his most popular pictures probably because its symbolism was immediately intelligible to the viewer.

The Wreck of the 'Hope'

1821. 98 × 128 (38½ × 51⅛) Kunsthalle, Hamburg

XXXIV GEORG FRIEDRICH KERSTING 1785–1847

Born at Güstrow, Kersting was attracted to the Copenhagen Academy by the reputation of Jens Juel and Abilgaard who taught there. During the wars of 1813 he executed several paintings inspired by military life or events. Afterwards he became drawing master to Princess Saprena of Warsaw. He was friendly with Caspar David Friedrich and indeed painted his portrait; from him he caught a feeling for cool, silent, 'introspective' interiors, charged with emotion. The most typical of these is his portrait of Friedrich in his studio, which gives an exact rendering of the atmosphere in which the 'master of the tragic landscape' worked. In 1818 he went to the porcelain manufactory of Meissen. He was considered one of the most outstanding exponents of the 'bourgeois intimism' which held an important place in Germany, though not in other countries.

Children at the Window

68 × 52 (26¾ × 20½) Kunstmuseum, Düsseldorf

XXXV MORITZ VON SCHWIND 1804–71

Von Schwind belonged to a group of Austrian artists which included Franz Schubert, Grillparzer and Lenau, and Kupelwieser, the Oliviers, and Krafft. He first won approval as an illustrator of contemporary poets and novelists such as Brentano, Wieland and Mörike, as well as the folk tales which were such a cult in Germany. His admiration for Runge, however, led him to attempt larger and more ambitious works. Modelling himself on Cornelius he learned fresco technique and embarked on large mural compositions at Munich, Hohenschwangau and Vienna. In 1847 he was made a professor of the Academy at Munich where he died at the age of sixty-seven. His murals are not without vigour or imagination but they are generally found less interesting than his smaller-scale paintings, with their greater intimacy, tenderness and fairytale atmosphere. He excelled all the German artists of his day in portraying the poetry of reality with refreshing simplicity and imagination.

In the Artist's House

c. 1860. 71 × 51 (28 × 20⅓) Schackgalerie, Munich

XXXVI JOSEPH ANTON KOCH 1768–1839

Koch came of a Tyrolean peasant family, and the Tyrol exerted a great influence on his work. He was one of the first painters to take an especial interest in mountains and to portray them with equal regard for their reality and their poetry. He first left his native Obergibeln when he was apprenticed to Ingerl, an Augsburg sculptor; later he studied under Hetsch and Harper at the Karlsschule, Stuttgart, but left this rigorously disciplined establishment to travel in Alsace and Switzerland where he perfected his landscape technique: his compositions are neither wholly realistic nor wholly imaginary, but composed of a number of elements observed from nature and arranged according to the poetic or musical feeling he wants to arouse. In short, he was one of the most active and original exponents of the new attitude towards the landscape developed by the Romantics. In 1795 he moved to Rome where he lived, with few interruptions, until the end of his life in 1839. After becoming friendly with the Nazarenes, Carstens and Thorwaldsen, he made a study of Italian painting and composed landscape in the 'heroic pastoral' style of the 17th century and historical scenes taken from the *Divina Commedia* or *Ossian*. In trying to produce 'symphonic' compositions he lost the early, almost Impressionist, sensitivity which had marked out his Swiss and Tyrolean landscapes. This charming composition shows the influence of Poussin, Claude and Salvator Rosa.

Waterfalls near Subiaco

1813. 58 × 68 (22⅞ × 26¾) Nationalgalerie, Berlin

XXXVII LUDWIG ADRIAN RICHTER 1803–84

At the age of seventeen Richter left his native city of Dresden to accompany Prince Narishkin on his travels; during these he painted the views which his noble companion found most pleasing. In 1823 he was granted a scholarship for a three-year visit to Italy by the bookseller Christoph Arnold. He stayed mainly in Rome, frequenting Nazarene circles, and became particularly friendly with Koch and Schnorr von Carolsfeld. On his return from Germany he taught at the Academy of Dresden and was a director of the Meissen porcelain factory. He himself recorded the more picturesque episodes of his life in his very amusing and instructive autobiography, *Lebenserinnerungen eines deutschen Malers*. Despite the not inconsiderable merits of his paintings, Richter was principally admired for his drawings; he illustrated many books of poems and stories with wood engravings remarkable in conception and execution. He excelled both in recreating the atmosphere of medieval towns and in imagining forests peopled by wood-nymphs and sprites, and the contrasts offered by the legendary scenes on the one hand, and the scenes of bourgeois German life on the other, are interesting and curious. *The Little Lake* was the only oil painting executed by Richter as a result of his tour of the Riesengebirge in 1823, undertaken at the suggestion of a Leipzig publisher who was planning a series of steel engravings on the region.

The Little Lake

1839. 63 × 88 (24¾ × 34¾) Nationalgalerie, Berlin

XXXVIII CARL SPITZWEG 1808–85

It is always surprising to the foreigner that German Romanticism—unlike that of England and France—contrived to include a sort of glorification of bourgeois simplicity, of the modest, kindly, unpretentious virtues beloved of Biedermeier. Carl Spitzweg was a remarkably sympathetic, if lively and amused, portraitist of the life of humble people, in both its gay and its sad aspects. While North German Romantics went out of their way to find tragic or fantastic subjects, the Bavarians and Austrians were moved and inspired by episodes from everyday life. This depiction of a picnic on the grass is characteristic of Spitzweg's light-handed gaiety, here applied to rustic pleasures rather than incidents from dramas or scenes in medieval towns. The brilliance and luminosity of the colour indicates that he took a considerable interest in contemporary investigations in painting technique.

The Outing

27 × 49 (10⅝ × 19¼) Neue Pinakothek, Munich

XXXIX CARL SPITZWEG

Like Hans Thoma and Arnold Böcklin, Spitzweg
belongs to a sort of Indian summer of Romanticism.
After studying pharmacy at Munich University in
1832 he went on a journey to Italy where his eyes
were opened to the splendours of Italian painting.
It was not until the following year, however, that
he began to teach himself to paint while conva-
lescing from brain fever. Later he was given some
lessons by Christian Heinrich Hansonn, and studied
the Dutch masters in the Munich Pinakothek
before asking the elder Eduard von Schleich to
teach him. While producing illustrations for the
review *Fliegende Blätter,* founded in 1844 by Braun
and Schneider, he also painted the charming genre
scenes which made his name—pictures with thick,
warm colour and a use of light which often recalls
stage designs. Spitzweg was one of the 'painter-
poets' of whom there were so many in Germany
in the Romantic and post-Romantic period. Their
influence lingered long in German art and is still
visible even in Expressionism.

Life in an Attic

1866. 54 × 31.5 (21¼ × 12⅜) Schackgalerie, Munich

XL ARNOLD BÖCKLIN 1827–1901

Böcklin was one of the few Romantics surviving in a predominantly Realist age; he stubbornly resisted the academic outlook of the school of Düsseldorf where he worked under Schirmer. As the industrialized Germany of the end of the 19th century struck him as unfavourable to art he settled in Italy, dying at Fiesole in 1901. Perhaps his lyricism is overdone, too declamatory and theatrical, but he certainly possesses many of the qualities of the true Romantic—the taste for mystery, obsession with death, aspiration towards the infinite. For some reason, the fact that he treated Romantic themes realistically, even naturalistically, has been used as a reproach against Böcklin, although it would seem to be to his credit that he used the means open to his generation to express his extreme sensitivity, sincere love of the Mediterranean landscape and insight into the sensuality of Greek mythology. His favourite subjects, *The Wedding Journey,* an exaltation of life and love, and *The Isle of the Dead,* a melancholy evocation of tragic, resigned solemnity, exist in several versions.

The version illustrated is one of the most restrained: the emotion in it is concentrated, unrhetorical. In all the many pictures inspired by this theme, Böcklin was looking for a representation of death which would be both tragic and serene. Possibly the Venetian cemetery on the Isola di San Michele suggested the general idea of *The Isle of the Dead*, but the initial image was transformed as the cliffs of red rock and dense, dark clumps of poplars came to accentuate the dramatic character of the scene more and more. The vessel solemnly carrying the corpse to its last rest, with a magnificent, if lugubrious, stateliness, admirably reflects the idea of death as also envisaged by Böcklin in his *Self-portrait with Skeleton*.

The Isle of the Dead

1880. Panel. 71 × 122 (29 × 48) Metropolitan Museum of Art, New York

XLI HANS THOMA 1839–1924

Born in Bernau in the Black Forest, his father a miller and his mother the descendant of a long line of artists and craftsmen, Thoma studied first with a lithographer, then with a painter in Basle, and finally with a decorator of clock-cases in Furtwangen. From 1860 to 1866 he spent every winter at the Karlsruhe Academy, studying under Schirmer and Descondres, but during the summers he returned to his native Black Forest from which he derived his broad, healthy outlook, love for everything natural, true and poetic. At Paris in 1868 he discovered Courbet and the Barbizon School. In 1873 he met and became friendly with Böcklin and Leibl in Munich. He remained always modest, happy in simple pleasures and the wide, sunlit landscapes we see in his pictures, although he rose to great eminence as a result of his exhibitions from 1890 onwards and his position as an officer of the Academy, professor at the School of Fine Art, and director of the Karlsruhe Museum—honours accorded him by Friedrich I, Grand Duke of Baden.

Although in some of his pictures Thoma may be reproached with sentimentality and a rather bourgeois *Gemütlichkeit* which have prevented him from acquiring a reputation outside Germany, *In the Sun* does not suffer from these faults. It has a tranquil, simple beauty; a magical light ripples over the trees and water, while the splashes of sunlight bring out the life in the material of the dress and veil, the straw of the hat, with a boldness unusual in this artist and, in fact, in any painter in 1867. In this picture, Hans Thoma, the 'Realist', approaches very close to Impressionism.

In the Sun

1867. 110 × 80 (43¼ × 31½) Staatliche Kunsthalle, Karlsruhe

IN 19TH-CENTURY FRANCE, painting entered on a frantic quest for the spirit and meaning of the age—an age which from the end of the Monarchy until the Commune consisted of an unending series of upheavals. And in pursuit of this aim Romantic painters called on all their feverish, sharpened emotionality, all their love of new pictorial techniques. While 18th-century painters such as Chardin, Watteau and Fragonard had attached little importance to the political events of Europe, their Romantic counterparts, from David to Courbet and Daumier, reacted with the sensitivity of seismographs to the undercurrents disturbing both society and individuals. The Romantic painter was deeply rooted in his own age; everything happening round him awoke in him an echo, a sympathetic resonance. It would be entirely erroneous to consider the Romantics in isolation from their period; not only were they strongly 'committed' artists but they derived subjects of a touching grandeur and variety from the Napoleonic campaigns.

If Napoleon paid less attention to the artistic currents of the day than Louis XIV, his exploits, the nobility of his campaigns and battles, contributed many novel themes to the pictorial repertoire and steered artists' activities into new channels. David himself toned down his Neo-Classicism to a sort of aulic realism in order to portray contemporary events, and his *Coronation* (1805, Louvre, Paris) is a magnificent illustration from contemporary history. But basically David was no Romantic; for him it was not the historical document, but the feeling it generated which counted. This feeling is often strong enough to transfigure reality and swell **it** to almost myth-like proportions. It was the painters, even more than the poets, who contributed to the formation of the Napoleonic myth with its strange but impressive brilliance.

Widely different artists shared in this hero-worship, this idolatry of the great man, but the most remarkable of them, the only one who can really be called a genius, was Baron Gros (1771–1835). Gros' distinction lies not only in his ability to portray battle scenes with such documentary accuracy that a historian might well go to them for information as to the uniforms of the various European armies, for instance, but also in his evocation of the spirit stimulating the military ardour of these armies and above all the very skilful way in which he makes the pathetic-mythical element harmonize with the visual (almost tactile and olfactory) realism. In all of his pictures where Napoleon is the hero, *The Plague-Hospital at Jaffa* (1804,

Louvre, Paris), *Napoleon Crossing the Bridge at Arcola* (1796, Louvre, Paris), *The Battle of Eylau* (1808, Louvre, Paris), he appears as a superhuman figure, a commander of men and almost of the elements; when he touches the wounds of the plague-sufferers he appears not merely to be making a heroic gesture, courageously defying the disease, but actually to be healing the sick man who sees him as a miracle-worker—as Gros probably did himself.

Gros studied with David, who long afterwards claimed to exercize a certain influence over his pupil, even when the latter had broken away from him and was already justly considered 'the most illustrious dissident' of the Davidian school. His lyrical temperament and richness of imagination were capable of transforming reality and made the strait-jacket of Classical realism unbearable to him. His forte was the sort of super-reality which appears in his battle pictures: these are visionary rather than naturalistic, however faithful they are to the facts, however accurate their documentation.

But most of all he was interested in translating reality into myth—and indeed the spirit of the Napoleonic campaigns could only be reproduced at this level. Delacroix hit the nail on the head when he said that Gros succeeded in 'raising a modern subject to the stature of the ideal', a description which might well be applied to Delacroix himself. Gros was so attached to the Napoleonic myth that the fall of the Empire, the return of the Bourbons, who made him a baron but completely failed to understand him, and the indifference of a later generation of artists and public drove him to suicide, a tragic end to an existence divided between luminary brilliance and epic defeat.

Compared with Gros, the other painters inspired by the campaigns appear mere chroniclers, almost anecdotists. Anne-Louis Girodet de Roucy-Trioson (1767–1824) used the Egyptian campaign as a subject for his *Revolt at Cairo* (c. 1810, Versailles), but this hardly bears comparison with *The Plague-Hospital at Jaffa*. Where Gros' picture is filled with the sinister smell of poverty, the charnel-house and infected death-beds, Girodet's is merely picturesque in an anecdotal way; Gros' power, so great that one can almost smell the wet skins, the sweating horse, the trampled snow and the bricks warmed by the sun, is completely missing in Girodet. The latter turned away from the Davidian Classicism of his youth and became addicted to an almost 'troubadour' Neo-Gothic. Inspired by Chateaubriand, he painted a representation of *The Funeral of Atala* (1808, Louvre, Paris), and with his curious composition of 1801, painted for Malmaison, entered the ranks of the Napoleonic-myth painters. An avid reader of Macpherson, he also embarked on the following unusual scene: '*The Shades of French Soldiers Having Been Led by Victory into the Palace of Odin are Received by the Homer of the North and the Warlike Ghosts of Fingal and his Descendants.*'

Ingres himself had turned Romantic in order to decorate the ceiling of Napoleon's room in the Quirinal with a *Dream of Ossian* whose fantastic feeling and visionary atmosphere make it one of the Romantic masterpieces; it is at least much more in the spirit of the movement than the 'troubadour'-type pictures such as *Paolo and Francesca* (1820, Musée Condé, Chantilly) and the 'Classical' subjects of François Gérard (1770–1837). On the other hand Gérard's *Corinne at Miseno* (1819, Musée des Beaux-Arts, Lyons, inspired by Madame de Staël's famous novel) is worth a mention for its authentically Romantic inspiration and lyrical execution.

Although Baudelaire, perhaps aiming at a paradox, maintained in his account of the 1855 Exhibition that in Guérin and Girodet 'it is not difficult to discern a few small germs of infection, a few sinister but intriguing symptoms of the Romanticism which was to come', this is hard to justify from any of Guérin's works. He confined himself to a Neo-Classicism which varied only between cold formalism and declamatory melodrama. Much more interesting than this painter, whose 'great works' clutter up the Louvre to this day without providing anything more than an academic interest, is the almost unknown Boissard de Boisdenier (1813–1866) who in 1835 painted his admirable *The Retreat from Russia*, now in the museum of Rouen.

THÉODORE PIERRE ETIENNE ROUSSEAU   see p. 162

1   *Marshy Landscape*

Charcoal and bistre with touches of white and green on buff paper. 59.5 × 89 (23⅜ × 35)
Musée Fabre, Montpellier

VICTOR HUGO 1802–85

The poet and dramatist, Victor Hugo, also had a gift for visual art. When seized by inspiration, he used whatever materials were at his disposal—including cigar ash, coffee grounds and soot. His drawings are a direct expression of his restless, questing spirit, predilection for the macabre and supernatural and fascinated love of the old castles on the Rhine.

2   *The Mouse-Tower*

1840. Pen, wash and pastel. 28 × 44 (11 × 17⅜)
Collections de la Maison de Victor Hugo, Paris

1

2

3

4

5

Another picture of the retreat from Russia, painted by Nicolas Toussaint Charlet (1792–1845) in 1836 (Musée des Beaux-Arts, Lyons), must be mentioned here. Auguste Raffet (1804–1860), another apostle of Napoleonism may perhaps be called the Béranger of painting; he was the humorist, the gossip columnist of the Napoleonic legend, the painter who had shared the military hardships and triumphs of the Emperor's Old Guard—not an 'officer's mess' painter like Gros but the chronicler of the private soldier, the hagiographer of the *fioretti* of the Grande Armée.

Is it possible to associate the word 'Romanticism' with Jean Auguste Dominique Ingres (1780–1867)? The critics of his own day and David's fanatical supporters came near to doing so when in 1806 they declared his portrait of Madame Rivière (Louvre, Paris), to be 'extraordinary, revolutionary, Gothic'. Today one would hardly apply such epithets to so well-behaved, so unrevolutionary a work. In reality Ingres was probably closer in one thing at least—the belief that there was something 'animal' in colour, while line alone represented the superior forces of the mind—to the Nazarenes. Nevertheless he did yield, in very Romantic fashion, to the temptation of exoticism in his *Odalisques* (Walters Art Gallery, Baltimore; Metropolitan Museum of Art, New York; Musée des Beaux-Arts, Lyons) and *Turkish Bath* (1852–1863, Louvre, Paris) but this was merely a result of his own sensual temperament and had nothing in common with the scholarly researches of the real Orientalists or even of minor members of the fraternity such as Marilhat and Fromentin. His taste for nature is, however, interesting; he himself remarked that 'nature is style' and Amaury Duval rightly said of him that 'he was an enemy of the ideal and had declared his love for nature', although this was by no means in the manner of the Barbizon School or even of Géricault.

Baudelaire, who, as a poet, was more perceptive than purely non-creative critics, divined affinities between Ingres and Courbet which would have astonished both Romantics and Neo-Classics; to an unbiased viewer the most striking quality of Ingres is the contrast between his desire for Raphaelesque, Roman form and his interior Romanticism, a Romanticism of temperament which he felt obliged to tame and suppress. This involved a conflict between his natural artistic inclinations and his desire for Classicism which was no less violent, and even perhaps painful, for being suppressed.

He was too attached to Antiquity ever to fling himself wholeheartedly into Gothic but for a time he indulged in Romantic (in both senses of the word) themes, as for instance *Rinaldo Rescuing Angelica*, and *Paolo Malatesta and Francesca da Rimini* (1813, Musée Condé, Chantilly); however, instead of reproducing Dante's sombre fire or Ariosto's tragic power, he endowed these dramatic episodes with such frigid formality that one sympathises with Lionello Venturi's description of them as 'congealed Romanticism'—a Romanticism whose savoury juices are covered with the cold white fat of Roman and Raphaelesque memories. Perhaps we have attained a greater freedom and, at the same time, precision in our aesthetic judgments; at least we have long ceased to see an absolute opposition between Ingres, the unaware Romantic, and Delacroix who brought Romanticism to its highest and most fruitful Classical period. In reality this opposition never amounted to more than a hostility (personal as much as artistic) between the two painters, which was aggravated and poisoned by the activities of their partisan pupils and admirers. These, of course, went much further than the two men themselves; a deep rift appeared between Delacroix' red-waistcoated supporters who wore their own hair and the 'bewigged' academicians.

When Théodore Géricault's (1791–1824) *Raft of the 'Medusa'* (1818, Louvre, Paris) was exhibited in 1819, artistic opinion was unprepared for its daring, novel qualities; although painted with enormous care for the objective truth of details (Géricault had studied everything written on this horrifying shipwreck), it attained an epic, almost mythological grandeur. After seeing it the twenty-one-year-old Delacroix ran home in a state of extreme exaltation, and for other artists the work acquired

EUGÈNE DELACROIX see p. 176

3 Study for '*Liberty Leading the People*'

One of many sketches from nature for the main figure in his composition of 1830 entitled *July 28, 1830: Liberty Leading the People*
1830. Drawing
Cabinet des Dessins, Musée du Louvre, Paris

PAUL HUET 1803–69
Huet's bold but tumultuous temperament, dramatic feeling for nature, and the lessons he had learned from the 1824 exhibition of English painters, show clearly in all his works, particularly his 'Shakespearian' landscapes.

4 *The Beach at Villiers*

Pencil and watercolour. 19.8 × 32.5 (7¾ × 12¾)
Musée du Louvre, Paris

JULES ROBERT AUGUSTE,
known as Monsieur AUGUSTE 1789–1850
Although only a minor artist, this sculptor, painter, Orient-lover, collector and crack rider was one of the most picturesque and characteristic figures of French Romanticism in the 1830's. In addition, his lively imagination and brilliant palette put him, it has been thought, on a par with Delacroix.

5 *Study of Arab Horses*

Watercolour. 20.2 × 25.3 (8 × 10)
Maurice Perret-Carnot Collection, France

a sort of symbolic significance. As Michelet said: 'It is France herself, our whole society which he put aboard the raft of the *Medusa*.' It was Michelet, too, who devised the very Romantic epithet of 'The Correggio of Suffering' for this painter of mad scenes, executions and shipwrecks.

Géricault, one feels, ought to have points in common with the great Baroque realists, with Caravaggio or Feti. And he had indeed been struck by Caravaggio (and Michelangelo) during a visit to Italy when he painted his splendid *Race of Riderless Horses on the Corso in Rome* (1817, Walters Art Gallery, Baltimore), one of the more sensational features of the Roman carnival. No other artist had such a love for horses as Géricault, himself no mean rider; in fact he was considered almost the equal of Franconi, the famous star of the circus ring. Few could paint them with his strong passion, almost attaining to a mysterious communion, although other fine painters of horses were Gros, Monsieur Auguste, John Wootton, George Stubbs, James Ward and Fuseli.

The Romantics' 'magic horse', the mount of medieval paladins, Valkyries and enchanted huntsmen, recurs more often in Géricault's work than in any other with a significant, almost obsessive, insistance. His famous portraits of hussar and dragoon officers, his *Artillery Attack* (c. 1814, Munich) and his *Death of Hippolytus* (c. 1815, Montpellier Museum) primarily provide him with opportunities for portraying the secret power of these noble, mysterious, almost incomprehensible animals in heroic revolt.

Even after his visit to London in 1820—he went with his *Raft of the 'Medusa'* which a clever travelling showman was exhibiting throughout England—where the Derby revealed to him a new kind of horse-racing and horse-personality, he still revelled in the sort of intuitive knowledge and physical intimacy that one finds in Auguste and Stubbs. In short, Géricault worshipped the horse because he saw that it provided him with a halfway house between objective, experimental reality and the super-real imagination which transfigures and deifies a living creature.

An analogous attitude can be sensed in his portraits of madmen, criminals and executed men, which in addition reveal a mind strangely attracted by scenes of horror, insanity and cruelty—a mind not, as in Goya, regarding these scenes with diabolical insouciance but primarily interested in them for their documentary value, their value as monstrous horrors, as anomalies. Delacroix said he was 'extreme in everything' but in fact his taste for the more sinister mysteries of the human mind reflects a teratological side of Romanticism in general which must not be ignored. In their revolt from ideal beauty and classical perfection, painters and poets often turned to monsters. To peer into the wild eyes of a madman or the glazed ones of a severed head, was, for Géricault, to plunge into the depths of the unconscious; in this he had something in common with Baudelaire.

This preoccupation wears a slightly morbid and pathological air, but it is, of course, of less interest than the beauty of the painting itself. However much the artist was haunted by the idea of madness (and, indeed, it led him to an almost clinical study of the characteristic expression of kidnappers, incendiaries, gamblers and kleptomaniacs), from the moment he picked up his palette and brushes he was interested in nothing but paint and pictorial values, colour inflamed by an internal light. His representation of a severed head beginning to decompose (Musée d'Art et d'Histoire, Geneva), his man under torture (1818, Art Institute of Chicago), the two severed heads (1818, Nationalmuseum, Stockholm) and the madman with military megalomania (1822–1823, Oskar Reinhart Collection, Winterthur) are of the same brand as Rembrandt's *Flayed Ox* (Louvre, Paris)—realism raised to the level of a visionary image, reality recreated by imagination, everyday things endowed with a monstrous and paradoxical splendour. This was one of the chief ambitions of Romanticism and Géricault, with his sombre, blinding genius, was one of the few to achieve it.

Eugène Delacroix (1798–1863) gave an illuminating description of himself in his *Journal*: 'If by my Romanticism people mean the free display of my personal impressions, my remoteness from the servile copies repeated *ad nauseam* in academies of art and my extreme distaste for academic formulae, then I am indeed a Romantic.' He also said that 'the finest works of art are those which express the pure imagination of the artist.' Delacroix' main contributions to the concept of Romanticism were indeed his horror of hard-and-fast recipes for pictorial techniques, his belief in aesthetic inspiration, in freedom of imagination, of the immediate impression. To these must be added his quest for musicality in colour (which for him was not 'animal' but could, on the contrary, become pure spirituality), his method of stimulating the emotions by increasing the importance given to contemporary dramatic events (as in his *Massacres at Chios, Greece Expiring on the Ruins of Missolonghi*, etc.) and the fact that he made full use of the discoveries and art of the Orient. Moreover he was influenced, both intellectually and emotionally, by poetry and music; he admired both Berlioz and Byron, for instance, and attempted to achieve in his painting the ideal of the German Romantics. No wonder, then, that Baudelaire should have described him as 'a volcanic crater artistically concealed beneath bouquets of flowers', just as Schumann described Chopin as 'a cannon hidden beneath roses'.

It was only to be expected that the public and critics should misunderstand an artist who himself owned that it took great courage to be oneself. When in 1822 his first big picture, *Dante and Virgil in Hell* (1821, Louvre, Paris), was exhibited—he was then twenty-four—it was received with the stupidity and blankness guaranteed to all true innovators. Just as, later, Cézanne's art was to be called 'the painting of a tipsy scavenger', so in 1822 Delacroix was said to paint with a 'drunken broomstick'. Naturally enough, Paul Delaroche (1797–1856), the idol of art-lovers and once ironically called 'a prince of mediocrities,' was considered infinitely preferable. Delacroix produced a Classical Romanticism; Delaroche, though not without talent or skill, succeeded in converting Romanticism into academicism. Though he cannot be excluded from an account of the Romantic Movement, he can only be classed as a history painter of a violently theatrical nature; his *Children of Edward* (1831, Louvre, Paris), *Execution of Lady Jane Grey* (1834, formerly Tate Gallery, London, destroyed) and *Death of Elizabeth* (1827, Louvre, Paris) evoked from Heine the witty comment that 'Monsieur Delaroche paints all the decapitated crowned heads of Europe.'

Apart from a journey to England in 1825, whither he was attracted by Bonington, and six months of 1832 spent in Morocco in the company of the Duc de Morny, Delacroix hardly ever left France; he never visited Italy although he resolved several times to go there and see Michelangelo's work. The brilliance, the flashing colour of his palette, were not simply means of expression, but the outpouring of his soul, his joy in letting his native music sing. He was too cultured an artist, too free of all sectarianism to use his Romanticism as an art-political weapon; on the contrary his instinct led him towards genius in whatever quarter it lay and his judgment was infallible. Instinctively he subdued his tumultuous inspiration by means of a rigorous concentration of space. The taut rhythms of the curves in his *Death of Sardanapalus* (1827, Louvre, Paris), the bold perspectives converging towards the centre of the most intensely dramatic portion of his *Entry of the Crusaders into Constantinople* (1840, Louvre, Paris), the ceiling of the Galerie d'Apollon in the Louvre, where he is revealed as the equal of the greatest Baroque designers, of Maulbertsch and Tiepolo—all these bear witness to his untiring intellectual activity. This is further demonstrated by the fact that, once his eyes had been opened by Constable, he repainted the landscape in the *Massacres at Chios* (1824, Louvre, Paris); that of the *Jacob Wrestling with the Angel* in the Church of St Sulpice, Paris (1861) is a piece of pure naturalism, of a *pleinairisme* culled from the Barbizon School.

Delacroix was a man of enormous imagination, a visionary with a tendency towards the fantastic. Not content with showing movement at its most intense and revealing, he boasted of having wanted to 'paint the flash of a sword', which may be called the height of ambition in this direction. It shows, moreover, how far removed he was from the beaten track, the trumpery Gothic and 'troubadour' idylls. Though excited by the sensuality of colour, extraordinarily sensitive to the degree of brilliance of a tone, the glinting spangles of light on silks and satins, Delacroix did not see in colour the animal voluptuousness which frightened Ingres; for him it set in motion a process belonging at once to the senses, the emotions and the intellect. It allowed him to challenge the musician, perhaps even to outdo him. ('Colours are the music of the eyes . . . Certain colour-harmonies produce sensations which even music cannot rival . . .') Never has the analogy between the pictorial and musical palette been so complete as in Delacroix' use of tones to parallel the characteristic sonorities of the horn, the oboe and the cor anglais, each quite individual but combining with the others in a marvellous concord. Without loss of clarity or intensity he modulates from one key to the next, secure in the knowledge that form is born of colour, from which it derives its life and richness. Handling light and what could be called 'the light of shade' with sovereign ease, he manipulates his ultra-sensitive colour to produce a streak of sunshine, the quick flash of a reflection, the warm ambers and pale ivories of living flesh. He makes the object and its refraction reflect each other and blend together so that the resultant complex unity resembles a halfway state between waking and dreaming. The true substance of objects becomes of small interest, only material to be painted, probably because the objective existence of things was of less importance to him than his mental picture of them. He once said that he fled before the 'cruel reality of objects' and it was to escape from them that he set up his own creation in opposition, the higher reality of the work of art which may lean on nature but insists on the right to be independent of it. He said, too, that painting was a bridge between the mind of the painter and that of the spectator; it is also, of course, a bridge between objective, natural reality, from which the painter borrows his forms, and the new substance, a distillation of the soul and mind, of which communication and communion are made.

Delacroix was particularly fond of Rubens and made several admirable copies from his works. He learned much from him, particularly where the rhythm of large compositions was concerned (*The Battle of Taillebourg*, 1837, Versailles Museum; *The Battle of Nancy*, 1834, Musée des Beaux-Arts, Nancy; *The Entombment*, 1848, Museum of Fine Art, Boston), but at twenty-four he already knew how much of Rubens he should keep and how much he should discard. 'This is Rubens improved,' said Baron Gros, a good judge, of the *Dante and Virgil in Hell* in 1822. With greater richness, variety and depth than Rubens, Delacroix sometimes even approaches Rembrandt, in particular when he ventures into the kingdom of night in pursuit of the troubled spirits of Medea and Hamlet.

There were, of course, a host of 'minor Romantics', eluded by celebrity and genius alike, possibly because they put their Romanticism into their lives rather than their works. Of these the one who followed most closely in Delacroix' footsteps was the strange man known as Monsieur Auguste. The son of a rich jeweller, a sculptor, horse-lover and connoisseur of 18th-century painting (rare in an age which, reacting against the previous century, detested all things Rococo), Jules Robert Auguste (c. 1789–1850) remains rather mysterious. Few finished paintings by him are known but his designs and studies seethe with a strange genius. Like Decamps he was constantly experimenting with new media, with rich and seductive paints, and the laboratory was almost more important to him than the studio. To him goes the honour of having discovered Géricault,—who made him give up sculpture for painting,—and of having contributed to the spread of Orientalism by his generosity in lending friends the magnificent costumes he had brought back from his visits to Africa.

Orientalism was not the transient, superficial fashion it had been in the previous century, when the chief demands made of Asia had been for picturesque knick-knacks, amusing oddities to fill out chinoiserie décors *à la* Boucher. In the 19th

DAVID PIERRE GIOTTINO HUMBERT DE SUPERVILLE, known as GIOTTINO 1770–1849
Though of French descent, Superville was born and educated in Holland. He was one of the first to admire the Italian primitives, who had until then been either unknown or despised. His artistic standpoint was closely bound up with his religious feeling, so that in many respects he resembled the Nazarenes.

6 *Angel and Devil Struggling for the Soul of an Old Man*

Pen, brown ink and wash. 30.2 × 25.2 (14¼ × 10)
Rijksmuseum, Amsterdam
The subject may be taken from the legend of Michael preventing the Devil from carrying off Moses' body.

EUGÈNE DELACROIX

7 *Study for Apollo's Chariot*

This drawing was a sketch for Delacroix' large allegorical composition in the Galerie d'Apollon, painted in 1851
Black chalk. 27.2 × 44 (10¾ × 17¾)
Cabinet des Dessins, Musée du Louvre, Paris

PIERRE PAUL PRUD'HON 1758–1823
Prud'hon's career coincided with the transition between the philosophical 18th century and the Romantic 19th. His choice of subjects and way of treating them reveal the complexity of a sensitive, receptive nature, both sensual and dreamy.

8 *Justice and Divine Vengeance Pursuing Crime*

Study for the large painting in the Louvre commissioned in 1804 by the Prefect of the Seine
Black chalk heightened with white on bluish paper.
40 × 50.5 (15¾ × 19⅞)
Musée du Louvre, Paris

6

7

8

9

10

11

12

14

13

15

16

18

17

19

ANTOINE LOUIS BARYE 1796–1875

9 *Lion and Snake*

Watercolour. 30×48 (11¾×20)
Musée Fabre, Montpellier

JEAN-FRANÇOIS MILLET 1814–75
With deep tenderness Millet devoted himself to evoking the
sad grandeur of the winter landscape, the hard toil of wood
and field, the private poetry of everyday tasks. His respect
and love for peasants at work often gives his pictures
sociological overtones, but his main concern is to express the
intense inner nobility of humble people, without brilliance
or even great happiness.

10 *The Wild Geese*

Charcoal
Cabinet des Dessins, Musée du Louvre, Paris

ADRIEN DAUZATS 1804–68
Dauzats worked with Delacroix who appointed him executor
of his will. His travels in Spain, Portugal, Egypt and Asia,
Minor provided him with material for an enormous number
of paintings, whose fidelity to local colour, so prized by the
Romantics, is perhaps their chief merit. With his brilliant
use of colour, luminosity and charm, Dauzats is one of the
more remarkable members of the French Romantic School.

11 *Orleans Cathedral*

1832. Watercolour. 38.5×27.5 (15¼×10¾)
Musée du Petit Palais, Paris

LOUIS BOULANGER 1808–67
A friend of Victor Hugo, for whose plays he designed the
first décors and many of whose books he illustrated,
Boulanger felt most at home in a supernatural atmosphere;
in this respect, there is a certain affinity between him and
Goya. His work also reveals to a certain extent the influence
of Delacroix, another friend of his.

12 *Sire de Gyac*

Watercolour.
Collections de la Maison de Victor Hugo, Paris

GUSTAVE DORÉ

13 *The Wandering Jew Crossing a Cemetery*

Lithograph
Cabinet des Estampes, Bibliothèque Nationale, Paris

CHARLES MERYON 1821–68
As a naval officer Meryon had ample opportunities for
ranging the world, but at twenty-seven he devoted himself
to art, and principally to engraving, for which he showed
great talent. Unfortunately his life was shortened by want,
sickness and the strain of an imagination tending towards
the gloomy and fantastic. His best etchings mingle a
documentary treatment of the Parisian landscape with
startling evocations of monsters and fabulous creatures.

14 *The Ghoul*

1853. Etching. 16.5×13 (6¼×5¼)
Grosjean-Maupin Collection, France

THÉODORE GÉRICAULT see p. 170

15 *The Retreat from Russia, or the Wounded Cuirassier*

c. 1813. Pen over pencil. 19.1×14.5 (7½×5¾)
École des Beaux-Arts, Paris

FRANÇOIS MARIUS GRANET 1775–1849
Although born in Provence, Granet spent most of his life in
Italy. In Rome he met Ingres, who painted his portrait.
His chief delight was Italy, which he saw through a
Romantic haze, with its picturesque monks, churches and
gardens. His sensitivity and talent as a watercolourist mark
him out as something more than the 'minor painter' he is
often considered to be.

16 *Louis Philippe Visiting the Galleries of the Louvre at Night*

Pen and wash. 32×31 (12⅝×12¼)
Musée du Louvre, Paris

JEAN AUGUSTE DOMINIQUE INGRES see p. 158

17 Study for *The Dream of Ossian*

1866. Black and white chalk and wash. 25.6×20.3 (10×8)
Musée Ingres, Montauban

ALFRED JOHANNOT 1800–37
Like his brother Tony (1803–52), Alfred Johannot was a
well known illustrator, particularly distinguished for his
'vignettes' and 'cathedral frontispieces', characteristic of
Romantic taste. He became famous principally for his
illustrations to translations of Byron, Cowper and Scott.

18 *Esmeralda Abducted by Quasimodo*

Drawing for Victor Hugo's *Notre Dame*
Charcoal heightened with white chalk.
17×13 (6¾×5¼)
Collections de la Maison de Victor Hugo, Paris

GUSTAVE DORÉ 1832–83
With his inexhaustible imagination, powerful vision and
fantastic temperament, his talent as a draughtsman and his
quest after new techniques and means of expression, Doré
is one of the most eminent members of the French Romantic
movement. His book illustrations won him immense
popularity.

19 *The Witches' Sabbath or the Witches from 'Macbeth'*

The subject is taken, as in so many Romantic pictures,
from Shakespeare
Unfinished. Pen and wash in Indian ink
with some body colour. 78×58 (30¾×22¾)
Musée des Beaux-Arts, Strasbourg

century the influence of Morocco, Algeria and Moorish Spain was not confined to forms and colours; it transformed the spirit of the age, at a fairly profound level, for psychological as well as aesthetic reasons. Like Gothic, and to an equal extent, it answered the Romantic need to escape from workaday reality to a 'different' world—whether 'different' in time or in space did not really matter—a world imagined to be freer, more beautiful, more deep-feeling.

The fashion for exoticism, of which the passion for the Middle Ages represents one aspect, was bound up with the rise to power of the middle classes and those whom Heine called 'Philistines.' Far away countries and past ages were credited with wondrous advantages: instincts allowed free reign, the reason ruled by the irrational, freedom for the passions and fulfilment of all desires. For the grey dankness of Paris and the middle-class way of life were substituted the noble splendours and polychrome brilliance of the East, a new way of seeing and experiencing, a new physical, moral and intellectual outlook. Of the artists who took themselves and their easels to the other side of the Mediterranean or even further the most notable are Gabriel Alexandre Decamps (1803–1860), Alfred Dehodencq (1822–1882), Eugène Fromentin (1820–1876), Marilhat (1811–1847), Dauzats (1804–1868) and Tournemine (1812–1872). All were equally fascinated by the desert and the bazaars, African life and Africa's wide spaces stretching to infinity and offering no petty barriers to limitless contemplation and meditation.

Decamps is the most interesting in that he shows how much Orientalism (like the Neo-Gothic fashion) was an essentially psychological, rather than aesthetic, phenomenon. Decamps created his own 'interior' Orient, comparable with an imaginary world. One short visit to Smyrna provided him with enough material for an enormous crop of Orientalist pictures; his memories of things seen and felt, kept fresh by a huge stock of costumes and accessories, produced a wealth of picturesque episodes which look as though they were painted from nature, the Orient in them is so vivid and alive. Though capable of a work as fine as his *Defeat of the Cimbri* (1833, Louvre, Paris), one of the most moving products of French Romanticism, Decamps was generally satisfied with amusing anecdotal pictures of a Turkey which he had only once glimpsed but which still filled his dreams and his art. Nevertheless *The Defeat of the Cimbri* marks him out as one of the finest history painters of an age which blindly considered Paul Delaroche (1797–1856), François Joseph Heim (1787–1865), Ary Scheffer (1795–1858) and Eugène Devéria (1805–1865) his superiors in this genre.

Athaliah Butchering the Royal Children (1827, Musée des Beaux-Arts, Nantes) indicates that Sigalon (1787–1837), might also have become one of Romanticism's most successful history painters, if throughout his life his ambitions had not been frustrated and his efforts stultified by poverty and misfortune. In the Salon of 1827 where his picture had an unparalleled success and Delaroche's *Death of Elizabeth* was hailed as a work of genius, Delacroix' *Death of Sardanapalus* passed completely unnoticed. But *Mazeppa*, a powerfully original picture revealed the dazzling talent of a twenty-one-year-old painter, Louis Boulanger (1806–1867).

He had not selected the most dramatic episode of the rebel's life—the scene where he is tied on to the back of a fiery stallion who gallops off with him across the forests of the steppes, painted by Géricault. For Géricault the horse was much more important than the rider; indeed, the horse, with its roots in ancient Germanic mythology, was the Romantic animal *par excellence*. Boulanger took a static phase of the Mazeppa story for his picture—the moment when the rebel is tied to his horse before the eyes of his implacable, hate-filled enemies. *Mazeppa* (c. 1827, Rouen Museum) is full of sustained violence, cramped and confined, ready to explode. It shows a Boulanger quite unlike the wild breathless Romantic—a sort of artistic equivalent of Petrus Borel, Napol or Aloysius Bertrand—of the *Hell Hunt* (1835) or the *Witches' Sabbath in a Church* (1828), the famous lithograph which harmonized perfectly with the 'Gothick' novels England had brought into fashion, or the *Scene of an Orgy* (1866, Musée des Beaux-Arts, Dijon) inspired by his friend Victor Hugo. He remained a constant favourite with the writers, probably because there was always some literary reference in his works; he was, however, equally influenced by the stage-designer Ciceri, who had divined instinctively how to present such Romantic dramas and operas as *Hernani* and *Robert le Diable*. Something of Ciceri's style filters not only into contemporary history painters and genre painters but even certain landscapists, such as Huet who, perhaps unconsciously, took over the spirit of the famous designer's backcloths.

Théodore Chassériau (1819–1856) is a good example of the multiplicity of ways in which Romanticism could be interpreted. Occupying a position diametrically opposed to that of Boulanger, Géricault and Delacroix he seems almost to merit the epithet Classical. Indeed he must have experienced unusual difficulties (and deserved proportionate merit) in throwing off the shackles of Classicism; seeing a sketch made by him at the age of twelve, Ingres declared that he would be 'the Napoleon of painting'. In fact he ceased to be a disciple of Ingres once he had attained his majority, but he never became fully associated with any other school. Throughout his short life—he died at thirty-seven—he remained isolated, a solitary figure. Moreover, his most important work, the great decorations for the Cour des Comptes, Paris (executed between 1844 and 1848) were fated to be destroyed by fire during the troubles of the Commune; the few vestiges which were saved were badly damaged by flood in 1909 so that today it is impossible to know the real Chassériau at his best. His *Sleeping Bather* (1850, Musée Calvet, Avignon), *Tepidarium* (1853), *Venus Anadyomene* (1839) and *Toilet of Esther* (1842), all in the Louvre, give no idea of what his monumental compositions must have been. These can only be deduced from his drawings and designs and a few fragments saved with great difficulty. Chassériau was a Creole (born in St Domingo) suffused by the Hellenism which continued from Thomas Couture to Puvis de Chavannes and Gustave Moreau.

However great, even definitive, the influence and consequences of Constable's pictures exhibited in the Salon at Paris in 1824, French Romantic landscape-painting did not begin with the 19th century; its origins go back as far as Watteau, Fragonard, Moreau the Younger, perhaps even Hubert Robert. Once established, however, the new attitude affected not only ways of seeing and recognizing nature, but the whole conception of the individual's position within the universe and his relation to objects and elements. Even with Watteau and Fragonard landscape had ceased to be objective fact or mere decoration; it had become a mood, a state of being in the same way as poetry and music. But while melancholy, disquiet or nostalgia were invading nature, artists also became more interested in truth, exactitude, so that conscientious objectivity became associated with an intense subjectivization of emotions and feeling. A 'mystique of landscape' took possession of the desire for realism and breathed into it a new spirit. More truthful, in the literal sense of the word, than Watteau and Fragonard, painting what they dreamed as much as what they saw, giving sight the stature of vision, the Romantic painters of the 19th century made great efforts to remain very close to 'facts'. They abandoned the studio in order to paint from nature, threw off the bonds of previous ideas to devise and elaborate a new aesthetic, an increasingly supple and rich technique. From these beginnings grew the great movement which was to culminate, later in the century, in the Impressionists, in Cézanne, Gauguin and Van Gogh, in whom one can easily find traces of the Romanticism which brought about this new conception.

At the time, this return to a nature both real and bound up with the emotions caused a great scandal; one academic critic took strong objection to the fact that Paul Huet 'tried to bring the landscape back to nature'; or in other words to eliminate the presence of man. The Classical view was that only man's presence justified the painting of landscape, which if it was neither historic or 'heroic' had no *raison d'être* at all. The first French Romantic landscapists, Georges Michel (1763–1843) and Paul Huet (1803–1869), had found precedents for a dramatic interpretation of nature in Dutch painters such as Everdingen, Ruisdael, Seghers and, most important of all, Rembrandt. Their instinctive, spontaneous, primordial lyricism was also stimulated by the poets among whom they lived; in the first half of the 19th century there were frequent exchanges of influence between poets and painters in the artistic coteries of the day. They were, of course, great readers of Shakespeare, steeped in the tragic splendours of *Macbeth* and *King Lear*, and eager to re-create them, far from Scotland or Cornwall, out of the country they had at their disposal when the play of light, storms, or clouds gave it a tragic grandeur. There is something very Shakespearian in Huet's *Sun Setting behind an Old Abbey* (1831), exhibited in the Salon in 1831, just as there is in Friedrich's *Ruins of Eldena under Snow*.

By their choice of scenes they show their predilection for places in harmony with their own temperament and acting as a stimulus to their feelings—desolate marshes, deserted shores, seas tossed by storms, thunder clouds, dark forests and naked rocks. Théodore Rousseau (1812–1867) summed up the ideal shared by the first landscapists in the following uncompromising way: 'Our art can achieve pathos only through sincerity.' It was no longer a question of a pathos furnished by the figures to which the landscape served as a background, but of an elemental pathos, that is, a pathos created by contemplation of the elements and sincere in that it was involuntary and immediate—pathetic fallacy, in fact.

The whole outlook was so incomprehensible to the critics of the day that Rousseau's *Descent of Cattle from Pasture* (1835, Mesdag Museum, The Hague) was nicknamed by an inane wit 'Descent of Cattle into Hell'. Rousseau's sober grandeur and pathos owed much to the fact that, as the years passed, he painted more and more from life, without polishing his sketches in the studio. He had a great gift for pinning down a place or moment, strongly individualizing it and charging it with all the emotional force at his command, as for instance in his *Gorges of Aspremont at Noon* (1857). Particularly fond of the forest of Fontainebleau with its variety of wild beauty, Rousseau settled in the village of Barbizon where several of his friends came to join him. Consequently this group of Romantic landscapists, including Charles Daubigny (1817–1878), Jules Dupré (1811–1889) and Diaz de la Peña (1807–1876), came to be known as the Barbizon School.

However, the influence of the English landscape-painters must not be under-estimated. Constable's pictures, exhibited in the Salon in 1824, had touched off a real aesthetic revolution and Bonington's friendship with several French painters had created a number of links between English and French art. Rousseau was, in Focillon's words, 'the noblest spirit and finest genius' of the whole group, but several of the others attained to a sort of Impressionism long before the term was ever coined, an original, highly personal way of feeling and representing nature, not with cold scholarly objectivity, but with a wealth of rich and fertile exchanges taking place, during the very act of artistic creation, between the thing seen, the artist's mind and the thing created. All this is to be found in Daubigny's pictures, bathed in a silvery, transparent light where every drop of humidity glistens and scintillates, in the vast skies of Dupré, who recaptured the spirit of Constable and the early Turner in his *Around Southampton* (1835), in the warm, brilliant impasto of Auguste Ravier (1814–1895) and the simultaneously dazzling and mellow greens of Antoine Chintreuil (1816–1873).

Even when Gustave Courbet (1819–1877) imagined that he was being eminently realistic and showing objects exactly as they are, without any idealization, in fact he was dominated by a typically Romantic subjectivity. His presence is perfectly visible in his smallest sketch, even when it is merely an objective representation of a rocky cliff overlooking a river, or a leaf-shaded pond where deer are drinking. The picture is only as it is because he sees it in that way; he alone was able to express this 'received experience' of nature in a state of intimate communion which has nothing forced or 'literary' but is merely an effusion of the sensibility, a total

DENIS AUGUSTE MARIE RAFFET 1804–60
Raffet was an eloquent supporter of the Napoleonic cult, having worshipped at the Emperor's shrine ever since his earliest years, when studying with Charlet and Gros. From 1831 he devoted himself almost exclusively to lithography, Senefelder's invention, which had become the most popular method of reproduction in the Romantic era.

20 *La Revue Nocturne 1834*

This drawing, which may have served as a sketch for the large picture on the same subject now in the Château de Compiègne, illustrates the famous ballad by Sedlitz
Lithograph
Cabinet des Estampes, Bibliothèque Nationale, Paris

ANNE-LOUIS GIRODET DE ROUCY-TRIOSON
see p. 168

21 *The Funeral of Atala*

Sketch for the picture of the same title painted in 1808, now in the Louvre. Innumerable pictures by various artists were inspired by Chateaubriand's Romantic novel *Atala*
1808. Black chalk heightened with white on brown paper
24.8 × 40 (9¾ × 15¾)
Musée du Louvre, Paris

HONORÉ DAUMIER see p. 182

22 *Don Quixote and Sancho Panza*

1865. Oil on canvas. 100 × 81 (39½ × 32)
Courtauld Institute of Art, London

20

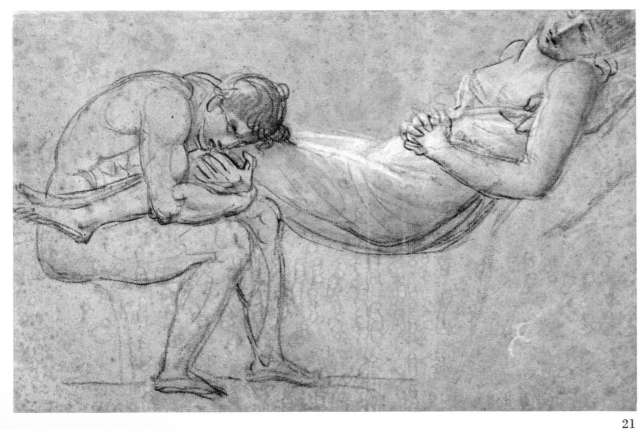

21

22

23

24

apprehension of the object by the individual who for the moment is one with the object itself.

The subject and idea behind Courbet's big compositions like *A Burial at Ornans* (1850, Louvre, Paris) and *The Painter's Studio* (1855, Louvre, Paris), and the social protest activating *The Stone-Breakers* (1850, Gemäldegalerie, Dresden) make them difficult to discuss at the present day. But the landscapes themselves, having no such overtones, live with that deep and secret life of things which seem to blossom more freely in the absence of man, unless of course man is, like Courbet, an element of nature, vibrating in sympathy with animals, rocks, trees and water. His only aim is truth in its deepest sense, the total truth obtained when the object is perceived by all the senses. (Courbet's tactile and olfactory faculties were particularly acute.) At the same time it is transmitted through a splendidly developed sensibility, a heart sharing fully in the mysterious essence of nature above and beyond its forms and appearances. And so Courbet's 'socialism' takes on a much deeper meaning and, going beyond a concern with the human condition, becomes communication on a cosmic scale.

Few of his contemporaries could have understood the message of this artist who, in his *Dame de Francfort* (1858, Kunsthaus, Zürich), expressed Romantic melancholy as nobody had ever done before him. In this picture the nostalgic sadness of the landscape harmonizes exactly with the wistful, sickly face of the woman and her despairing expression reflects the death-struggles of the setting sun. Yet, as always, there were insensitive reactionaries to reproach him with being a mere 'craftsman', 'realistic out of sheer ignorance' or to declare that he was 'making fun of himself, others and his art'; the Germans understood him better and, after the exhibition of 1856 in Munich, recognised in him the master of a Romantic realism which was to enrich, later on, the realism of Hayden, Trübner and Leibl.

The same Romantic realism, perhaps here even social realism, dominates the work of Jean François Millet (1814–1875), who worshipped at the twin shrines of nature and Poussin. With deep humility he devoted himself to portraying the life of the fields and the woods, aiming always to raise them to a style comparable with that of the painter of *The Funeral of Phocion*. Even if the sentimentality of the over-famed *Angelus* (1857–1859, Louvre, Paris) now alienates us, there can be no doubt that he has no rival in the way in which he makes us smell the log-fire at the verge of the forest in the dim autumn twilight, the damp paths, the sodden wood, the unconscious, unstressed poetry of things in their humble, everyday reality. Nevertheless the secret of his immense power is that he is really depicting what lies behind this visible truth, its hidden interior, its innermost, passionate, pure vibrations.

This is equally true of Honoré Daumier (1808–1879)—not Daumier the satirist, whose wit lashed out at foolishness, baseness and narrow-mindedness, the genius of the *Charivari* and *Caricature*, but the Daumier who painted *The Washerwoman*, (1861, Louvre, Paris) and *Don Quixote* (1865, Courtauld Institute of Art, London) riding alone through the plains and gullies of La Mancha. Few figures are as essentially Romantic as Don Quixote and it is not surprising that he so often inspired Daumier, with his bitter contempt for human mediocrity, his pessimism verging on melancholia, his misanthropy counterbalanced by loving contemplation of the mysterious life of inanimate objects. Banville said of him, with justice, that 'he was the first to jerk nature and material objects out of their indifference and oblige them to play their part in the Comedy of Man, making trees join in ridicule of their owner or the bronzes on a family table creak with an ironic rage.' This turning of things against man, which Grandville pushed to the point of exasperated delirium, remains always within the bounds of reality with Daumier. Despite the variety of tone in his reddish-brown and gold colouring, which, though almost monochrome, permits him to express all the nuances of the pathetic, he is strangely indifferent to the use of colours to heighten the emotional content in his pictures. Only Daumier, apart from Rembrandt whom he almost equals in

THÉODORE GÉRICAULT

23 *The Murder of Fualdès*

Sepia. 22.5 × 29 (8⅞ × 11⅜)
Musée Wicar, Lille

HONORÉ DAUMIER

24 *Rue Transnonain on April 15, 1834*

Lithograph. 29 × 44 (11¼ × 17⅜)
Antoine de Halasz Collection, France

this respect, has succeeded in showing how ardently God's fire burns within man's mortal clay and how much the spirit shines through this translucent outer casing.

At the Ny Carlsberg Glyptothek in Copenhagen there is a curious picture by Camille Corot (1796–1875) called *Melancholy*. The picture of a figure, gazing into space, probably dates from 1855, ten years before the *Interrupted Reading* in the Art Institute of Chicago which is treated in the same spirit. It raises the question of whether Corot was in fact a Romantic. The Italian landscapes suggest that he was not, as do the French landscapes of the last decades of his life which, in their excess of idyllic haze, miss the true depth of Romantic feeling. But his female figures, silent, motionless, strangers to their surroundings, isolated in a space with which they seem to have no communication, empty of passion and waiting, perhaps in vain, for something to fill up this emotional and spiritual vacuum, show us a Corot less familiar than the landscapist, less immediately accessible and only intelligible within the context of Romanticism. The discreet, tender delicacy with which the artist approaches these solitary women, verging on phantoms, is the only technique capable of capturing 'the spiritual beauty which is grace, precisely because it is natural' as Lionello Venturi says. It needed Corot's prophetic spirit to divine their secret, without unveiling it, without deflowering it and to let it speak through their unquiet faces and arrested movements.

Fantasy, which played an essential role in Romantic painting, as in literature, found magnificent interpreters in the draughtsmen and engravers of the day. Gustave Doré (1832–1883), best known as the illustrator of Dante, Shakespeare, Cervantes and Rabelais, was also a talented painter whose *Ship Trapped by Icebergs* in the Strasbourg Museum has something in common with Wagner's phantom-ships or Friedrich's *Wreck of the 'Hope'* (1821, Kunsthalle, Hamburg). A true vision-ary, Doré made his great skill as a painter and engraver serve his inexhaustible imagination. Another such visionary was Rodolphe Bresdin (1825–1885) whose etchings evoke nightmare scenes set in luxuriant landscapes. He knew only too well the depths of despair and was dominated by a sinister feeling which, as in the 16th-century Swiss engravers, led him to transform the branches of dead trees into spectral figures and portray demon faces peering out from the folds in the bark. Charles Meryon (1821–1868), who died insane at the age of forty-six, was a virtuoso in the black-white gymnastics made possible by etching. By means of vigorous accentuation of light and shade he was able to express the mysterious presences haunting Paris' older buildings, which he depicted with the care and exactitude of an architect—dragons flying round the spires of Notre Dame, spectres creeping along walls. In connection with Bresdin and Meryon mention must be made of Grandville (1803–1847), a master of the extraordinary and abnormal who may well be called an ancestor of the Surrealists. Ingenious in his inventions of monsters with every kind of disquieting deformity, he metamorphoses men into animals and vice versa and brings to his fierce, demonic depiction of the most innocent objects the morbid, tainted imagination of a Hieronymus Bosch.

The Romantic engravers revived all the past techniques, restored wood-cuts to favour and explored the possibilities of lithography, recently invented by Senefelder. It had been known since the beginning of the century but the outcrop of new newspapers, reviews and book-illustrations enlarged its sphere of action considerably. The Romantic age produced a number of talented illustrators in every country and the 'cathedral frontispieces' of Celestin Nanteuil are among the most interesting and characteristic expressions of the spirit of the age. Edouard May, Camille Rogier, Jean Gigoux, the two Johannot brothers, Tony and Alfred, Achille and Eugène Devérin and, at a later date, Bertall, probably give a more complete and accurate idea of Romanticism than the painters—because, in engraving, all peculiarities are underlined and exaggerated. And finally, few painters conveyed the fantastic atmosphere of the Rhine castles dear to Romantic imaginations with such gusto as Victor Hugo who, in his moments of inspiration, drew with whatever came to hand: with a cigar dipped in coffee dregs or ash he could create diabolical figures, medieval towns bathed in moonlight and dream landscapes plunged in the deepest, most Romantic, gloom.

XLII THÉODORE CHASSÉRIAU 1815–56

Chassériau was led to become a Romantic by his admiration of Delacroix and a visit to Algeria, to which he was invited by the Caliph of Constantine in 1846. If he had not died at the early age of forty he would undoubtedly have developed a very personal idiom of his own, less pathetic than that of Courbet and Delacroix, nearer to reality, more subtle in feeling and ideas. The tragic fate of Mazeppa inspired a number of Romantic pictures, but for Chassériau it may well have had an added attraction, the fatal ride being almost a symbol of his own dramatically shortened life.

Cossack Girl Finding the Body of Mazeppa

1851. 55.5 × 37 (22 × 14½) Musée des Beaux-Arts, Strasbourg

XLIII JEAN DÉSIRÉ GUSTAVE COURBET 1819–77

From his childhood years spent in Franche-Comté Courbet retained memories of a landscape filled with a wild intensity and mysterious solemnity, in which the animals appeared like nature-gods or wood-sprites. His pictures almost smell of dead leaves, damp stones, warm fur, appealing to other senses besides that of sight. He is too aware of the 'spirit' of objects to embrace pure, superficial naturalism. The figures in *The Painter's Studio* have an extraordinary feeling of 'presence', which almost makes them resemble the characters in dreams or hallucinations. Whether or not Courbet ever met them in reality, they still possess this 'super-real' quality. The picture was refused by the Salon of 1855, because the jury found it 'incomprehensible', but Courbet showed it in a hut which he set up in the grounds of the Universal Exhibition. Painted at Ornans between November 1854 and March 1855, it was called 'a Real Allegory summarizing a seven-year Phase of my Life' by the artist. 'The picture is divided into two parts,' he wrote to Champfleury. 'I am in the middle painting; on the right are the shareholders, that is my friends, fellow-workers and art-lovers. On the left, the other side of life—the proletariat, poverty, penury, capitalism, exploitation, the men who live on death'. In 1897 the picture was bought by Victor Desfosses who adapted it into a curtain for his private theatre. It is a strange, complex work in which Courbet tries to show the figures, both real and symbolical, who had made up part of his own life as allegories of human destiny; it is, as it were, a manifesto of his æsthetic and social ideals. Certain details have great naturalistic beauty—for example, the naked model by the easel—but the whole is inspired by a truly Romantic feeling, expressing the tragedy of the everyday world, although it is not merely the 'slice of Life' beloved of the systematic Realists, for the whole composition is dominated by a tragic conception of human destiny.

Detail from *The Painter's Studio*

1855. 359 × 596 (141⅜ × 234⅝) Musée du Louvre, Paris

XLIV JEAN DÉSIRÉ GUSTAVE COURBET

Courbet presents the animal with the approach of a peaceful nature-lover, a 'man of the soil' who has made friends with all the inhabitants of his native region. In other pictures he shows the wild grandeur of the stag-fights in the forests of the Jura in the rutting season and the almost total solitude of the waterholes where they drink at night. The deep resonance of the greens, browns and greys used in these pictures gives them solidity together with a certain grace.

The Roebuck in the Forest

1867. 94 × 131 (37 × 51⅝) Musée du Louvre, Paris

XLV JEAN BAPTISTE CAMILLE COROT 1796–1875

Corot's Romanticism is not principally revealed, as is generally thought, in the misty landscapes of his later years, with their nymphs and dancing shepherds, but in his pensive, dreaming female portraits, his studies of women who seem to have directed their gaze inward. Probably he himself was unaware of the oppressive nostalgia weighing down these gracious heads, the secret emotion which paralyzes them, turns them to stone for a moment, and gives that moment eternal majesty. Some of these figures hold guitars, others sit thinking before an easel; this one has let fall on to her lap the letter which she has stopped reading. In every case the beauty of the painting and the warm hues of the flesh provide a striking contrast with the withdrawn quality of the inner spirit towards which each woman seems to be turning. The serenity, with which the young woman in *The Letter* is reading, is heightened by the strong, but delicate and sober, background in which she is set. There is nothing to distract the eye from what is essential to what is mere accessory or to weaken the immense power emanating from the work. The colour-harmony is made up of a discrete mixture of grey and brown tones peculiar to Corot so that anything brighter or more lively, even if it is the smallest detail, stands out with tremendous effect. His figure-studies have the same atmosphere as his landscapes— homely yet silent, suffused with a feeling of modest simplicity and intimacy.

The Letter

54 × 38 (21¼ × 15) Metropolitan Museum of Art, New York

XLVI JEAN AUGUSTE DOMINIQUE INGRES 1780–1867

Ingres would have been annoyed to have been called a Romantic, but his Classicism was always an arbitrarily adopted manner rather than the product of his temperament. Nevertheless his vigour brings him very close to the avowed Romantics whose excesses he condemned. He even entered into the 'troubadour' manner with *Paolo and Francesca* and paid homage to the Romantic idol *Ossian* at Napoleon's request. At twenty-seven, when he painted this portrait of Granet, a painter friend of his, Ingres laid stress, rather strikingly on the sympathy between the Roman landscape behind the sitter and the interior landscape expressed in his eyes. The formal perfection of the work is only a means of revealing with modesty and discretion, its tender, moving nostalgia. The tactile sensitivity with which he indicates the texture of the various objects—the leather of the book, the material of the cloak, etc.—is not intended primarily to create an illusion of reality but to add depth to the allure of colour and subject by appealing to other senses besides sight. It is interesting that the landscape of the Trinità dei Monti behind the sitter is painted in a style very like that of Granet himself who, unlike Ingres, was principally a landscape artist; this has given rise to the theory that Ingres let Granet paint in his own background. Whether or not this is the case, Ingres produced few other works so beautiful and satisfying.

Portrait of Granet

1807. 73 × 61 (28¾ × 24) Musée Granet, Aix-en-Provence

XLVII CHARLES FRANÇOIS DAUBIGNY 1817–78

Daubigny entered on to the scene of French Romanticism at a time when the lyrical, almost idealized conception of landscape was giving place to a more simple approach, and direct communion with nature. The dramatic landscape painted in the studio was giving way to a more objective version, often painted from nature. The whole transition can be seen in Daubigny who, after studying with Delaroche and Granet, rejected the academicism of the first and the Italianism of the second, in favour of the 'return to nature' begun by the Barbizon School and perfected by the Impressionists. Sincere and sensitive, his favourite subjects were familiar places, woods, ponds reflecting the setting sun. The colour of *Evening* suggests that it was painted from nature, with all the intensity of the 'first rapture', or at least completed in the studio when the forms and colours were still fresh in the painter's mind. The impasto is thick and warm, with a density which suggests the weight and depth of the things shown, the actual consistency of the wet grass, the heaviness of the earth. This 'poetry of reality', in which Daubigny excelled, remained one of the richest sources of beauty for the Barbizon painters and their successors, the Impressionists.

Evening

58 × 93 (22¾ × 36½) Metropolitan Museum of Art, New York

XLVIII THÉODORE PIERRE ETIENNE ROUSSEAU 1812–67

When Rousseau at the age of twenty-four settled in the unknown little village of Barbizon in the forest of Fontainebleau, he unwittingly opened a new chapter in the history of painting. His new methods were indeed revolutionary, for in his desire to preserve the closest contact with nature and to avoid the subjective modifications which are inevitable in the studio, he set up his easel out of doors—an unheard-of act of temerity. To the 'pathetic' attitude towards nature typical of Romanticism he added a desire to penetrate to its humblest as well as its most impressive aspects. He had already made a study of the peculiarities of the various regions of France— Auvergne, the Landes, Normandy, etc. The rough reception accorded to his *Descent of Cattle* by the Salon in 1835 showed how much his rigorous, energetic art was out of tune with contemporary taste. For fourteen years after this failure he lived in obscurity, which enabled him to mature, untroubled by Salons and Academies, in almost total solitude. He himself summed up his essential virtues as a painter in a phrase which condemns the theatrical qualities often present in Romanticism: 'Our art can reach true pathos only through sincerity'.

Sunset at Arbonne

64 × 99 (25¼ × 39) Metropolitan Museum of Art, New York

XLIX   ANTOINE JEAN GROS   1771–1835

In this picture showing one of the young Napoleon's exploits during the Italian campaign, Gros presents us with a 'portrait of a hero', rather than a 'great heroic epic' as in *The Field of Battle at Eylau,* for instance. He had met Napoleon in Milan in 1796 and at Josephine's request began a study of the Arcola episode, when the general picked up the flag a dying soldier had dropped and spurred on his regiment to attack the bridge which was well covered by the enemy artillery. Napoleon was too busy and impatient to give Gros long sittings, and even short snatches bored him so that Josephine had to restrain him forcibly. This picture, full of youthful ardour and dynamism, marks Gros' definitive conversion from the Davidian Classical ideal to Romanticism, at least in spirit; in form it still echoes the Davidian precepts. It was finished at Versailles from the sketches made in Milan and, without being an idealized portrait—on the contrary its documentation is very exact—it has a fascinating 'super-reality'.

Napoleon Crossing the Bridge at Arcola

1796. 72 × 59 (28⅝ × 23¼) Musée du Louvre, Paris

L   ANTOINE JEAN GROS

One of David's pupils, Gros was commanded by 'the master', after he had been exiled to Brussels, to take charge of his school which was to develop truly 'Classical' painters. However, he himself turned from Classical subjects to themes taken from the Revolution or the Imperial wars. He reaches epic stature in the choice of his subjects and the force of his treatment of dramatic scenes. The fidelity of his realistic detail, the care he takes to produce a composition which is both 'modern' and traditional, and to assemble all the elements which would go to make up local colour, ensure that his pictures are reliable historical documents. Although he almost 'deified' Napoleon in his pictures, it was not until the monarchy was restored that he was created a baron. However his lack of success in his later years and the onset of a mental illness, which he feared would be fatal, drove him to suicide. Although less dramatic than his large compositions his portraits establish a deep, secret relationship between the sitter and the background against which he is set.

Portrait of Christina Boyer

1800. 214 × 134 (84¼ × 52¾) Musée du Louvre, Paris

LI ANNE-LOUIS GIRODET DE ROUCY, known as GIRODET DE ROUCY-TRIOSON 1767–1824

A pupil of David and Gros and much influenced by the Italians during a stay in Rome, Girodet remained filled with the spirit of the 18th century; his Romanticism resembles that of the *fin de siècle* rather than the beginning of the century up to 1830. He has been compared with Correggio and Prud'hon, but in fact his imagination was fired by Celtic legends and *Ossian*, so popular in France at the time. He painted several fine portraits, religious pictures and mythological scenes. The subject of his most popular picture, *The Funeral of Atala,* is taken from Chateaubriand's intensely Romantic novel about the New World, with its wide open spaces and 'noble savages'. Reflecting the sentimentality of a whole era, it was exhibited in the Salon of 1808 and belonged to the private collection of Louis XVIII. A replica painted in 1813 is in the museum at Amiens. The work lacks all local colour; perhaps Girodet should have accompanied Chateaubriand to the land of the Natchez. His Atala and Red Indians seem to belong to Rousseau's theories on the basic goodness of man, but the picture has a calm, modest beauty having more in common with the elegiac sentimentality of the day than with the real America, as later revealed by Catlin to the great delight of Baudelaire, among others.

The Funeral of Atala

1808. 210 × 267 (82⅝ × 105⅜) Musée du Louvre, Paris

LII THÉODORE GÉRICAULT 1791–1824

Like so many of the French Romantic painters, Géricault was a product of David's studio and although he studied for a time with Guérin, he learned the basic principles of his art and his rich technique from the old masters. Unlike Delacroix, who refused to visit Italy, he made several visits to Rome and Florence, familiarizing himself with Michelangelo and Raphael (some of whose works he had already copied in the Louvre), Titian, Rubens and Rembrandt. His character was a mixture of numerous opposites: a brilliant horseman, to whom life was full of excitement, he was nevertheless subject to fits of melancholy and often took as the subjects for his paintings the more dramatic, even melodramatic aspects of human nature. He was passionately fond of the animals in whom the nobility of nature still seems to reign untamed, such as horses, and these inspired some of his finest pictures. As with Stubbs and Fuseli, his horses seem to be charged with mystery and magic. The picture illustrated was painted in England, probably between 1820 and 1821; it is one of the best examples of Géricault's deep intimacy with the equine character; he does not strain after Romantic picturesqueness but portrays, quite simply, an ultra-sensitive creature, capable of emotions which man either does not know or interprets clumsily. The daring and sureness of the execution are equally remarkable and the picture may be compared with certain paintings by James Ward, *The Fall of Phaeton* in the Lord Camrose Collection, for instance, or his *Horse Attacked by a Boa Constrictor* refused by the Royal Academy in 1803.

Horse Frightened by Thunder and Lightning

1820–21. 49 × 60 (19¼ × 25⅝) National Gallery, London

LIII THÉODORE GÉRICAULT

The Romantics specialized in the macabre, the extraordinary, the least-known and most astounding aspects of reality. Géricault carried this taste to the extreme of painting severed heads and portraits of madmen and criminals. In many of his portraits he made a conscious effort to capture the particular shade of peculiarity or madness of the sitter. *La Folle* (*The Madwoman*) in the Lyons Museum was painted between 1821 and 1824, probably in 1822, for Dr Georget, the doctor in charge of the mental cases at the Salpétrière hospital. This patient was nicknamed 'the Hyena' and her obsession was a form of pathological jealousy carried to the extreme of monomania and complete insanity. It is interesting to note how closely the portrait corresponds with Dr Georget's clinical notes; these describe the disease as causing an increase of circulation, violent pulsation of the arteries in the head and bloodshot eyes shining with a wild fury. Realistic accuracy here reaches an almost unbearable intensity.

La Folle (The Madwoman)

c. 1822. 72 × 58 (28¼ × 22¾) Musée des Beaux-Arts, Lyons

LIV   THÉODORE GÉRICAULT

When it was exhibited in the Salon in 1819 the *Raft of the 'Medusa'* caused a great scandal, shocking academic critics and visitors with the 'repulsive realism' of its details. On the other hand it was a revelation to young painters, particularly Delacroix, who found it a magnificent expression of all that Romanticism was trying to achieve in the sphere of art—true feeling for nature, emotion elevated to its highest degree, an exact and faithful representation of details taken from nature. In accordance with this ideal, Géricault, before beginning the large composition, collected all possible documents and oral testimonies about the shipwreck of the frigate *Medusa,* lost at sea in July 1816. He even set up a studio opposite a hospital in order to be able to study sick, dying and dead men with greater ease. Because of violent opposition from official sources the picture was not bought for the state, and he was awarded only a gold medal instead of first prize. From 12th June to 31st December, 1820, however, an enterprizing Englishman called Bullock exhibited the enormous canvas in London; he also took it to Dublin and showed it from 5th February to 31st March, 1821. In both places he was rewarded with an immense success, probably more from curiosity than from artistic interest.

Raft of the 'Medusa'

1819. 491 × 716 (193 × 282) Musée du Louvre, Paris

LV EUGÈNE DELACROIX 1798–1863

After seeing the *Raft of the 'Medusa'* Delacroix was inspired to adopt artistic principles very like, if not identical with, those of Géricault. A man of wide culture, he added every possible additional layer of meaning to painting; nevertheless, though he often took historical and literary subjects as the basis for his compositions he never forgot that a picture is, above all, 'painting'. His largest compositions, which bear comparison with the Venetians and Rubens, and his landscapes reveal a new sensitivity to nature, a new conception of it, while his crowded, forceful, historical pictures display all the resources of his art. He was, too, one of the first and most important artists to become enthusiastic about the Orient, which was to figure so largely in French Romanticism. Many of his themes were taken from the works of Byron, Shakespeare and Walter Scott, all of whom he read with great avidity. And, in addition, he was deeply influenced by Constable; his ideas as to landscape painting were transformed after he had studied the Englishman's works. As the most complex and complete of the early 19th-century painters, the one who was perhaps the first to throw off the shackles of Neo-Classicism, he may be considered the father of modern painting in every respect.

The tragic intensity of this scene of Greek insurrection and Turkish cruelty is brought out by many evocative details: the naked woman tied to the rider's saddle, the dying man breathing his last, and the unforgettable 'old Greek Woman' symbolizing the pride and misery of a noble country oppressed by foreigners. Each individual object comes alive by means of vivid colour, the exciting gleam of metal, silk or leather. This is a Romantic picture *par excellence,* in the pathos of the subject itself and the communion established between the landscape with its distant fires flaming up and the figures devoured by an 'interior fire'.

Detail from *Scenes of the Massacre at Chios*

1822. 422 × 352 (166⅛ × 138⅝) Musée du Louvre, Paris

LVI EUGÈNE DELACROIX

This famous painting depicts the spirit of the July uprisings of 1830 in both realistic and symbolical fashion. An ardent liberal, the young Delacroix attempted to show the way in which all classes of society were brought together at the barricades, middle-classes and working-classes, children and grown men. The very figure of 'Liberty' is almost a manifesto of Romanticism in itself; instead of contenting himself with a feeble allegory as the Neo-Classicists would have done, the artist has made this vigorous woman, shown with bosom bared, spurring men into battle by her warlike fury, into a living creature. The 'olfactory values' are almost as striking as the tactile ones; the smell of blood, sweat, bare flesh, burning cloth, metal and powder, so dear to the Romantics (e.g. Géricault, Courbet), after having been ignored or shown only with repugnance throughout the whole of the Neo-Classical period, figure largely in this picture.

Liberty Leading the People

1830. 260×325 (102¼×128) Musée du Louvre, Paris

LVII EUGÈNE DELACROIX

Scott's novels appealed to the Romantics for their lively, individualistic depiction of history, and they provided the inspiration for a number of paintings. Delacroix was particularly fond of *Ivanhoe* and made several versions of one of its most dramatic episodes, the abduction of Rebecca. The one dating from 1858 which is in the Louvre shows vast differences from the version illustrated here, being invested with a certain Classical balance which is entirely lacking in the New York version. The velvety colour, at once brilliant and rich, the daring, almost Expressionistic treatment of the burning castle, and the way in which all the elements are subordinated to the dramatic feeling, make this one of the works most representative of French Romanticism in general and Delacroix' tragic vein in particular. In this picture his fiery brushwork and freedom in colouring attain their highest power.

The Abduction of Rebecca

1846. 100 × 82 (39½ × 32½) Metropolitan Museum of Art, New York

LVIII HONORÉ DAUMIER 1808–79

In the eyes of his contemporaries Daumier was chiefly a graphic artist and caricaturist. Today his talent as a painter is recognized—the sumptuousness of his treatment, the effects of the lights gleaming mysteriously out of his (usually monochrome) colour, the dramatic realism of his subject-matter, taken from the amusing or touching incidents of everyday life, the 'small ironies of the humdrum'. It has been said that he was a sort of amalgam of Michelangelo and Goya, but in fact he owes little to either artist. In all his work—in the political cartoons he did for opposition newspapers of the day, in his pathetic pictures of laundresses carrying washing, in his equally touching depiction of the lofty Don Quixote riding across the plains of La Mancha—Daumier always shows himself to be a man of great generosity, an enemy to injustice and stupidity who rebelled against all forms of oppression. To him art itself was yet another weapon to be used by liberalism against despotism. With his 'sombre manner', he exerted a great influence on the early works of Cézanne who, like him, came from Southern France.

The Print Collector

Oil on panel. 34 × 26 (13⅜ × 10¼) Philadelphia Museum of Art

VI   OTHER EUROPEAN COUNTRIES

SPAIN

MOST BIOGRAPHIES of Francisco Goya (1746–1828) attribute his transformation from a man of the 18th-century Rococo into a Romantic to his serious illness in 1792. But for whatever reason, Goya certainly became a Romantic, almost Romanticism incarnate, in whom painful, passionate anguish attained its maximum intensity. In 1792 the painter was forty-six, at the height of his fame; for twelve years he had been acknowledged by Spanish society to be a portrait painter of genius for whom it was a distinction to pose—the Court had taken him up and named him Painter of the Chamber in 1789. The Tapestry Manufactory of Madrid had commissioned from him the 'series' in which he depicted, with the verve of a Tiepolo and the chromatic richness of a Fragonard, the Spanish people at work and play. He exuded *joie de vivre*, innocent wit and health, and succeeded marvellously in giving expression, with tumultuous colour and almost 'folk' liveliness, to this superabundance of vigour.

A superb draughtsman, he possessed a brilliant palette, rich in enamel-like colours and shifting iridescences; from Velasquez he had inherited the very Spanish gift (it has passed to Picasso) of making tones attain their highest frequency and combine in their most subtle melodies, merely by surrounding them by very rich and delicate greys and browns. He was also skilled in bringing out the sumptuousness of black. The drawing merely helped him to work out form; this once established it came to fruition through colour, simultaneously receiving and giving out light.

'Always lines and never solid bodies. But where are these lines in nature? I see only bodies which are lit up and bodies which are not, planes which approach and planes which recede, objects in relief and objects in recession.' Until 1792 he lived in a blaze of sunlight which lit up his pictures and himself equally. In his joyously greedy and vulgar way of gobbling up life he remained plebeian, although capable of aristocratic refinement. He took over from Rococo its elegant sensuality and taste for hedonism but otherwise he remained a true son of his austere, grave country. Passionate and governed by his instincts, he seems to have been fairly indifferent to currents of thought, and, after his illness, plunged into extreme pessimism, surrendered wholly to night and the devil with the same blind vehemence with which in happier days he had seen absolute beauty in a woman's body bathed in pearl-white light. Everything in him points to a man primitive in his instincts;

this was probably why the illness which left him deaf caused a complete metamorphosis, so that he became melancholic, bitter, seeing only the ugliness and tragedies of life. Although he turned back to the palette of his early days for the dome of S Antonio de la Florida at Madrid where the forms emerge and are submerged at one and the same time in a ripple of satin and pearl, the same year saw the engraving of the *Caprichos*, that *danse macabre* in which a disquieting troop of monsters, frightening in that they are too human, rises out of a shadowy night.

Baudelaire, as usual, summed him up accurately. 'Goya's great achievement is that he makes the monstrous credible. His monsters are very harmonic. No other artist has ventured so far in the direction of believable absurdity. All his contortions, bestial faces and diabolical grimaces are permeated with *humanity*.'

It almost seems as though during his early period of peace, happiness and euphoria, Goya had only seen the artificial façade and surface graces of humanity. Only when his deafness with its allied annoyance, shame and inhibitions caused him to cut himself off, did he see through the outer husk and discover yawning chasms beneath the outward appearances. Once he had rejoiced in portraying picturesque and joyous scenes, the most beautiful women and distinguished men of the age. Now, isolated from the public, clients and even his friends, no longer working on commissions, he deliberately chose to chronicle the most dramatic and painful aspects of life. Lunatic asylums, where naked madmen tear at each other, cannibal Red Indians devouring Canadian priests; the plague-hospital beneath whose roof the plague-germs joyfully dance out their murderous ballet in the dusty shafts of sunlight; the Inquisition tribunal before which the unfortunates convicted of heresy crumble, humiliated and defeated; processions of screaming blind men, drunken beggars and sufferers from convulsions miming a demoniac, lunatic dance; the platform on which the man sentenced to death, with his head already in the noose, still clutches at the crucifix which has failed to save him: all these make up Goya's new world, a world without pardon, redemption or salvation. The Christ of *The Betrayal of Judas* (1798, Cathedral of Toledo) and *Christ in the Garden of Olives* (1818, S Antonio, Madrid) has lost his halo of divinity, indeed every spark of spirituality: he is merely a man like any other, condemned to suffering, despair and death.

Goya's palette becomes progressively dimmer and darker; the sharp dissonances of his sullen blacks, acid greens, greys and livid whites make themselves felt. Like out-of-tune instruments, although played with the sure instinct of the master, the colours grate against each other, shriek, mingle their fellow miseries. Not that he became careless as a craftsman; he was never so skilled as when the task itself had become hateful to him. Always eager to learn, he had himself taught lithography at the age of seventy-three; this new technique, which he used for the *Tauromachia*, gave him a simplicity of execution and suppleness, opened up new possibilities in light and shade. All this had been impossible with etching, the medium he had used for the nightmarish *Disparates* (also called the *Proverbs*), engraved between 1816 and 1824, and the *Disasters of War* inspired by the horrors of the French invasion, the Spanish resistance and the ensuing reprisals.

Goya's national feeling and patriotic hate of the French must not be exaggerated; it was in France that he found a refuge when he had to leave Spain and he died at Bordeaux. His attachment to his country was that of the Aragon peasant who regards any stranger as an intruder or enemy. He puts side by side the cold, nocturnal execution of the Spanish prisoners in the *Third of May* (1814, Prado, Madrid) and the swift, joyous revolt of the Madrid people ripping open the Mamelukes' horses the previous day in the *Second of May* (1814, Prado, Madrid) and in doing so he displays the same plebeian brutality, perfectly sincere and unaffected, with which he sets himself in opposition, as a proletarian to the aristocrats, as a Spaniard to the French.

This fondness for fighting scenes reflects the attraction which tragedy, ugliness, everything which reveals human foolishness, cruelty or wickedness, had for this

FRANCISCO DE GOYA Y LUCIENTES see p. 208

1   *Man Walking among Phantoms*

Engraving from the *Proverbios*
Etching, aquatint and drypoint. 24 × 35.5 (9½ × 14)
Tomas Harris Collection. England

2   *The Carnivorous Vulture*

From *The Disasters of War*, plate 76
c. 1820. Etching and aquatint. 17.5 × 21.5 (6⅞ × 8½)
Tomas Harris Collection. England

3   *The Dream of Reason Produces Monsters*

From the *Caprichos*, plate 43
c. 1810–15. Etching and aquatint. 21.5 × 15 (8⅜ × 5⅞)
Philadelphia Museum of Art.

1

El buitre carnívoro.

2

3

4

5

6

7

pessimist held prisoner by his deafness. Most of his time was spent at his country house which he decorated with ghastly scenes as though his real nightmares were not enough and he must always have before his eyes the terrifying figures of Saturn eating his children, giants fighting in a marsh, men flying as one flies in a dream into nothingness, sorcerers shaking with laughter as they stir their hell-brews and men twisted by the joy of unpardonable vices.

His neighbours called this temple of nightmare 'the deaf man's house' (*La Quinta del Sordo*) and wondered how he could find pleasure in living with these terrifying forms seen as though in distorting mirrors; what they did not understand was that pleasure no longer entered into it. Goya now belonged entirely to the powers of darkness, to the devil who appeared, in the form of a buck, to the sorcerers meeting in the plain of Aquelare. His only pleasure was his joy in painting, for his grey-green compositions are prodigies of refinement; one might say that his virtuosity as a colourist was never so great as when he rejected all the bright colours and kept only the dull, flat, sober, sad ones—the colours of Seville, of Burnt Siena ... To restrict himself to such an austere gamut was to force his genius into acts of supreme daring, resulting in magnificent successes, more difficult (though less immediately attractive) than the dewy, sun-lit iridescences of the *Naked Maya* (1800–1802, Prado, Madrid).

Baudelaire spoke of Goya's 'love of things difficult to grasp, feeling for violent contrasts, for the terrors of nature and human physiognomies strangely animalized by circumstances' and these had, in fact, become the main elements of his vision and painting. They can be seen to perfection in the beggars of the *Romeria di S Isidro*, with their grimaces like masks in a tragic, demoniac carnival, stretched out, contracted, flattened, swollen by the fire of a furious hatred. These faces so haunted Spanish artists of the day that they did their utmost to see, think and paint like Goya, to come as close to him as the difference between talent and genius permitted.

It must be admitted that the chief virtue of the few Spanish Romantics—Leonardo Alenza (1807–1845), Eugenio Lucas y Padilla (1824–1870), and his son Eugenio Lucas y Villaamil and Jose Parcerisa (born 1840)—is their sincerely, sometimes naively, imitative Goyism. Others, such as the Madrazo father and son, followed in the footsteps of David and Delaroche respectively, and their discipleship was a very indolent, spiritless, unoriginal affair. For a whole generation Madrid was occupied by 'Davidians' carrying on a lifeless Classicism which served only to destroy the heritage which Tiepolo had left to Spain. One exception was Alenza who created some dramatic etchings steeped in Goya's atmosphere of hell, madness, sorcery and crime. Nevertheless, he had enough humour to satirize Romanticism in the two versions of his *Romantic Suicide* (the better of the two is in the Romantic Museum, Madrid), rather similar in tone to the English skits on 'Gothick' novels. The two Lucases further exaggerated Goya's teachings, hurling themselves without restraint into fantasy and absurdity and relinquishing all perspective or balance in favour of forms that seem born of a sick mind. The monsters of Goya's pupils and imitators are often unconvincing and seem to belong to a stock of figures which have already become a convention. In reality Romanticism in Spain began and ended with Goya alone, and such men as the Lucases, Alenza and Parcerisa merely prolonged his personality rather than being truly personal and original creators. It is beyond the scope of this book to examine whether the expressionism of Solana, so strongly marked by Goya's influence should be considered as a form of Post-Romanticism. And what about Dali's 'Goyism'? At the very least, it must be acknowledged that Goya's Romanticism was not foreign to Spain but rooted in an ancient tradition capable of constant fruitful renewals.

LEONARDO ALENZA 1807–45

A pupil of Juan Rozera and José de Madrazo, Alenza painted scenes of Spanish low life in a style resembling Goya's. He was also a respected portraitist and his graphic work won him great fame.

4 *Study of Heads*

Etching. 13.6 × 10 (5⅜ × 3⅞)
British Museum, London

ADAM WOLFGANG TOEPFFER 1766–1847

Toepffer began his working life as an engraver at Lausanne but during a visit to Paris (ended in 1789) he turned to painting. He visited England in 1816 and greatly admired Hogarth's work which influenced his own from that date onward.

5 *Girl with Bowed Head*

Drawing. 25.5 × 19.9 (10 × 7¾)
British Museum, London

HENRY FUSELI 1741–1825

Although born in Zürich, Fuseli early moved to London where he made the acquaintance of Blake and won immense popularity, becoming Professor of Painting, and later Principal of the Royal Academy. He was an excellent teacher. His ruling passions were Michelangelo, whose dramatic dynamism he attempted to imitate, and, in the sphere of literature, 'Ossian', Dante, Shakespeare and Milton. All these provided him with material for strange compositions combining tragedy and humour, nightmare and satirical verve. Herder said of him that 'his laughter stung like the Devil's mockery, and his love lit up its object like a flash of destructive lightning'.

6 *The Body of Buonconte da Montefeltre being Carried off by the Devil*

The scene is taken from Dante's *Purgatorio* where Buonconte describes how he fell dead from his wounds with the Virgin's name on his lips and his body was swept down the stream into the Arno
Pen and wash. 47 × 35.2 (18½ × 13⅞)
British Museum, London

HENRY FUSELI

7 *Odin Foreseeing Balder's Death*

Drawing and wash. 28 × 40 (11 × 15⅞)
British Museum, London

SWITZERLAND

IT WAS THE AGE when Albert von Haller was writing his great poem on the Alps, which was to stir up Romantic sensibility as much as Young's *Night Thoughts* or Rousseau's *Rêveries d'un Promeneur Solitaire;* when heavily equipped expeditions including physicians, geologists and alpinists were making the first climbs of the Alps for scientific rather than sporting motives; when Joseph Anton Koch, from Tyrol, was remarking, for almost the first time, the majestic beauty in the wildernesses of waterfalls and glaciers. In the sphere of art Swiss painters were discovering and marvelling at the rich fund of aesthetic emotions, surprises and joys offered by the mountains of their country. Perhaps for the first time they saw them not as 'hostile peaks' and 'terrifying gulfs' but as landscapes worth painting for their own sake and not merely as the background to a regional or dramatic 'plot'.

To the Renaissance minds of men such as Manuel Deutsch, Graf or Leu, the mountains and forests were tragic elements in themselves, but they were still tied up with events, actions in which man was implicated: the 'man of nature' of the German Renaissance was a hybrid creature part animal, part rustic god, but nevertheless a kind of man. Altdorfer, Cranach and Wolf Huber had sensed that wooded and alpine landscapes might be animated by invisible presences represented, without anthropomorphism, in trees, rocks and torrents like ancient earthly deities, and Hercules Seghers' empty landscapes breathe an atmosphere of pagan divinity; but with the Swiss painters of the end of the 18th century and beginning of the 19th —not to say Segantini, the hermit of la Maloja—the haughty, distant beauty of the mountains acquires a certain cosy good-fellowship, an idyllic sweetness which tempers their inaccessible severity. 'The finest view leaves a certain emptiness in the spirit if it is not animated by some more approachable object which suggests the presence of our fellow-creatures,' wrote Karl Albert Kasthofer.

Liotard painted the little gardens of Geneva's suburbs dominated by the Saleve, but only as an adjunct to his portrait of himself and, perhaps, in order to add documentary value to his own garden. Although the two Gabriel Lorys, father and son (1763–1840 and 1784–1846) of Berne and Johann Ludwig Aberli (1723–1786) studied the nature of rocks, waterfalls and torrents with almost scientific exactitude, they brought to their pictures of the wildest localities a sort of idyllic grace which lessened both the majesty and the intimidating austerity of the mountains. They also added an admixture of Rousseauesque theism and, like Klopstock, discerned in each waterfall an 'inspiration of the Creator'. Their sensibilities were not directly touched and they tended at times to subside into mere bucolicism.

The true Romantic spirit appears with J. J. Hürlimann (1793–1850) from Riedikon, J. J. Biedermann (1763–1830) of Winterthur, and P. Birmann (1758–1844) of Basle, Aberli's best pupil. Birmann's *Devil's Bridge*, the *Splügen Pass* of J. J. Meyer (1787–1858), and *Gorges of la Douanne* of Dunker (1746–1807) are filled with the rustling of trees and singing of waterfalls; in them the high wind of the peaks sounds more loudly than the picturesque Alpine horn but, even so, these painters still lag behind the poets of the day. None of them succeeds in making us aware, as did Byron, that beneath these ice-domes is 'dark-heaving—boundless, endless and sublime, the image of eternity'. This achievement was reserved, though still in miserly measure, for the Swiss artists to whom mountains were a commonplace of life in which there was almost nothing more to discover, but only to feel and express.

Certain of the Swiss painters cannot possibly be called true Romantics—Léopold Robert (1794–1835) despite his taste for painting truculent theatrical brigands, the anecdotal Friedrich Rudolf Simon (1828–1862), Jacques Laurent Agasse

(1767–1849) who, like his compatriot Fuseli, became a favourite of the English in his later years on account of his solid, but rigorous and elegant craftsmanship, Wolfgang Adam Toepffer (1766–1847) who readily gave way to sentimental or comically banal genre scenes, Alfred van Mayden (1818–1898), imprisoned by a rather mawkish sensibility.

With great eclecticism, Hans Heinrich Füssli (1741–1825), who made his home in England and changed his name to Fuseli, produced, like some German eclectic painters, work which was an amalgam of equal parts of the old German epic poems and the Greek tragedies all covered by an overlay of Shakespeare. In painting he was mostly influenced by Michelangelo and Rubens of the old masters, and Reynolds of the 'moderns', but his imagination led him to investigate the darker sides of life; he was frequently visited by macabre apparitions and nightmares, and himself said of his progress, that it was like that of a sleepwalker, groping his way through mists of fantasy, that he advanced 'through a sea without shores or bottom'.

The stars of Swiss Romantic landscape painting are Maximilien de Meuron (1785–1868) from Neuchâtel, who set up his easel at the lake-side, beneath high mountains and sketched in the midst of avalanches, and the sincere, vigorous François Diday (1802–1877). Only thirty or forty years separate his *Cascade de Pissevache* (1852, Musée d'Art et d'Histoire, Geneva) from that by Gabriel Lory (the younger) but in those few decades a great change had taken place in the Swiss technique and aesthetic of mountain-painting. Gabriel Lory remains naive and clumsy, because he is intimidated by the subject and the mountain has not yet taken possession of his being; Diday, on the other hand, is at one with Nature, unlike the painters of the preceding generation who seem to remain town-dwellers not quite familiar with the Nature around them. His *Mont Blanc Seen from Sallanches* (Geneva Museum) unfolds with the breadth and harmony of a symphony. This harmony is found also in the pictures of Barthélémy Menn (1815–1893), who must be regarded as a Post-Romantic rather than a Romantic; his painting, ample, supple, musical, exercised a considerable influence on Ferdinand Hodler (1853–1918).

But the greatest of this generation, the artist in closest communion with a landscape which no longer held mysteries or terrors, was Alexandre Calame (1810–1864). Although he was very fond of Italy and profited greatly from what it had to offer him, he did not allow it to overcome his own individuality. Eclectic in his tastes, fond of working in the open air, Calame was intimately bound up with the Nature of the cantons over which he ranged and retained enough of the idyllic tradition of the previous century to portray an everyday Switzerland, both wild and well-kept. However, Calame's real genius was not to reach its highest point in portraying the sweet, careless pleasure to be gained from living in well-kept localities. It is the tragic power of mountains which really awakens his spirit; storms held for him the same fascination as for all the Romantics, whether they acknowledged it or not, and his universe is that of the forests lashed by tempests, torrents bursting their banks, grey glaciers across which heavy storm-clouds throw their leaden shadows. *The Storm at Handeck* (Musée d'Art et d'Histoire, Geneva) is his most characteristic work, at least with regard to this aspect of his personality. Calame is aware of powers in Nature which come to the surface all the more freely when man is excluded from these haunts of gods and demons. Böcklin's mythological figures, in their incongruous nudity or stage costumes, would be entirely out of place here.

Calame's Romanticism remains within the limits of a Realism saturated with supernatural qualities, strangely fantastic and unfamiliar. We do not need to see gods depicted to sense how much they cast their aura over his *Summer on the Plain* (1850, Musée d'Art et d'Histoire, Geneva). A sort of Swiss honesty, or perhaps timidity, or a desire to remain within the bounds of the familiar, restrains Calame from letting these powers peer out from the rocks or tree-bark. But one could also say that it is a mark of his art's nobility that, in its most dramatic moments, it preserves a certain modest reserve.

RUSSIA

COMPARED with Russia's Romantic literature, with its Pushkin and Lermontov, her pictorial art seems of much less significance. At least two artists, however, Brullov (1800–52) (a descendant of French emigrés called Brulleau) and Ivanov, deserve a less patronizing attitude than that normally meted out to them and, to varying degrees and for different reasons, deserve to be remembered. The poverty of Russian Romanticism compared with that of France, England and Germany was due to the tyranny of æsthetic tradition rather than its absence. While religious art voluntarily confined itself to repeating forms established centuries earlier by the schools of Pskov, Moscow and Novgorod, themselves deriving from Byzantium, secular art followed obediently at the heels of Paris and Berlin fashion, as required by Russian high society which considered 'derussification' its ultimate aim; folk art, produced by countryfolk for countryfolk, was more or less static and merely repeated *ad nauseam* unchanging themes with unchanging means.

The genre painting of Alexis Venetsianov (1780–1847) and Paul Andrevitch Fedotov (1815–1852) is skilful, theatrical, humorous, documentary—never reaching above the level of a careful, unexceptionable academism. Consequently, Brullov's large canvases are almost moving in that they at least possess something lacking in Venetsianov's and Fedotov's 'petit-bourgeois' or, rather, 'small-town nobility' works. His ideal painters were Michelangelo and the Raphael of the *Stanze*. His well-known *Last Day of Pompeii* (1833, Tretyakov Gallery, Moscow) is the best (that is to say, the worst) example of how far he lags behind them.

Although painted in 1833, when the artist had had ample opportunities of seeing the horrors of the war, this picture is pathetically bombastic and does not show any of the realities of a catastrophe, even if it is not entirely without grandeur. However the mood of this catastrophe overtaking a charming town of the *campagna* now buried under lava and ashes is not at all academic, and although the scene is Classical and the 'plot' taken from history, the tragic episodes are treated with real feeling. It is hardly important whether Brullov got the idea for the picture when listening in Naples to an opera on the subject of Pompeii, as tradition would have it; enough that the Romantic character of the work reaches a height of tragic feeling which lends it an exciting rhythm and gives unity to the various elements of the story.

Alexander Ivanov (1806–1858) is quite different. Turgenev summed up the contrast between these two widely opposed but equally famed personalities when he said: 'Brullov had the gift of being able to express all he wanted to, but he had nothing to say. Ivanov had much to say, but an impediment in his speech.' At Rome, Ivanov had frequented the circle of the Nazarenes and became particularly friendly with Overbeck whom he much admired while adopting the æsthetics and ideals of the Brotherhood generally. By temperament a philosopher and mystic, he devoted almost his entire energies to a painting showing Jesus appearing to the Jews on the banks of the Jordan, *Appearance of Christ before the People* (Roumanziev Museum, Moscow) which was to be the fine distillation of his whole religious thought.

This self-imposed project was so important to him that he felt himself unready, artistically and spiritually, to express the religious feeling bound up with it; he literally devoted his whole life to it, piling up studies and sketches. Only practical difficulties prevented him from going to Palestine to imbibe the atmosphere and local colour which might give added life to his picture. As might be expected, however, the picture, born with such labour pains, constantly worked over by an artist impossible to satisfy, emerged cold, lifeless, with a certain undeniable nobility but altogether lacking in the spirit Ivanov had meant to express.

HENRY FUSELI see p. 210

8 *Dante Meeting Ugolino in the Frozen Cocytus*

This drawing and Plate 6 show episodes from Dante's *Divine Comedy* and were executed in Rome between 1774 and 1777
Drawing and wash. 47 × 35 (18½ × 13⅞)
British Museum, London

ALEXANDRE CALAME 1810–64
Painter, engraver and lithographer, Calame studied under Diday in 1829. He made many visits to Holland and Italy, but remained faithful to the scenery of his native Switzerland which he immortalized in so many of its aspects.

9 *Landscape with Two Figures*

Watercolour. 16.2 × 24.3 (6¼ × 9½)
British Museum, London

ALEXANDRE CALAME

10 *Mountain Landscape*

Sepia. 36.8 × 26.5 (14½ × 10⅜)
British Museum, London

CARL BRULLOV 1800–52
This Russian painter, specializing in portraits and historical scenes, had a particular feeling for large tragic works, but he did not completely escape extravagance and pomposity. Along with the virtues of Romanticism he also suffered from its defects. His genre scenes show greater simplicity.

11 *Design for a Fountain*

Watercolour. 52.6 × 36.3 (20¾ × 14¼)
British Museum, London

8

10

9

11

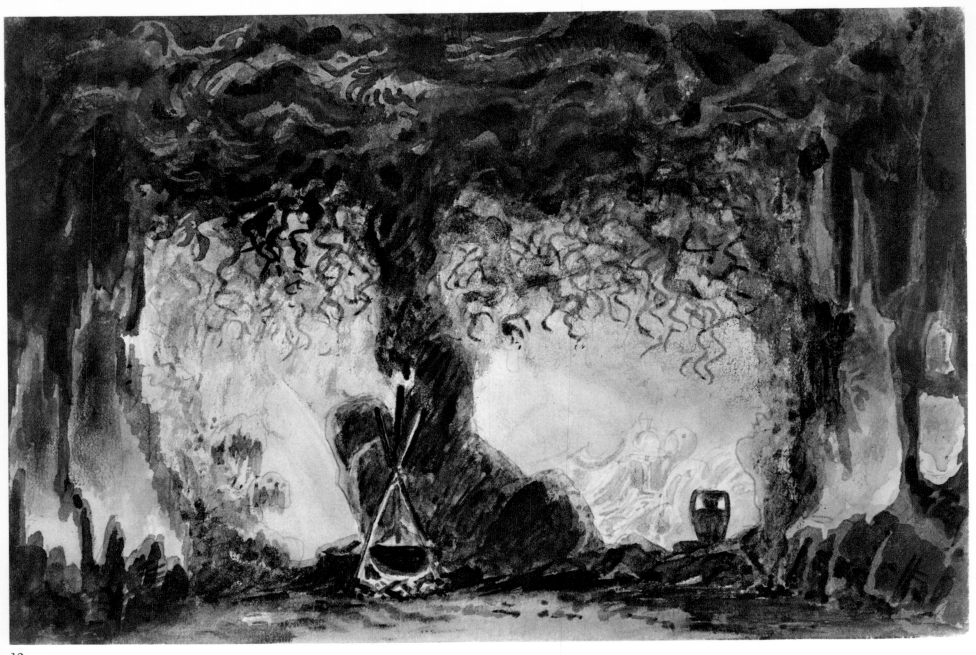

12

13

14

15

16

17

18

19

20

21

AUGUST FREDERICK AHLGRENSSON 1838–1902

Swedish. Ahlgrensson's early training as a scenic designer in Stockholm bore fruit in a large number of designs for stage décors. After spending considerable periods in Paris and Vienna where he perfected his technique he was engaged by the State Theatre of Copenhagen, for which he designed and carried out many stage decorations.

12 *Grotto*

Gouache. 20.4×30 (8⅛×11¾)
Kgl. Teaters Bibliotek, Copenhagen

THOMAS BRUUN 1742–1800

Danish. After studying at the Academy in Copenhagen he specialized in stage designs and created décors for several Danish plays and Italian operas. He was attached to the State Theatre, Copenhagen as stage designer for eighteen years, from 1782 to 1800.

13 *Grotto*

Décor for the play *Balders Död* by J. Ewald
Pencil, Indian ink and watercolour. 38.5×45.8 (15¼×17¾)
Statens Museum for Kunst, Copenhagen.

SVEND LUDVIG VALDEMAR GYLLICH 1837–95

Danish. Gyllich represents the Realistic strain of Scandinavian stage decoration which, in the second half of the 19th century, began to usurp the place of fairy-tale idealism. He went so far as to attempt illusionist effects, following the theories then current in Austria, Germany and France.

14 *The Valkyries*

Décor for a ballet
1861. Gouache. 17.5×25.7 (6⅞×10⅛)
Kgl. Teaters Bibliotek, Copenhagen.

JENS PETERSEN LUND 1730–after 1793

Danish. Lund began as a house painter in Copenhagen, but later entered the Academy, paid visits to Paris and Rome and, in his last years, was appointed landscape painter to the Danish Court. He also painted allegorical compositions, panoramas (which were then in high fashion) and stage décors.

15 *Punch in Prison*

Pen and watercolour. 27.6×41.4 (10⅞×16⅜)
Statens Museum for Kunst, Copenhagen

PETER CRAMER 1726–82

Danish. Cramer was nicknamed 'the Danish Teniers' because of his predilection for genre scenes in the Netherlandish manner. He was also well known as a stage designer and devoted a large part of his activities to the theatre. His designs are mostly for plays in the repertoire of Danish theatres during the second half of the 18th century.

16 *Death of Balder*

Study, showing the last scene of the play *Balders Död* by J. Ewald, for the painting of the same name also in the Statens Museum for Kunst
Pencil drawing. 38×46.9 (15×18½)
Statens Museum for Kunst, Copenhagen

NICOLAI ABRAHAM ABILDGAARD 1743–1809

Danish. Abildgaard's work reveals the influence of both Fuseli and the 16th- and 17th-century Italian painters whom he studied during his visit to Rome from 1772 to 1777. For the subjects of his paintings and drawings he frequently went to Nordic mythology, Milton, Shakespeare, Macpherson's *Ossian* and the theatre generally.

17 *Fingal's Ancestors Appearing to him by Moonlight*

Pen, Indian ink, and wash. 22.1×22.3 (8¾×8⅞)
Statens Museum for Kunst, Copenhagen

JENS CHRISTIAN CLAUSEN DAHL 1788–1857

Norwegian. Dahl, who worked in Copenhagen and Dresden, learned much from the Germans and in return influenced North German landscape painters. He succeeds in bringing out the spirit of a landscape with remarkable force and intensity.

18 *Landscape*

1826. Watercolour. 17.2×24.5 (7½×9¾)
Billedgalleri, Bergen

AUGUST CAPPELEN 1827–52

Norwegian. Although he died at twenty-five, this remarkable painter was the most gifted and original Norwegian artist of the Romantic Age. He had worked with Gude in Oslo and with Schirmer in the Düsseldorf School. His landscapes are taken from the Telemark region where he lived at the end of his life.

19 *Brook in a Forest*

Watercolour. 34.8×51 (13¾×20⅛)
Nasjonalgalleriet, Oslo

CARL WAHLBOM 1810–58

Swedish. The flowering of Romanticism in Sweden ran roughly parallel to the vogue for 'Swedish drill'. Wahlbom was a professor at the Ling Institute of Gymnastics in Stockholm as well as being a painter. His most striking works are his illustrations for history books and Nordic legends and mythology.

20 *Braga the Ancient*

Pencil. 22.4×14.6 (8¾×5¾)
Nationalmuseum, Stockholm

LOUIS GALLAIT 1810–87

After studying with Hennequin and at the Tournai Academy, Gallait turned to historical painting and produced successful versions of several dramatic episodes from Netherlandish history, especially the Spanish occupation.

21 *Two Children*

Drawing. 16.8×12.6 (6⅝×5)
British Museum, London

By attempting to give a particular significance to each figure, every slight movement having something to say, he produced a composition both static and emphatic and cluttered up with anecdotal details. In a sense he improves on the excessively medievalist Nazarenes in the beauty of his background landscape and the moral grandeur of the tiny figure of Christ advancing towards the crowd of John the Baptist's disciples; the nudes are treated with a certain vigour and the faces are expressive. Despite its undeniable faults, resulting from the superabundance of qualities which the artist tried to squeeze in, the work is not a complete failure; it has nobility and, if the heat of inspiration has cooled somewhat through the long years of execution, the distribution of the masses at least reveals a more gifted and original painter than Brullov. Perhaps Ivanov would have shown his true measure if he had ever carried out the colossal decorative compositions for a monumental Temple of Humanity of which he dreamed. But here too an excess of zeal caused him to protract his preparations for years, studying not only Palestinian but Egyptian and Assyrian archaeology, until at last he was hamstrung by his own scrupulousness. If he had lived twenty years longer perhaps the Temple of Humanity would have been one of the most grandiose manifestations of Slav Romanticism; even so, Russian art would still have lacked a genius of the stature of Gogol and Tchaikovsky.

SCANDINAVIA

Asmus Jacob Carstens (1754–1798) is often compared with Blake, Fuseli and Flaxman, and not without reason. He achieved the apparently impossible: a synthesis of Romanticism and Classicism. Passionately devoted to Italy and Michelangelo, he nevertheless exercised a tremendous influence on German Romanticism, more in fact than on that of his own country. It is unfortunate that he died at forty-four, one of those *Frühvollendeten* who hardly emerge from their apprentice years and are thus never able to complete their oeuvre and give the final measure of their genius. His principle originality lies in his deliberate repudiation of colour, whether because his large drawings were only sketches or because he thought (which is more likely) that a great artist can model in black and white or in colour with equal ease.

For him drawing was sufficient to embrace form and express it in all its fullness; he would have agreed with Ingres that 'drawing is the better part of art'. Forced to take up commerce for a living, it was not until late in life and in his spare time that he could work with Abildgaard in Copenhagen. Abildgaard introduced him to Fuseli's work and he himself turned instinctively to Homer, Klopstock, Shakespeare and 'Ossian'. A plaster cast of the Apollo Belvedere moved him to tears when he saw it for the first time. His ambition was to attain the pathos inherent in the grandeur and simplicity of Antiquity which Neo-Classicism, with its mistaken attitudes, had overlooked. Although he had never seen the Sistine Chapel—on his visit to Italy in 1783 he was forced to turn back at Mantua for lack of money—he understood Michelangelo's genius better than any of his contemporaries. He only knew Giulio Romano's work from the Palazzo del Tè but he saw in his frescoes, however removed from his own artistic ideals, an indication of the route he should follow; it was not until 1792 that a patron's generosity enabled him to return to Italy and this time to reach Rome, where he had determined to end his days. Yet, far from breaking with Scandinavian traditions as such, he wrote mythological dramas with Wotan and Baldur for heroes, Scaldic poems and fervent imitations of 'Ossian'.

His genius was eclectic enough for him to absorb everything which violently excited his imagination, from Milton to Aeschylus. Through drawing alone he gave tremendous animation and life to his figures. Only the vast walls of a palace or the dome of a great church could have allowed his tumultuous vision full scope. When, finally, he took up colour, a medium strange and unnatural to him, he used it with a rare, imposing strength.

The present fashion of reproaching Carstens for his 'coldness', meaning a certain formalism in his nudes, is unjust to the anguish and passion of these gigantic figures. His imagination pushed him on too fast for him to have the patience to model—this is the principle defect of his sculptures, although they too are full of spirit and violence. An avid reader, he was launched by each new book into new experiments in which a less hardy talent would have exhausted itself and died: Dante, the Bible, the Edda, the Nibelungenlied, Goethe and Plato, each provided him with a new image and the poets' inventions immediately took on gigantic dimensions in his mind. And because he had an exceptional knowledge and mastery of black-and-white, each drawing was a complete and perfect whole.

His giant figures floating in space, as in *The Birth of Light* or *Night and her Children* (Staatliche Kunstsammlungen, Weimar) are massively, vibrantly three-dimensional; they evolve in a sort of concrete space where atmosphere itself is form and in turn gives form to all the figures within it. These are spiritual forces charged with a potentially material intensity, sources of cosmic energy. Goethe was able to appreciate Carstens' magnificent fire because it was applied to Classical subjects and the function of form was always scrupulously respected. Where in Thorwaldsen form congeals and blurs, with Carstens it leaps out from the portrayed object. Despite his great imagination he always remained very close to Nature and even in the excesses of his dreams there is a strict concordance between movement and form, a temperance, if this word is not too paradoxical, for such an essentially Romantic artist.

Apparently Carstens was too consistently individual to attract disciples in the Scandinavian countries where one might have looked for the natural heirs to his genius; these, however, are to be found in Germany. But one aspect of his work was developed by the Scandinavian painters who continued to take their inspiration from the old Nordic literature, bound up with the deepest characteristics of these peoples. Long after the fashion for 'Ossian' or Wotan had disappeared from England and France and even Germany, where this mythology originated, the sagas and old religious poems retain all their popularity in Denmark and Norway, and trolls and giants continued to hold their sway.

Of the sculptors, the Swede Bengt Erland Fogelberg (1786–1854) was one of the most assiduous portrayers of Wotan, the solemn and terrible. Of the painters, Nils Johan Olsson Blommer (1816–1853) gave idyllic or tragic treatment to the gods of the Edda or the Scaldic heroes, but one senses that this mythology was no longer as living, as real to him as to Carstens or Runge; it had become matter for 'historical painting', with even a touch of formalism although his *Water Sprite and Daughters of Agir* (1850, National Museum, Stockholm) bears witness to a real talent which deserves wider appreciation. The same is true of the Dane Nicolaj Abraham Abildgaard (1743–1809), another eclectic who painted the large historical scenes in the castle of Christianborg, later destroyed by fire. Early influenced by Italy and the Venetians in particular—his ambition was to transplant their colour into the Northern countries—he was obsessed by Michelangelo and Antiquity; like Carstens he dreamed of blending ideal Classical beauty with the dark, dreamy power of Nordic mythology. Despite their qualities of force and sincerity, his compositions with 'Ossian' and Fingal as heroes (Statens Museum for Kunst, Copenhagen) still breathe a certain air of academicism. Perhaps this Italian-trained Dane was more at home with subjects from Greek mythology—his *Philoctetus* in Copenhagen is the best example—or his favourite comic illustrations after plays by Holberg, half farce, half comedies of manners.

Another eclectic is the Dane Jörgen Valentin Sonne (1801–1890), who worked in Italian and Bavarian academies before establishing himself in his own country. He painted battle pictures, compositions on contemporary subjects (the Tyrolean revolt against Napoleon I, the war of Schleswig-Holstein), as well as religious scenes which caused him to be called the father of the revival of religious art, although they are not, if the truth be told, either very forceful or very original. He had been the best pupil of Christoffer Wilhelm Eckersberg (1783–1853), rightly considered the founder of modern Danish painting.

An idea of what this new art was to be can be glimpsed from the fact that Eckersberg studied for three years in David's studio in Paris and in Rome with Thorwaldsen, or at least under his influence. Fortunately he cast aside the shackles of Davidian academicism, still visible in his *Israelites Crossing the Red Sea* (1816, Statens Museum for Kunst, Copenhagen), to become in his last years a poetic and subtle interpreter of Danish landscape.

It is interesting that, whereas the Nordic sagas and mythology became less and less important to painters, they remained a fruitful source of inspiration for illustrators and, unlikely as it may seem, stage-designers. A book could be written on Romanticism's influence on stage décor; in Germany, for instance, Blechen came to true Romanticism through having painted back-cloths for *Sturm und Drang* dramas under the direction of Schinkel. Schinkel himself, before covering Berlin with Greek imitation temples which won him official approbation, had given free rein to his passion for a certain Gothic giganticism in his stage-designs and paintings. In France too, it was a stage-designer, Ciceri, who had a very recognizable influence

LUIGI SABATELLI 1772–1850

He painted frescoes in Milan and Florence, his birthplace, and later in Rome and Venice. An acquaintance of Ingres, he blended the Classical style with a Romantic temperament which is distinguished by its temperance and balance.

22 *Scene with a Doge*

Charcoal on yellow paper. 18.7×20 (7¼×7¾)
Gabinetto Disegni e Stampe, Florence

FRANCESCO MORELLI c. 1768–1830

Born in Franche-Comté, Morelli nevertheless spent most of his life at Rome, engraving religious pictures and landscapes after Claude, Carracci, etc.

23 *View of the Ponte Lamentano, outside the Old Porta Pia, Rome*

Engraving. 9×5 (3½×2½)
Victoria and Albert Museum, London

FELICE GIANI 1758–1823

This painter was always interested in politics and, although a Jacobin at the time of the Revolution, became Napoleon's favourite painter, in which character he worked in several Italian and French palaces. In him Romantic ardour is combined with a Neo-Classical subtlety.

24 *The Sorcerer*

Ink and watercolour. 22.6×17.6 (9×7)
Gabinetto Disegni e Stampe, Florence

TOMMASO MINARDI 1787–1871

Minardi, a professor at the Academy of St Luke in Rome from 1821 to 1858, worked principally on restorations of religious pictures in various churches. He also produced a number of drawings.

25 *Trojan Women Lamenting over the Body of Hector*

Engraving after a drawing of 1823. 48×23 (18¾×9½)
British Museum, London

22

da A.Franzetti *Ponte Lamentano* a Bisangaigne

23

24

25

26

27

28

on most of his colleagues such as the Johannots, Nanteuil and the Déveria, as well as on a number of painters whose main contact with Gothic was through the décors of operas and melodramas.

In Denmark the work of at least five stage-designers, preserved in the Statens Museum, Copenhagen, may be placed among this country's best and most significant contributions to European Romanticism. Two of them, Thomas Bruun (1742–1800) and Peter Cramer (1726–1782), composed striking décors, at once tragic and mysterious, for one of the most dramatic episodes of the Edda, the death of Baldur, the White God, killed by Loki, the God of Fire. The grottos of Frederik August Ahlgrensson (1838–1902) have a strange, mysterious appearance which reflects well the shades of Scandinavian mythology and Svend Valdemar Gyllich (1837–1895) filled his designs for the Valkyries with all the fire and brilliance of Wagnerian orchestration. Jens Petersen Lund (1730–after 1793) hovers on the boundary between Rococo and Romanticism. In time he belongs purely to the 18th century and his work has overtones of the great Italian Baroque artists, Buornacini and Galli-Bibiena, together with Servandoni. He is particularly important as a link between two periods, and introduced certain elements of the *commedia dell'arte*, as interpreted by the two Tiepolos, into the art of the Northern countries.

Few of the portrait painters can be called Romantics: they tend to be Realists, sometimes in the grand style but always doggedly concerned with truth. The only one who perhaps merits the epithet is Jens Juel (1745–1802), a pupil of Abildgaard who afterwards studied at Hamburg and Rome and is best known for having painted the finest portrait of the young Goethe. He took as his motto a sentence which may have saved him from the tyranny of academicism: 'Paint what you like, as you like.' This is what he did, and with great success, for his portraits are full of spirit and his genre scenes of graceful humour and a delicate, elegant realism.

Among Caspar David Friedrich's successors was a young Norwegian who had studied at Copenhagen before settling at Dresden, Johan Christian Clausen Dahl (1788–1857). The remembered beauties of his native country, its wild mountains, primeval forests, storm-tossed fjords and glaciers turning up their tormented white faces towards Infinity, introduced into his sensitive work a dramatic element rare in the Scandinavian landscapists of the period. No doubt he had heard Friedrich say that 'the painter should not paint only what he sees outside but what he sees in himself: if he sees nothing in himself then he should cease to paint what he sees outside'. Probably he had also been struck by the terrible dictum of the master of Greifswald, that these pictures of the interior eye are like screens behind which one expects to find only sick men or corpses. His *Views of the Elbe* (Gemäldegalerie, Dresden), *Storms in the Forest* (1835) and *Shipwreck* (c. 1822, both Nasjonalgalleriet, Oslo) are animated by a genuine and forceful empathy with Nature. Dahl was not content merely to look at landscape; he experienced it in the secret places of his heart, was haunted by the tragic presences to be sensed therein, which later would haunt Edvard Munch's landscapes. In this he represents a noble and quite remarkable exception to the main body of Scandinavian landscapists who in general suffer from a sort of idyllic quietism.

The landscapes of the Swede Elias Martin (1739–1818) constitute an exception to this rule, although their lyricism is not always truly *felt*. Retaining something of Rococo formalism they nevertheless admit new passions. Per Hilleström (1732–1816), a sympathetic painter of genre scenes and conversation pieces, at least once rose to heights of real originality and grandeur in his *Foundry* in the National Museum, Stockholm.

The more favoured genre painters such as Wilhelm Marstrand (1810–1873) or Constantin Hansen (1804–1880) hardly count in the history of Romanticism, to which they contributed little. They are skilful, likeable minor masters, anecdotalists specializing in charming depictions of the life of Danish painters at Rome or the amusing surprises to be encountered in the Copenhagen streets. Neither Rörbye

GIACINTO GIGANTE 1806–76

Gigante always worked from Nature in the manner of Corot, whom he may perhaps have met in Rome in 1826. He produced many thousands of watercolours and drawings which were avidly competed for by visitors to Naples, where he lived. With his great facility, sensitivity and generosity he characterizes the Romanticism of Southern Italy.

26 *Fountain of the Temple of Serapis, Pozzuoli*

1841. Watercolour. 37×57 (14¼×22½)
Museo Nazionale di San Martino, Naples

GIUSEPPE BERNADINO BISON 1762–1844

Best known as an engraver, Bison acquired a great reputation for the frescoes with which he covered palaces and villas in the Venice area. Heir to the style and imagination of the great Venetian painters, he transposed their visionary feeling into fantastic compositions which reveal the stage designer.

27 *Temptation of St Anthony*

Gouache on paper. 34.5×30 (13½×11¾)
Alessandro Morandotti Collection, Italy

FORTUNATO DURANTI 1786–1863

Duranti lived in a fantastic world peopled with strange figures, demons, monsters and angels moving in a tragic world of chiaroscuro. The influence of Giani and Camuccini does not sufficiently explain the strangeness of his personality and art, both of which show curious affinities with Goya.

28 *Two Saints and an Angel*

Watercolour. 25.5×18.5 (10×7¼)
Gabinetto Nazionale delle Stampe e Disegni, Rome

(1803–1848) nor Christen Köbke (1810–1848) is distinguished by any strong Romantic accent. In their love for reality there is a touching naiveté, inspiring respect and sympathy, but the interior life which Friedrich considered indispensable is generally lacking from their pictures. Far from being the home of the gods their landscapes are made to man's measure, arranged for his use and pleasure.

Peter Kristian Skovgaard (1817–1875), Christen Daalsgaard (1824–1907), Johan Thomas Lundbye (1818–1848), Johan Gustaf Sandberg (1782–1854) and Per Gabriel Wickenberg (1812–1846) almost seem to belong to 17th-century Dutch painting rather than to the Romanticism of the 19th century. Art-historically it is surprising and thought-provoking that the Scandinavians should so often have brought such timidity to their concept of Romanticism and their way of interpreting it, the more so in view of the strong links between Northern Germany and Copenhagen and the artistic pre-eminence of the latter city, where so many Germans came to study; its importance at the time was second only to that of Paris.

A possible reason for this inadequacy is that the excesses of the Scandinavian, and especially the Norwegian, landscape, though acting as a stimulus to Dahl, paralyzed and even completely vanquished artists less capable of coping with such awe-inspiring all-powerful elements. Moreover the existing artistic tradition had not been rich or complex enough to afford material for a truly effective new movement. Consequently, with the exception of its few great artists, Scandinavian Romanticism remains a provincial art, a local variant of the Romantic phenomenon.

ITALY

WHAT IS THE REASON for Italy's almost total absence from the picture of Romantic art? Not political circumstances alone, for during the 19th century Romantic music and literature flourished in the peninsula—one has only to think of Verdi and Boito, Leopardi, Carducci and Foscolo. There must be another reason why Italy, after six centuries of incomparable artistic genius, sank into near-sterility until with the advent of Realism she regained a semblance of its earlier position.

The first thing to be borne in mind is that in Italy Romanticism did not answer an irresistible necessity, a racial-hunger, as it did in England and Germany. Again, Italy had in a sense already elaborated and completed her Romanticism in the Baroque Age, and had no need to do it all again, to say what had already been said. Théophile Gautier's remark, though too absolute, contains a good deal of truth: 'Italy is resting on her laurels. Her schools of art are nothing but museums.' Her opulent past proved a disadvantage rather than the contrary for it continually obtruded upon artists' notice eminently 'copiable' masterpieces; as a result genius was at a premium although there were many men of talent at work during the Romantic period. Their productions are by no means insignificant even if none of them are, properly speaking, Romantic.

Who were the Italian contemporaries of Delacroix, Constable and Friedrich? There were the painters deriving more or less directly from Pompeo Batoni or Mengs, such as Gasparè Landi (1756–1830) or Vincenzo Camuccini (1773–1844); there were Neo-Classical painters such as Andrea Appiani (1754–1844) and Giuseppe Bossi (1777–1815); there were the Davidians Pietro Benvenuti (1769–1844) and Francesco Hayez (1791–1882). The last-named generally painted respectable, worthy portraits and achieved his greatest success in rather 'troubadour' genre scenes, half theatrical and half domestic, such as his overpraised *Romeo and Juliet* (1859) in the Milan Gallery of Modern Art. If the David-imitators looked to France for their lead, another group turned towards the German Nazarenes and modelled their aesthetics on the doctrines of S Isidoro and frescoes of the Bartholdy Casino. Like the Nazarenes, they too cultivated the ideal of medieval, almost monastic, purity; their aim was to revive truly religious art according to Wackenroder's principles, as revealed to them by Overbeck and Cornelius, and, following in the latter's footsteps, they went in search of what they considered medieval painting—Renaissance painting, in fact.

These Purists, as they called themselves, recognized Luigi Mussini (1813–1888) as their leader, although he was the youngest of them all; he was, however, the one with the greatest talent. Maximilian Seitz (1811–1888), an Italianized German, Antonio Marini (1788–1861) and Tommaso Minardi (1787–1871) deserve a mention if only for the fact that, in a country so famed for its artistic originality and daring, they deliberately confined themselves to imitation, if not pastiche.

The Verists are more interesting in every respect. Remaining within the mainstream of Italian genius, always interested in faithfully observing and reproducing reality, they reacted strongly, almost hostilely, against the idealism, tainted with artificiality, of the Purists. Italian painting, ever since Giotto and Cavallini, had always derived new strength from its periodic returns to reality. Unfortunately Verism produced hardly more creative geniuses than Purism but at least these supporters of Realism directed painting into less sterile channels than those in which the post-Nazarene painters were stuck fast. Moreover the aesthetics of Realism are altogether more complex and subtle than those of simple naturalism. A good many 'literary' overtones still cling to the compositions of Nicolò Barabino (1832–1892), Francesco Netti (1834–1894) and the best of the group, Domenico Morelli (1826–1901); they specialize in a sort of stage reality rather than truthful portrayal of the reality of every day; that is, they treat banal subjects taken from history, literature or the theatre with a sort of affected naturalism. Gaetano Gigante's *Festa della Madonna dell'Arco* (c. 1811, Naples Museum), Gabriele Smargiassi's (1798-1882) *St Francis' Vision of the Cross* (Private Collection, Naples) and Bernardo Celentano's (1835–1863) *Death of Tasso* derive from an arbitrary aesthetic scheme which might be compared with those of Verdi and Puccini in music.

Perhaps there is more easy emotion than true Romanticism in the austere simplicity of the Purists and slightly declamatory rhetoric of the Verists. The influence of Delacroix on Morelli, particularly in his *Daughter of Jairus* (1874) is also interesting to note; like the painter of *Women of Algiers*, Morelli had discovered the fascination of Africa and touched off a trend of Orientalism which for a while enjoyed a certain success.

However, after Massimo d'Azeglio (1798-1866) gave them a lead, the Italians turned, for preference, to their own landscape which had aroused the passion and nostalgia of so many English, French, German and Scandinavian painters. The Neapolitan painters known collectively as the Posillipo School (Edoardo Dalbono (1841-1915), Filippo Palizzi (1818-1899) etc.) made a sincere attempt to portray the appearance and spirit of these southern landscapes faithfully. In their tenderness and care for Nature and the poetic feeling animating their interpretation, they are indeed Romantics of a sort.

Is there anything Romantic in the Macchiaioli (literally 'Tachistes') of the second half of the 19th century, among whom figure many minor masters of considerable originality and interest? This can only be gauged if one appreciates the true nature of Italian Romanticism and the characteristics distinguishing it from the Romanticism of other countries. At its best it combines the spirit of folk art with literary themes, theatrical realism and plain reality and is wielded between 1850 and 1900 by Romantic naturalists like Tranquillo Cremona (1837–1878), Giacomo Favretto (1849–1887), Paolo Michetti (1851-1929) and Telemaco Cremono, who enjoyed tremendous success during their own lifetimes, for they provided Italian society with exactly what it wanted. They were equally appreciated by the middle class and the working class, who found in them something of the aesthetics of the theatre, opera, music—the pleasures most generally (indeed almost universally) preferred. They ought perhaps to be discussed in a history of artistic taste rather than a pure history of art, if such a distinction can be drawn. Nevertheless they and Italy's other leading Romantic artists have a very real charm and outstanding pictorial qualities, even if as a whole Romanticism was less natural to Italy than to other countries.

THE NETHERLANDS

BELGIUM'S CONTRIBUTION to European Romanticism can be summed up quite briefly: a few history painters combining the traditional virtues of the Netherlands painting with a sincere lyricism and realistic care for the objective truth of the objects portrayed; one painter of genius, Wiertz—paradoxical, morbid, unequal, hesitating between social-naturalistic sentimentality and a visionary imagination not unlike that of his successor, James Ensor. The Belgians, stimulated by the ideas of liberty, independence and social progress animating the generation of 1830, made a point of re-establishing their links with the country's artistic past. 'Long live Belgium, long live Rubens', was the rallying cry of the painters as they rushed to portray the great moments of national history or, alternatively, continued in the traditional style without, apparently, any desire for novelty or even originality. The height of their ambition was to demonstrate their antipathy towards the ideas and forms of the 18th century and to proclaim their patriotism—almost the predominant sentiment in every social class in the 19th century, owing to the course of political events.

Claiming kinship with Rubens, historical painters such as Louis Gallait (1810–1887), Henri Leys (1815–1869) and Gustave Wappers (1803–1874) remained faithful to the respectable, healthy ideals of the traditional 'fine work of art'. *Barthall de Haze in his Thirties* (Musées Royaux, Brussels) by Henri Leys, *The Last Moments of Count Egmont* (1858, National-Galerie, Berlin) by Gallait, and *Episode from the Belgian Revolution* (Musées Royaux, Brussels) by Wappers are all, in effect, tributes to the masters of the past, but their 19th-century feeling should not be ignored; here we have, once again, the Romantic conception of the 'page of history'.

Gallait erred on the side of excessive admiration of the French and Delaroche in particular; Leys, on the other hand, was closer to the Germans of the Düsseldorf School and frequently gives evidence of a modern approach to both composition and colour treatment; he might perhaps have been capable of raising Belgian art to new heights, had he not died prematurely at the age of fifty-four. It was even more unfortunate that the madness of Antoine Joseph Wiertz (1806–1865) and the flights of caprice of his extravagant imagination exposed him to ridicule, when in fact his great talent and impetuous originality were worthy of a very different fate. The *trompe-l'oeil* effects of his fair-booths, the melodramatic horrors of his *Buried Alive* (1854) and *Woman Eating her Child* (1853, Musée Wiertz, Brussels), of whose photographic naturalism Wiertz was extremely proud, are justified by their primitive sincerity, a 'folk' naiveté tempering their almost pathological megalomania. It is a pity that Wiertz's work is spoilt by his perverse cultivation of the horrible and monstrous, for its sombre inspiration and fiery execution make him not unfit to rank with the great Romantic 'eccentrics', those curious and incomplete geniuses who attract our curiosity and sympathy.

In Holland the great landscape tradition of the 17th century was resumed, after an interim of more than a century, in the admirable works of W. J. J. Nuyen (1813–1839), Barend Cornelis Koekkoek (1803–1862) and J. Willem Pieneman (1779–1853). The last was also a remarkably fine portrait-painter.

LIX FRANCISCO DE GOYA Y LUCIENTES 1746–1828

In their way, Goya's portraits are as Romantic as his tragic, almost monochrome pictures in the 'Quinta del Sordo'—the scenes of torture, madness, and hallucination emanating from the world of darkness and misery in which he lived in his later years—and as his engravings showing the 'dream of reason giving free rein to monstrous creatures of the brain'. Implacably he draws to the surface of each face the dramatic conflicts taking place in the sitter, who is forced, willynilly, to display all his inmost personality. The pictorial beauty, the gleam of the grey material, the tremor and crackle of the striped, flowered silk—all these provide a powerful contrast with the rock-like hardness of the face, lofty and stern as a landscape of Old Castile. Although he could take a delight in succulent feminine beauty, Goya was also the painter of the more severe, unattractive qualities—arrogance, and scorn.

In its sober colouring, economy of form and concentration of emotion this portrait is one of the best Goya ever painted. The figure of Dr Peral, a friend of the painter, occupies the picture with almost provoking authority and sculptural solidity; it impresses the spectator as a 'thing in itself', quite independent of its meaning or provenance, born of the painter's mind but charged with a forceful, almost painful, humanity.

Portrait of Dr Peral

c. 1795. Panel. 95 × 66 (37⅜ × 25⅞) National Gallery, London

LX HENRY FUSELI 1741–1825

Although a native of Zürich, Fuseli made England his home, and was honoured by London society as one of the most illustrious artists of the day. He had the unusual gift of being able to reconcile his position as an academic teacher with an imaginative temperament which tended towards the supernatural and macabre. His fantastic visions were expressed with a sombre, earnest exaltation. It was said that he 'went on the wings of the wind', and he himself felt as though he were perpetually hovering over abysses. Certainly solid earth was altogether too humdrum for this painter, who, in his imagination rode on griffins and lived in a world peopled by nightmarish figures and characters from his beloved Shakespeare.

Lady Macbeth Grasping the Daggers

c. 1801. 102 × 127 (40 × 50) Mrs J. Stanley-Clarke Collection, England

VII THE UNITED STATES

IN THE ROMANTIC PERIOD America had some remarkable painters but few outstanding sculptors. Hezekiah Augur (1791-1858), William Rush (1756-1833), John
Browere (1792-1834) (who produced several energetic portraits in a serious vein),
John Rogers (1829-1904), and Horatio Greenough (1805-1852) are unimportant in the
history of three-dimensional art. Nor can high claims be made for a sculptor like
Powers, who is in a sense Romantic, despite the Classical style of his work. The
sculptors in wood, anonymous or otherwise, who made figureheads, are much more
interesting in their originality, their freedom, whether born of simplicity or extreme
skill, their rusticity or their refinement. This figurehead-sculpture still belongs more
to the sphere of craft than that of art but nevertheless it reflects the true American
spirit much more accurately than the more academic works of the period. The spirit
in question continues until the present day: what more magnificent craftsman than
Calder! Wax models, too, had a great vogue; this art-form had much in common
with figurehead-sculpture.

Curiously enough, American painters continued to derive from, if not imitate,
famous European (English or French) artists, during the end of the 18th and early
part of the 19th century. It was a long time before a truly national art threw off
the bonds of the Old World and looked with new eyes and a fresh sensibility at
the American landscape and its inhabitants. One of the most interesting phenomena,
in this respect, is the discovery of the aesthetic value of the Red Indian, both as a
picturesque figure and as possessing the sort of Romantic glamour proper to
'natives'. This of course did not deter the settlers from persecuting them whenever they coveted their ancient hunting grounds.

It was George Catlin (1794–1872) who brought Red Indians into fashion. He
lived amongst them, listing and studying the objects they used with the assiduity
and method of an ethnographer, and collected the results of his researches in a
curious work, published in 1841, *The Manners, Customs and Conditions of the North
American Indians*. The themes which he popularized were to be made famous by
Fenimore Cooper and Longfellow and it was mainly for their novelty and exotic
quality, to European eyes, that Catlin was honoured by the Paris Salon in 1846.

Baudelaire, unimpressed by his art as Romanticism, nevertheless appreciated the way in which 'by their beautiful attitudes and the ease of their movements, these savages give us a closer insight into the sculpture of Antiquity'.

Catlin's chief concern was to preserve an image of Indian life and attributes, 'before they go to join the shades of their fathers in the setting sun'. In other words he attached more importance to the documentary, or informative, value of his works than to their artistic character as such. Abandoning portraiture, which he had practised with some success at the beginning of his career, he left Washington and his main clients behind him and set out for the West, where lived his beloved Red Indians. Five years later he returned with a multitude of paintings and drawings and the components of his 'Indian Museum'—tents, clothes, weapons and everyday objects which were to demonstrate the complete accuracy and documentary precision of his paintings.

These preoccupations give a cold, over-careful effect to his compositions; not a feather is missing, not a stripe of war-paint. He would have been an excellent illustrator, as was Seth Eastman (1808-1875) who in 1830 settled in Minnesota and became both the friend and 'portraitist' of the Sioux and Chippewas. In this he had better fortune than John Mix Stanley (1814-1872) who on one occasion was in danger of being assassinated by his models. Of the other 'Indian-painters' the best are James Otto Lewis (dates unknown), Charles Bird King (1785/6-1862), Alfred Miller (died 1874) and George Caleb Bingham (1811-1879). The last, however, was as much interested in frontier and river subjects as in the Red Indians themselves; their interest for him was limited to the savage atmosphere of their life. In his famous genre scene in the Metropolitan Museum, New York, *Fur Traders Descending the Missouri* (c. 1845), intense and direct truth is combined with a feeling for Nature which goes far beyond the limits of the nominal 'subject'.

Many artists were inspired by the American landscape and made faithful portraits of it in the Romantic idiom. The 'Hudson River School', with Thomas Doughty, Asher Durand and Thomas Cole, was so called by Sydney Keller. It was united by a sort of 'Hudson Romanticism', going in for discussions on the nature of the 'picturesque' and the 'sublime' in which writers of the day also took a part. Emerson's theories about nature encouraged this Romantic inclination, in that they demanded that landscape should be illuminated and transfigured by the spirit, rather than painted in a spirit of strict realism.

Before a truly authentic native school of American landscape painting could emerge, the whole body of traditions taken over from Europe, including Crome, Wilson, Claude and even Salvator Rosa had to be repudiated. On the other hand, since these Continental artists were either Romantic in feeling or embryo Romantics, they had some favourable influence on American painting. Dutch painting of the 17th century had some effect on artists such as John Kensett (1818–72) and George Durrie, while Poussin inspired Washington Allston (1779–1843).

Thomas Cole (1801–1848) was basically an instinctive painter whose work is a direct though emotionalized reflection of the landscape of the White Mountains. He was, however, an enthusiastic reader of the English Romantics and admired Salvator Rosa; indeed he preferred him to Claude because he felt closer to him both as man and as artist: 'I feel more at home with the wild and tormented.' The poet Bryant's description of his vision as wild and primeval is accurate enough. His *Oxbow of the Connecticut* (1836, Metropolitan Museum of Art, New York), with its contrasts between the harmonious distant background and the storm wind tossing the foreground trees and cloud, is a good example of this art of the immediate impression, this way of seizing at one blow both the anecdotic details and inner spirit of nature. Cole's landscapes are always animated by a passion which adds drama to each shower of rain or stormy squall. His vision of reality was very like that of the German Romantics, and Caspar David Friedrich in particular, whose works he must have studied during his three-year stay in Europe. In addition to

ROBERT HAVELL died 1878

1 *Niagara Falls Seen from the Chinese Pagoda*

1845. Watercolour. 45×69.5 (17¾×27¼)
Phelps Stokes Collection, New York Public Library

THOMAS DOUGHTY 1793–1856

Doughty was one of the painters commissioned by Colonel Stevens of Hoboken to decorate his steamship *Albany*. Originally a leather merchant, he abandoned this trade in 1820 and went to Philadelphia where he devoted himself entirely to art. Although he was entirely self-taught, his landscapes are remarkable for their depiction of light and the poetic feeling they express.

2 *River Landscape*

Pencil. 14×19 (5¼×7½).
Metropolitan Museum of Art, New York

ASHER B. DURAND see p. 228

3 *Sketch from Nature*

Pencil on grey paper. 36×25 (14×10).
Metropolitan Museum of Art, New York

THOMAS COLE see p. 224

4 *Landscape with Tower*

Pencil. 22×16.5 (8½×6½)
Metropolitan Museum of Art, New York

9 *Landscape*

Pencil. 10×13 (3¾×5¼)
New York Historical Society, New York

1

2

3

4

7

5

8

6

9

11

14

12

15

13

16

REMBRANDT PEALE 1778–1860
Peale was one of three sons christened Raphael, Rembrandt and Rubens. Rembrandt attained distinction chiefly as a portraitist, influenced sometimes by David's dryness, sometimes by the mellower qualities of Reynolds. His portrait of Jefferson, painted in 1806, won him considerable renown and many commissions. With his father, Charles Wilson Peale, he worked on a 'Gallery of Famous Men' which was to include all the celebrities, both American and European, of the day.

5 *Harpers Ferry in 1812*

1812. Watercolour. 25×33 (10×13)
Municipal Museum of the City of Baltimore, Baltimore, Maryland

WASHINGTON ALLSTON see p. 226

6 *Romantic Landscape*

Sepia. 17×17 (6¾×6¾)
Carolina Art Association, Gibbes Art Gallery, Charleston, South Carolina

THOMAS SULLY 1783–1872
This painter's childhood was spent in the picturesque milieu of a travelling theatrical company in the southern states. Later he studied for four years with Gilbert Stuart, a famous portraitist, afterwards becoming a pupil of Lawrence in London. In England he abandoned the rather dry realism of the American school for the more supple, generous and lyrical manner of his best pictures.

7 *Woman and Child Reading*

Pencil and wash. 21×18 (8⅛×7)
New York Historical Society, New York

SAMUEL F. B. MORSE 1791–1872
Morse was gifted in many different fields; he was, for instance, interested in scientific inventions, particularly telegraphy and photography. His expressed wish was to advance the scientific progress of humanity, an aim which seemed to him more worthy than the progress of art. Nevertheless he had studied the early Romantics in Paris and made copies of the Classics. He founded the National Academy of Graphic Arts, which was to encourage the growth of truly American painting.

8 *Romantic Scene*

Pencil. 7×12 (2⅞×4¾)
New York Historical Society, New York

THOMAS MORAN 1837–1926
Moran was a hugely successful artist and Congress paid $10,000 (an enormous sum at the time) for his picture of the Grand Canyon. He was both a good landscape painter, sensitive to the picturesque grandiose qualities of the American scene, and a skilful engraver.

10 *Solitude*

1869. Lithograph. 52×41 (20⅜×16)
Prints Division, New York Public Library

MARY CUSHMAN early 19th century
Mary Cushman was a member of the Cushman family of Attleboro, Massachusetts. Her work is representative of the popular folk art of the time, in which embroidery and needlework were used for pictorial purposes. Today she would be classified amongst the 'Naives', who belong to one of the most characteristic and fertile strains of American art, which also produced Hicks and Erastus Field.

11 *Mourning Picture—Jacob Cushman*

c. 1810. Needlework on silk. 47.5×46.5 (18¾×18¼)
Abby Aldrich Rockefeller Folk Art Collection, Williamsburg, Virginia

JOHN TRUMBULL 1756–1843
Trumbull first studied drawing at Harvard and later worked in the studio of Benjamin West. After visits to both France and England he turned to history painting, in which field he acquired an immense reputation. His portraits have life and originality and he had sufficient imaginative power to be able to treat epic subjects with great brilliance. His ambition was to free American art from the shackles and mentorship of Europe.

12 *Death of Hotspur*

Sepia and brush drawing. 22×18 (8¾×7)
Vassar College Museum, Poughkeepsie, N.Y.

ALFRED J. MILLER 1810–74
Miller was much admired for his 'Indian' pictures and scenes of life in the far West; collectors vied with each other to obtain copies of these works. He was able to study his subjects in the flesh when he visited the Sioux with Captain William Stewart. His landscapes are endowed with a quite exceptional force of expression and suggestion.

13 *The Trapper's Bride*

Drawing. 31×24 (12×9⅜)
Walters Art Gallery, Baltimore

REMBRANDT PEALE

14 Study for *The Court of Death*

Sepia, pen and wash. 21×37 (8¼×14½)
Charles Coleman Sellers Collection, Carlisle, Pennsylvania

WASHINGTON ALLSTON

15 *Ships at Sea*

Chalk on canvas. 121×151 (47½×59½)
Fogg Museum of Art, Harvard University, Cambridge, Massachusetts

KARL BODMER 1809–93
One of the first painters to be attracted by the 'Indians' as a subject, Bodmer accompanied Prince Maximilian of Neuwied on his travels to Yellowstone, the Rocky Mountains and various Indian villages in order to collect the material for illustrations of these visits.

16 *Indians Hunting Bison*

1843. Watercolour. 30×44 (11⅞×17¼)
New York Public Library

his use of the pathetic fallacy he shared the tendency to mysticism of Friedrich and John Martin, an artist he much admired. This mysticism led him to a symbolic conception of history shown in the allegorical compositions of his latter years—ambitious, incomplete, full of strokes of genius and unsuccessful feats of daring. In *The Course of Empire* (1836, Coll. New York Historical Society) he shows the sad fate to which man is heir and which condemns to ultimate decay even the strongest and most magnificent civilizations.

Cole's Romanticism, which came more and more to resemble that of Martin, took on a tragic flavour in his *Voyage of Life* (1840-41, St Luke's Hospital, New York) and *The Cross and the World* (c. 1847, Brooklyn Museum, New York): the landscape here is a sort of code message in the manner of Philipp Otto Runge, in which the emotions are used to convey allegory. Without ever turning away from reality, Cole introduced the symbolic landscape into the United States, adapting it to the nature of the country, whose wild and primitive character he so much admired. In Europe, he was wont to say, man had domesticated the elements.

American painters were very enthusiastic about the new invention of photography which appealed, of course, to their taste for objective reality, and they came, on occasion, to look at landscape with an almost camera-like eye, while always endowing it with their very individual emotional qualities. None of them went so far as to eliminate all feeling or thought from their photographic naturalism. John Neagle (1799–1865) is a representative example: extremely naturalistic details in his pictures are combined to form a pathetic, musical whole. His well-known *View on the Schulkill* (1827, Art Institute of Chicago) is typically American in this respect, as is the celebrated *In the Catskills* of Thomas Doughty (1793-1856) (1836, Anderson Gallery of Arts, Andover, Mass.). Although possibly inspired by English landscapes these paintings display an entirely different conception of space, more vast, more dynamic: distance is no longer equivalent with nostalgia for the inaccessible, as in the German Romantics, but a calm assured taking-possession of the scene. Man is no longer intoxicated by the infinite any more than he is hemmed in by irksome limits. The day of the 'topographers' is past; artists like Vanderlyn, who painted a view of Niagara in 1802, content with merely making a detailed, documentary copy of a landscape and unconcerned as to its grandeur and majesty, had passed out of fashion. Vanderlyn, born in 1776 and thus only about twenty years older than Doughty, had hardly been touched by the growing Romantic contagion. The vogue for panoramas, very strong in the first third of the 19th century, laid more emphasis on the documentary interest of a landscape than its emotional qualities. The best known panorama-painters (many of them began their careers as scenic designers and were solid craftsmen rather than artists) included Frederick Catherwood, John Banvard and Henry Lewis whose works astonish by their extraordinary size even more than by their real aesthetic value. The panorama is a Romantic phenomenon in that it indicates a desire (often unconscious) to escape from the prison of the finite, a desire for 'wide open spaces' expressed with a sort of external illusionism instead of by exploring the mind within. Although in itself a Baroque phenomenon, *trompe-l'oeil* was a feature of the Romantic period in America; there was a considerable market for Harnett's and Peto's illusionist still-lifes. As for the panoramas, Lewis' 1200-yard canvas showing the Mississippi and Banvard's prodigy, three miles in length deserve attention only in so far as they are symptomatic of the very American taste for hugeness as such, for the colossal, the super-colossal, evidenced also in skyscrapers, and in the sculptures of various United States presidents carved out of a mountainside.

Illusionism in still-life answered a need for absolute objective reality, another of the abiding American characteristics. John Peto's (1854-1905) virtuosity resides chiefly in his way of giving a striking spatial value to the various objects he portrays hanging on the wall, in the favourite tradition of the 18th century. Peto was not so naive or puerile as to be content with merely hoodwinking spectators into (almost) believing his painted objects real. Whereas the true Romantic painter tries to establish the individual's place in the space he occupies, his relation to it, his physical and moral position in the universe, Peto tries to detach each object from its surroundings and background, thus emphasizing its autonomy, the independence of each element of a still-life. Again, whereas a 17th-century Dutch still-life, for instance, or a Chardin still-life is constructed symphonically, the volumes and colours related like the various subjects of a first movement, Peto's objects stand alone in a kind of isolation which may be, perhaps, indicative of the artist's own interior solitude. Instead of being amusing or charming, his visual and tactile illusionism, probably unequalled within its own limits, is almost tragic, a fortuitous coming together of individually isolated elements grimly associated by chance.

William Harnett (c. 1848-1892) is equally complex, equally enigmatic. Born in 1848, he would seem to be a late Romantic but is, at the same time, very archaic. His pictures call to mind Kalf, Chardin, even Flegel or Baschenis, although he is less lyrical than the last-named. Larkin defined the nature of his illusionism exactly: 'When he painted the glowing embers of a pipe one felt their heat, and when he included a five-dollar bill in his pictures the Treasury Department began to get worried.' But he also adds something which suggests greater artistic scope: 'The critic of today realizes that Harnett did not merely reproduce what he saw but intensified it: he divined imagined skeletons behind the closed doors of his cupboards'.

This is what makes Harnett a Romantic among still-life painters, as opposed to the 17th-century Dutch and Germans, and 18th-century French—his intensification of reality, the strange suggestive power emanating from his closed doors with their possible contents. A composition like *Old Models* (Museum of Fine Arts, Boston), strongly and subtly built up with a geometric sub-structure almost as rigorous as that of a Mondrian picture, can only be understood in the context of the old tradition of the *'vanitas'* still-life. What does this cupboard with its medieval ironwork and broken planks contain? What do these musical instruments hanging on its doors, these sad, hopeless, abandoned objects suggest, if not the elements of a *'vanitas'* or *'memento mori'*? There is a heavy incurable sadness about the violin and trumpet, left to their silence, the books which will never again be opened, the inexorable severity of the closed door whose key has been lost and which has successfully resisted all attempts at a forced entry. Despite its acknowledged theme, which ought really to suggest nothing more than objective realism, this work has an indefinable atmosphere which puts it on quite a different plane from the *trompe-l'oeil* pure and simple.

The works of Edward Hicks and Erastus Field, two early American precursors of Surrealism, tend in the direction of fantasy. Hicks is not unlike the so-called 'naive painters', while Field is curiously close to the mysterious Monsù Desiderio, although he had certainly never seen any of his pictures.

It is hard to imagine a stranger character than Hicks, (the Quaker convert from Pennsylvania) a sort of New World Douanier Rousseau who, despite painful scruples and self-condemnation, spent his leisure time in painting. He compromised with his conscience by taking care that his works should be both innocent and useful; thus, he felt, they would escape the inherent profanity of art. Hicks, the travelling preacher, was eager that painting too should preach a moral, and commonly used, as subjects for his simple but delightful paintings, the same Bible verses which provided the texts for his sermons.

His favourite text and the one which inspired his best works, was that from Isaiah heralding a future heaven on earth in which universal peace would be re-established for the benefit of all creatures. The two best versions of *The Peaceable Kingdom* are in the Brooklyn Museum, New York, and the Phillips Collection, Washington, but more than eighty are said to exist and amongst them certain themes are repeated. As a rule he added, in one corner of the picture, a group of white settlers negotiating with Indians a voluntary and honourable settlement of American territory. If this should happen America would really become a 'kingdom of peace' and all quarrels between the newcomers and ancient owners of the continent would cease. In this Eden the lion would lie down with the lamb, the prowling wild beast with the cow, the deer and the sheep. In vain do Hicks' lions and tigers fix their large, proud eyes on the spectator, with an impressive air of command; we know that they can no longer harm us, that children can lie down between their paws or scramble over their backs in safety.

Hicks' *Peaceable Kingdoms* are the projection on to canvas of his own honest longing for universal reconciliation. For him triumph could come only through the joint forces of truth and love; and so he has the typically 'Naive' attachment to Realism, alongside the Naives' childlike lyricism. His picture of Washington painted in 1846, three years before his death, is the best and most harmonious synthesis of all the aesthetic and moral preoccupations which had filled his life. The landscape is more important, more successfully arranged, more musical. The technique is still that of the 'Naive' but the feelings inspiring the work belong to the purest and most moving Romanticism.

Erastus Salisbury Field (1805–1900) lacks Hicks' piquant clumsiness and his childlike spirit; he seems to be haunted by scholarly preoccupations, by memories of grand, mysterious architecture culled from old books. He had been greatly struck by Egypt's gigantic monuments and also by her relations with the Hebrews, as recounted in the Bible. Apart from painting portraits and landscapes he also reproduced his architectural visions which breathe the spirit of Martin's Old Testament and *Paradise Lost*. At the same time he aimed at a monumental syncretism in which were mingled reality and invention, and which, at its best, is the work of a true visionary, a true descendant of Monsù Desiderio with his tragic 'fancies'.

His most remarkable work in this field is his extraordinary *Historical Monument of the American Republic* (c. 1876, Coll. Mrs H. S. Williams, Springfield, Mass), painted about 1876 for the glorification of his country. It certainly has no fellow in American art, and is probably unequalled in the art of Europe. On an enormous canvas he painted an extraordinary family of Towers of Babel linked at the top by aerial bridges, swarming with sculptures, bas-reliefs and colonnades; he mingles the styles of India, Egypt, Greece, Mesopotamia and Rome with the quiet, imperturbable daring of a man perfectly confident that his dreams are not only real but within his grasp.

The picture is neither the raving of a madman nor an archaeologist's nightmare but a harmonious, well-built decorative arrangement, of impressive majesty, magnificent in its very excess. Significantly, it is a Classical vision, and only the feeling inspiring it is Romantic; here Neo-Gothic has no place. With his inexhaustible imagination, Field crams the huge structure with an infinity of architectural and decorative details. In its way the picture is a masterpiece, although a paradoxical one in which impossibility is allowed free play within the limits of a logical construction. Erastus Field deserves more attention from the Surrealists; they should recognize in him an early ancestor whose strange genius is probably unequalled.

LXI GEORGE C. BINGHAM 1811–79

Bingham was born in Virginia but when he was still a child the family moved to Franklin, a small town in Missouri. He began by painting portraits with a dry, detailed realism which earned him a great success. During a visit to Philadelphia in 1837 his eyes were opened to the possibilities of genre painting and he devoted himself to portraying the picturesque figures of Indians, trappers, and politicians haranguing the constituents. An ardent democrat, he entered into a contest in 1850 with the supporters of the 'Free Earth' movement. He also painted banners for electoral campaigns. At forty-six he spent three years in Düsseldorf to which he was attracted by the reputation of the town's painters, and the visit had a certain influence on his æsthetic ideas and style of painting in the last years of his life. His art shows the warmth of his feeling for the American scene.

Fur Traders Descending the Missouri

c. 1845. 74×93 (29×36½) Metropolitan Museum of Art, New York

LXII THOMAS COLE 1801–48

Born in Lancashire, Cole emigrated to Ohio with his parents in 1819. Although he was attracted at first by Salvator Rosa and Claude, the gods of the American Romantics, he later returned to a faithful portrayal of the landscape of his own country which had been his first love. His tastes were eclectic enough to embrace both Caspar David Friedrich and John Martin, whom he admired for his visionary mysticism. In the later part of his life he abandoned his delicate realism and charming depictions of idyllic landscapes for large symbolical evocations of the ruins he had seen in Europe. These 'programme-pictures' bear allusive titles: *The Cross and the World, The Voyage of Life,* etc. To present-day eyes, Cole's best works are his fresh, unaffected landscapes of Connecticut.

In the Catskills

99 × 160 (39 × 63) Metropolitan Museum of Art, New York

LXIII WASHINGTON ALLSTON 1779–1843

In his early years Allston came under the spell of Italy, where he lived for a certain period, and professed admiration for Poussin from whom he caught a taste for distance and bucolism. Later he attempted to rival Salvator Rosa, imitating his sombre manner and tragic subjects. At a time when the Pre-Raphaelites were at work in England, Allston too dreamed of knights-at-arms and tales of chivalry. He was a friend of the poet Coleridge and, with his idyllic landscapes in the tradition of Claude and Turner, transplanted the complete stock-in-trade of European legend and history to his native Boston. In the United States as well as Europe, Romanticism often meant a flight into distance—in time and space—and Allston was typical of this trend; his work is full of escapist nostalgia and second-hand memories.

The Flight of Florimel

91 × 72 (35¾ × 28½) Detroit Institute of Arts

LXIV ASHER B. DURAND 1796–1886

Until he was thirty-five Durand had devoted himself exclusively to engraving, so that when he took up painting he was virtually self-taught. He was one of the first American landscapists who took an interest in representing the richness and variety of the New World itself, even though their vision was still cluttered up with memories of England and Italy and their 'reality' was somewhat distorted by their habit of seeing everything with Claude's eyes. Durand abandoned this formalist attitude for a direct, though delicate, realism. He declared that there was no need to idealize reality, and that painters should stop coating the summer greens with muddy brown. There are striking analogies between this picture and some of the Swiss Romantic landscapes by Calame, Lory, Diday or Aberli.

With many of the American artists of this period one is conscious that they still derived their inspiration and technique to a large extent from Europe and European æsthetic traditions. Even when taking his subjects from reality, Durand still saw them through a haze of English or French assumptions; his is a limited reality which ignores much that is extravagant and naturally Romantic in the American scene— the prairies, the Rocky Mountains, the Red Indians, who had such an influence on Catlin and, now relegated to Westerns, continue to perpetuate the essential character of American Romanticism.

Kindred Spirits

1849. 117×91 (44×36) New York Public Library

CONCLUSION

FEW PERIODS have been as unsusceptible to Romanticism as our own, not so much because of incompatibility of sensibility as because of our current opinion that the line of progress followed by Romantic art will never again produce living works of art, and consequently that continued allegiance to Romantic sensibility is a waste of time.

Although it would be absurd to advocate a 'return to Romanticism' for the artists of today, it is equally foolish to steel oneself against the appeal which Romantic art can still exert, however remote from the present day it may seem. Its vitality lies not only in the qualities praised by the art-historians, who are, in any case, too much influenced by modern aesthetic standpoints to do it full (or impartial) justice, but much more in its discreet resonances and understated emotion, which demand a true state of communion. Romantic art is a 'living art', calling on the deepest sources of our sensibility; it owes nothing to fashion but is eternally valid and unceasingly invigorating, precisely because it expresses profound emotion with a warmth which has never detracted from the genius of any artist capable of feeling it. In our period, particularly, when abstract art seems to have become the most varied and moving expression of the dramatic anguish at the very root of our conception of existence and growth, one might imagine that Romantic painting would have a profound appeal, in that it deals with a similar anguish. It is no paradox to say that in abstract art there seems to be something which might be a late form, a distant echo of Romanticism, with its desire for a stormy subjectivism. This is not contradicted by the fact that, in abstract painting, subject is completely absent, whereas it was of great importance, as aforesaid, in Romantic art; perhaps the abstract picture represents Pater's 'musical state' in a form unforeseeable in the 19th century. Perhaps, again, abstraction represents a real, fully Romantic achievement, in its essence if not in its outward forms. The cosmic feeling inspiring Marc, Klee and Kandinsky corresponds to the ideals of Carus and Friedrich, even if the means adopted by them to attain this communion with Nature are entirely different.

In the final analysis, the work of art must be judged by its power to unite the individual and the universe, by its faithfulness to the spirit of the world it reflects, and the 19th-century German Romantics would have agreed with Klee's statement that 'our heart beats to carry us down into the depths, the unfathomable depths of the primordial Breath'. The actual processes of Romantic sensibility are reflected in the 'philosophy of Nature' with which Klee's painting is strongly impregnated and which leads him to say that 'art does not reproduce the visible; it renders visible'. Obviously his idea of infinitely 'open' space is an extension of the conception of landscape shared by Constable, Turner, Huet and Friedrich, and all of them aspire equally, though they may express it differently, to go beyond the perceptible, to blend experience and imagination; all consider that they have failed if they do not arrive, *via* nature, at a point 'beyond nature'.

A close examination of the aesthetic ideals of the great innovators of the end of the 19th and beginning of the 20th centuries reveals strong links with the Romantics of the first half of this century, even if they repudiated all relationship with an art which seemed to them remote from their own aspirations. What could be more Romantic than the lives of Gauguin, Van Gogh or Edvard Munch? And certainly their works betray longings very like those animating the generation of 1800–1850.

The less obvious comparisons are often the most fruitful: we have already identified true Romantics among the Baroque masters, and among the post-Romantics, too, there are many artists who, without belonging to any school, or accepting categorizations which would certainly have been inadequate to describe their talents, come of the same stock—a family extending through the centuries and characterized by a common uncertainty about the relationship of man to the outside world. Cézanne's art, for instance, follows a process analogous with that of the Romantic landscapists and Turner in particular. For what were the laws governing Cézanne's long development from the tectonic constructions of the Gardanne period to the last *Mont Sainte-Victoires* where matter is transcended by spirit and where form is cancelled out and at the same time sublimated into pure irradiation? What else but to convert painting into pure vibration, so that the weight and opacity of matter should not war with the atmosphere, to transform objects into light—the light they give out and the light they receive—to fill space with a profound empathetic feeling for Nature, to abolish, finally, all distinction between observer and thing observed, finite humanity and the infinity of the universe.

At the other extreme of the post-Romantic artistic gamut stands the Douanier Rousseau, a painter both skilful and naive, who surely must be called yet another descendant of the Romantics. Rousseau's escape-routes to Infinity, to the super-reality sought by Moritz von Schwind in fairy tales and by Richter in the small towns of medieval Germany, were different from those of the typical Romantic; instead of the Gothic spire and the Middle Ages, he dreamed of the tropics with their virgin forests, tigers, monkeys and naked women lying on couches amid baobab-trees and mangroves, the same faraway glories which enflamed Bresdin's imagination and drove Gauguin to the South Sea Islands. It was merely the difference between the Paris of 1900 and that of 1830, the customs-officer behind his barrier and the 'head-in-the-air young man' whiling away his time in a Gothic tavern with poets and musicians equally intent on reviving the Middle Ages. Current opinion, in any case hostile to Romanticism, holds this to be a symptom of inferiority, but such judgments can only be based, in the final analysis, on individual taste and aesthetic preferences.

Nobody can deny the importance of the spiritual message preached by Romanticism or the deep resonances which it added to art by allowing it to speak the language of the soul. It is this we should hear, this 'spontaneous overflow of powerful feelings' that should be recollected in tranquillity, so that spectator and picture are merged once again in intimate fusion, just as the painter and his canvas had been in that flash of divine illumination out of which the work was born.

LIST OF ILLUSTRATIONS

Colour plates are indicated by Roman numbers, black-and-white illustrations by Arabic numbers

I FORERUNNERS OF ROMANTICISM

II ARCHITECTURE AND SCULPTURE

III ENGLAND

IV GERMANY

V FRANCE

VI OTHER EUROPEAN COUNTRIES

VII THE UNITED STATES

INDEX OF NAMES

Ordinary arabic numbers refer to the main text, those in brackets refer to captions; roman numbers correspond to the colour plates; arabic numbers in italics preceded by a section title refer to black-and-white illustrations